SCARECROW AREA BIBLIOGRAPHIES
Edited by Jon Woronoff

1. *Middle East,* by Sanford R. Silverburg. 1992.
2. *Eastern Europe,* by Rebecca Gates-Coon. 1993.
3. *U.S. Foreign Relations with the Middle East and North Africa,* by Sanford R. Silverburg and Bernard Reich. 1994.
4. *South Asia,* by David N. Nelson. 1994.
5. *Bibliography of the Soviet Union, Its Predecessors, and Successors,* by Bradley L. Schaffner. 1995.
6. *Asian States' Relations with the Middle East and North Africa: A Bibliography, 1950–1993,* by Sanford R. Silverburg and Bernard Reich. 1994.
7. *East and Northeast Africa: A Bibliography,* by Hector Blackhurst. 1996.
8. *Caribbean,* by Marian Goslinga. 1996.
9. *Western Europe Since 1945: A Bibliography,* by Joan F. Higbee. 1996.

East and Northeast Africa Bibliography

Hector Blackhurst

Scarecrow Area Bibliographies, No. 7

The Scarecrow Press, Inc.
Lanham, Md., & London

Ref
DT
365.18
B55
1996

SCARECROW PRESS, INC.

Published in the United States of America
by Scarecrow Press, Inc.
4720 Boston Way
Lanham, Maryland 20706

4 Pleydell Gardens, Folkestone
Kent CT20 2DN, England

British Cataloguing-in-Publication Information Available

Library of Congress Cataloging-in-Publication Data

Blackhurst, Hector.
East and Northeast Africa bibliography / by Hector Blackhurst.
p.   cm. — (Scarecrow area bibliographies ; no. 7.)
1. Africa, East—Bibliography.   2. Africa, Northeast—Bibliography.   I. Title.
II. Series: Scarecrow area bibliographies ; 7.
Z3516.B55   1996   [DT365.18]   016.9676—dc20   95-40627   CIP

ISBN 0-8108-3090-6 (cloth : alk. paper)

Contents

Editor's Foreword

East and Northeast Africa have, unfortunately, been very newsworthy of late. I say unfortunately because, for Africa at any rate, this usually means that the media are busily exposing one case or another of drought, famine, refugee flight, civil unrest, or political coup. While such problems do exist, there is more to the region than that. Yet most of the more positive achievements or, indeed, the solutions to earlier crises receive much less attention from the media. Fortunately, they are described in more serious works by authors who dig deeper and consider less sensational aspects as well. These other works are essential to provide the background for what is happening in East and Northeast Africa now, whether they deal with anthropology, economics, history, political science, sociology, or other fields.

Such, on the whole more serious, works can be found in profusion in this *East and Northeast Africa Bibliography*. They cover the eight countries of the region, delving into an amazing number of significant aspects. Thanks to detailed categorization, titles can readily be located by looking under the relevant subjects. Works can also be traced through an author's index. Unlike many others, this bibliography also includes numerous works that have not appeared in English but make a definite contribution. Readers thus have a very handy key to literature on a region that, despite any problems, remains one of the more important and promising parts of Africa.

This bibliography was compiled by someone who knows the region very well, and not just from books. Dr. Hector Blackhurst is both a librarian and a teacher, presently occupying the posts of Assistant Librarian at the John Rylands University Library and Honorary Lecturer at the Department of Social Anthropology, University of Manchester. From 1969 to 1971, he did field work in Ethiopia and has written on the Oromo people of that country. For nearly a decade he produced *Africa Bibliography*. That was excellent preparation for the *East and Northeast Africa Bibliography*.

Jon Woronoff
Series Editor

Acknowledgments

This listing would never have seen the light of day without the assistance in computer matters and text processing of my colleagues in the John Rylands University Library of Manchester: Charles Hulme, Anne Parkinson, and Judith Kent. I am grateful to them for the patience they showed in their dealings with a technological illiterate. Unfortunately, errors and omissions cannot ultimately be blamed on computers; responsibility for these rests entirely with the compiler.

Introduction

This bibliography has the principal aim of providing the student of any of the eight countries covered—Djibouti, Eritrea, Ethiopia, Kenya, Somalia, Sudan, Tanzania, Uganda—with a convenient and broadly based listing of the significant published material. An attempt has also been made to include a selection of material that is less scholarly but of general interest and publications that, although by no means essential reading, contain useful insights either on specific topics or issues or on the development of a discussion or an author's thinking.

These general aims have been pursued within a set of guidelines that has limited both the amount and the type of material included. The bibliography lists only books or booklets with a minimum of about forty pages, and it lists only material published from 1960 to the present. There is inevitably an element of arbitrariness in the choice of such criteria. The first is purely practical. To have included periodical articles, items in collective works, and other types of publications would have made the compilation unworkably long. The second does have some bibliographic justification. Over the period covered there has been a rapid increase in the rate of publication on Africa. The initial impetus to this was undoubtedly the interest aroused by the promise and processes of decolonisation, but, more recently, concern with the continent has been sustained by a series of political and environmental difficulties and disasters. During the period there also has been an expansion in higher education, including African studies, both in Africa and elsewhere. This has further added to the flow of publications. This bibliography provides a structured introduction to the literature of this period of expansion and change.

The limitation to one form of publication, the book, has had a number of unintended consequences, the principal one being the lack of representation of some subject areas. Most writing on health and medical matters has been produced either as periodical articles or chapters in edited volumes. Such material is therefore not well represented here. A similar caveat applies to work in the fields of technology and science. Examples of both types of material will be found in the bibliography but the main bias of the listing is towards the humanities and social sciences.

A second consequence of the limitation by date is that many works that are considered classics of either interpretation or description are not included in the bibliography. Thus, for example, people versed in the anthropological study of the Sudan will notice many gaps in the entries for E. E. Evans-Pritchard since most of his major works were published before 1960. Similarly, those familiar with the missionary and exploration literature of the region will note the absence of such names as Isenberg, Krapf, and Roscoe. These lacunae are, however, easily filled by the use of other bibliographies. Many of these are entered at the appropriate place in the listing, others I mention in the second section of this introduction.

The listing contains no items of creative literature, though some compilations of folk literature are present. A relatively small number of reports from international organisations, principally the World Bank and the International Labour Organisation is included, but government reports and documents have been excluded. In other areas, because of the threat to the overall balance of the bibliography, I have had to exclude a significant amount of material. Kenya and Tanzania are two countries that have inspired a large literature dealing with wildlife, photography, tourism, and the like, as did Ethiopia until the events of 1974 and after. I have no prejudice against coffee-table books about the Maasai or Serengeti, but a complete listing of them would be out of place here. I have therefore left out more than I have included. For reasons of my own linguistic incompetence, no items in African languages have been included, though a good deal of material about them has. Most of the entries are in English but there is a strong presence of books written in French, Italian, and German. Languages with non-Latin scripts are not covered.

One particular excluded category that should be mentioned here is that of the facsimile reprint. During the late 1960s and the 1970s a number of publishers specialised in the production of photographic reprints of the classics of African exploration and travel. The regions covered by this bibliography were well represented in this enterprise and many works that had been difficult or expensive to obtain were again made available to private scholars. Some of these editions also benefited from new introductions by contemporary researchers, which put the work into context and assessed its value as an historical document. Despite this, these books remain of their own time and would be out of place in the present listing. Further information about this phenomenon and details of the main publishers in the field can be found in "The Scramble for Africana" by A. H. M. Kirk-Greene in *African Affairs,* 70, 278 (1971).

In the course of searching for material for inclusion in this bibliography, I have come across a number of reviews of other bibliographies in the field, a great many of them hostile. Three aspects of a bibliography seem to have the potential to excite the ire of reviewers: coverage, arrangement, and appropriateness. So far as coverage is concerned, I hope I have laid out clearly the aims of this listing and the criteria on which it was compiled. If I have omitted works falling within the category of essential reading, then I have erred. Arrangement refers essentially to the ease of use of the bibliography while appropriateness seeks some congruence between the bibliography and the historical experience of the country or region covered. The two are inevitably linked and have caused me a good deal of thought in relation to the present listing.

The bibliography is part of a series of Area Bibliographies. Unlike other areas, for example the Middle East, there is not a large literature which deals with East and Northeast Africa as a unit. There is a body of regional literature on "East Africa," which is usually Anglophone East Africa. Of recent years, and largely as a result of the international politics of the region, there has developed a literature on the Horn or Northeast Africa, though depending on the topic under discussion, this may or may not include parts of Kenya, Somalia, and the Sudan. In general, however, the geographical focus in the literature has been the country.

Nonetheless, many of the peoples, personalities, and events dealt with in the books listed here, although "belonging" to a specific country, have a regional if not a continental or worldwide significance.

The arrangement of the bibliography is intended to accommodate these regional, country, and topically specific items. There are subject entries for East Africa and Northeast Africa, country entries, divided by subjects that reflect the nature of the literature on that country rather than some predetermined scheme, and direct entries for people or events of general significance, all arranged in one alphabetical sequence. There is a limited amount of dual entry of items, but this has been kept to a minimum. If a topic is not found under a general heading, for example, there is no entry for Jomo Kenyatta under Kenya, it should be searched for directly. The author index uses the item number as the link between the index and the main listing.

Other Bibliographies and Sources of Information

All of the countries covered here have already been the subject of bibliographical works, and many of these will be found in the listing either in the bibliography section for that country or, if the bibliography is subject specific, with the appropriate subject. Particularly useful, especially for access to pre-1960 publications, is the *African Historical Dictionary Series* published by Scarecrow Press, each of which contains a substantial bibliography covering books, periodical articles, reports, and other documentation. Those relevant to the present area published up to now are:

Historical Dictionary of Ethiopia and Eritrea. Second edition. By Chris Prouty and Eugene Rosenfeld. 1993.
Historical Dictionary of Kenya. By Bethwell A. Ogot. 1981.
Historical Dictionary of Somalia. By Margaret F. Castagno. 1975.
Historical Dictionary of the Sudan. Second edition. By Carolyn Fluehr-Lobban, Richard Lobban, and John O. Voll. 1992.
Historical Dictionary of Tanzania. By Laura Kurtz. 1978.

Information about a vast range of other bibliographies of both countries and subjects can be traced using Yvette Scheven's *Bibliographies for African Studies, 1970–1986* (London, Hans Zell, 1988). This is a practically exhaustive account of bibliographies available not only in book form but also those tucked away or "hidden" in journal articles or books. Another noteworthy bibliography of bibliographies covering earlier periods is Theodore Besterman: *A World Bibliography of African Bibliographies,* revised by J. D. Pearson (Oxford, Blackwell, 1975). Also covering bibliographies of bibliographies as well as general reference and research tools is *Guide to Research and Reference Works on Sub-Saharan Africa,* compiled by Helen F. Conover and Peter Duignan (Stanford, Hoover Institution Press, 1971). A more recent publication, which covers reference material such as encyclopaedias, handbooks, gazetteers, and statistical sources, is *Africa: A Guide to Reference Material,* by John McIlwaine (London, Hans Zell, 1993).

For current bibliographical information, it is usually necessary to consult sources covering the whole of Africa, rather than specific countries or regions.

Three publications are invaluable here. The *International African Bibliography* appears quarterly and lists books, essays in edited volumes, and periodical articles from a wide range of journals. The *Africa Bibliography,* from the International African Institute in London, covers similar ground and appears as an annual compilation. These two indexes, with wide coverage, are complemented by *African Studies Abstracts,* formerly *Documentatieblad,* from the African Studies Centre, Leiden, which gives abstracts from a smaller number of journals and edited volumes. This is also a quarterly publication.

Two bibliographic periodicals are worthy of note here: *Africana Journal* and *Current Bibliography on African Affairs.* Both journals have listings of new books, review sections, and publish bibliographies on particular subjects or personalities. *African Research and Documentation,* a quarterly publication from the Standing Committee on Library Materials from Africa in London, specialises in archives and documentation concerned with Africa and has useful reviews and news sections. Although government publications themselves are not included in this listing, some country bibliographies of these have been entered. Other, more general guides include Boston University Libraries: *Catalog of African Government Documents* (3rd ed. Boston, G. K. Hall, 1976). Also published by G. K. Hall is *Bibliographic Guide to Government Publications: Foreign.*

One major area of difficulty is access to titles published in Africa. East Africa has long had a healthy publishing industry and many scholarly titles have appeared there. Unfortunately, it has not always been possible to find out about these publications, though the flow of information has improved recently. African publishers have become somewhat more active in promoting their own products and a number of European and American sources of information are now available. The *African Book Publishing Record* is a quarterly that lists by subject, author, and country of publication material published in Africa. It also has a useful book review section. The Library of Congress's *Accessions List: East Africa* also gives details of African imprints acquired by the library.

Finally, although this short review has concentrated on printed material, it should be noted that a mass of material of relevance to the student of Africa is now available via electronic media, be these commercially produced databases or library resources made widely available through computer networks. Whether such databases will substitute completely for the conventional bibliography remains to be seen. The death of the book has long been forecast, but as yet, it and its synergistic companion, the bibliography, remain remarkably healthy.

The Bibliography

Acholi—Education

1. Ocitti, J. P. *African indigenous education as practised by the Acholi of Uganda*. Nairobi, East African Literature Bureau, 1973.

Acholi—Ethnography

2. Girling, F. K. *The Acholi of Uganda*. London, H.M.S.O., 1960.

Acholi—Politics

3. Leys, Colin. *Politicians and politics: an essay on politics in Acholi, Uganda, 1962–65*. Nairobi, East African Publishing House, 1967.

Addis Ababa—Centenary

4. Ahmed Zekaria, et al. (eds.) *Proceedings of the International Symposium on the centenary of Addis Ababa, November 24–25, 1986*. Addis Ababa, Addis Ababa University, Institute of Ethiopian Studies, 1987.

Addis Ababa—Libraries

5. Yonas, T. *The organization and management of libraries in Addis Ababa, with special emphasis on public libraries, 1985–1986*. Addis Ababa, Department of National Libraries and Archives, 1987.

Addis Ababa—Prostitution

6. Laketch Dirasse. *The commoditization of female sexuality: prostitution and socio-economic relations in Addis Ababa, Ethiopia*. New York, AMS Press, 1991.

Administration—East Africa

7. Jacobs, B. L. *Administration in East Africa: six case studies*. Entebbe, Government Printer, 1965 [actually published in 1986].

8. Schaffer, B. (ed.) *Administrative training and development: a comparative study of East Africa, Zambia, Pakistan and India*. New York, Praeger, 1974.

Afar—Ethnography

9. Chailley, Marcel. *Notes sur les Afar de la région de Tadjoura: Tadjoura, Sismo, Djibouti, novembre 1935–septembre 1937*. Paris, Académie des Sciences d'Outre-Mer, 1980.

1

Afar—Geology

10. Varet, J. *Geology of central and southern Afar (Ethiopia and Djibouti Republic)*. Paris, Centre National de la Recherche Scientifique, 1978.

Afar—Language

11. Bliese, Loren F. *A generative grammar of Afar*. Dallas, Summer Institute of Linguistics, 1981.

12. Parker, E. M., and Richard J. Hayward. *An Afar-English-French dictionary, with grammatical notes in English*. London, University of London, School of Oriental and African Studies, 1985.

Agau Languages

13. Böhm, Gerhard. *Der Bau des Prädikats in den Agau-Sprachen*. Wien, Afro-Pub, 1983.

Agricultural Equipment—East Africa

14. Minto, S. D., and S. B. Westley. *Low cost rural equipment suitable for manufacture in East Africa*. Nairobi, University of Nairobi, Institute for Development Studies, 1975.

Agriculture—East Africa

15. Acland, Julian Dyke. *East African crops: an introduction to the production of field and plantation crops in Kenya, Tanzania and Uganda*. London, Longman, 1971.

16. Amann, V. F. (ed.) *Agricultural policy issues in East Africa*. Kampala, Makerere University, 1973.

17. Bevan, David, et al. *Peasants and governments: an economic analysis*. Oxford, Clarendon Press, 1989.

18. Engelhard, Karl. *Die wirtschaftsräumliche Gliederung Ostafrikas*. München, Weltforum-Verlag, 1974.

19. Helleiner, G. K. (ed.) *Agricultural planning in East Africa: proceedings of a conference held at the University College, Dar es Salaam, April, 1967*. Nairobi, East African Publishing House, 1968.

20. Ker, A. D. R., et al. *Agriculture in East Africa*. London, Edward Arnold, 1978.

21. Kirkby, Roger A. (ed.) *Crop improvement in eastern and southern Africa: research objectives and on-farm testing. A regional workshop held in Nairobi, Kenya, 20–22 July, 1983*. Ottawa, International Development Research Centre, 1984.

22. Kokwaro, J. O. *Classification of East African crops*. Nairobi, Kenya Literature Bureau, 1980.

23. Kyesimira, Yoeri. *Agricultural export development*. Nairobi, East African Publishing House, 1969.

24. Leakey, C. L. A. *Crop improvement in East Africa*. Farnham Royal, Commonwealth Agricultural Bureaux, 1970.

25. Lundahl, Mats. *Incentives and agriculture in East Africa*. London, Routledge, 1990.

26. Moris, Jon R., and Gerald Saylor (eds.) *Technical innovation and farm development in East Africa: proceedings of the East African Agricultural Economics Society Conference, University of Nairobi, 23–25 June, 1969*. Kampala, Makerere University, 1975.

27. Ngugi, D. *East African agriculture*. Revised edition. London, Macmillan, 1982.

28. Yoshida, Masao. *Agricultural marketing intervention in East Africa: a study in the colonial origins of marketing policies, 1900–1965*. Tokyo, Institute of Developing Economies, 1984.

Aidid, Mohammed Farah

29. Ruhela, Satya Pal (ed.) *Mohammed Farah Aidid and his vision of Somalia*. New Delhi, Vikas, 1994.

Aksum

30. Kobishchanov, Iurii. *Axum*. University Park, Pennsylvania State University Press, 1979.

31. Meck, Barbara. *Über die Stelen von Axum, Äthiopien: ein Beitrag zur Astro-Archäologie*. Frankfurt am Main, Peter Lang, 1979.

32. Munro-Hay, S. C. *Aksum: an African civilisation of late antiquity*. Edinburgh, Edinburgh University Press, 1991.

33. Munro-Hay, S. C. *Excavations at Aksum: an account of research in the ancient Ethiopian capital directed in 1972–74 by the late Dr. Neville Chittick*. Nairobi, British Institute in Eastern Africa, 1989.

Alur—Language

34. Ukoko, Joseph, et al. *Essai de dictionnaire Dho Alur*. Leiden, E. J. Brill, 1964.

Alwa—History

35. Zarroug, M. El-Din A. *The kingdom of Alwa*. Calgary, University of Calgary Press, 1991.

Amaa—Ethnography

36. Gafour, Ayyoub-Awaga Bushara. *My father the spirit-priest: religion and social organisation in the Amaa tribe, southwestern Sudan*. Lewiston, Edwin Mellen Press, 1989.

Amhara—Ethnography

37. Hoben, Allan. *Land tenure among the Amhara of Ethiopia: the dynamics of cognatic descent.* Chicago, University of Chicago Press, 1973.

38. Messing, Simon D. *Highland plateau Amhara of Ethiopia.* New Haven, Human Relations Area Files, 1985. 3 vols.

Amharic—Language

39. Bender, Marvin Lionel, and Haile Fulass. *Amharic verb morphology.* East Lansing, Michigan State University, African Studies Center, 1978.

40. Hartmann, Josef. *Amharische Grammatik.* Stuttgart, Franz Steiner, 1980.

41. Kane, Thomas Leiper. *Amharic-English dictionary.* Wiesbaden, Otto Harrassowitz, 1990.

42. Kapeliuk, Olga. *Nominalization in Amharic.* Stuttgart, Franz Steiner, 1988.

43. Leslau, Wolf. *Concise Amharic dictionary: Amharic-English, English-Amharic.* Wiesbaden, Otto Harrassowitz, 1976.

44. Leslau, Wolf. *English-Amharic context dictionary.* Wiesbaden, Otto Harrassowitz, 1973.

45. Mulugeta Kebede, and John D. Murphy (eds.) *An Amharic newspaper reader.* Kensington, Dunwoody Press, 1984.

46. Polacek, Zdenek, et al. *A concise sociopolitical dictionary: English-Amharic.* Wiesbaden, Otto Harrassowitz, 1990.

47. Ullendorff, Edward. *An Amharic chrestomathy: introduction, grammatical tables, texts, Amharic-English glossary.* Second edition. London, University of London, School of Oriental and African Studies, 1978.

Amharic—Literature

48. Gerard, Albert G. *Four African literatures: Xhosa, Sotho, Zulu, Amharic.* Berkeley, University of California Press, 1971.

49. Kane, Thomas Leiper. *Ethiopian literature in Amharic.* Wiesbaden, Otto Harrassowitz, 1975.

50. Molvaer, Reidulf Knut. *Tradition and change in Ethiopia: social and cultural life as reflected in Amharic fictional literature, ca. 1930–1974.* Leiden, E. J. Brill, 1980.

Amin, Idi

51. Atwoki, K., et al. *Amin.* London, Walton Press, 1979.

52. Decalo, Samuel. *Psychoses of power: African personal dictatorships.* Boulder, Westview Press, 1989.

53. Grahame, Iain. *Amin and Uganda: a personal memoir.* London, Granada, 1980.

54. Gwyn, David N. *Idi Amin: death-light of Africa.* Boston, Little, Brown, 1977.

55. Jamison, Martin. *Idi Amin and Uganda: an annotated bibliography.* Westport, Greenwood Press, 1992.

56. Kiwanuka, M. S. M. Semakula. *Amin and the tragedy of Uganda.* Munich, Weltforum-Verlag, 1979.

57. Kleinschmidt, Harald. *Amin collection: bibliographical catalogue of materials relevant to the history of Uganda under the military government of Idi Amin.* Heidelberg, Éditions Bantoues, 1983.

58. Kyemba, Henry. *State of blood: the inside story of Idi Amin.* London, Corgi, 1977.

59. Listowel, Judith Hare. *Amin.* Dublin, Irish University Press, 1973.

60. Martin, D. *General Amin.* Revised edition. London, Sphere, 1978.

61. Melady, Thomas P., and Margaret B. Melady. *Idi Amin Dada: Hitler in Africa.* Kansas City, Sheed Andrews, 1977.

62. Oppong-Affi, A. M. *My experience in Idi Amin's Uganda.* Legon, Adwinsa, 1982.

63. Smith, George Ivan. *Ghosts of Kampala: the rise and fall of Idi Amin.* London, Weidenfeld and Nicolson, 1980.

64. Strate, Jeffrey T. *Post-military coup strategy in Uganda: Amin's early attempts to consolidate political support.* Athens, Ohio University, Center for International Studies, 1973.

65. Wiedemann, E. *Idi Amin: ein Held von Afrika?* Wien, Paul Zsolnay, 1976.

Ankole — Ethnography

66. Kreuer, Werner. *Ankole.* Stuttgart, Franz Steiner, 1979.

Ankole — Fertility

67. Ntozi, James P., et al. *Some aspects of determinants of fertility in Ankole, Uganda.* Kampala, Makerere University, 1990.

Ankole — Markets

68. Good, Charles M. *Rural markets and trade in East Africa: a study of the functions and development of exchange institutions in Ankole, Uganda.* Chicago, University of Chicago, Department of Geography, 1970.

Ankole — Music

69. Thiel, Paul W. F. van. *Multi-tribal music of Ankole: an ethnomusicological study.* Tervuren, Musée Royale de l'Afrique Centrale, 1977.

Ankole—Politics

70. Doornbos, Martin R. *Not all the king's men: inequality as a political instrument in Ankole, Uganda.* The Hague, Mouton, 1978.

71. Doornbos, Martin R. *Regalia galore: the decline and eclipse of Ankole kingship.* Nairobi, East African Literature Bureau, 1975.

Ankole—Proverbs

72. Cisternino, Marius. *The proverbs of Kigezi and Ankole, Uganda.* Rome, Museum Combonianum, 1987.

Arbore—Language

73. Hayward, Richard J. *The Arbore language: a first investigation.* Hamburg, Helmut Buske, 1984.

Archaeology—East Africa

74. Hodder, Ian. *Symbols in action: ethnoarchaeological studies of material culture.* Cambridge, Cambridge University Press, 1982.

75. Kirkman, James S. *Men and monuments of the East African coast.* London, Lutterworth Press, 1964.

76. Kryzaniak, L., and M. Kobusiewicz (eds.) *Origin and early development of food-producing cultures in north-eastern Africa.* Poznan, Polish Academy of Sciences and Poznan Archaeological Museum, 1984.

77. Sutton, J. E. G. *A thousand years of East Africa.* Nairobi, British Institute in Eastern Africa, 1990.

Archaeology—Northeast Africa

78. Sadr, Karim. *The development of nomadism in ancient Northeast Africa.* Philadelphia, University of Pennsylvania Press, 1991.

Ariaal—Social Conditions

79. Fratkin, E. M. *Surviving drought and development: Ariaal pastoralists of northern Kenya.* Boulder, Westview Press, 1990.

Art and Artists—East Africa

80. Agthe, Johanna. *Wegzeichen: Kunst aus Ostafrika, 1974–89.* Frankfurt am Main, Museum für Völkerkunde, 1990.

81. Burt, Eugene C. *An annotated bibliography of the visual arts of East Africa.* Bloomington, Indiana University Press, 1980.

82. Miller, Judith von D. *Art in East Africa: a contemporary guide to East African art.* London, Muller, 1975.

Asians—East Africa

83. Bharati, Agehananda. *The Asians in East Africa: Jayhind and Uhuru*. Chicago, Nelson-Hall, 1972.

84. Delf, George. *Asians in East Africa*. London, Oxford University Press, 1963.

85. Don Nanjira, D. D. C. *The status of aliens in East Africa: Asians and Europeans in Tanzania, Uganda and Kenya*. New York, Praeger, 1976.

86. Ghai, Dharam P., and Yash P. Ghai (eds.) *Portrait of a minority: Asians in East Africa*. Second edition. London, Oxford University Press, 1970.

87. Gregory, Robert G. *India and East Africa: a history of race relations within the British Empire, 1890–1939*. Oxford, Clarendon Press, 1971.

88. Gregory, Robert G. *Quest for equality: Asian politics in East Africa, 1900–67*. London, Sangam, 1993.

89. Gregory, Robert G. *South Asians in East Africa: an economic and social history*. Boulder, Westview Press, 1993.

90. Gregory, Robert G. *The rise and fall of philanthropy in East Africa: the Asian contribution*. New Brunswick, Transaction Books, 1992.

91. Hollingsworth, Lawrence William. *The Asians of East Africa*. London, Macmillan, 1960.

92. Mangat, J. S. *A history of the Asians in East Africa, c. 1886–1945*. Oxford, Clarendon Press, 1969.

93. Mohamed, H. E. *The Asian legacy in Africa and the white man's color culture*. New York, Vantage Press, 1979.

94. Rai, Kauleshwar. *Indians and British colonialism in East Africa, 1883–1939*. Patna, Associated Book Agency, 1979.

Asu—Religion

95. Omari, C. K. *God and worship in traditional Asu society*. Erlangen, Evangelical Lutheran Church of Tanzania, 1990.

Athletes—East Africa

96. Hartmann, Robert. *Schwarzes Gold: auf den Spuren der afrikanischen Läufer*. Düsseldorf, Edition Spiridon, 1988.

Atuot—Ethnography

97. Burton, John W. *A Nilotic world: the Atuot-speaking peoples of the southern Sudan*. New York, Greenwood Press, 1987.

98. Burton, John W. *God's ants: a study of Atuot religion*. St. Augustin, Anthropos Institute, 1981.

Ba'iso—Ethnography

99. Haberland, Eike, and Marcello Lamberti. *Ibaaddo ka-Ba'iso: culture and language of the Ba'iso*. Heidelberg, Carl Winter, 1988.

Baggara—Ethnography

100. Cunnison, Ian. *Baggara Arabs: power and lineage in a Sudanese nomad tribe*. Oxford, Clarendon Press, 1966.

Bahr al—Ghazal—History

101. Santandrea, Stefano. *A tribal history of the western Bahr El Ghazal*. Bologna, Nigrizia, 1964.

102. Santandrea, Stefano. *Ethno-geography of the Bahr al-Ghazal, Sudan: an attempt at historical reconstruction*. Bologna, Editrice Missionaria Italiana, 1981.

Banking—East Africa

103. Abdi, Ali Issa. *Commercial banks and economic development: the experience of eastern Africa*. New York, Praeger, 1977.

104. Pauw, E.-J. *Das Bankwesen in Ostafrika*. München, Weltforum-Verlag, 1969.

Bantu Languages

105. Hinnebusch, Thomas J., et al. *Studies in the classification of eastern Bantu languages*. Hamburg, Helmut Buske, 1981.

106. Möhlig, Wilhelm J. G. *Die Stellung der Bergdialekte im Osten des Mt. Kenya: ein Beitrag zur Sprachgliederung im Bantu*. Berlin, Dietrich Reimer, 1974.

107. Nurse, Derek. *Description of sample Bantu languages of Tanzania*. London, International African Institute and OAU Inter-African Bureau of Languages, 1979.

108. Rombi, Marie-Françoise (ed.) *Études sur le bantu oriental: Comores, Tanzanie, Somalie, Kenya*. Paris, SELAF, 1982.

Bantu—Ethnography

109. Taylor, Brian K. *The western lacustrine Bantu*. London, International African Institute, 1962.

Barabaig—Ethnography

110. Klima, George J. *The Barabaig: East African cattle-herders*. New York, Holt, Rinehart, 1970.

Bari—Language

111. Spagnolo, Lorenzo M. *Bari English Italian dictionary*. Verona, Missioni Africane, 1960.

Beadwork—East Africa

112. Carey, Margret. *Beads and beadwork of East and South Africa*. Aylesbury, Shire, 1986.

Beja—Ethnography

113. Hjort af Ornäs, Anders, and Gudrun Dahl. *Responsible man: the Atmaan Beja of north-eastern Sudan*. Uppsala, SSSA in cooperation with Scandinavian Institute of African Studies, 1991.

114. Palmisano, Antonio L. *Ethnicity: the Beja as representation*. Berlin, Das Arabische Buch, 1991.

Beri—Ethnography

115. Tubiana, Marie-José. *Des troupeaux et des femmes: mariage et transferts de biens chez les Beri du Tchad et du Soudan*. Paris, L'Harmattan, 1985.

Berti—Ethnography

116. Holy, Ladislav. *Neighbours and kinsmen: a study of the Berti people of Darfur*. London, Hurst, 1974.

117. Holy, Ladislav. *Religion and custom in a Muslim society: the Berti of Sudan*. Cambridge, Cambridge University Press, 1991.

Beta Israel—History

118. Kaplan, Steven. *Beta Israel (Falasha) in Ethiopia: from earliest times to the twentieth century*. New York, New York University Press, 1992.

119. Kessler, David. *The Falashas: the forgotten Jews of Ethiopia*. London, Allen & Unwin, 1982.

120. Ochs, Edith, and Bernard Nantet. *Les Falasha: la tribu retrouvé*. Levallois-Perret, Manya, 1992.

121. Parfitt, T. *Operation Moses: the story of the exodus of the Falasha Jews from Ethiopia*. London, Weidenfeld and Nicolson, 1985.

122. Quirin, James. *Evolution of the Ethiopian Jews: a history of the Beta Israel (Falasha) to 1920*. Philadelphia, University of Pennsylvania Press, 1992.

123. Rapoport, Louis. *The lost Jews*. Second edition. New York, Stein and Day, 1983.

124. Safran, Claire. *Secret exodus*. New York, Prentice Hall, 1987.

125. Shelemay, Kay Kaufman. *Music, ritual and Falasha history*. East Lansing, Michigan State University, African Studies Center, 1986.

126. Trevisan Semi, Emanuela. *Allo specchio dei Falascià: Ebrei ed etnologia durante il colonialismo fascista*. Firenze, Giuntina, 1987.

Beta Israel—Missionaries

127. Payne, Eric. *Ethiopian Jews: the story of a mission.* London, Olive Press, 1972.

Beta Israel—Religion

128. Kaplan, Steven. *Les Falashas.* Turnhout, Éditions Brepols, 1990.

Bibliography—East Africa

129. Ofcansky, Thomas P. *British East Africa, 1856–1963: an annotated bibliography.* New York, Garland, 1985.

Bibliography—Northeast Africa

130. Darch, Colin. *A Soviet view of Africa: an annotated bibliography on Ethiopia, Somalia and Djibouti.* Boston, G. K. Hall, 1980.

131. Marcus, Harold G. *The modern history of Ethiopia and the Horn of Africa: a select and annotated bibliography.* Palo Alto, Hoover Institution Press, 1972.

Biology—East Africa

132. Hicken, N. E. *African notebook: the notes of a biologist in East Africa.* London, Hutchinson, 1969.

Bongo—Ethnography

133. Kronenberg, Waltraud, and Andreas Kronenberg. *Die Bongo: Bauern und Jäger in Südsudan.* Stuttgart, Franz Steiner, 1981.

Boni—Language

134. Heine, Bernd. *Boni dialects.* Berlin, Dietrich Reimer, 1980.

Botany—Northeast Africa

135. Hulton, Paul, et al. (eds.) *Luigi Balugani's drawings of African plants from the collection made by James Bruce of Kinnaird on his travels to discover the source of the Nile, 1767–73.* New Haven, Yale Center for British Art, 1991.

Boundaries—East Africa

136. McEwen, A. C. *International boundaries of East Africa.* Oxford, Clarendon Press, 1971.

Boundaries—Northeast Africa

137. Hoskyns, Catherine (ed.) *The Ethiopia-Somalia-Kenya dispute, 1960–1967.* Dar es Salaam, Oxford University Press, 1969.

Bukusu—History

138. Makila, F. E. *An outline history of Babukusu of western Kenya.* Nairobi, Kenya Literature Bureau, 1978.

Bukusu—Language

139. Blois, K. F. de. *Bukusu generative phonology and aspects of Bantu structure*. Tervuren, Musée Royale de l'Afrique Centrale, 1975.

Bukusu—Religion

140. Wolf, Jan de. *Differentiation and integration in western Kenya: a study of religious innovation and social change among the Bukusu*. The Hague, Mouton, 1977.

Chagga—Ethnography

141. Moore, Sally Falk. *Social facts and fabrications: "customary" law on Kilimanjaro, 1880–1980*. Cambridge, Cambridge University Press, 1986.

142. Moore, Sally Falk, and P. Puritt. *The Chagga and Meru of Tanzania*. London, International African Institute, 1977.

Chagga—History

143. Stahl, Kathleen M. *History of the Chagga people of Kilimanjaro*. The Hague, Mouton, 1964.

Chagga—Language

144. Nurse, Derek. *Classification of the Chaga dialects: language and history on Kilimanjaro, the Taita hills and the Pare mountains*. Hamburg, Helmut Buske, 1979.

145. Philippson, G. *"Gens des bananeraie," Tanzanie: contribution linguistique à l'histoire culturelle des Chaga du Kilimanjaro*. Paris, Éditions Recherche sur les Civilisations, 1984.

Chagga—Social Conditions

146. Lawuo, Z. E. *Education and social change in a rural community: a study of colonial education and local response among the Chagga between 1920–1945*. Dar es Salaam, Dar es Salaam University Press, 1984.

Chamus—Ethnobotany

147. Heine, Bernd, and I. Heine. *Plant concepts and plant use: an ethnobotanical survey of the semi-arid and arid lands of East Africa. Part I: plants of the Chamus, Kenya*. Saarbrücken, Breitenbach, 1988.

Chamus—Language

148. Sim, Ronald J. *A sociolinguistic profile of Maasai-Samburu-Ilchamus languages, Kenya*. Dallas, Summer Institute of Linguistics, 1980.

Chiga—Proverbs

149. Cisternino, Marius. *The proverbs of Kigezi and Ankole, Uganda*. Rome, Museum Combonianum, 1987.

Chiga—Religion

150. Turyahikayo-Rugyema, Benoni. *Philosophy and traditional religion of the Bakiga in southwest Uganda*. Nairobi, Kenya Literature Bureau, 1983.

Chiga—Social Conditions

151. Ngologoza, P. *Kigezi and its people*. Nairobi, East African Literature Bureau, 1969.

Christianity—East Africa

152. Anderson, William B. *The church in East Africa, 1840–1974*. Nairobi, Uzima Press, 1977.

153. Church, J. E. *Quest for the highest*. Exeter, Paternoster Press, 1981.

154. Muga, Erasto. *African response to western Christian religion: a sociological analysis of African separatist religious and political movements*. Kampala, East African Literature Bureau, 1975.

155. Nthamburi, Zablon (ed.) *From mission to church: a handbook of Christianity in East Africa*. Nairobi, Uzima, 1991.

156. Okullu, J. Henry. *Church and marriage in East Africa*. Nairobi, Uzima Press, 1976.

157. Okullu, J. Henry. *Church and politics in East Africa*. Nairobi, Uzima Press, 1974.

158. Pfeiffer, Baldur E. (ed.) *Seventh-day Adventist contributions to East Africa, 1903–1983*. Frankfurt am Main, Peter Lang, 1985.

159. Shorter, Aylward, and Eugene Kataza (eds.) *Missionaries to yourselves: African catechists today*. Maryknoll, Orbis Books, 1972.

160. Shorter, Aylward (ed.) *Church and marriage in eastern Africa*. Eldoret, Association of Episcopal Conferences in Eastern Africa, 1978.

Civil Service—East Africa

161. Kiapi, Abraham. *Civil service laws in East Africa*. Kampala, East African Literature Bureau, 1974.

Climate—East Africa

162. Brown, L. H., and J. Cocheme. *A study of agroclimatology in the highlands of East Africa*. Rome, FAO, 1969.

Coastal Ecology—East Africa

163. Brown, Leslie H. *East African coasts and reefs*. Nairobi, East African Publishing House, 1975.

Colonial History — East Africa

164. Archer, Geoffrey Francis. *Personal and historical memoirs of an East African administrator*. Edinburgh, Oliver & Boyd, 1963.

165. Atieno Odhiambo, E. S. *Siasa: politics and nationalism in East Africa, 1905–1939*. Nairobi, Kenya Literature Bureau, 1981.

166. Brett, Edwin Allan. *Colonialism and underdevelopment in East Africa: the politics of economic change, 1919–1939*. London, Heinemann, 1973.

167. Büttner, Karl, and Heinrich Loth (eds.) *Philosophie der Eroberer und koloniale Wirklichkeit: Ostafrika 1884–1918*. Berlin, Akademie Verlag, 1981.

168. Galbraith, John S. *Mackinnon and East Africa, 1878–1895: a study in the "New Imperialism."* Cambridge, Cambridge University Press, 1972.

169. Gillett, Mary. *Tribute to pioneers: Mary Gillett's index of many of the pioneers of East Africa*. Oxford, J. M. Considine, 1986.

170. Golding, J. A. *Colonialism: the golden years*. Ashford, Birlings, 1987.

171. Gregory, Robert G. *Sidney Webb and East Africa: Labour's experiment with the doctrine of native paramountcy*. Berkeley, University of California Press, 1962.

172. Horrut, Claude. *Les décolonisations est-africaines*. Paris, Pedone, 1971.

173. Lord, John. *Duty, honor, empire: the life and times of Colonel Richard Meinertzhagen*. London, Hutchinson, 1977.

174. Rotberg, Robert I. (ed.) *Imperialism, colonialism and hunger: East and Central Africa*. Lexington, D. C. Heath, 1983.

175. Strayer, Robert W., et al. *Protest movements in colonial East Africa: aspects of early African response to European rule*. Syracuse, Syracuse University Press, Maxwell School of Citizenship and Public Affairs, 1973.

176. Youé, Christopher P. *Robert Thorne Coryndon: proconsular imperialism in southern and eastern Africa, 1897–1925*. Waterloo, Wilfrid Laurier University Press, 1986.

Colonial History — Northeast Africa

177. Aquarone, Alberto. *Dopo Adua: politica e amministrazione coloniale*. Roma, Ministero per i Beni Culturali e Ambientali, Ufficio Centrale per i Beni Archivistici, 1989.

178. Boca, Angelo del. *Gli italiani in Africa Orientale: dall'unità alla marcia su Roma*. Bari, Laterza, 1976.

179. Boca, Angelo del. *Gli italiani in Africa Orientale: la caduta dell'impero*. Bari, Laterza, 1982.

180. Boca, Angelo del. *Gli italiani in Africa Orientale: la conquista dell'impero*. Bari, Laterza, 1979.

181. Bongiovanni, Alberto. *La fine dell'Impero: Africa orientale 1940–1941.* Milano, Mursia, 1974.

182. Grassi, Fabio, and Luigi Goglia (eds.) *Il colonialismo italiano da Adua all'impero.* Bari, Laterza, 1981.

183. Poggiali, Ciro. *Diario AOI, 15 giugno 1936–4 ottobre 1937: gli appunti segreti dell'inviato del Corriere della Serra.* Milano, Longanesi, 1971.

184. Rossi, Gianluigi. *L'Africa italiana verso l'indipendenza, 1941–49.* Milano, Giuffrè, 1980.

185. Stella, Gian Carlo. *Africa Orientale, Eritrea, Abissinia, Somalia, e colonialismo italiano: bibliografia. Catalogo delle opere possedute.* Ravenna, G. C. Stella, 1986.

186. Taddia, Irma. *La memoria dell'Impero: autobiografie d'Africa orientale.* Manduria, Lacaita, 1988.

187. Zaghi, Carlo. *La conquista dell'Africa: studi e ricerche.* Napoli, Istituto Universitario Orientale, 1984. 2 vols.

Cooperatives—East Africa

188. Hyden, Goren. *Efficiency versus distribution in East African cooperatives: a study in organizational conflicts.* Nairobi, East African Literature Bureau, 1973.

189. Widstrand, Carl Gosta (ed.) *Co-operatives and rural development in East Africa.* New York, Africana Publishing, 1970.

Cushitic Languages

190. Bechhaus-Gerst, Marianne, and Fritz Serzisko (eds.) *Cushitic-Omotic: papers from the international symposium on Cushitic and Omotic languages, Cologne, January 6–9, 1986.* Hamburg, Helmut Buske, 1989.

191. Ehret, Christopher. *The historical reconstruction of southern Cushitic phonology and vocabulary.* Berlin, Dietrich Reimer, 1980.

192. Hudson, Grover. *Highland East Cushitic dictionary.* Hamburg, Helmut Buske, 1989.

193. Lamberti, Marcello. *Kuliak and Cushitic: a comparative study.* Heidelberg, Carl Winter, 1988.

194. Leslau, Wolf. *Fifty years of research: selection of articles on Semitic, Ethiopian Semitic and Cushitic.* Wiesbaden, Otto Harrassowitz, 1988.

195. Wedekind, K. *Generating narratives: interrelations of knowledge, text variants and Cushitic focus strategies.* Berlin, Mouton de Gruyter, 1990.

196. Zaborski, Andrzej. *The morphology of nominal plural in the Cushitic languages.* Vienna, Afro-Pub, 1986.

197. Zaborski, Andrzej. *The verb in Cushitic*. Warsaw, Panstwowe Wydawnictwo Naukowe, 1975.

Dams—East Africa

198. Roggeri, Henri. *African dams: impacts in the environment. The social and environmental impact of dams at the local level: a case study of five manmade lakes in eastern Africa*. Nairobi, Environment Liaison Centre, 1985.

Danagla—Agriculture

199. Omer, El Haj Abdalla Bilal. *The Danagla traders of northern Sudan: rural capitalism and agricultural development*. London, Ithaca, 1985.

Dar es Salaam—Geography

200. Blij, Harm J. de. *Dar es Salaam: a study in urban geography*. Evanston, Northwestern University Press, 1963.

201. Sutton, J. E. G. (ed.) *Dar es Salaam: city, port and region*. Dar es Salaam, Tanzania Society, 1970.

Dar es Salaam—Social Conditions

202. Leslie, J. A. K. *A survey of Dar es Salaam*. London, Oxford University Press, 1963.

203. Vorlaufer, Karl. *Dar es Salaam: Bevölkerung und Raum einer afrikanischen Grossstadt unter dem Einfluss von Urbanisierungs- und Mobilitätsprozessen*. Hamburg, Deutsches Institut für Afrika-Forschung, 1973.

Darfur—Archaeology

204. Mohammed, Ibrahim Musa. *The archaeology of central Darfur, Sudan, in the 1st millennium A.D*. Oxford, British Archaeological Reports, 1986.

Darfur—Bibliography

205. Bjørkelo, Anders, and G. E. Wickens. *A bibliography of the Dar Fur/Wadai region*. Bergen, Historisk Institut, Universitetet i Bergen, 1981.

Darfur—Description and Travel

206. Nachtigal, Gustav. *Sahara and Sudan. Vol. IV: Wadai and Darfur*. London, Christopher Hurst, 1972.

Darfur—Desertification

207. Ibrahim, Fouad N. *Desertification in Nord-Darfur: Untersuchungen zur Gefährdung des Naturpotentials durch nicht angepasste Landnutzungsmethoden in der Sahelzone der Republik Sudan*. Hamburg, F. Hirt, 1980.

208. Ibrahim, Fouad N. *Ecological imbalance in the Republic of Sudan, with reference to desertification in Darfur*. Bayreuth, Druckhaus Bayreuth Verlagsgesellschaft, 1984.

Darfur—Economy

209. Abdel-Rahman El-Rasheed, Fatima. *Activités commerciales et dynamisme socio-économique au Darfur*. Bruxelles, Académie Royale des Sciences d'Outre-Mer, 1991.

Darfur—Famine

210. Waal, Alex de. *Famine that kills: Darfur, Sudan, 1984–1985*. Oxford, Clarendon Press, 1989.

Darfur—History

211. Adelberger, J. *Von Sultanat zur Republik: Veränderungen in der Sozialorganisation der Fur (Sudan)*. Stuttgart, Franz Steiner, 1990.

212. Kapteijns, Lidwien, and Jay Spaulding. *After the millennium: diplomatic correspondence from Wadai and Dar Fur on the eve of colonial conquest, 1885–1916*. East Lansing, Michigan State University Press for the African Studies Center, 1988.

213. O'Fahey, Rex S. *State and society in Dar Fur*. New York, St. Martin's Press, 1980.

214. Theobald, A. B. *Ali Dinar: last Sultan of Darfur, 1898–1916*. London, Longmans, 1965.

Darfur—Land

215. O'Fahey, Rex S., et al. *Land in Dar Fur: chapters and related documents from the Dar Fur Sultanate*. Cambridge, Cambridge University Press, 1983.

216. Runger, Mechthild. *Land law and land use control in western Sudan: the case of southern Darfur*. London, Ithaca Press, 1987.

Darfur—Language

217. Jakobi, Angelika. *A Fur grammar: phonology, morphophonology, and morphology*. Hamburg, Helmut Buske, 1990.

Dassenetch—Ethnography

218. Almagor, Uri. *Pastoral partners: affinity and bond partnerships among the Dassenetch of southwest Ethiopia*. Manchester, Manchester University Press, 1978.

219. Carr, Claudia. *Pastoralism in crisis: the Dasanetch and their Ethiopian lands*. Chicago, University of Chicago, Department of Geography, 1977.

Description and Travel—East Africa

220. Beddow, Tim. *East Africa: an evolving landscape*. London, Thames and Hudson, 1988.

221. Hanley, Gerald. *Warriors and strangers*. London, Hamish Hamilton, 1971.

222. Heaton, Tom. *In Teleki's footprints*. London, Macmillan, 1989.

223. Hickman, Gladys Minnie. *Lands and peoples of East Africa*. Third edition. Harlow, Longman, 1986.

224. Hills, Denis. *Man with a lobelia flute: a new view of East Africa*. London, Allen & Unwin, 1969.

225. Richards, Charles, and James Place (eds.) *East African explorers*. Revised edition. London, Oxford University Press, 1968.

Description and Travel—Northeast Africa

226. Beckwith, C., et al. *African ark: the peoples and ancient cultures of Ethiopia and the Horn of Africa*. London, Collins-Harvill, 1990.

227. Weber, Olivier (ed.) *Corne de l'Afrique*. Paris, Autrement, 1987.

Dinka—Ethnography

228. Deng, Francis Mading. *Africans of two worlds*. New Haven, Yale University Press, 1978.

229. Deng, Francis Mading. *Dinka cosmology*. London, Ithaca Press, 1980.

230. Deng, Francis Mading. *The Dinka of the Sudan*. New York, Holt, Rinehart and Winston, 1972.

231. Lienhardt, Godfrey. *Divinity and experience: the religion of the Dinka*. London, Oxford University Press, 1961.

232. Nebel, Arturo. *I dinca sono così: ricordi di una vita fra i dinca del Bahr el Ghazal, Sudan*. Bologna, Nigrizia, 1968.

Dinka—Folktales

233. Deng, Francis Mading. *Dinka folktales: African stories from the Sudan*. London, Holmes and Meier, 1974.

Dinka—History

234. Mawut, Lazarus Leek. *The Dinka resistance to condominium rule, 1902–1932*. Khartoum, University of Khartoum, Graduate College, 1983.

Dinka—Language

235. Malou, Job. *Dinka vowel system*. Dallas, Summer Institute of Linguistics, 1988.

236. Nebel, Arturo. *Dinka-English, English-Dinka dictionary.* Bologna, Editrice Missionaria Italiana, 1979.

237. Tucker, A. N. *Dinka orthography.* Khartoum, University of Khartoum, Institute of African and Asian Studies, 1978.

Dinka—Law

238. Deng, Francis Mading. *Tradition and modernization: a challenge for law among the Dinka of Sudan.* New Haven, Yale University Press, 1971.

239. Khadouf, Hunud Abia. *An outline of Dinka customary law in the Jonglei area.* Khartoum, University of Khartoum, Faculty of Law, 1977.

240. Makec, John Wuol. *The customary law of the Dinka people of Sudan, in comparison with aspects of Western and Islamic laws.* London, Afroworld, 1988.

Dinka—Song

241. Deng, Francis Mading. *The Dinka and their songs.* Oxford, Clarendon Press, 1973.

Dizi—Ethnography

242. Haberland, Eike. *Hierarchie und Kaste: zur Geschichte und politischen Struktur der Dizi in Südwest-Äthiopien.* Stuttgart, Franz Steiner, 1993.

Djibouti—Agriculture

243. Amat, J. P., et al. *L'agriculture maraîchère et fruitière traditionnelle en République de Djibouti.* Paris, Agence de Coopération Culturelle et Technique, 1981.

Djibouti—Bibliography

244. Aubry, Marie-Christine. *Djibouti: bibliographie fondamentale.* Paris, L'Harmattan, 1990.

245. Schraeder, Peter J. *Djibouti.* Oxford, Clio Press, 1991.

Djibouti—Description and Travel

246. Aubry, Marie-Christine. *Djibouti l'ignoré: récits de voyages.* Paris, L'Harmattan, 1988.

247. Hancock, Graham, and Stephen Lloyd. *Djibouti: crossroads of the world.* Nairobi, H & L Associates, 1982.

248. Martineau, André. *Djibouti.* Nouvelle édition. Boulogne-Billancourt, Éditions Delroisse, 1977.

249. Poinsot, Jean Paul. *Djibouti et la Côte Française des Somalis.* Paris, Hachette, 1964.

250. Tazieff, Haroun. *L'odeur du soufre: expédition en Afar*. Paris, Stock, 1975.

251. Weiss, Eric. *Djibouti: évasion*. Paris, Éditions du Fer à Marquer, 1990.

Djibouti—Economy

252. Abdallah, Anis, et al. *Djibouti, developing city and country*. Djibouti, Republic of Djibouti, 1983.

253. Aden Hersi, Mahamoud. *Économie et développement de la ville de Djibouti*. Bordeaux, Université de Bordeaux III, Faculté des Lettres et des Sciences Humaines, Institut de Géographie et d'Études Regionales, 1984.

254. Clarke, Walter Sheldon. *A developmental bibliography for the Republic of Djibouti*. Djibouti, Institut Supérieur d'Études et de Recherches Scientifiques et Techniques, 1979.

255. Wais, I. *Dschibouti: Entwicklungsprobleme und Perspektiven kleiner Staaten. Ein Fallbeispiel*. Osnabruck, Forschungsinstitut Dritte Welt, 1991.

Djibouti—Electricity

256. Dhai, Shibu. *Conventional electricity in Djibouti: challenges and opportunities for the future*. Arlington, Volunteers in Technical Assistance, 1985.

257. Petcu, Mihai. *Perspectives de développement du système éléctrique et tarification de l'éléctricité*. Djibouti, Institut Supérieur d'Études et de Recherches Scientifiques et Techniques, 1986.

Djibouti—Energy

258. Milukas, Matthew, et al. *Djibouti energy initiatives: national energy assessment*. Arlington, Volunteers in Technical Assistance, 1984.

Djibouti—Female Circumcision

259. Erlich, Michel. *La femme blessée: essai sur les mutilations sexuelles féminines*. Paris, L'Harmattan, 1986.

Djibouti—Fisheries

260. DeRito, Paul A., et al. *Development of fishing and fisheries in Djibouti*. Diamond Springs, Resources Development Associates, 1982.

Djibouti—Folktales

261. Mumin, Hassan Shekh, et al. *Contes de Djibouti*. Paris, Conseil International de la Langue Française, 1980.

Djibouti—Foreign Relations

262. Koburger, Charles W. *Naval strategy east of Suez: the role of Djibouti*. New York, Praeger, 1992.

Djibouti—Forestry

263. Bowen, M. Roderick. *A bibliography of forestry in Somalia and Djibouti.* Mogadishu, British Forestry Project Somalia, Overseas Development Administration, 1990.

Djibouti—History

264. Diehl, Jean-Pierre. *Le regard colonial ou 'il y a peu de coloniaux qui n'aient fait escale à Djibouti au moins une fois dans leur vie'.* Paris, Éditions Régine Defordes, 1986.

265. Farah, Gaouad. *La République de Djibouti: naissance d'un état. Chronologie.* Tunis, Imprimerie Officielle, 1982.

266. Laudouze, André. *Djibouti: nation-carrefour.* Deuxième édition. Paris, Karthala, 1989.

267. Oberlé, Philippe. *Afars et Somalis: le dossier de Djibouti.* Paris, Éditions Présence Africaine, 1971.

268. Oberlé, Philippe, and Pierre Hugot. *Histoire de Djibouti: des origines à la république.* Paris, Éditions Présence Africaine, 1985.

269. Trampont, J. *Djibouti hier: de 1887 à 1939.* Paris, Hatier, 1990.

Djibouti—Industry

270. UNIDO. *Djibouti: economic diversification through industrialisation.* Vienna, UNIDO, 1989.

Djibouti—Informal Economy

271. International Labour Office. *Le secteur non-structuré à Djibouti: caractéristiques des entreprises et de le main-d'oeuvre du secteur, contribution à l'emploi et la formation des revenus. Rapport d'une enquête réalisée par le Programme des Emplois et des Compétences Techniques pour l'Afrique.* Addis Abeba, PECTA, 1982.

Djibouti—Music

272. Nourrit, Chantal, and William Pruitt. *Musique traditionnelle de l'Afrique noire: discographie. Vol. 17: Djibouti.* Paris, Radio-France Internationale, Centre de Documentation Africaine, 1983.

Djibouti—Pastoral Production

273. Audru, J., et al. *La végétation et les potentialités pastorales de la République de Djibouti.* Maisons-Alfort, Institut d'Élévage et de Médecine Vétérinaire des Pays Tropicaux, 1987.

Djibouti—Politics

274. Coubba, Ali. *Djibouti: une nation en otage.* Paris, L'Harmattan, 1993.

275. Rabeh, Omar Osman. *Le cercle et la spirale*. Paris, Les Lettres Libres, 1984.

276. Rabeh, Omar Osman. *République de Djibouti ou roue de secours d'Éthiopie*. Ivry, Silex, 1985.

277. Robleh Awaleh, Aden. *Djibouti, clef de la Mer Rouge*. Paris, Caractères, 1986.

278. Tholomier, Robert. *Djibouti: pawn of the Horn of Africa*. Metuchen, Scarecrow Press, 1981.

279. Thompson, Virginia, and Richard Adloff. *Djibouti and the Horn of Africa*. Stanford, Stanford University Press, 1968.

280. Warsama, Absieh Omar, and Maurice Botbol. *Djibouti: les institutions politiques et militaires*. Paris, Banque d'Information et de Documentation de l'Océan Indien, 1986.

Documentation — East Africa

281. Conover, Helen F., and Audrey Walker. *Official publications of British East Africa. Pt. 1: The East Africa High Commission and other regional documents*. Washington, Library of Congress, 1960.

282. Easterbrook, David L., et al. *Microfilms relating to eastern Africa, Pt. 3: Kenya and miscellaneous. A guide to recent acquisitions of Syracuse University*. Syracuse, Syracuse University, Maxwell School of Citizenship and Public Affairs, Program of Eastern African Studies, 1975.

283. Leigh, David, and R. F. Morton. *Microfilms relating to eastern Africa, Pt. 2: Kenya, Asian and miscellaneous. A guide to recent acquisitions of Syracuse University*. Syracuse, Syracuse University, Maxwell School of Citizenship and Public Affairs, Program of Eastern African Studies, 1973.

284. Thurston, Anne. *Guide to archives and manuscripts relating to Kenya and East Africa in the United Kingdom*. London, Hans Zell, 1991.

Documentation — Northeast Africa

285. Luciani, Silvia, and Irma Taddia (eds.) *Fonti comboniane per la storia dell'Africa nord-orientale. Vol. I*. Bologna, Università degli Studi di Bologna, Dipartimento di Politica, Istituzioni, Storia, 1986.

Dodoth — Description

286. Thomas, Elizabeth Marshall. *Warrior herdsmen*. London, Secker & Warburg, 1966.

Drums — East Africa

287. Wymeersch, Patrick. *Ritualisme et fonction des tambours en Afrique interlacustre*. Roma, Istituto Italo-Africano, 1979.

Earthquakes — Northeast Africa

288. Gouin, Pierre. *Earthquake history of Ethiopia and the Horn of Africa*. Ottawa, International Development Research Center, 1979.

Economy—East Africa

289. Bevan, David, et al. *Controlled open economies: a neoclassical approach to structuralism.* Oxford, Clarendon Press, 1990.

290. Bevan, David, et al. *East African lessons on economic liberalization.* Aldershot, Gower, 1987.

291. Bohnet, M., and H. Reichelt. *Applied research and its impact on economic development: the East African case.* Munich, Weltforum-Verlag, 1972.

292. Butt, Safdar Ali. *Essentials of commerce in East Africa.* London, Cassell, 1976.

293. Eshetu Chole, et al. *The crisis of development strategies in eastern Africa.* Addis Ababa, Organization for Social Research in Eastern Africa, 1990.

294. Killick, Tony. *The economies of East Africa* [Bibliography]. Boston, G. K. Hall, 1976.

295. Killick, Tony, et al. *The economies of East Africa: a bibliography, 1974–1980.* Boston, G. K. Hall, 1984.

296. Livingstone, Ian, and H. W. Ord. *Economics for eastern Africa.* Revised and enlarged edition. Nairobi, Heinemann, 1980.

297. Rutz, W. (ed.) *Ostafrika: Themen zur wirtschaftlichen Entwicklung am Beginn der siebziger Jahre.* Stuttgart, Franz Steiner, 1974.

298. Seidman, Ann. *Comparative development strategies in East Africa.* Nairobi, East African Publishing House, 1972.

Economy—Northeast Africa

299. Heinrich, Wolfgang (ed.) *Entwicklungsperspektiven am Horn von Afrika.* Hamburg, Dienste in Übersee, 1991.

Education—East Africa

300. Abidi, Syed A. H. *The future of education in East Africa.* Kampala, World Peace Academy, 1988.

301. Bogonko, Sorobea Nyachieo. *Reflections on education in East Africa.* Nairobi, Oxford University Press, 1991.

302. Castle, Edgar Bradshaw. *Growing up in East Africa.* London, Oxford University Press, 1966.

303. Furley, O. W., and Tom Watson. *A history of education in East Africa.* New York, NOK Publishers, 1978.

304. Gorman, Thomas Patrick (ed.) *Language in education in eastern Africa.* Nairobi, Oxford University Press, 1970.

305. Hartwell, Ash, and Gerard Bennaars (eds.) *School and community in East Africa.* Kampala, Makerere Institute of Social Research, 1975.

306. Hazlewood, Arthur (ed.) *Education, work and pay in East Africa.* Oxford, Clarendon Press, 1989.

307. Ishumi, Abel G. M., et al. (eds.) *Education and social change: readings on selected issues and cases.* Dar es Salaam, Black Star Agencies, 1980.

308. King, Kenneth. *Pan-Africanism and education: a study of race philosophy and education in the southeastern states of America and East Africa.* London, Oxford University Press, 1971.

309. Knight, John B., and Richard H. Sabot. *Education, productivity and inequality: the East African natural experiment.* New York, Oxford University Press for the World Bank, 1990.

310. Lugumba, S. M. E. *A history of education in East Africa, 1900–1973.* Kampala, Kampala Bookshop Publishing Department, 1973.

311. Lutsenburg Maas, Jacob van, and Geert Criel. *Distribution of primary school enrollments in eastern Africa.* Washington, World Bank, 1982.

312. Maliyamkono, T. L., et al. *Higher education and development in East Africa.* London, Heinemann, 1982.

313. Mutibwa, O. M. N. *Education in East Africa, 1970: a selected bibliography.* Kampala, Makerere University Library, 1971.

314. Prewitt, Kenneth (ed.) *Education and political values.* Nairobi, East African Publishing House, 1971.

315. Southall, Roger. *Federalism and higher education in East Africa.* Nairobi, East African Publishing House, 1974.

316. Ssekamwa, J. C. *Readings in the development of education in East Africa.* Kampala, Makerere University, 1971.

317. Umbima, W. E. *Research in education on East Africa (Kenya, Tanzania, Uganda): periodical articles, theses, research papers, 1900–1976.* Nairobi, University of Nairobi, Library, 1977.

Eldoret—Land Use

318. Olima, Washington H. A. *The land use planning in provincial towns of Kenya: a case study of Kisumu and Eldoret towns.* Dortmund, Projekt Verlag, 1993.

Embu—Ethnography

319. Saberwal, S. *The traditional political system of the Embu of central Kenya.* Nairobi, East African Publishing House, 1970.

Embu—History

320. Mwaniki, Henry Stanley Kabeca. *Embu historical texts.* Nairobi, East African Literature Bureau, 1974.

Embu—Songs

321. Mwaniki, Henry Stanley Kabeca. *Categories and substance of Embu traditional songs and dances*. Nairobi, Kenya Literature Bureau, 1986.

Emin Pasha

322. Caillou, A. *South from Khartoum: the story of Emin Pasha*. New York, Hawthorn Books, 1974.

323. Jones, Roger. *The rescue of Emin Pasha*. London, Allison and Busby, 1972.

324. Smith, Iain R. *The Emin Pasha relief expedition, 1886–90*. Oxford, Clarendon Press, 1972.

Employment—East Africa

325. Ishumi, Abel G. M. *The urban jobless in eastern Africa*. Uppsala, Scandinavian Institute of African Studies, 1984.

Energy—East Africa

326. Amann, H. *Energy supply and economic development in East Africa*. Munich, Weltforum-Verlag, 1969.

English Language—East Africa

327. Schmied, Josef J. (ed.) *English in East and Central Africa*. Bayreuth, Eckhard Breitinger, 1989–92. 2 vols.

Entebbe Raid

328. Ben-Porat, Yeshayahu. *Entebbe rescue*. New York, Delacorte Press, 1977.

329. Ofer, Yehuda. *Operation thunder*. Harmondsworth, Penguin, 1976.

330. Stevenson, William. *90 minutes at Entebbe*. London, Bantam, 1976.

331. Williamson, Tony. *Counterstrike Entebbe*. London, Collins, 1976.

Environment—East Africa

332. Berglund, Björn. *Noah's ark is stranded*. London, Macdonald and Jane's, 1977.

333. Brown, Leslie H. *East African mountains and lakes*. Nairobi, East African Publishing House, 1971.

334. Pratt, D. J., and M. D. Gwynne (eds.) *Rangeland management and ecology in East Africa*. London, Hodder & Stoughton, 1977.

Environment—Northeast Africa

335. Molvaer, Reidulf Knut (ed.) *Environmental cooperation and confidence building in the Horn of Africa*. London, Sage, 1993.

Eritrea—Bibliography

336. Research and Information Centre on Eritrea. *Bibliography on Eritrea.* Rome, Research and Information Centre on Eritrea, 1982.

Eritrea—Colonial History

337. Taddia, Irma. *L'Eritrea, colonia 1890–1952: paesaggi, strutture, uomini del colonialismo.* Bologna, Franco Angeli, 1986.

338. Tekeste Negash. *Italian colonialism in Eritrea, 1882–1941: policies, praxis and impact.* Uppsala, University, 1987.

339. Tekeste Negash. *No medicine for the bite of the white snake: notes on nationalism and resistance in Eritrea, 1890–1940.* Uppsala, University, 1986.

340. Trevaskis, G. K. N. *Eritrea: a colony in transition, 1941–52.* London, Oxford University Press, 1960.

341. Yemane Mesghenna. *Italian colonialism, a case study of Eritrea, 1869–1934: motive, praxis and result.* Lund, Ekonomisk-Historiska Fvreningen i Lund, 1988.

Eritrea—Health and Medicine

342. Agneta, Francesca, et al. *Cooperazione e sanità in Eritrea.* Roma, Istituto Italo-Africano, 1990.

Eritrea—Land Tenure

343. Ambaye Zekarias. *Land tenure in Eritrea.* Addis Ababa, Addis Printing Press, 1966.

Eritrea—Law

344. Mellana, V. (ed.) *L'amministrazione della giustizia in Eritrea e Somalia.* Roma, Istituto Poligrafico dell Stato, 1971.

Eritrea—Politics

345. Becker, E., and C. Mitchell. *Chronology of conflict resolution initiatives in Eritrea.* Fairfax, George Mason University, Institute for Conflict Analysis and Resolution, 1991.

346. Bereket Habte Selassie. *Eritrea and the United Nations and other essays.* Trenton, Red Sea Press, 1989.

347. Cahsai Berhane and E. Cahsai-Williamson. *Érythrée: un peuple en marche, 19e–20e siècles.* Paris, L'Harmattan, 1985.

348. Cliffe, Lionel, and Basil Davidson (eds.) *The long struggle of Eritrea for independence and constructive peace.* Trenton, Red Sea Press, 1988.

349. Comité Belge de Secours à L'Érythrée. *Revolution in Eritrea: eyewitness reports.* Brussels, the Committee, 1979.

350. Connell, Dan. *Against all odds: a chronicle of the Eritrean revolution.* Trenton, Red Sea Press, 1993.

351. Davidson, Basil, et al. (eds.) *Behind the war in Eritrea.* Nottingham, Spokesman, 1980.

352. Fenet, Alain, et al. *La question de l'Érythrée: droit international et politique des deux grands.* Paris, Presses Universitaires de France, 1979.

353. Firebrace, J., and S. Holland. *Never kneel down: drought, development and liberation in Eritrea.* Nottingham, Spokesman, 1984.

354. Furrer-Kreski, E., et al. *Handbuch Eritrea: Geschichte und Gegenwart eines Konflikts.* Zürich, Rio Verlag, 1990.

355. Gamacchio, Piero. *La resistenza eritrea.* Cosenza, Lerici, 1978.

356. Habtu Ghebre-Ab. *Ethiopia and Eritrea: a documentary study.* Trenton, Red Sea Press, 1992.

357. Iversen, Ola. *Eritrea!* Oslo, Oktober, 1978.

358. Machida, Robert. *Eritrea: the struggle for independence.* Trenton, Red Sea Press, 1987.

359. Matthies, Volker. *Der Eritrea-Konflikt: ein 'vergessener Krieg' am Horn von Afrika.* Hamburg, Institut für Afrika-Kunde, 1981.

360. Okbazghi Yohannes. *Eritrea: a pawn in world politics.* Gainesville, University of Florida Press, 1991.

361. Papstein, R. *Eritrea: revolution at dusk.* Trenton, Red Sea Press, 1991.

362. Pateman, Roy. *Eritrea: even the stones are burning.* Trenton, Red Sea Press, 1991.

363. Pool, David. *Eritrea: Africa's longest war.* Revised edition. London, Anti-Slavery Society, 1982.

364. Pool, David. *Establishing movements' hegemony: the Eritrean Peoples Liberation Front and the cities, 1977.* Manchester, University of Manchester, Department of Government, 1992.

365. Research and Information Centre on Eritrea. *The Eritrean case.* Rome, Research and Information Centre on Eritrea, 1982.

366. Sherman, R. *Eritrea: the unfinished revolution.* New York, Praeger, 1980.

367. Tesfatsion Medhane. *Eritrea: dynamics of a national question.* Amsterdam, Gruener, 1986.

368. Wolde-Yesus Ammar. *Eritrea: root causes of war and refugees.* Baghdad, Sinbad Printing Co., 1992.

369. Zimmerman, Martin. *Eritrea: Aufbruch in die Freiheit.* Second edition. Essen, Neuer Weg, 1992.

Eritrea—Refugees

370. Gaim Kibreab. *Refugees and development in Africa: the case of Eritrea.* Trenton, Red Sea Press, 1987.

Eritrea—Social Conditions

371. Gebre Medhin, Jordan. *Peasants and nationalism in Eritrea: a critique of Ethiopian studies.* Trenton, Red Sea Press, 1989.

372. Marando, Joseph. *Life in liberated Eritrea: portrait of a people who are constructing a new society.* Rome, Research and Information Centre on Eritrea, 1987.

Eritrea—Women

373. Abeba Tesfagiorgis. *A painful season and a stubborn hope: the odyssey of an Eritrean woman in prison.* Trenton, Red Sea Press, 1992.

374. Kemink, Friederike. *Die Tegreñña-Frauen in Eritrea: eine Untersuchung der Kodizes des Gewohnheitsrechts, 1890–1941.* Stuttgart, Franz Steiner, 1991.

375. Shuckar, Monica. *Lebensbedingungen, Widerstand und Verfolgung von Frauen vor dem Hintergrund des eritreischen Unabhängigkeitskampfes.* Berlin, Berliner Institut für Vergleichende Sozialforschung, 1990.

376. Wilson, Amrit. *The challenge road: women and the Eritrean revolution.* Trenton, Red Sea Press, 1991.

Ethiopia—Agriculture

377. Adams, Dale W. *Agriculture development strategies in Ethiopia, 1950–1970.* Columbus, Ohio State University, 1970.

378. Franzel, S., and H. van Wouten (eds.) *Research with farmers: lessons from Ethiopia.* Wallingford, Commonwealth Agricultural Bureaux, 1992.

379. Göricke, Fred V. *Revolutionäre Agrarpolitik in Äthiopien.* Saarbrücken, Verlag der SSIP-Schriften Breitenbach, 1977.

380. Green, David Alfred George. *Ethiopia: an economic analysis of technological change in four agricultural production systems.* East Lansing, Michigan State University, African Studies Center, 1974.

381. Haile Yesus Abegaz. *The organization of state farms in Ethiopia after the land reform of 1975: planning, realization, potential and problems.* Saarbrücken, Breitenbach, 1982.

382. Hartl, Philipp von, et al. *Agricultural carrying capacity and regional development planning in Ethiopia.* Stuttgart, Universität Stuttgart, Institut für Raumordnung, 1990.

383. Huffnagel, H. P. (ed.) *Agriculture in Ethiopia.* Rome, FAO, 1961.

384. Kidane Mengisteab. *Ethiopia: failure of land reform and agricultural crisis.* New York, Greenwood Press, 1990.

385. Kirsch, O. C., et al. *Agricultural revolution and peasant emancipation in Ethiopia: a missed opportunity.* Saarbrücken, Breitenbach, 1989.

386. Leander, Lars. *A case study of peasant farming in the Digelu and Yeloma areas, Chilalo Awraja, Ethiopia.* Addis Ababa, Chilalo Agricultural Development Unit, Planning and Evaluation Section, 1969.

387. Leithmann-Früh, Gudrun A. *Scope of quantitative analysis of development strategies in subsistence-oriented farms: the case of smallholder development in the Ethiopian highlands.* Krefeld, Günter Marchal, und Hans-Jochen Matzenbacher Wissenschaftsverlag, 1983.

388. Miller, Clarence John, et al. *Production of grains and pulses in Ethiopia.* Menlo Park, Stanford Research Institute, 1969.

389. Pickett, J. *Economic development in Ethiopia: agriculture, the market and the state.* Paris, OECD, 1991.

390. Robinson, Harry Joseph, and Mammo Bahta. *An agricultural credit program for Ethiopia.* Menlo Park, Stanford Research Institute, 1969.

391. Ståhl, Michael. *Contradictions in agricultural development: a study of three minimum package projects in southern Ethiopia.* Uppsala, Scandinavian Institute of African Studies, 1973.

392. Ståhl, Michael. *Ethiopia: political contradictions in agricultural development.* Stockholm, Liber Treyk, 1974.

393. Storck, Harmen, et al. *Farming systems and farm management practices of smallholders in the Hararghe highlands: a baseline survey.* Kiel, Vauk, 1991.

394. Westphal, E. *Agricultural systems in Ethiopia.* Wageningen, Centre for Agricultural Publishing and Documentation, 1974.

Ethiopia—Archaeology

395. Bernand, Etienne, et al. *Recueil des inscriptions de l'Éthiopie des périodes pré-Axoumite et Axoumite.* Paris, Boccard, 1991. 2 vols.

396. Drewes, Abraham Johannes. *Inscriptions de l'Éthiopie antique.* Leiden, E. J. Brill, 1962.

397. Jäger, Otto A., and Ivy Pearce. *Antiquities of north Ethiopia: a guide.* Stuttgart, Brockhaus, 1974.

398. Leroy, Jules. *L'Éthiopie: archéologie et culture.* Paris, Desclée De Brouwer, 1973.

Ethiopia—Art and Artists

399. Biasio, Elisabeth. *Die verborgene Wirklichkeit: drei äthiopische Maler der Gegenwart.* Zürich, Völkskundemuseum der Universität, 1989.

400. Chojnacki, Stanislaw. *Major themes in Ethiopian painting: indigenous developments, the influence of foreign models and their adaptation, from the 13th to the 19th century.* Stuttgart, Franz Steiner, 1983.

401. Gerster, Georg (ed.) *Kirchen in Fels: Entdeckungen in Äthiopien.* Zürich, Atlantis Verlag, 1972.

402. Girma Fisseha and Walter Raunig. *Mensch und Geschichte in Äthiopiens Volksmalerei.* Innsbruck, Pinguin-Verlag, 1985.

403. Grierson, Roderick (ed.) *African Zion: the sacred art of Ethiopia.* New Haven, Yale University Press, 1993.

404. International Conference on the History of Ethiopian Art. *Proceedings of the first International Conference on the History of Ethiopian Art.* London, Pindar Press, 1989.

405. Leroy, Jules. *Ethiopian painting in the late middle ages and under the Gondar dynasty.* London, Merlin Press, 1967.

406. Pankhurst, Richard. *Afewerk Tekle.* Addis Ababa, Artistic Printers, 1987.

407. Raunig, Walter. *Religöse Kunst Äthiopiens: religious art of Ethiopia.* Stuttgart, Institut für Auslandsbeziehungen, 1973.

408. Taye Tadesse. *Short biographies of some Ethiopian artists.* Revised edition. Addis Ababa, Kuraz Publishing Agency, 1991.

Ethiopia—Atlases

409. Mesfin Wolde Mariam. *An atlas of Ethiopia.* Revised edition. Addis Ababa, [the Author], 1970.

Ethiopia—Banking

410. Mauri, Arnaldo, and Clara Caselli. *Moneta e banca in Etiopia.* Milano, Giuffrè, 1986.

Ethiopia—Bible

411. Cowley, Roger W. *Ethiopian biblical interpretation: a study in exegetical tradition and hermeneutics.* Cambridge, Cambridge University Press, 1989.

412. Cowley, Roger W. *The traditional interpretation of the Apocalypse of St. John in the Ethiopian Church.* Cambridge, Cambridge University Press, 1982.

413. Ullendorff, Edward. *Ethiopia and the Bible.* London, Oxford University Press, 1968.

Ethiopia—Bibliography

414. Abbink, J. *Ethiopian society and history: a bibliography of Ethiopian studies.* Leiden, African Studies Centre, 1991.

415. Alula Hidaru and Dessalegn Rahmato. *A short guide to the study of Ethiopia: a general bibliography.* Westport, Greenwood Press, 1976.

416. Brown, Clifton E. *Ethiopian perspectives: a bibliographical guide to the history of Ethiopia.* Westport, Greenwood Press, 1978.

417. Lockot, Hans Wilhelm. *Bibliographia Aethiopica: die äthiopienkündliche Literatur des deutschsprachigen Raums.* Stuttgart, Franz Steiner, 1982.

418. Milkias, Paulos. *Ethiopia: a comprehensive bibliography.* Boston, G. K. Hall, 1989.

Ethiopia—Biography

419. Belaynesh Michael, et al. *The dictionary of Ethiopian biography. Volume 1: from early times to the end of the Zagwé dynasty, c. 1270 AD.* Addis Ababa, Addis Ababa University, Institute of Ethiopian Studies, 1975.

Ethiopia—Calendar

420. Neugebauer, Otto. *Chronography in Ethiopic sources.* Vienna, Verlag der Österreichischen Akademie der Wissenschaften, 1989.

421. Neugebauer, Otto. *Ethiopic astronomy and computus.* Vienna, Österreichischen Akademie der Wissenschaften, 1979.

422. Tubiana, Joseph. *Ethioconcord: a computerized concordance of the Ethiopian and Gregorian calendars.* Rotterdam, Balkema, 1988.

Ethiopia—Ceramics

423. Fattovich, Rodolfo. *Materiali per lo studio della ceramica pre-aksumita etiopica.* Napoli, Istituto Orientale di Napoli, 1980.

Ethiopia—Child Welfare

424. Pirenne, Jacqueline. *Mes fils de la rue—Addis Abeba.* Paris, Fayard, 1989.

Ethiopia—Coffee Production

425. Sadler, Peter. *Regional development in Ethiopia: a cost benefit appraisal.* Cardiff, University of Wales Press, 1976.

Ethiopia—Community Development

426. Baier, E. *Sozialstruktur, community development und Entwicklungsplanung in Äthiopien.* München, Weltforum-Verlag, 1974.

Ethiopia—Constitution

427. Paul, James C., and Christopher Clapham. *Ethiopian constitutional development: a sourcebook.* Addis Ababa, Haile Selassie I University, Faculty of Law, 1966.

428. Yohannes Petros. *Constitutional history of Ethiopia.* London, Ethio-International, Center of Documentation and Translation, 1989.

Ethiopia—Cooperatives

429. Poluha, E. *Central planning and local reality: the case of a producers co-operative in Ethiopia.* Stockholm, University of Stockholm, Department of Social Anthropology, 1989.

Ethiopia—Craftsmen

430. Amborn, Hermann. *Differenzierung und Integration: vergleichende Untersuchungen zu Spezialisten und Handwerken in südäthiopischen Agrargesellschaften.* München, Trickster, 1990.

431. Karsten, Detlev. *The economics of handicrafts in traditional societies: an investigation in Sidamo and Gemu Goffa Province, southern Ethiopia.* Munich, Weltforum-Verlag, 1972.

Ethiopia—Crosses

432. Hecht, Elisabeth Dorothea. *The hand crosses of the IES collection.* Addis Ababa, Addis Ababa University, Institute of Ethiopian Studies, 1990.

433. Korabiewicz, W. *The Ethiopian cross.* Addis Ababa, Holy Trinity Cathedral, 1973.

Ethiopia—Description and Travel

434. Alvares, Francisco. *The Prester John of the Indies: a true relation of the lands of the Prester John being the narrative of the Portuguese embassy to Ethiopia in 1520 . . . The translation of Lord Stanley of Alderley, 1881, revised and edited with additional material by C. F. Beckingham and G. W. B. Huntingford.* London, Hakluyt Society, 1961. 2 vols.

435. Balsan, François. *Embuscade en Éthiopie.* Paris, Éditions de l'Amitié Rageot, 1971.

436. Buxton, David. *The Abyssinians.* London, Thames and Hudson, 1970.

437. Cropp, Wolf-Ulrich. *Äthiopien: im Land der Mursi.* Stuttgart, Pietsch, 1991.

438. Davy, André. *Éthiopie d'hier et d'aujourd'hui.* Paris, Le Livre Africain, 1970.

439. Edmonds, I. G. *Ethiopia: land of the Conquering Lion of Judah.* New York, Holt, Rinehart and Winston, 1975.

440. Forbes, Duncan. *The heart of Ethiopia.* London, Robert Hall, 1972.

441. Galperin, Georgii Lvovich. *Äthiopische Reise.* Leipzig, Brockhaus, 1972.

442. Gerster, Georg, et al. *Äthiopien: das Dach Afrikas.* Zürich, Atlantis Verlag, 1974.

443. Gouvenain, Marc de. *Retour en Éthiopie.* Paris, Actes Sud, 1990.

444. Hasselblatt, Gunnar. *Äthiopien: Menschen, Kirchen, Kulturen.* Stuttgart, Radius-Verlag, 1979.

445. Henze, Paul B. *Ethiopian journeys: travels in Ethiopia, 1969–72.* London, Benn, 1977.

446. Lobo, Jeronimo. *The "Itinerario" . . . Translated by D. M. Lockhart from the Portuguese text established and edited by M. G. da Costa. With an introduction and notes by C. F. Beckingham.* London, Hakluyt Society, 1984.

447. Marsden-Smedley, Philip. *A far country: travels in Ethiopia.* London, Century, 1990.

448. Murphy, Dervla. *In Ethiopia with a mule.* London, Century, 1984.

449. Pankhurst, Richard, and L. Ingrams. *Ethiopia engraved: an illustrated catalogue of engravings by foreign travellers from 1681 to 1900.* London, Kegan Paul International, 1988.

450. Prutky, Remedius. *Prutky's travels in Ethiopia and other countries.* Translated by J. H. Arrowsmith-Brown. London, Hakluyt Society, 1991.

451. Rittlinger, Herbert. *Das Geheimnis des Abai.* Wiesbaden, Brockhaus, 1960.

452. Shelemay, Kay Kaufman. *A song of longing: an Ethiopian journey.* Urbana, University of Illinois Press, 1991.

453. Snailham, R. *The Blue Nile revealed: the story of the Great Abbai expedition.* London, Chatto and Windus, 1970.

454. Vanderlinden, Jacques. *L'Éthiopie et ses populations.* Bruxelles, Éditions Complexe, 1977.

455. Wohlenberg, Hellmut. *Im südlichen Abessinien: Reiseberichte von Oktober 1934 bis Mai 1935, mit einem Schriftenverzeichnis des Autors und einem Register von Ilse Wohlenberg.* Hildesheim, Georg Olms, 1988.

456. Woodhead, Leslie. *Box full of spirits: adventures of a film-maker in Africa.* London, Heinemann, 1987.

Ethiopia—Documentation

457. Steffanson, Borg G., and Ronald K. Starrett (eds.) *Documents on Ethiopian politics.* Salisbury, N.C., Documentary Publications, 1976–77. 3 vols.

Ethiopia—Economy

458. Assefa Bekele and Eshetu Chole. *A profile of the Ethiopian economy.* London, Oxford University Press, 1969.

459. Cherian, K. A. *Ethiopia today: an up-to-date, illustrated review of economic development.* Addis Ababa, Central Printing Press, 1969.

460. Daniel Teferra. *Economic development and nation building in Ethiopia.* Bid Rapids, Ferris State College, 1986.

461. Daniel Teferra. *Social history and theoretical analyses of the economy of Ethiopia.* Lewiston, Edwin Mellen Press, 1990.

462. Ege, Svein (ed.) *Development in Ethiopia: proceedings from a conference at the University of Trondheim, 9–10 March, 1987.* Trondheim, University of Trondheim, College of Arts and Science, Ethiopia Research Programme, 1988.

463. Ege, Svein (ed.) *Ethiopia: problems of sustainable development. A conference report.* Trondheim, University of Trondheim, 1990.

464. Galperin, Georgii Lvovich. *Ethiopia: population, resources, economy.* Moscow, Progress, 1981.

465. Gill, P. (ed.) *Readings on the Ethiopian economy.* Addis Ababa, Haile Selassie I University, Institute of Development Research, 1974.

466. Griffin, Keith (ed.) *The economy of Ethiopia.* Basingstoke, Macmillan, 1992.

Ethiopia—Education

467. Fassil R. Kiros. *Implementing educational policies in Ethiopia.* Washington, World Bank, 1990.

468. Geda Worku. *Bibliography of educational publications on Ethiopia.* Addis Ababa, National University, Faculty of Education, Research Center Library, 1975.

469. Hanson, John W. *Secondary level teachers: supply and demand in Ethiopia.* East Lansing, Michigan State University, Institute for International Education and African Studies Center, 1970.

470. McNab, C. *Language policy and language practice: implementation dilemmas in Ethiopian education.* Stockholm, Stockholm University, Institute of International Education, 1989.

471. Searle, Chris. *A blindfold removed: Ethiopia's struggle for literacy.* London, Karia Press, 1991.

472. Sjöström, Margareta, and Rolf Sjöström. *How do you spell development? A study of a literacy campaign in Ethiopia.* Uppsala, Scandinavian Institute of African Studies, 1993.

473. Sjöström, Margareta. *Literacy and development.* Umea, Umea Universitet, Pedagogiska Institutionen, 1982.

474. Sjöström, Rolf, and Margareta Sjöström. *YDLC: a literacy campaign in Ethiopia. An introductory study and a plan for further research.* Uppsala, Scandinavian Institute of African Studies, 1973.

475. Summerskill, John. *Haile Sellassie I University: a blueprint for development.* New York, Ford Foundation, 1970.

476. Tekeste Negash. *The crisis of Ethiopian education: some implications for nation-building.* Uppsala, University of Uppsala, Department of Education, 1990.

477. Teshome G. Wagaw. *Education in Ethiopia: prospect and retrospect.* Ann Arbor, University of Michigan Press, 1979.

478. Teshome G. Wagaw. *The development of higher education and social change: an Ethiopian experience.* East Lansing, Michigan State University Press, 1990.

Ethiopia—Employment

479. International Labour Office. *Employment and unemployment in Ethiopia: report of the exploratory Employment Policy Mission organized by the International Labour Office.* Geneva, International Labour Office, 1973.

480. International Labour Office. *Socialism from the grass roots: accumulation, employment and equity in Ethiopia.* Addis Ababa, International Labour Office, Jobs and Skills Programme for Africa, 1982.

481. Osterkamp, R. *Vom Händler zum Industrieunternehmer? Zur beruflichen Mobilität in Entwicklungsländern am Beispiel Äthiopiens.* München, Weltforum-Verlag, 1974.

Ethiopia—Environment

482. Böhm, Karlheinz. *Äthiopien: mein Traum für ein Land.* Stuttgart, Horizonte/Libri F, 1993.

483. Brown, Leslie H. *Conservation for survival: Ethiopia's choice.* Addis Ababa, Haile Selassie I University, 1973.

484. Mesfin Wolde Mariam. *Suffering under God's environment: a vertical study of the predicament of peasants in north-central Ethiopia.* Bern, Arbeitsgemeinschaft Geographica Bernensia, 1991.

Ethiopia—Ethnobotany

485. Mooney, H. F. *A glossary of Ethiopian plant names.* Dublin, Dublin University Press, 1963.

Ethiopia—Ethnography

486. Bender, Marvin Lionel (ed.) *Peoples and cultures of the Ethio-Sudan borderlands.* East Lansing, Michigan State University, African Studies Center, 1981.

487. Hultin, Jan. *Man and land in Wollega, Ethiopia.* Göteborg, University of Göteborg, Department of Social Anthropology, 1977.

488. Leiris, Michel. *La possession et ses aspects théâtraux chez les Éthiopiens de Gondar.* Paris, Le Sycomore, 1980.

489. Levine, Donald. *Greater Ethiopia: the evolution of a multiethnic society*. Chicago, University of Chicago Press, 1974.

490. Levine, Donald. *Wax and gold: tradition and innovation in Ethiopian culture*. Chicago, University of Chicago Press, 1965.

491. Lord, Edith. *Queen of Sheba's heirs: cultural patterns of Ethiopia*. Washington, Acropolis Books, 1970.

492. Minker, Gunter. *Burji, Konso-Gidole, Dullay: Materialien zur Demographie, Landwirtschaft und Siedlungsstruktur eines südäthiopischen Kulturareals*. Bremen, Übersee-Museum, 1986.

493. Minker, Gunter. *Der sakrale Charakter der Macht: Legitimation von Autorität, Macht und Herrschaft des pogolho in den oralen Traditionen Dullay-sprachiger Völker Süd-Äthiopiens*. Bremen, Übersee-Museum, 1988.

494. Rodinson, Maxime. *Magie, médecine et possession à Gondar*. Paris, Mouton, 1967.

495. Shack, William A. *The central Ethiopians: Ahmara, Tigrina and related peoples*. London, International African Institute, 1974.

496. Straube, Helmut. *Westkuschitische Volker Süd-Äthiopiens*. Stuttgart, Kohlhammer, 1963.

497. Tippett, Alan R. *Peoples of southwest Ethiopia*. South Pasadena, William Carey Library, 1970.

Ethiopia—Exports

498. Schwarz, William L. K. *Ethiopia's export trade in major agricultural commodities*. Menlo Park, Stanford Research Institute, 1969.

Ethiopia—Famine

499. Alemneh Dejene. *Environment, famine and politics in Ethiopia: a view from the village*. Boulder, Lynne Rienner, 1990.

500. Article 19. *Starving in silence: a report on famine and censorship*. London, Article 19, 1990.

501. Banga, Luther (ed.) *Reducing people's vulnerability to famine: an evaluation of Band Aid and Live Aid financed projects in Africa. Vol. 4: Ethiopia, country annexe and case studies*. London, Band Aid, 1991.

502. Clay, Jason W., and Bonnie K. Holcomb. *Politics and the Ethiopian famine, 1984–1985*. Cambridge, Mass., Cultural Survival, 1986.

503. Dawit Wolde Giorgis. *Red tears: war, famine and revolution in Ethiopia*. Trenton, Red Sea Press, 1989.

504. Dessalegn Rahmato. *Famine and survival strategies: a case study of northeast Ethiopia*. Uppsala, Scandinavian Institute of African Studies, 1991.

505. Finn, James (ed.) *Ethiopia: the politics of famine.* New York, Freedom House, 1990.

506. Gill, P. *A year in the death of Africa: politics, bureaucracy and the famine.* London, Grafton Books, 1986.

507. Hancock, Graham. *Ethiopia: the challenge of hunger.* London, Gollancz, 1985.

508. Harris, Myles F. *Breakfast in hell: a doctor's eyewitness account of the politics of hunger in Ethiopia.* New York, Poseidon, 1987.

509. Hussein, Abdul Mejid. *Rehab: drought and famine in Ethiopia.* London, International African Institute, 1976.

510. Hutchinson, B. *Famine mitigation bibliography, with special emphasis on Ethiopia, Sudan and Angola.* Tucson, University of Arizona, Arid Lands Information Center, 1992.

511. Jansson, Kurt, et al. *The Ethiopian famine.* London, Zed Books, 1987.

512. Jean, François. *Éthiopie: du bon usage de la famine.* Paris, Médecins sans Frontières, 1986.

513. Kaplan, R. D. *Surrender or starve: the wars behind the famine.* Boulder, Westview Press, 1988.

514. Lundstrom, Karl Johan. *North-Eastern Ethiopia: society in famine.* Uppsala, Scandinavian Institute of African Studies, 1976.

515. Mesfin Wolde Mariam. *Rural vulnerability to famine in Ethiopia, 1958–1977.* New Delhi, Vikas, 1984.

516. Nolan, Liam. *The forgotten famine.* Dublin, Mercier Press, 1974.

517. Pankhurst, Richard. *The great Ethiopian famine of 1888–1892: a new assessment.* Addis Ababa, Haile Selassie I University, 1964.

518. Pankhurst, Richard. *The history of famine and epidemics in Ethiopia prior to the twentieth century.* Addis Ababa, Relief and Rehabilitation Commission, 1985.

519. Penrose, A. (ed.) *Beyond the famine: an examination of the issues behind famine in Ethiopia.* Geneva, International Institute for Relief and Development, 1988.

520. Purcell, Deirdre. *Ethiopia: the dark hunger.* Dublin, Magill, 1984.

521. Solberg, Richard W. *Miracle in Ethiopia: a partnership response to famine.* New York, Friendship Press, 1991.

522. Varnis, S. L. *Reluctant aid or aiding the reluctant: US food aid policy and Ethiopian famine relief.* New Brunswick, Transaction Books, 1990.

523. Waller, James. *Fau: portrait of an Ethiopian famine.* Jefferson, McFarland, 1990.

524. Webb, Patrick, et al. *Famine in Ethiopia: policy implications of coping failure at national and household levels.* Washington, International Food Policy Research Institute, 1992.

Ethiopia—Fertility

525. Dahl-Jørgensen, Carla. *Fertility behavior in a peasant society of northern Shäwa, Ethiopia.* Trondheim, University of Trondheim, 1991.

Ethiopia—Finance

526. Mauri, Arnaldo. *Il mercato del credito in Etiopia.* Milano, Giuffrè, 1967.

Ethiopia—Folksong

527. Lange, Werner. *Domination and resistance: narrative songs of the Kafa highlands.* East Lansing, Michigan State University, 1979.

Ethiopia—Folktales

528. Bachrach, Shlomo. *Ethiopian folk-tales.* Addis Ababa, Oxford University Press, 1967.

529. Hopfmann, Jürgen. *Altäthiopische Volksweisheiten im historischen Gewand: Legenden, Geschichten, Philosophien.* Frankfurt am Main, Peter Lang, 1992.

Ethiopia—Food and Nutrition

530. Abebe Haile Gabriel. *Generating marketed surplus of food through state farms: a critical evaluation of Ethiopian experience.* The Hague, Institute of Social Studies, 1990.

531. Holmberg, Johan. *Grain marketing and land reform in Ethiopia: an analysis of the marketing and pricing of food grains in 1976 after the land reform.* Uppsala, Scandinavian Institute of African Studies, 1977.

532. Holt, Julius, and Mark Lawrence. *Making ends meet: a survey of the food economy of the Ethiopian north-east highlands.* London, Save the Children UK, 1993.

533. Selinus, Ruth. *The traditional food of the central Ethiopian highlands.* Uppsala, Scandinavian Institute of African Studies, 1971.

Ethiopia—Foreign Aid

534. Dettbarn, Günter. *Äthiopienhilfe: Menschen für Menschen.* Kiel, Magazin-Verlag, 1990.

Ethiopia—Foreign Relations

535. Bairu Tafla. *Ethiopia and Germany: cultural, political and economic relations, 1871–1936.* Stuttgart, Franz Steiner, 1981.

536. Buccianti, Giovanni. *L'egemonia sull'Etiopia, 1918–1923: lo scontro diplomatico tra Italia, Francia e Inghilterra.* Milano, Giuffrè, 1977.

537. Dimetros, Namrud. *Die äthiopische Revolution und deren aussenpolitische und wirtschaftspolitische Orientierung, unter besonderer Berücksichtigung der Europäischen Gemeinschaft.* Münster, Lit-Verlag, 1985.

538. Donzel, E. van. *Foreign relations of Ethiopia, 1642–1700: documents relating to the journeys of Khodja Murad.* Leiden, Nederlands Historisch-Archaeologisch Instituut te Istanbul, 1979.

539. Hagos Mehary. *The strained US-Ethiopian relations.* Stockholm, Almqvist & Wiksell, 1989.

540. Korn, D. A. *Ethiopia, the United States and the Soviet Union.* London, Croom Helm, 1986.

541. Lefebvre, Jeffrey A. *Arms for the Horn: U.S. security policy in Ethiopia and Somalia, 1953–1991.* Pittsburgh, University of Pittsburgh Press, 1991.

542. Magri, Pier Giacomo. *La politica estera etiopica e la questione eritrea e somala, 1941–1960.* Milano, Giuffrè, 1980.

543. Marcus, Harold G. *Ethiopia, Great Britain, and the United States, 1941–1974: the politics of empire.* Berkeley, University of California Press, 1983.

544. Potholm, Christian P. *Liberation and exploitation: the struggle for Ethiopia.* Washington, University Press of America, 1976.

545. Ram, K. V. *The barren relationship: Britain and Ethiopia, 1805–1868.* New Delhi, Concept Publishing, 1985.

546. Ulm-Erbach, C. F. von. *Äthiopiens Beitrag zur Gründung der Organisation für Afrikanische Einheit: eine Studie zur Rezeption des Panafrikanismus in die afrikanische Politik und Anpassung Äthiopiens in diese Entwicklung.* Frankfurt am Main, Peter Lang, 1974.

547. Yakobson, Sergius. *The Soviet Union and Ethiopia: a case of traditional behavior.* Notre Dame, Ind., University of Notre Dame Press, 1965.

548. Zaghi, Carlo. *I Russi in Etiopia.* Napoli, Guida Editori, 1972–73. 2 vols.

Ethiopia—Forestry

549. Chaffey, D. R. *South-West Ethiopia Forest Inventory Project: a glossary of vernacular plant names and a field key to the trees.* Surbiton, Land Resources Development Centre, 1980.

550. Poschen-Eiche, P. *The application of farming systems research to community forestry: a case study in the Harage highlands, eastern Ethiopia.* Werksheim, Josef Margraf, 1989.

Ethiopia—Geography

551. Imbrighi, Gastone. *L'Etiopia: lineamenti antropogeografici.* L'Aquila, Japadre, 1970.

552. Mesfin Wolde Mariam. *An introductory geography of Ethiopia*. Addis Ababa, Berhanena Selam HSI Printing Press, 1972.

553. Stitz, Volker. *Studien zur Kulturgeographie Zentraläthiopiens*. Bonn, Dümmlers, 1974.

Ethiopia—Geology

554. Abul-Haggag, Y. *A contribution to the physiography of northern Ethiopia*. London, Athlone Press, 1961.

555. Morton, Bill. *A field guide to Ethiopian minerals, rocks and fossils*. Addis Ababa, Addis Ababa University Press, 1978.

Ethiopia—Hagiography

556. Kriss, Rudolf, and Hubert Kriss-Heinrich. *Volkskundliche Anteile in Kult und Legende äthiopischer Heiliger*. Wiesbaden, Otto Harrassowitz, 1975.

Ethiopia—Handbook

557. Nelson, Harold D., and Irving Kaplan (eds.) *Ethiopia: a country study*. Third edition. Washington, American University, 1981.

Ethiopia—Health and Medicine

558. Kloos, Helmut, and Zein Ahmed Zein (eds.) *Ecology of health and disease in Ethiopia*. Boulder, Westview Press, 1992.

559. Kloos, Helmut, and Zein Ahmed Zein. *Health and disease in Ethiopia: a guide to the literature, 1940–1985*. Addis Ababa, Ministry of Health, 1988.

560. Kloos, Helmut, and Zein Ahmed Zein. *Health, disease, medicine and famine in Ethiopia: a bibliography*. London, Greenwood Press, 1991.

561. Messing, Simon D. *A holistic reader in applied anthropology: the target of health in Ethiopia*. New York, MSS Information Corporation, 1972.

562. Pankhurst, Richard. *An introduction to the medical history of Ethiopia*. Trenton, Red Sea Press, 1990.

563. Schneider, H. *Leprosy and other health problems in Hararghe, Ethiopia*. Groningen, Rijksuniversiteit, 1975.

564. Slikkerveer, L. J. *Plural medical systems in the Horn of Africa: the legacy of "Sheikh" Hippocrates*. London, Kegan Paul International, 1990.

Ethiopia—History

565. Abir, Mordechai. *Ethiopia and the Red Sea: the rise and decline of the Solomonic dynasty and Muslim-European rivalry in the region*. London, Frank Cass, 1980.

566. Abir, Mordechai. *Ethiopia, the era of the princes: the challenge of Islam and the re-unification of the Christian empire, 1769–1855*. London, Longmans, 1968.

567. Anfray, Francis. *Les anciens Éthiopiens: siècles d'histoire*. Paris, Armand Colin, 1990.

568. Appleyard, David L., et al. *Letters from Ethiopian rulers, early and mid-nineteenth century. Preserved in the British Library, the Public Record Office, Lambeth Palace, the National Army Museum, India Office Library and Records*. Translated by D. L. Appleyard from Ge'ez and Amharic and by A. K. Irvine from Arabic and annotated by R. K. P. Pankhurst with an appendix by Bairu Tafla. London, Oxford University Press for the British Academy, 1986.

569. Arnold, Percy. *Prelude to Magdala: Emperor Theodore of Ethiopia and British diplomacy*. London, Bellew Publishing, 1991.

570. Asfa-Wossen Asserate. *Die Geschichte von Sawa (Äthiopien), 1700–1865, nach dem Tarika Nagast des Belatten Geta Heruy Walda Sellase*. Stuttgart, Franz Steiner, 1980.

571. Bahru Zewde. *A history of modern Ethiopia, 1855–1974*. London, James Currey, 1991.

572. Bairu Tafla. *A chronicle of Emperor Yohannes IV, 1872–89*. Stuttgart, Franz Steiner, 1977.

573. Bartnicki, Andrzej, and Joanna Mantel-Niecko. *Geschichte Äthiopiens, von den Anfängen bis zur Gegenwart*. Berlin, Akademie-Verlag, 1978. 2 vols.

574. Bates, Darrell. *The Abyssinian difficulty: the Emperor Theodorus and the Magdala campaign, 1867–1868*. London, Oxford University Press, 1979.

575. Casbon, Eleanor. *The incurable optimists: Chris and Dan Sandford of Ethiopia*. Penzance, United Writers, 1993.

576. Darkwah, R. H. Kofi. *Shewa, Menilek and the Ethiopian empire, 1813–1889*. London, Heinemann, 1975.

577. Dombrowski, Franz Amadeus. *Ethiopia's access to the sea*. Leiden, E. J. Brill, 1985.

578. Dombrowski, Franz Amadeus. *Tanasee 106: eine Chronik der Herrscher Äthiopiens*. Stuttgart, Franz Steiner, 1983. 2 vols.

579. Donham, Donald L., and Wendy James (eds.) *The southern marches of imperial Ethiopia: essays in history and social anthropology*. Cambridge, Cambridge University Press, 1986.

580. Ellert, Gerhart. *Afrikas christliche Festung: Äthiopien im Bild der Geschichte*. Wien, Kremayr und Scheriau, 1972.

581. Erlich, Haggai. *Ethiopia and Eritrea during the scramble for Africa: a political biography of Ras Alula, 1875–1897*. East Lansing, Michigan State University, African Studies Center, 1982.

582. Erlich, Haggai. *Ethiopia and the challenge of independence*. Boulder, Lynne Rienner, 1986.

583. Garavaglia, Lino. *Ethiopia: XXV secoli di civiltà e di storia.* Milano, Missioni Estere Cappuccini, 1973.

584. Gebre I. Elyas, and Reidulf Knut Molvaer. *Prowess, piety and politics: the chronicle of Abeto Iyasus and Empress Zewditu of Ethiopia, 1909–1930.* Stuttgart, Franz Steiner, 1993.

585. Gebru Tareke. *Ethiopia: power and protest. Peasant revolts in the twentieth century.* Cambridge, Cambridge University Press, 1991.

586. Gilkes, Patrick. *The dying lion: feudalism and modernization in Ethiopia.* London, Julian Friedmann, 1975.

587. Greenfield, Richard. *Ethiopia: a new political history.* London, Pall Mall Press, 1965.

588. Haberland, Eike. *Untersuchungen zum äthiopischen Königstum.* Stuttgart, Franz Steiner, 1965.

589. Habtu Ghebre-Ab. *Ethiopia and Eritrea: a documentary study.* Trenton, Red Sea Press, 1992.

590. Hammerschmidt, Ernst. *Äthiopien: Christliches Reich zwischen Gestern und Morgen.* Wiesbaden, Otto Harrassowitz, 1967.

591. Hansberry, William Leo. *Pillars in Ethiopian history.* Washington, Howard University Press, 1974.

592. Holcomb, Bonnie K., and Sisai Ibssa. *The invention of Ethiopia: the making of a dependent colonial state in Northeast Africa.* Trenton, Red Sea Press, 1990.

593. Huntingford, G. W. B. *The glorious victories of 'Amda Seyon, King of Ethiopia.* Oxford, Clarendon Press, 1965.

594. Huntingford, G. W. B. *The historical geography of Ethiopia from the first century AD to 1704.* Oxford, Oxford University Press for the British Academy, 1989.

595. Labanca, N. *In marcia verso Adua.* Torino, Einaudi, 1993.

596. Malécot, G. R. *Les voyageurs français et les relations entre la France et l'Abyssinie de 1835 à 1870.* Paris, Société Française d'Histoire d'Outre-Mer, 1972.

597. Marcus, Harold G. *A history of Ethiopia.* Berkeley, University of California Press, 1994.

598. Marcus, Harold G. *The life and times of Menilek II: Ethiopia, 1844–1913.* Oxford, Clarendon Press, 1983.

599. Masotti, Pier Marcello. *Ricordi d'Etiopia di un funzionario coloniale.* Milano, Pan, 1981.

600. Massaia, Guglielmo. *Lettere e scritti minori.* Roma, Istituto Storico dei Cappuccini, 1978. 5 vols.

601. McCann, James. *From poverty to famine in rural northeast Ethiopia: a rural history, 1900–1935.* Philadelphia, University of Pennsylvania Press, 1987.

602. McClellan, Charles W. *State transformation and national integration: Gedeo and the Ethiopian Empire, 1895–1935.* East Lansing, Michigan State University, African Studies Center, 1988.

603. Mulatu Wubneh and Yohannis Abate. *Ethiopia: transition and development in the Horn of Africa.* Boulder, Westview Press, 1988.

604. Myatt, Frederick. *The march to Magdala: the Abyssinian war of 1868.* London, Leo Cooper, 1970.

605. Norberg, Viveca Halldin. *Swedes in Haile Sellassie's Ethiopia. 1924–1952: a study in early development cooperation.* Uppsala, Scandinavian Institute of African Studies, 1977.

606. Oyegoke, Bisi. *The history of Ethiopia: the earliest times to the present day, 600–1916, Aksum to Addis Ababa.* Ibadan, Claverianum Press, 1982.

607. Pankhurst, Richard. *A social history of Ethiopia: the northern and central highlands from early medieval times to the rise of Emperor Tewodros II.* Addis Ababa, Addis Ababa University, Institute of Ethiopian Studies, 1990.

608. Pankhurst, Richard. *Economic history of Ethiopia, 1800–1935.* Addis Ababa, Haile Selassie I University, 1968.

609. Pankhurst, Richard. *Introduction to the economic history of Ethiopia: from early times to 1800.* London, Sidgwick and Jackson, 1961.

610. Pankhurst, Richard. *State and land in Ethiopian history.* Nairobi, Oxford University Press, 1966.

611. Pankhurst, Richard. *The Ethiopian royal chronicles.* Addis Ababa, Oxford University Press, 1967.

612. Pankhurst, Richard. *An introduction to the history of the Ethiopian army.* Addis Ababa, Imperial Ethiopian Air Force, 101st Training Centre, 1967.

613. Petridès, Pierre. *Le héros d'Adoua: Ras Makonnen, Prince d'Éthiopie.* Paris, Plon, 1966.

614. Pranovi, Remo. *Etiopia: l'ex impero del re dei re.* Vicenza, Stocchiero, 1978.

615. Prather, Ray. *The King of Kings of Ethiopia, Menelik II.* Nairobi, Kenya Literature Bureau, 1981.

616. Prouty, Chris. *Empress Taytu and Menilek II: Ethiopia, 1883–1910.* Trenton, Red Sea Press, 1986.

617. Prouty, Chris, and E. Rosenfeld. *Historical dictionary of Ethiopia and Eritrea.* Second edition. Metuchen, Scarecrow Press, 1994.

618. Rosenfeld, Chris Prouty. *A chronology of Menilek II of Ethiopia, 1844–1913.* East Lansing, Michigan State University, African Studies Center, 1976.

619. Rouaud, Alain. *Afä-wärq: un intellectuel éthiopien, témoin de son temps, 1868–1947.* Paris, CNRS, 1991.

620. Rubenson, Sven. *King of Kings: Tewodros of Ethiopia.* Addis Ababa, Haile Selassie I University, 1966.

621. Rubenson, Sven. *The survival of Ethiopian independence.* London, Heinemann, 1978.

622. Rubenson, Sven, et al. (eds.) *Acta Æthiopica. Vol. I: correspondence and treaties, 1800–1854.* Evanston, Northwestern University Press, 1987.

623. Sergew Hable Selassie. *Ancient and medieval Ethiopian history to 1270.* Addis Ababa, United Printers, 1972.

624. Sorenson, John. *Imagining Ethiopia: struggles for history and identity in the Horn of Africa.* New Brunswick, Rutgers University Press, 1993.

625. Spencer, J. H. *Ethiopia at bay: a personal account of the Haile Sellassie years.* Algonac, Reference Publications, 1984.

626. Taddele Seyoum Teshale. *The life history of an Ethiopian refugee, 1944–1991.* Lewiston, Edwin Mellen Press, 1991.

627. Taddese Beyene, et al. (eds.) *Kasa and Kasa: papers on the lives, times and images of Tewodros II and Yohannes IV, 1855–1889.* Addis Ababa, Addis Ababa University, Institute of Ethiopian Studies, 1993.

628. Taddese Beyene, et al. (eds.) *The centenary of Dogali: proceedings of the International Symposium, Addis Ababa-Asmara, January 24–25, 1987.* Addis Ababa, Addis Ababa University, Institute of Ethiopian Studies, 1988.

629. Taddesse Tamrat. *Church and state in Ethiopia, 1270–1527.* Oxford, Clarendon Press, 1972.

630. Tekle S. Mekouria. *Ethiopian history from Tewodros to Haile Sellassie.* Addis Ababa, Giyorgis Press, 1968.

631. Theodore II, Emperor of Ethiopia. *The Amharic letters of Emperor Theodore of Ethiopia to Queen Victoria and her special envoy, preserved in the India Office Library and the Public Records Office.* Oxford, Oxford University Press, 1979.

632. Triulzi, Alessandro. *Salt, gold and legitimacy: prelude to the history of a no-man's land, Bela Shangul, Wallagga, Ethiopia, ca. 1800–1898.* Napoli, Istituto Universitario Orientale, 1981.

633. Ullendorff, Edward. *The Ethiopians: an introduction to country and people.* Third edition. Oxford, Oxford University Press, 1973.

634. Zewde Gabre Sellassie. *Yohannes IV of Ethiopia: a political biography.* Oxford, Clarendon Press, 1975.

Ethiopia—Human Rights

635. Africa Watch. *Evil days: thirty years of war and famine in Ethiopia*. New York, Africa Watch, 1991.

636. Amnesty International. *Ethiopia: end of era of brutal repression*. London, Amnesty International, 1991.

Ethiopia—Incunabula

637. Wright, Stephen G. *Ethiopian incunabula . . . from the collections in the National Library of Ethiopia and the Haile Sellassie I University*. Addis Ababa, Commercial Printing Press, 1967.

Ethiopia—Industry

638. Abraham Medhane. *Die Wirtschaft Äthiopiens und die Möglichkeiten der Industrialisierung*. Wien, Verlag Notring, 1970.

639. Mulatu Wubneh. *A spatial analysis of urban-industrial development in Ethiopia*. Syracuse, Syracuse University, Maxwell School of Citizenship and Foreign Affairs, 1982.

640. UNIDO. *Ethiopia: new directions of industrial policy*. Oxford, Blackwell, 1991.

Ethiopia—Islam

641. Cuoq, Joseph. *L'Islam en Éthiopie des origines au XVIe siècle*. Paris, Nouvelles Éditions Latines, 1981.

Ethiopia—Italian Invasion

642. Asante, S. K. B. *Pan-African protest: West Africa and the Italo-Ethiopian crisis, 1934–1941*. London, Longman, 1977.

643. Baer, G. W. *Test case: Italy, Ethiopia and the League of Nations*. Stanford, Hoover Institution Press, 1976.

644. Baer, G. W. *The coming of the Italian-Ethiopian war*. Cambridge, Mass., Harvard University Press, 1967.

645. Barker, A. J. *The civilizing mission: a history of the Italo-Ethiopian war of 1935–1936*. London, Cassell, 1968.

646. Boca, Angelo del. *The Ethiopian war, 1935–1941*. Chicago, University of Chicago Press, 1969.

647. Chukumba, Stephen U. *The big powers against Ethiopia*. Washington, University Press of America, 1977.

648. Coffey, T. M. *Lion by the tail: the story of the Italian-Ethiopian war*. London, Hamish Hamilton, 1974.

649. Dugan, J., and L. Lafore. *Days of emperor and clown: the Italo-Ethiopian war, 1935–36*. New York, Doubleday, 1973.

650. Giovana, Mario. *L'avventura fascista in Etiopia*. Milano, Teti, 1976.

651. Glover, M. *An improvised war: the Ethiopian campaign, 1940–1941*. London, Leo Cooper, 1987.

652. Goglia, Luigi. *Storia fotografica dell'impero fascista, 1935–1941*. Bari, Laterza, 1985.

653. Hardie, Frank. *The Abyssinian crisis*. London, Batsford, 1974.

654. Harris, Brice. *The United States and the Ital-Ethiopian crisis*. Stanford, Stanford University Press, 1964.

655. Kacza, Thomas. *Äthiopiens Kampf gegen die italienischer Kolonialisten, 1935–41*. Pfaffenweiler, Centaurus, 1993.

656. Lenzi, Giulio. *Diari africani*. Pisa, Giardini, 1973.

657. Minardi, Salvatore. *Alle origini dell'incidente Ual Ual*. Caltanissetta, Sciascia, 1990.

658. Mockler, Anthony. *Haile Selassie's war*. London, Oxford University Press, 1984.

659. Mori, Renato. *Mussolini e la conquista dell'Etiopia*. Firenze, Le Monnier, 1978.

660. Pieroni, Piero. *L'Italia in Africa*. Firenze, Vallecchi, 1974.

661. Pignatelli, L. *La guerra dei sette mesi*. Napoli, Mezzogiorno, 1961.

662. Sbacchi, A. *Ethiopia under Mussolini: fascism and the colonial experience*. London, Zed Books, 1985.

663. Stella, Gian Carlo. *Bibliografia politico-militare del conflitto italo-abissino, 1935–36*. Ravenna, G. C. Stella, 1988.

664. Verich, Thomas M. *The European powers and the Italo-Ethiopian war, 1935–1936: a diplomatic study*. Salisbury, N.C., Documentary Publications, 1980.

665. Waley, Daniel P. *British public opinion and the Abyssinian war, 1935–36*. London, Temple Smith, 1975.

Ethiopia—Jesuits

666. Caraman, P. *The lost empire: the story of the Jesuits in Ethiopia, 1553–1634*. London, Sidgwick & Jackson, 1985.

Ethiopia—Land

667. Aster Akalu. *The process of land nationalization in Ethiopia: land nationalization and the peasants*. Lund, Gleerup, 1982.

668. Berhanou Abbebe. *Évolution de la propriété foncière au Choa (Éthiopie) du règne de Ménélik à la constitution de 1931*. Paris, Paul Geuthner, 1971.

669. Cohen, John M., and Dov Weintraub. *Land and peasants in imperial Ethiopia: the social background to a revolution.* Assen, Van Gorcum, 1975.

670. Huntingford, G. W. B. *Land charters of northern Ethiopia.* Addis Ababa, Haile Selassie I University, Institute of Ethiopian Studies, 1965.

671. Mantel-Niecko, Joanna. *The role of land tenure in the system of Ethiopian imperial government in modern times.* Warsaw, Wydawnictwa Uniwersytetu Warszawskiego, 1980.

672. Reilly, P. M. *Ethiopia: land resource bibliography.* Surbiton, Ministry of Overseas Development, Land Resources Division, 1978.

Ethiopia—Land Reform

673. Cohen, John M., et al. *Revolution and land reform in Ethiopia: peasant associations, local government and rural development.* Ithaca, Cornell University, Center for International Studies, Rural Development Committee, 1976.

674. Dessalegn Rahmato. *Agrarian reform in Ethiopia.* Uppsala, Scandinavian Institute of African Studies, 1984.

675. Göricke, Fred V. *Social and political factors influencing the application of land reform measures in Ethiopia.* Saarbrücken, Breitenbach, 1979.

676. Hoben, Allan. *Social soundness analysis of agrarian reform in Ethiopia.* Washington, United States Agency for International Development, 1976.

677. Mengistu Woube. *Problems of land reform implementation in rural Ethiopia: a case study of Dejen and Wolmera districts.* Uppsala, Kulturgeografiska Institutionen vid Uppsala Universitet, 1986.

678. Pausewang, Siegfried. *Peasants and local society in Ethiopia: land tenure, social structure and land reform.* Bergen, Chr. Michelsen Institute, 1978.

679. Pausewang, Siegfried. *Peasants, land and society: a social history of land reform in Ethiopia.* Munich, Ifo-Institut für Wirtschaftsforschung, 1983.

680. Ståhl, Michael. *New seeds in old soil: a study of the land reform in western Wollega, Ethiopia, 1975–1976.* Uppsala, Scandinavian Institute of African Studies, 1981.

Ethiopia—Languages

681. Bender, Marvin Lionel. *The non-Semitic languages of Ethiopia.* East Lansing, Michigan State University, African Studies Center, 1976.

682. Bender, Marvin Lionel, et al. (eds.) *Language in Ethiopia.* London, Oxford University Press, 1976.

683. Böhm, Gerhard. *Die Sprache der Aithiopen im Lande Kusch.* Wien, Afro-Pub, 1988.

684. Ehrensvärd, Ulla, and Christopher Toll (eds.) *On both sides of al-Mandab: Ethiopian, South-Arabic and Islamic studies presented to Oscar Löfgren*

on his ninetieth birthday, etc. Stockholm, Swedish Research Institute in Istanbul, 1989.

685. Hetzron, Robert. *Ethiopian Semitic: studies in classification.* Manchester, Manchester University Press, 1972.

686. Segert, S., and J. E. Bodrogligeti (eds.) *Ethiopian studies. Dedicated to Wolf Leslau on the occasion of his seventy-fifth birthday, November 14th, 1981, by friends and colleagues.* Wiesbaden, Otto Harrassowitz, 1983.

687. Unseth, Peter. *Bibliography of the non-Semitic languages of Ethiopia.* East Lansing, Michigan State University, African Studies Center, 1990.

Ethiopia—Law

688. Conte, Carmelo, and Guglielmo Gobbi. *Ethiopia: introduzione alla etnologia del diritto.* Milano, Giuffrè, 1976.

689. Ewing, W. (ed.) *The consolidated laws of Ethiopia.* Addis Ababa, Haile Selassie I University Press, 1971. 2 vols.

690. Rossi, M. *Matrimonio e divorzio nel diritto abissino.* Milano, Edizioni Unicopli, 1982.

691. Scholler, Heinrich, and Paul Brietzke. *Ethiopia: revolution, law and politics.* Munich, Weltforum-Verlag, 1976.

692. Scholler, Heinrich. *The Special Court of Ethiopia, 1920–1935.* Stuttgart, Franz Steiner, 1985.

693. Vanderlinden, Jacques. *Introduction au droit de l'Éthiopie moderne.* Paris, Librairie Générale de Droit et de Jurisprudence, 1971.

694. Vosikis, Nicolas. *Le trust dans le code civil éthiopien: étude de droit éthiopien avec référence au droit anglais.* Genève, Librairie Droz, 1975.

Ethiopia—Literature

695. Fusella, L., et al. *Trois essais sur la littérature éthiopienne.* Antibes, Aresae, 1984.

Ethiopia—Local Government

696. Cohen, John M., and Peter Koehn. *Ethiopian provincial and municipal government: imperial patterns and postrevolutionary changes.* East Lansing, Michigan State University, African Studies Center, 1980.

Ethiopia—Magic Scrolls

697. Mercier, Jacques. *Ethiopian magic scrolls.* New York, G. Braziller, 1978.

698. Raineri, Osvaldo. *Catalogo dei rotoli protettori etiopici della collezione Sandro Angelini.* Roma, Sanguis, 1990.

Ethiopia—Manpower

699. Getatchew Metaferia and Maigenet Shifferraw. *The Ethiopian revolution of 1974 and the exodus of Ethiopia's trained human resources.* Lewiston, Edwin Mellen Press, 1991.

700. Ginzberg, Eli, and H. A. Smith. *Manpower strategy for developing countries: lessons from Ethiopia.* New York, Columbia University Press, 1967.

Ethiopia—Manuscripts

701. Appleyard, David L. *Ethiopian manuscripts.* London, Jed Press, 1993.

702. Hammerschmidt, Ernst, and Otto A. Jäger. *Illuminierte äthiopische Handschriften.* Stuttgart, Franz Steiner, 1968.

703. Jankowski, A. *Die Königen von Saba and Salomo: die amharische Version der Handschrift Berlin Hs. or. 3542. Text, Übersetzung und Erläuterungen.* Hamburg, Helmut Buske, 1987.

704. Macomber, William F., and Getatchew Haile. *A catalogue of Ethiopian manuscripts microfilmed for the Ethiopian Manuscript Microfilm Library, Addis Ababa, and for the Monastic Manuscript Microfilm Library, Collegeville. Vols. 1–9.* Collegeville, Monastic Manuscript Microfilm Library, 1975–87.

705. Strelcyn, Stefan. *Catalogue des manuscrits éthiopiens de l'Accademia Nazionale dei Lincei.* Roma, Accademia Nazionale dei Lincei, 1976.

706. Strelcyn, Stefan. *Catalogue of Ethiopic manuscripts in the John Rylands University Library of Manchester.* Manchester, Manchester University Press, 1974.

Ethiopia—Mass Media

707. Janas, J. *History of the mass media in Ethiopia.* Warsaw, University of Warsaw, Institute of Oriental Studies, 1991.

Ethiopia—Minerals

708. Jelenc, Danilo A. *Mineral occurrences of Ethiopia.* Addis Ababa, Ministry of Mines, 1966.

Ethiopia—Missionaries

709. Aleme Eshete. *Activités politiques de la Mission Catholique (Lazariste) en Éthiopie (sous la règne de l'empereur Johannes, 1869–1889).* Paris, Études Documentaires, 1970.

710. Aren, Gustav. *Evangelical pioneers in Ethiopia: origins of the Evangelical Church Mekane Yesus.* Stockholm, EFS, 1978.

711. Bockelman, W., and E. Bockelman. *Ethiopia: where Lutheran is spelled 'Mekane Yesus.'* Minneapolis, Augsburg, 1972.

712. Crummey, Donald E. *Priests and politicians: Protestant and Catholic missions in Orthodox Ethiopia, 1830–1868.* Oxford, Clarendon Press, 1972.

713. Davis, Raymond J. *Fire on the mountains, the story of a miracle: the church in Ethiopia.* London, Oliphants, 1966.

714. O'Mahoney, Kevin. *The ebullient phoenix: a history of the Vicariate of Abyssinia. Vol. 1: 1839–1860.* Asmara, Ethiopian Studies Centre, 1982.

715. O'Mahoney, Kevin. *The ebullient phoenix: a history of the Vicariate of Abyssinia. Vol. 2: 1860–1881.* Asmara, Ethiopian Studies Centre, 1987.

716. Saeverås, O. *On church-mission relations in Ethiopia, 1944–69, with special reference to Evangelical Church Mekane Yesus and the Lutheran missions.* Lunde, Forlag og Bokhandel, 1974.

717. Wassmann, Dietrich. *Als fünftes Rad am Wagen: ein Missionshandwerker in Äthiopien.* Erlangen, Verlag der Evangelisch-Lutherischen Mission, 1979.

718. Wesenick, J. *Viyale Kirche in Äthiopien: Versuch einer Analyse des Aira District der Western Synod der Evangelical Churche Mekane Yesus in Äthiopien.* Hermannsburg, Verlag des Missionshandlung Hermannsburg, 1976.

Ethiopia—Music

719. Powne, Michael. *Ethiopian music: an introduction.* London, Oxford University Press, 1966.

720. Zenebe Bekele. *Music in the Horn: a preliminary analytical approach to the study of Ethiopian music.* Stockholm, Evrfattares Bokmaskin, 1987.

Ethiopia—Oilseed Industry

721. DeRafols, Wilfredo, et al. *Development of the Ethiopian oilseeds industry.* Menlo Park, Stanford Research Institute, 1969.

Ethiopia—Orthodox Church

722. Andersen, Knut. *Ethiopiens Orthodokse Kirke.* Copenhagen, Dansk Ethiopei Mission, 1971.

723. Aymro Wondmagegnehu and Motovu Joachim (eds.) *The Ethiopian Orthodox Church.* Addis Ababa, The Ethiopian Orthodox Mission, 1970.

724. Bonk, Jon. *An annotated and classified bibliography of English literature pertaining to the Ethiopian Orthodox Church.* Metuchen, Scarecrow Press, 1984.

725. Ephraim Isaac. *The Ethiopian Church.* Boston, H. N. Sawyer, 1968.

726. Furioli, Antonio. *La separazione della chiesa d'Etiopia da Roma: nota storico-teologica.* Brescia, Paideia Editrice, 1981.

727. Girma Beshah and Merid Wolde Aregay. *The question of the union of churches in Luso-Ethiopian relations, 1500–1632*. Lisboa, Junta de Investigaçôes de Ultramar Centro, 1964.

728. Haberland, Eike (ed.) *Haymanotä abäw qäddämt: la foi des pères anciens. I: texte éthiopien, enseignements de mamher Kefla Giyorgis, etc.* Stuttgart, Franz Steiner, 1986.

729. Hammerschmidt, Ernst. *Stellung und Bedeutung des Sabats in Äthiopien.* Stuttgart, Kohlhammer, 1963.

730. Hammerschmidt, Ernst. *Studies in the Ethiopic anaphoras.* Berlin, Akademie-Verlag, 1961.

731. Heyer, Friedrich. *Die Kirche Äthiopiens: eine Bestandsaufnahme.* Berlin, Walter de Gruyter, 1971.

732. Heyer, Friedrich. *Die Kirche in Dabra Tabor.* Erlangen, Lehrstuhl für Geschichte und Theologie des Christlichen Ostens, 1981.

733. Kaplan, Steven. *The monastic holy man and the Christianization of early Solomonic Ethiopia.* Stuttgart, Franz Steiner, 1984.

734. Mara, Yolande. *The church of Ethiopia: the national church in the making.* Asmara, Il Poligrafico, 1972.

735. Mercer, Samuel. *The Ethiopic liturgy: its sources, development, and present form.* New York, AMS Press, 1970.

736. Molnar, E. C. *The Ethiopian Orthodox church: a contribution to the ecumenical study of less known Eastern churches.* Pasadena, Bloy House Theological School, 1969.

737. Sergew Hable Selassie. *The Church of Ethiopia: a panorama of history and spiritual life.* Addis Ababa, Ethiopian Orthodox Church, 1970.

738. Stoffregen-Pedersen, K. *Les Éthiopiens.* Turnhout, Brepols, 1990.

739. Verghese, Paul (ed.) *Koptisches Christentum: die orthodoxen Kirchen Ägyptens und Äthiopiens.* Berlin, Walter de Gruyter, 1974.

740. Yaqob Beyene (ed.) *L'unzione do Cristo nella teologia etiopica.* Roma, Pontificium Institutum Studiorum Orientalium, 1981.

Ethiopia—Pastoralists

741. Faye, B. *Éleveurs d'Éthiopie.* Paris, Karthala, 1990.

Ethiopia—Philosophy

742. Sumner, Claude. *Ethiopian philosophy. Vol. 1: "The book of the wise philosophers."* Addis Ababa, Central Printing Press, 1974.

743. Sumner, Claude. *Ethiopian philosophy. Vols. 2–3: the treatise of Zar'a Yaqob and of Walda Heywat.* Addis Ababa, Addis Ababa University, 1976–78. 2 vols.

744. Sumner, Claude. *Ethiopian philosophy. Vol. 4: the life and maxims of Skandas.* Addis Ababa, Commercial Printing Press, 1981.

745. Sumner, Claude. *Ethiopian philosophy. Vol. 5: the Fisalgwos.* Addis Ababa, Commercial Printing Press, 1982.

746. Sumner, Claude. *Sagesse éthiopienne.* Paris, Éditions Recherche sur les Civilisations, 1983.

747. Sumner, Claude. *The source of African philosophy: the Ethiopian philosophy of man.* Stuttgart, Franz Steiner, 1986.

Ethiopia—Planning

748. Treuner, Peter, et al. (eds.) *Regional planning and development in Ethiopia, 1.* Stuttgart, Universität Stuttgart, Institut für Raumordnung und Entwicklungsplanung, 1985.

749. Treuner, Peter (ed.) *Regional planning and development in Ethiopia, 2: a seminar report.* Stuttgart, Universität Stuttgart, Institut für Raumordnung und Entwicklungsplanung, 1988.

Ethiopia—Political Art

750. Sahlstrom, B. *Political posters in Ethiopia and Mozambique: visual imagery in a revolutionary context.* Uppsala, Almqvist and Wiksell, 1990.

Ethiopia—Politics

751. Abraham, Kinfe. *Ethiopia: from bullets to the ballot box. The bumpy road to democracy and the political economy of transition.* Trenton, Red Sea Press, 1993.

752. Addis Hiwet. *Ethiopia: from autocracy to revolution.* London, Merlin Press, 1975.

753. Clapham, Christopher. *Haile Selassie's government.* London, Longmans, 1969.

754. Clapham, Christopher. *Transformation and continuity in revolutionary Ethiopia.* Cambridge, Cambridge University Press, 1988.

755. Cole, Ernest. *Ethiopia: political power and the military.* Paris, Banque d'Information et de Documentation de l'Océan Indien, 1985.

756. Gallais, Jean. *Une géographie politique de l'Éthiopie: le poids de l'état.* Paris, Fondation Liberté sans Frontières, 1989.

757. Girma Kebbede. *The state and development in Ethiopia.* Atlantic Highlands, Humanities Press, 1992.

758. Glucksmann, André, and Thierry Wolton. *Politik des Schweigens.* Berlin, Ullstein-Taschenbuch-Verlag, 1989.

759. Gstrein, Heinz. *Äthiopien blickt in die Zukunft: vom Negus zu Revolution und Reform.* Stein/Nurnberg, Laetare, 1975.

760. Haile Kiros Asmerom. *Emergence, expansion and decline of patrimonial bureaucracy in Ethiopia.* Amsterdam, Haile Kiros Asmerom, 1978.

761. Harbeson, John Willis. *The Ethiopian transformation: the quest for the post-imperial state.* Boulder, Westview Press, 1988.

762. Hasselblatt, Gunnar. *Äthiopien am Rande des Friedens: Tigre, Oromo, Eritreer, Amharen im Gespräch.* Stuttgart, Radius-Verlag, 1992.

763. Henze, Paul B. *Ethiopia in early 1989: deepening crisis.* Santa Monica, Rand Corporation, 1989.

764. Hess, Robert L. *Ethiopia: the modernization of autocracy.* Ithaca, Cornell University Press, 1970.

765. Janssen, V. *Politische Herrschaft in Äthiopien.* Freiburg, Klaus Schwarz, 1976.

766. Keller, E. *Revolutionary Ethiopia: from empire to people's republic.* Bloomington, Indiana University Press, 1988.

767. Markakis, John. *Ethiopia: anatomy of a traditional polity.* Oxford, Clarendon Press, 1974.

768. Moffa, Claudio. *Etiopia dietro la trincea.* Milano, Celuc Libri, 1978.

769. Ottaway, Marina (ed.) *The political economy of Ethiopia.* New York, Praeger, 1990.

770. Perham, Margery. *The government of Ethiopia.* Second edition. London, Faber & Faber, 1969.

771. Pongratz, Philip. *Revolution und kommunistische Gleichschaltung in Äthiopien.* München, Tuduv-Verlagsgesellschaft, 1989.

772. Sauldie, Madan M. *Ethiopia: dawn of the red star.* New York, Apt Books, 1982.

773. Schwab, Peter. *Decision-making in Ethiopia: a study of the political process.* London, Hurst, 1972.

774. Schwab, Peter. *Ethiopia: politics, economics and society.* London, Pinter, 1985.

775. Schwab, Peter (ed.) *Ethiopia and Haile Selassie.* New York, Facts on File, 1972.

776. Tamene Bitema and Jürgen Steuber. *Die ungelöste nationale Frage in Äthiopien: Studie zu den Befreiungsbewegungen der Oromo und Eritreas.* Frankfurt am Main, Peter Lang, 1983.

Ethiopia—Ports

777. Adams, Phillip L., and Benjamin V. Andrews. *Improvement of Ethiopian ports.* Menlo Park, Stanford Research Institute, 1968.

Ethiopia—Pottery

778. Hecht, Elisabeth Dorothea. *The pottery collection.* Addis Ababa, Haile Selassie I University, Institute of Ethiopian Studies, Museum, 1969.

Ethiopia—Prehistory

779. Chavaillon, Nicole. *Gotera: un site paléolithique récent d'Éthiopie.* Paris, Éditions Recherche sur les Civilisations, 1985.

780. Deribéré, Paulette, and Maurice Deribéré. *L'Éthiopie, berceau de l'humanité.* Paris, Société Continentale d'Éditions Modernes Illustrées, 1972.

781. Johanson, Donald C., and James Shreeve. *Lucy's child: the discovery of a human ancestor.* New York, Morrow, 1989.

782. Johanson, Donald C. *Lucy.* London, Granada, 1981.

783. Wendorf, Fred, and Romuald Schild. *A middle Stone Age sequence from the central Rift Valley, Ethiopia.* Wroclaw, Wydawnictwo Polskiej Akademii Nauk, 1974.

Ethiopia—Psychology

784. Korten, D. C., and F. Korten. *Planned change in a traditional society: psychological problems of modernization in Ethiopia.* New York, Praeger, 1972.

Ethiopia—Railways

785. Loepfe, Willi. *Alfred Ilg und die äthiopische Eisenbahn.* Stuttgart, Franz Steiner, 1974.

786. Rosso, Max. *Le rail franco-éthiopien en détresse.* Paris, Pensée Universelle, 1983.

Ethiopia—Readership Survey

787. Conacher, John R. *An initial readership survey of Ethiopia.* Addis Ababa, Bible Churchman's Missionary Society, 1969.

Ethiopia—Refugees

788. Ellman, Anthony O. *An agricultural and socio-economic survey of south Sudan refugee settlements and surrounding areas in Gambela awraja, Ethiopia.* Addis Ababa, Institute of Agricultural Research, 1972.

789. Mekuria Bulcha. *Flight and integration: causes of mass exodus from Ethiopia and problems of integration in the Sudan.* Uppsala, Scandinavian Institute of African Studies, 1988.

Ethiopia—Regional Development

790. Ayele Tirfie. *Regionalisierte Entwicklungsstrategien: Ansätze und Möglichkeiten am Beispiel Äthiopiens.* Stuttgart, Universität Stuttgart, Institut für Raumordnung, 1986.

791. Ayele Tirfie. *Towards a regionalized development strategy for Ethiopia.* Stuttgart, Universität Stuttgart, Institut für Raumordnung, 1987.

Ethiopia — Revolution

792. Aleme Eshete. *Songs of the Ethiopian revolution.* Addis Ababa, Ministry of Culture, 1979.

793. Andargachew Tiruneh. *The Ethiopian revolution, 1974–1987: a transformation from an aristocratic to a totalitarian autocracy.* Cambridge, Cambridge University Press, 1993.

794. Bailey, Glen. *An analysis of the Ethiopian revolution.* Athens, Ohio University, Center for International Studies, 1980.

795. Balsvik, R. R. *Haile Sellassie's students: the intellectual and social background to revolution, 1952–1977.* East Lansing, Michigan State University, African Studies Center, 1985.

796. Benzing, Brigitta, and Kahsai Wolde-Giorgis. *Das neue Äthiopien, vom Kaiserreich zur Revolution: Darstellung und Dokumente.* Köln, Pahl-Rugenstein, 1980.

797. Brietzke, Paul H. *Law, development and the Ethiopian revolution.* Lewisburg, Bucknell University Press, 1982.

798. Brüne, Stefan. *Äthiopien: Unterentwicklung und radikale Militarherrschaft. Zur Ambivalenz einer scheinheiligen Revolution.* Hamburg, Institut für Afrika-Kunde, 1986.

799. Bureau, Jacques. *Éthiopie: un drame impérial et rouge.* Paris, Éditions Ramsay, 1987.

800. Dummer, Egon. *Äthiopien im Aufbruch.* Berlin, Dietz, 1984.

801. Falkenstörfer, Helmut. *Äthiopien: Tragik und Chancen eine Revolution.* Stuttgart, Radius, 1986.

802. Gavrilov, N., et al. (eds.) *Ten years of the Ethiopian revolution.* Moscow, Progress, 1986.

803. Halliday, Fred, and Maxine Molyneaux. *The Ethiopian revolution.* London, Verso, 1981.

804. Kaufeler, Heinz. *Modernization, legitimacy and social movement: a study of socio-cultural dynamics and revolution in Iran and Ethiopia.* Zürich, Ethnologisches Seminar der Universität Zürich, 1988.

805. Lefort, René. *Ethiopia: an heretical revolution?* London, Zed Press, 1983.

806. Legum, Colin. *Ethiopia: the fall of Haile Sellassie's empire.* London, Rex Collings, 1975.

807. Markakis, John, and Nega Ayele. *Class and revolution in Ethiopia.* Nottingham, Spokesman, 1978.

808. Moffa, Claudio. *La rivoluzione etiopica: testi e documenti.* Urbino, Argalìa, 1980.

809. Ottaway, David, and Marina Ottaway. *Ethiopia: empire in revolution.* New York, Africana Publishing, 1978.

810. Thomson, Blair. *Ethiopia: the country that cut off its head.* London, Robson Books, 1975.

811. Tubiana, Joseph, et al. (eds.) *La révolution éthiopienne comme phénomène de société: essais, témoignages et documents.* Paris, L'Harmattan, 1990.

812. Vivó, Raúl Valdés. *Ethiopia's revolution.* London, Zed Press, 1978.

Ethiopia—Rural Conditions

813. Andargatchew Tesfaye. *Basic needs and services in rural Ethiopia.* Addis Ababa, UNICEF, 1982.

814. Aspen, Harald. *Competition and co-operation: North Ethiopian peasant households and their resource base.* Trondheim, University of Trondheim, UNIT Centre for Environment and Development, 1993.

815. Baker, J. *The rural-urban dichotomy in the developing world: a case study from northern Ethiopia.* Oslo, Norwegian University Press, 1986.

816. Dessalegn Rahmato. *The dynamics of rural poverty: case studies from a district in southern Ethiopia.* Dakar, Codesria, 1992.

817. Teka Tegegn. *Rural poverty alleviation: the case of Ethiopia.* Addis Ababa, Addis Ababa University, Institute of Development Research, 1983.

818. Wudnesh Hailu. *Rural family of Ethiopia: economic activities, household analysis, and standard household type comparisons.* Hamburg, Weltarchiv, 1991.

Ethiopia—Rural Development

819. Alemneh Dejene. *Peasants, agrarian socialism, and rural development in Ethiopia.* Boulder, Westview Press, 1987.

820. Betru Gebregziabher. *Integrated development in rural Ethiopia: an evaluative study of the Chilalo Agricultural Development Unit.* Bloomington, Indiana University, 1975.

821. Böhm, Karlheinz. *Nagaya: ein neues Dorf in Äthiopien.* Hamburg, Rowohlt, 1986.

822. Cohen, John M. *Integrated rural development: the Ethiopian experience and the debate.* Uppsala, Scandinavian Institute of African Studies, 1987.

823. Cohen, John M. *Integrated rural development in Ethiopia: CADU after 1974.* Cambridge, Mass., Harvard Institute for International Development, 1986.

824. Haile Selassie Belay. *Principles and strategies for rural development in Ethiopia*. Debre Zeit, Agricultural Research Centre and College of Agriculture, 1979.

825. Haile Selassie Belay. *Problems, practices and strategies for rural development in Ethiopia*. Debre Zeit, Debre Zeit Agricultural Experiment Station, 1977.

826. Harbeson, John Willis, and Paul H. Brietzke (eds.) *Rural development in Ethiopia*. East Lansing, Michigan State University, African Studies Center, 1975.

827. Makin, M. J., et al. *Development projects in the southern Rift Valley, Ethiopia*. Surbiton, Ministry of Overseas Development, Land Resources Division, 1975.

828. Nekby, Bengt. *CADU: an Ethiopian experiment in developing peasant farming*. Stockholm, Prisma, 1971.

829. Pausewang, S., et al. (eds.) *Ethiopia: options for rural development*. London, Zed Books, 1990.

830. Pausewang, Siegfried. *Methods and concepts of social research in a rural developing society: a critical appraisal based on experience in Ethiopia*. Munich, Weltforum-Verlag, 1973.

831. Schmale, Matthias. *The role of local organizations in Third World development: Tanzania, Zimbabwe, and Ethiopia*. Aldershot, Avebury, 1993.

832. Tesfai Tecle. *The evolution of alternative rural development strategies in Ethiopia: implications for employment and income distribution.* East Lansing, Michigan State University, Department of Agricultural Economics, 1975.

833. Zewdie Shibre. *Förderung von Klein- und Mittelbetrieben im Produktionsbereich als Instrument der regionalen Entwicklungspolitik Äthiopiens*. Stuttgart, Universität Stuttgart, Institut für Raumordnung, 1986.

Ethiopia—Science and Technology

834. Kesete Belay. *Ethiopia: a bibliography of science*. Gaborone, National Institute of Development Research and Documentation, University of Botswana, 1982.

Ethiopia—Settlement Schemes

835. Clarke, J. *Resettlement and rehabilitation: Ethiopia's campaign against famine*. London, Harney and Jones, 1986.

836. Cohen, John M., and N. I. Isaksson. *Villagization in the Arsi region of Ethiopia: report prepared by SIDA*. Uppsala, Swedish University of Agricultural Sciences, International Rural Development Centre, 1987.

837. Colchester, M., and Virginia Luling. *Ethiopia's bitter medicine: settling for disaster. An evaluation of the Ethiopian government's resettlement programme*. London, Survival International, 1986.

838. Dieci, P., and C. Viezzoli. *Resettlement and rural development in Ethiopia: social and economic research training and technical assistance in the Beles Valley.* Milan, Angeli, 1992.

839. Niggli, P. *Ethiopia: deportations and forced labour camps. Doubtful methods in the struggle against famine.* Berlin, Berliner Missionwerk, 1985.

840. Pankhurst, Alula. *Resettlement and famine in Ethiopia: the villagers' experience.* Manchester, Manchester University Press, 1992.

Ethiopia—Social Conditions

841. Bjerén, Gunilla. *Migration to Shashemene: ethnicity, gender and occupation in urban Ethiopia.* Uppsala, Scandinavian Institute of African Studies, 1985.

842. Fekadu Bekele. *Gesellschaftsformation und Artikulation von Produktionweisen in Äthiopien.* Saarbrücken, Breitenbach, 1989.

843. Heinrich, Wolfgang. *Ethnische Identität und nationale Integration: eine vergleichende Betrachtung traditioneller Gesellschaftssysteme und Handlungsorientierungen in Äthiopien.* Aachen, Alano-Verlag, 1984.

844. Lipsky, George Arthur. *Ethiopia: its people, its society, its culture.* New Haven, HRAF Press, 1962.

845. Simoons, Frederick J. *Northwest Ethiopia: peoples and economy.* Madison, University of Wisconsin Press, 1960.

Ethiopia—Soils

846. Donahue, Roy L. *Ethiopia: taxonomy, cartography and ecology of soils.* East Lansing, Michigan State University, African Studies Center, 1972.

847. Weigel, Gerolf. *The soils of the Maybar/Wello area: their potential and constraints for agricultural development.* Bern, Arbeitsgemeinschaft Geographica Bernensia, 1986.

Ethiopia—Studies

848. Alula Hidaru. *A short guide to the study of Ethiopia.* Westport, Greenwood Press, 1976.

849. Congresso Internazionale di Studi Etiopici, 1972. *IV congresso internazionale di studi etiopici, Roma 10–15 aprile, 1972.* Roma, Accademia dei Lincei, 1974.

850. Convegno Internazionale di Studi Etiopici, Roma, 1959. *Atti del Convegno internazionale di studi etiopici, Roma, 2–4 aprile, 1959.* Roma, Accademia dei Lincei, 1960.

851. Goldenberg, G. (ed.) *Ethiopian studies: proceedings of the sixth international conference, Tel-Aviv, 14–17 April, 1980.* Rotterdam, Balkema, 1986.

852. Hess, Robert L. (ed.) *Proceedings of the fifth international conference on Ethiopian Studies, Session B, Chicago, 13–16 June, 1978.* Chicago, Office of Publications Services, University of Illinois at Chicago Circle, 1978.

853. International Conference of Ethiopian Studies, 1966. *Proceedings of the third international conference of Ethiopian studies, Addis Ababa, 3–7th April, 1966.* Addis Ababa, Haile Selassie I University, Institute of Ethiopian Studies, 1969–1970.

854. Marcus, Harold G. (ed.) *Proceedings of the first United States conference on Ethiopian studies, 1973.* East Lansing, Michigan State University, African Studies Center, 1975.

855. Pankhurst, Richard, and Taddese Beyene (eds.) *Silver jubilee of the Institute of Ethiopian Studies: proceedings of the symposium, Addis Ababa, November 24–26, 1988.* Addis Ababa, Addis Ababa University, Institute of Ethiopian Studies, 1990.

856. Rubenson, Sven (ed.) *Proceedings of the seventh International Conference of Ethiopian Studies, University of Lund, 26–29 April, 1982.* Uppsala, Scandinavian Institute of African Studies, 1984.

857. Scholz, Piotr O. (ed.) *Orbis Aethiopicus: studia in honorem Stanislaus Chojnacki natali septuagesimo quinto dicata, septuagesima septimo oblata.* Albstadt, Karl Schuler, 1992. 2 vols.

858. Taddese Beyene (ed.) *Proceedings of the Eighth International Conference of Ethiopian Studies, University of Addis Ababa, 1984.* Huntingdon, Elm Publications, 1988. 2 vols.

859. Tubiana, Joseph (ed.) *Modern Ethiopia, from the accession of Menilek II to the present: proceedings of the fifth international conference of Ethiopian studies, 19–22 December, 1977.* Rotterdam, Balkema, 1980.

860. Uhlig, S., and Bairu Tafla (eds.) *Collectanea aethiopica.* Stuttgart, Franz Steiner, 1988.

Ethiopia — Taxation

861. Pankhurst, Richard. *Tax records and inventories of Emperor Tewodros of Ethiopia, 1855–1868.* London, School of Oriental and African Studies, 1979.

Ethiopia — Towns

862. Pankhurst, Richard. *History of Ethiopian towns, from the mid-nineteenth century to 1935.* Stuttgart, Franz Steiner, 1985.

863. Pankhurst, Richard. *History of Ethiopian towns from the middle ages to the early 19th century.* Stuttgart, Franz Steiner, 1982.

Ethiopia — Treaties

864. Jacomy-Millette, A. *Treaties in force, 1889–1971: draft list of treaties and other international agreements of Ethiopia.* Addis Ababa, Haile Selassie I University, Faculty of Law, 1973.

Ethiopia—Volcanos

865. Zanettin, Bruno. *Evolution of the Ethiopian volcanic province.* Roma, Accademia Nazionale dei Lincei, 1992.

Ethiopia—Water Supply

866. Alula Abate. *Evaluation of the impact of UNICEF-assisted water supply projects in Bale, Harerge, Shewa and Wello, Ethiopia.* Addis Ababa, Addis Ababa University, Institute of Development Research, 1986.

Ethiopia—Wildlife

867. Nicol, C. W. *From the roof of Africa.* New York, Knopf, 1972.

Ethiopia—Women

868. Pankhurst, Helen. *Gender, development and identity: an Ethiopian study.* London, Zed Books, 1992.

869. Tsehai Berhane-Selassie (ed.) *Gender issues in Ethiopia: proceedings of the first university seminar on gender issues in Ethiopia, Addis Ababa, December 24–26, 1989.* Addis Ababa, Addis Ababa University, Institute of Ethiopian Studies, 1991.

Ethnography—East Africa

870. Baxter, P. T. W., and Uri Almagor (eds.) *Age, generation and time: some features of East African age organizations.* London, Christopher Hurst, 1980.

871. Braukämper, Ulrich. *Migration und ethnischer Wandel: Untersuchungen aus der östlichen Sudanzone.* Stuttgart, Franz Steiner, 1992.

872. Brewer, Marilynn Bolt, and Donald T. Campbell. *Ethnocentrism and intergroup attitudes: East African evidence.* Beverly Hills, Sage, 1976.

873. Kashamura, A. *Famille, sexualité et culture: essai sur les moeurs sexuelles des peuples des Grands Lacs africains.* Paris, Payot, 1973.

874. Kesby, John D. *The cultural regions of East Africa.* London, Academic Press, 1977.

875. Mair, Lucy. *Primitive government: a study of traditional political systems in eastern Africa.* Revised edition. Harmondsworth, Penguin, 1962.

876. Middleton, John, and E. H. Winter (eds.) *Witchcraft and sorcery in East Africa.* London, Routledge & Kegan Paul, 1963.

877. Shorter, Aylward. *East African societies.* London, Routledge & Kegan Paul, 1974.

Ethnography—Northeast Africa

878. Grottanelli, Vinigi Lorenzo. *Gerarchie etniche e conflitto culturale: saggi di etnologia nordest-africana.* Milano, Angeli, 1976.

879. Lewis, I. M. *Peoples of the Horn of Africa: Somali, Afar and Saho*. Second edition. London, International African Institute, 1969.

880. Panetta, E. (ed.) *L'Italia in Africa: studi italiani di etnologia e folklore dell' Africa orientale, Eritrea, Etiopia, Somalia*. Roma, Istituto Poligrafico dello Stato, 1973–74. 2 vols.

Exports—East Africa

881. Stein, Leslie. *The growth of East African exports and their effect on economic development*. London, Croom Helm, 1979.

Famine—East Africa

882. Seavoy, R. E. *Famine in East Africa: food production and food policies*. New York, Greenwood Press, 1989.

Farm Equipment—East Africa

883. Ahmed, I., and H. B. Kinsey (eds.) *Farm equipment innovations in eastern and central southern Africa*. Aldershot, Gower, 1984.

Feroge—Language

884. Santandrea, Stefano. *Note grammaticali e lessicali sul gruppo Feroge e sul Mundu, Sudan*. Napoli, Istituto Universitario Orientale, 1969.

Finance—East Africa

885. Malkamäki, M. *Banking the poor: informal and semi-formal financial systems serving the microenterprise*. Helsinki, Helsinki University, Institute of Development Studies, 1991.

886. Marlin, P. von (ed.) *Financial aspects of development in East Africa*. Munich, Weltforum-Verlag, 1970.

Fipa—Ethnography

887. Willis, Roy G. *The Fipa and related peoples of south-west Tanzania and north-east Zambia*. London, International African Institute, 1966.

Fipa—Folktales

888. Willis, Roy G. *There was a certain man: spoken art of the Fipa*. Oxford, Clarendon Press, 1978.

Fipa—History

889. Willis, Roy G. *A state in the making: myth, history and social transformation in pre-colonial Ufipa*. Bloomington, Indiana University Press, 1981.

Flora—East Africa

890. Milne-Redhead, E., and R. M. Polhill (eds.) *Flora of tropical East Africa.* London, Ministry for Overseas Development, 1968.

Folktales—East Africa

891. Arewa, Erastus Ojo. *A classification of the folktales of the northern East African cattle area by types.* New York, Arno, 1980.

892. Kohl-Larsen, Ludwig. *Der Hasenschelm: Tiermärchen und Volkserzählungen aus Ostafrika.* Kassel, Erich Röth, 1976.

Food and Nutrition—East Africa

893. Kraut, Heinrich, and Hans-Diedrich Cremer (eds.) *Investigations into health and nutrition in East Africa.* Munich, Weltforum-Verlag, 1969.

894. May, Jacques M., and Donna L. McLellan. *The ecology of malnutrition in eastern Africa and four countries of western Africa, etc.* New York, Hafner, 1970.

895. Porter, Philip Wayland. *Food and development in the semi-arid zone of East Africa.* Syracuse, Syracuse University, Maxwell School of Citizenship and Public Affairs, 1979.

Foreign Aid—East Africa

896. Mazzeo, D. *Foreign assistance and the East African common services, 1960–1970, with special reference to multilateral contributions.* Munich, Weltforum-Verlag, 1975.

Foreign Relations—East Africa

897. Agyeman, Opoku. *Nkrumah's Ghana and East Africa: Pan-Africanism and African interstate relations.* Rutherford, Fairleigh Dickinson University Press, 1992.

898. Bezboruah, M. *The U. S. strategy in the Indian Ocean: the international response.* New York, Praeger, 1977.

899. Cottrell, Alvin J., and R. M. Burrell (eds.) *The Indian Ocean: its political, economic and military importance.* New York, Praeger, 1972.

900. Vali, Ferenc A. *Politics of the Indian Ocean region: the balances of power.* New York, The Free Press, 1976.

Foreign Relations—Northeast Africa

901. Bell, J. Bowyer, and R. M. Burrell (eds.) *The Horn of Africa: strategic magnet in the seventies.* New York, Crane, Russak, 1973.

902. Bereket Habte Selassie. *Conflict and intervention in the Horn of Africa.* New York, Monthly Review Press, 1980.

903. Cao Huy, Than, et al. *La Corne de l'Afrique: questions nationales et politique internationale.* Paris, L'Harmattan, 1986.

904. Halliday, Fred. *Threat from the East? Soviet policy from Afghanistan and Iran to the Horn of Africa.* London, Penguin Books, 1982.

905. Makinda, Samuel M. *Security in the Horn of Africa.* London, Institute of Strategic Studies, 1992.

906. Makinda, Samuel M. *Superpower diplomacy in the Horn of Africa.* New York, St. Martin's Press, 1987.

907. Matthies, Volker. *Das "Horn von Afrika" in den internationalen Beziehungen: internationale Aspekte eines Regionalkonflikts in der Dritten Welt.* München, Weltforum-Verlag, 1976.

908. Ottaway, Marina. *Soviet and American influence in the Horn of Africa.* New York, Praeger, 1982.

909. Patman, R. G. *The Soviet Union in the Horn of Africa: the diplomacy of intervention and disengagement.* Cambridge, Cambridge University Press, 1990.

910. Ratliff, W. E. *Follow the leader in the Horn: the Soviet-Cuban presence in East Africa.* Washington, Cuban American National Foundation, 1986.

911. Sauldie, Madan M. *Superpowers in the Horn of Africa.* London, Oriental University Press, 1987.

912. Woodward, Peter. *The Horn of Africa: politics and international relations.* London, British Academic Press, 1993.

Forestry—East Africa

913. Burley, J. *Forestry research in eastern and southern Africa.* Oxford, Oxford Forestry Institute, 1989.

Forests—Northeast Africa

914. Friis, Ib. *Forests and forest trees of northeast tropical Africa: their natural habitats and distribution patterns in Ethiopia, Djibouti and Somalia.* London, H.M.S.O., 1992.

Fort Jesus

915. Kirkman, James S. *Fort Jesus: a Portuguese fortress on the East African coast.* Oxford, Clarendon Press, 1974.

Gabbra—Ethnography

916. Tablino, Paolo. *I Gabbra del Kenya.* Bologna, Editrice Missionaria Italiana, 1980.

Gamo—Ethnography

917. Bureau, Jacques. *Les Gamo d'Éthiopie: étude du système politique.* Paris, Société d'Ethnographie, 1981.

Ganda — Agriculture

918. Richards, Audrey I., et al. (eds.) *Subsistence to commercial farming in present-day Buganda: an economic and anthropological survey.* Cambridge, Cambridge University Press, 1973.

Ganda — Art and Artists

919. Lugira, A. M. *Ganda art: a study of the Ganda mentality with respect to possibilities of acculturation in Christian art.* Kampala, Osasa, 1970.

Ganda — Colonial History

920. Low, Donald Anthony, and Cranford Pratt. *Buganda and British overrule, 1900–1955: two studies.* London, Oxford University Press, 1960.

921. Pawlikova-Vilhanová, Viera. *History of anti-colonial resistance and protest in the kingdoms of Buganda and Bunyoro, 1890–1899.* Prague, Oriental Institute of the Czechoslovak Academy of Sciences, 1988.

Ganda — Ethics

922. Sempebwa, Joshua W. *African traditional moral norms and their implication for Christianity: a case study of Ganda ethics.* St. Augustin, Steyler Verlag, 1983.

Ganda — Ethnography

923. Fallers, Margaret Chave. *The eastern lacustrine Bantu: Ganda and Soga.* London, International African Institute, 1960.

924. Jensen, Jürgen. *Kontinuität und Wandel in der Arbeitsteilung bei den Baganda.* Berlin, Springer, 1967.

925. Robertson, A. F. *Community of strangers: a journal of discovery in Uganda.* London, Scolar Press, 1978.

Ganda — Folktales

926. Lubega, Bonnie. *The burning bush.* Nairobi, East African Literature Bureau, 1970.

Ganda — History

927. Füsser, Wilhelm K. *Rebellion in Buganda: eine Staatskrise in vorkolonialen Ostafrika.* Hamburg, Ergebnisse, 1989.

928. Kaggwa, Apolo. *The Kings of Buganda.* Nairobi, East African Publishing House, 1971.

929. Kavuma, Paulo. *Crisis in Buganda, 1953–55: the story of the exile and return of the Kabaka, Mutesa II.* London, Rex Collings, 1979.

930. Kiwanuka, M. S. M. Semakula. *A history of Buganda from the foundation of the kingdom to 1900.* London, Longman, 1972.

931. Kiwanuka, M. S. M. Semakula. *Muteesa of Uganda*. Nairobi, East African Literature Bureau, 1967.

932. Low, Donald Anthony. *Buganda in modern history*. London, Weidenfeld and Nicolson, 1971.

933. Low, Donald Anthony. *The mind of Buganda: documents of the modern history of an African kingdom*. London, Heinemann, 1971.

934. Mutesa II, Kabaka of Buganda. *Desecration of my kingdom*. London, Constable, 1967.

935. Rusch, W. *Klassen und Staat in Buganda vor der Kolonialzeit: über die Entwicklung der Produktionsverhältnisse in Buganda bis zum Ende des 19. Jahrhunderts und die Herausbildung eines Staates, seinen Aufbau und seine Funktionen. Ein Beitrag zur Erforschung der Geschichte der Buganda*. Berlin, Akademie-Verlag, 1975.

936. Wright, Michael. *Buganda in the heroic age*. London, Oxford University Press, 1971.

Ganda—Labour

937. Richards, Audrey I. (ed.) *Economic development and tribal change: a study of immigrant labour in Buganda*. Revised edition. Nairobi, Oxford University Press, 1973.

Ganda—Land

938. West, H. W. *Land policy in Buganda*. Cambridge, Cambridge University Press, 1972.

939. West, H. W. *The mailo system in Buganda: a preliminary case study in African land tenure*. Entebbe, Government Printer, 1964.

940. West, H. W. *The transformation of land tenure in Buganda since 1896*. Leiden, Afrika-Studiecentrum, 1969.

Ganda—Language

941. Nsereko, Ntanda. *English-Luganda law dictionary*. Gaborone, Magezi Muliro, 1993.

942. Snoxall, R. A. (ed.) *Luganda-English dictionary*. Oxford, Clarendon Press, 1967.

Ganda—Law

943. Haydon, Edwin Scott. *Law and justice in Buganda*. London, Butterworth, 1960.

Ganda—Mental Illness

944. Orley, John. *Culture and mental illness*. Nairobi, East African Publishing House, 1970.

Ganda—Music

945. Wegner, Ulrich. *Xylophonmusik aus Buganda, Ostafrika.* Wilhelmshaven, Flarian Noetzel Verlag, 1990.

Ganda—Politics

946. Coulibaly, Lenissongui. *L'autorité dans l'Afrique traditionnelle: étude comparative des états mossi et ganda.* Abidjan, Nouvelles Éditions Africaines, 1984.

947. Fallers, Lloyd A. (ed.) *The king's men: leadership and status in Buganda on the eve of independence.* London, Oxford University Press, 1964.

Ganda—Proverbs

948. Walser, Ferdinand. *Luganda proverbs.* Berlin, Dietrich Reimer, 1982.

Ganda—Religion

949. Kyewalyanga, Francis-Xavier S. *Traditional religion, custom and Christianity in East Africa as illustrated by the Ganda with references to other African cultures and reference to Islam.* Hohenschäftlarn, Karl Renner, 1976.

Ganda—Social Conditions

950. Klein, Eberhard C. *Sozialer Wandel in Kiteezi/Buganda: ein Dorf im Einflussbereich der Stadt Kampala.* München, Weltforum-Verlag, 1969.

951. Richards, Audrey I. *The changing structure of a Ganda village: Kisozi, 1892–1952.* Nairobi, East African Publishing House, 1966.

Ge'ez—Language

952. Lambdin, Thomas O. *Introduction to classical Ethiopic (Ge'ez).* Missoula, Scholars Press, 1978.

953. Leslau, Wolf. *Comparative dictionary of Ge'ez, classical Ethiopic: Ge'ez-English/English-Ge'ez.* Wiesbaden, Otto Harrassowitz, 1987.

954. Leslau, Wolf. *Concise dictionary of Ge'ez (classical Ethiopic).* Wiesbaden, Otto Harrassowitz, 1989.

955. Makonnen Argaw. *Matériaux pour l'étude de la pronunciation traditionnelle du guèze.* Paris, Éditions Recherche sur les Civilisations, 1984.

Geography—East Africa

956. Berger, Herfried, and Ernst Weigt (eds.) *Ostafrikanische Studien.* Nürnberg, Im Selbstverlag der Wirtschaft- und Sozialgeographischen Instituts der Friedrich-Alexander Universität, 1968.

957. Curutchet, M. *Bibliography on human settlements in developing countries: references with relevance to eastern Africa.* Lusaka, University of Zambia, Institute of African Studies, 1982.

958. Denis, Jacques, et al. *L'Afrique, central et orientale*. Paris, Presses Universitaires de France, 1971.

959. Hecklau, Hans. *Ostafrika: Kenya, Tanzania, Uganda*. Darmstadt, Wissenschaftliche Buchgesellschaft, 1989.

960. Morgan, W. T. W. *East Africa: its people and resources*. Nairobi, Oxford University Press, 1969.

961. Morgan, W. T. W. *Geography of East Africa*. London, Longmans, 1973.

962. O'Connor, Anthony M. *An economic geography of East Africa*. Second edition. London, Bell, 1971.

963. Ominde, Simeon H. (ed.) *Studies in East African geography and development: essays presented to S. J. K. Baker*. London, Heinemann, 1971.

Geology—East Africa

964. Bishop, Walter W. (ed.) *Geological background to fossil man: recent research in the Gregory Rift Valley, East Africa*. Edinburgh, Scottish Academic Press, 1978.

965. Hamilton, A. C. *Environmental history of East Africa: a study of the quaternary*. London, Academic Press, 1982.

Geology—Northeast Africa

966. Pilger, A., and A. Rösler (eds.) *Proceedings of an international symposium on the Afar region and related rift problems, held in Bad Bergzabern, F.R. Germany, April 1–6, 1974*. Stuttgart, E. Schweizerbart'sche Verlagsbuchhandlung, 1974–1976. 2 vols.

Gezira Scheme

967. Abdelmagid, Salah Abdelgadir. *The economic impact of faba bean introduction in smallholdings: a case study of the Gezira scheme, Sudan*. Kiel, Wissenschaftsverlag Vauk, 1992.

968. Ali Taha, Salah Abdel Rahman. *Society, food and nutrition in the Gezira: a social and medical study*. Khartoum, Khartoum University Press, 1977.

969. Barnett, Tony, and A. Abdelkarim. *Sudan: the Gezira scheme and agricultural transition*. London, Frank Cass, 1991.

970. Barnett, Tony. *The Gezira scheme: an illusion of development*. London, Frank Cass, 1977.

971. Bartsch, Reinhart. *Economic problems of pest control examined for the case of the Gezira/Sudan*. Munich, Weltforum-Verlag, 1978.

972. Fakki, H. *Economics and management of irrigation in the Sudan Gezira scheme*. Hohenheim, Universität Hohenheim, Fakultät IV-Agrarwissenschaften II, 1982.

973. Plusquellec, Hervi L. *The Gezira irrigation scheme in Sudan: objectives, design and performance.* Washington, World Bank, 1990.

Giriama—Colonial History

974. Brantley, C. *The Giriama and colonial resistance in Kenya, 1800–1920.* Berkeley, University of California Press, 1981.

Giriama—Ethnography

975. Parkin, David. *Palms, wine and witnesses: public spirit and private gain in an African farming community.* San Francisco, Chandler, 1972.

976. Parkin, David. *Sacred void: spatial images of work and ritual among the Giriama of Kenya.* Cambridge, Cambridge University Press, 1991.

Gisu—Ethnography

977. Heald, Suzette. *Controlling anger: the sociology of Gisu violence.* Manchester, Manchester University Press, 1989.

Gisu—Language

978. Brown, G. *Phonological rules and dialect variation: a study of the phonology of Lumasaaba.* Cambridge, Cambridge University Press, 1972.

Gisu—Markets

979. Bunker, Stephen G. *Peasants against the state: the politics of market control in Bugisu, Uganda, 1900–1983* [reprinted with a new afterword]. Chicago, University of Chicago Press, 1991.

Gogo—Ethnography

980. Rigby, Peter. *Cattle and kinship among the Gogo: a semi-pastoral society of central Tanzania.* Ithaca, Cornell University Press, 1969.

Gondo—Social Conditions

981. Vincent, Joan. *African elite: the big men of a small town.* New York, Columbia University Press, 1971.

Gonga—History

982. Lange, Werner. *History of the southern Gonga, southwestern Ethiopia.* Stuttgart, Franz Steiner, 1982.

Gordon, Charles George

983. Featherstone, Donald. *Khartoum 1885: General Gordon's last stand.* London, Osprey, 1993.

984. Garrett, Richard. *General Gordon.* London, Barker, 1974.

985. Johnson, Peter. *Gordon of Khartoum*. Wellingborough, Patrick Stephens, 1985.

986. MacGregor-Hastie, R. *Never to be taken alive: a biography of General Gordon*. London, Sidgwick & Jackson, 1985.

987. Nutting, Anthony. *Gordon: martyr and misfit*. London, Constable, 1966.

988. Pollock, John. *Gordon: the man behind the legend*. London, Constable, 1993.

989. Trench, Charles Pocklington Chenevix. *Charley Gordon: an eminent Victorian reassessed*. London, Allen Lane, 1978.

990. Turnbull, P. *Gordon of Khartoum*. Folkestone, Bailey Brothers and Swinfen, 1975.

Gulu—Geography

991. Ocitti, J. P. *The urban geography of Gulu*. Kampala, Makerere University, 1973.

Gurage—Ethnography

992. Gabreyesus Hailemariam. *The Guragué and their culture*. New York, Vantage Press, 1991.

993. Shack, William A. *The Gurage: a people of the ensete culture*. London, Oxford University Press, 1966.

Gurage—Folktales

994. Leslau, Wolf (ed.) *Gurage folklore: Ethiopian folktales, proverbs, beliefs, and riddles*. Wiesbaden, Franz Steiner, 1982.

995. Shack, William A., and Habte-Mariam Marcos (eds.) *Gods and heroes: oral traditions of the Gurage of Ethiopia*. London, Oxford University Press, 1974.

Gurage—Language

996. Hetzron, Robert. *The Gunnän-Gurage languages*. Napoli, Istituto Orientale di Napoli, 1977.

997. Leslau, Wolf. *Etymological dictionary of Gurage*. Wiesbaden, Otto Harrassowitz, 1979. 3 vols.

Gusii—Colonial History

998. Maxon, Robert M. *Conflict and accommodation in western Kenya: the Gusii and the British, 1907–1963*. Rutherford, Fairleigh Dickinson University Press, 1989.

Gusii—Ethnography

999. Hakansson, T. *Bridewealth, women and land: social change among the Gusii of Kenya*. Uppsala, University, 1988.

Gusii—History

1000. Ochieng', William Robert. *A pre-colonial history of the Gusii of western Kenya from c. A.D. 1500 to 1914.* Kampala, East African Literature Bureau, 1974.

Gusii—Women

1001. LeVine, Sarah, and Robert A. LeVine. *Mothers and wives: Gusii women of East Africa.* Chicago, University of Chicago Press, 1979.

Hadiya—History

1002. Braukämper, Ulrich. *Geschichte der Hadiya Süd-Äthiopiens, von den Anfängen bis zur Revolution 1974.* Stuttgart, Franz Steiner, 1980.

Haile Selassie I

1003. Askele Negash. *Haile Selassie.* New York, Chelsea House, 1989.

1004. Gorham, Charles. *The Lion of Judah: a life of Haile Selassie I, Emperor of Ethiopia.* New York, Farrar, Straus and Giroux, 1966.

1005. Haile Selassie I. *The autobiography of Emperor Haile Selassie I: "My life and Ethiopia's progress," 1892–1937.* London, Oxford University Press, 1976.

1006. Juniac, G. de. *Le dernier roi des rois.* Paris, Plon, 1979.

1007. Kapuscinski, Ryszard. *The emperor: downfall of an autocrat.* London, Quartet Books, 1983.

1008. Lockot, Hans Wilhelm. *The mission: the life, reign and character of Haile Selassie I.* London, Hurst, 1989.

1009. Marcus, Harold G. *Haile Sellassie I: the formative years, 1892–1936.* Berkeley, University of California Press, 1987.

1010. Mosley, Leonard O. *Haile Selassie: the conquering lion.* London, Weidenfeld and Nicolson, 1964.

1011. Potyka, C. *Haile Selassie, der Negus Negesti in Frieden und Krieg: zur Politik des äthiopischen Reformherrschers.* Bad Honnef, Osang, 1974.

1012. Schwab, Peter. *Haile Selassie I: Ethiopia's lion of Judah.* Chicago, Nelson-Hall, 1979.

1013. Tunstall, Bill (ed.) *Addis 1930: the coronation of H.I.M. Emperor Haile Sellassie.* London, Africa Archive, 1992.

Hamar—Ethnography

1014. Lydall, Jean, and Ivo Strecker. *The Hamar of southern Ethiopia.* Hohenschäftlarn, Klaus Renner, 1979. 3 vols.

1015. Strecker, Ivo. *The social practice of symbolism: an anthropological analysis*. London, Athlone Press, 1988.

Hamito—Semitic Languages

1016. Fronzaroli, Pelio (ed.) *Atti del secondo congresso internazionale di linguistica camito-semitica*. Firenze, Istituto di Linguistica e di Lingue Orientali, 1978.

1017. Jungraithmayr, H., and W. W. Müller (eds.) *Proceedings of the fourth international Hamito-Semitic Congress, Hamburg, September 20–22, 1983*. Amsterdam, John Benjamins, 1987.

Harar—History

1018. Garad, Abdurahman. *Harar: Wirtschaftsgeschichte eines Emirats Horn von Afrika, 1825–75*. Frankfurt am Main, Peter Lang, 1990.

Harar—Social Conditions

1019. Koehn, Peter, and S. R. Waldron. *Afocha: a link between community and administration in Harar, Ethiopia*. Syracuse, Syracuse University, Maxwell School of Citizenship and Public Affairs, 1978.

Harar—Women

1020. Hecht, Elisabeth Dorothea. *Die traditionellen Frauenvereine, Afoca, der Harari in Harar und in Addis Ababa, Äthiopien*. Berlin, Dietrich Reimer, 1994.

Harari—Language

1021. Wagner, Ewald. *Harari-Texte in arabischer Schrift*. Stuttgart, Franz Steiner, 1983.

Haya—Language

1022. Byarushengo, E., et al. (eds.) *Haya grammatical structure*. Los Angeles, University of Southern California, Department of Linguistics, 1977.

Health and Medicine—East Africa

1023. Beck, Ann. *A history of the British medical administration of East Africa, 1900–1950*. Cambridge, Mass., Harvard University Press, 1970.

1024. Muller, A. S., et al. *Bibliography of health and disease in East Africa*. Amsterdam, Elsevier, 1988.

1025. Wood, Michael. *Go an extra mile: the adventures and reflections of a flying doctor*. London, Collins, 1978.

Hima—Ethnography

1026. Elam, Yitzchak. *The social and sexual roles of Hima women.* Manchester, Manchester University Press, 1973.

History—East Africa

1027. Allen, James de Vere, and Thomas H. Wilson (eds.) *From Zinj to Zanzibar: studies in history, trade and society on the eastern coast of Africa.* Stuttgart, Franz Steiner, 1982.

1028. Anderson, John D. *West Africa and East Africa in the nineteenth and twentieth centuries.* London, Heinemann, 1972.

1029. Arens, William (ed.) *A century of change in eastern Africa.* The Hague, Mouton, 1976.

1030. Atieno Odhiambo, E. S., et al. *A history of East Africa.* London, Longmans, 1977.

1031. Ayot, Henry Okello. *Historical texts of the lake region of East Africa.* Nairobi, Kenya Literature Bureau, 1977.

1032. Ayot, Henry Okello. *Topics in East African history, 1000–1976.* Kampala, East African Literature Bureau, 1976.

1033. Bennett, Norman R. *Arab versus European: diplomacy and war in nineteenth-century East Central Africa.* New York, Africana Publishing, 1985.

1034. Berger, Iris. *Religion and resistance: East African kingdoms in the pre-colonial period.* Tervuren, Musée Royale de l'Afrique Centrale, 1981.

1035. Chittick, Neville, and Robert I. Rotberg (eds.) *East Africa and the Orient: cultural syntheses in pre-colonial times.* New York, Africana Publishing, 1975.

1036. Collins, Robert O. *Eastern African history.* New York, Wiener, 1990.

1037. Davidson, David. *A history of East and Central Africa to the late nineteenth century.* New York, Anchor Books, 1969.

1038. Ehret, Christopher. *Southern Nilotic history: linguistic approaches to the study of the past.* Evanston, Northwestern University Press, 1971.

1039. Ehret, Christopher. *Ethiopians and East Africans.* Nairobi, East African Publishing House, 1974.

1040. Ehret, Christopher, and M. Posnansky (eds.) *The archaeological and linguistic reconstruction of East African history.* Berkeley, California University Press, 1982.

1041. Fischer, Rudolf. *Korallenstädte in Afrika: die vorkoloniale Geschichte der Ostküste.* Oberdorf, Edition Piscator, 1984.

1042. Freeman-Grenville, G. S. P. *The Swahili coast, 2nd to 19th centuries: Islam, Christianity and commerce in East Africa.* London, Variorum Reprints, 1988.

1043. Freeman-Grenville, G. S. P. (ed.) *The East African coast: select documents from the first to the earlier nineteenth century*. Oxford, Clarendon Press, 1962.

1044. Gallagher, Joseph T. (ed.) *East African culture history*. Syracuse, Syracuse University, Maxwell School of Citizenship and Public Affairs, 1976.

1045. Haight, Mabel Violet Jackson. *European powers and south-east Africa: a study of international relations on the south-east coast of Africa, 1796–1856*. Revised edition. London, Routledge & Kegan Paul, 1967.

1046. Harlow, V., et al. (eds.) *History of East Africa. Vol. II*. Oxford, Clarendon Press, 1976.

1047. Ingham, Kenneth. *A history of East Africa*. Third edition. London, Longmans, 1965.

1048. Low, Donald Anthony, and A. Smith (eds.) *History of East Africa, Vol. III*. Oxford, Clarendon Press, 1976.

1049. Marsh, Zoë, and G. W. Kingsnorth. *A history of East Africa: an introductory survey*. Fourth edition. Cambridge, Cambridge University Press, 1974.

1050. Maxon, Robert M. *East Africa: an introductory history*. Morgantown, West Virginia University Press, 1986.

1051. McCall, D. F., et al. (eds.) *Eastern African history*. London, Pall Mall, 1969.

1052. McIntosh, B. G. (ed.) *Ngano: studies in traditional and modern East African history*. Nairobi, East African Publishing House, 1969.

1053. Moorehead, Alan. *The White Nile*. London, Hamish Hamilton, 1960.

1054. Nicholls, C. S. *The Swahili coast: politics, diplomacy and trade on the East African littoral, 1798–1856*. London, Allen and Unwin, 1971.

1055. Ogot, Bethwell A., and J. A. Kieran (eds.) *Zamani: a survey of East African history*. Revised edition. Nairobi, East African Publishing House, 1978.

1056. Ogot, Bethwell A. (ed.) *Hadith 1: proceedings of the conference of the Historical Association of Kenya, 1967*. Nairobi, East African Publishing House, 1968.

1057. Ogot, Bethwell A. (ed.) *Hadith 2: proceedings of the 1968 conference of the Historical Association of Kenya*. Nairobi, East African Publishing House, 1970.

1058. Ogot, Bethwell A. (ed.) *Hadith 3: proceedings of the conferences of the Historical Association of Kenya, 1969/70*. Nairobi, East African Publishing House, 1971.

1059. Ogot, Bethwell A. (ed.) *Hadith 4: politics and nationalism in colonial Kenya*. Nairobi, East African Publishing House, 1973.

1060. Ogot, Bethwell A. (ed.) *Hadith 5: economic and social history of East Africa.* Nairobi, East African Literature Bureau, 1975.

1061. Ogot, Bethwell A. (ed.) *Hadith 6: history and social change in East Africa.* Nairobi, East African Literature Bureau, 1976.

1062. Ogot, Bethwell A. (ed.) *Hadith 7: ecology and history in East Africa.* Nairobi, Kenya Literature Bureau, 1980.

1063. Oliver, Roland, and Gervase Mathew (eds.) *History of East Africa. Vol. 1.* Oxford, Clarendon Press, 1963.

1064. Rosenthal, Ricky. *The sign of the ivory horn: eastern African civilizations.* Dobbs Ferry, Oceana Publications, 1971.

1065. Simpson, Donald. *Dark companions: the African contribution to the exploration of East Africa.* London, Paul Elek, 1975.

1066. Ssekamwa, J. C. *A sketch map history of East Africa.* New enlarged edition. Amersham, Hulton Educational, 1984.

1067. Strandes, Justus. *The Portuguese period in East Africa.* Nairobi, East African Literature Bureau, 1961.

1068. Ward, W. E. F., and L. W. White. *East Africa: a century of change, 1870–1970.* London, Allen and Unwin, 1971.

1069. Webster, James Bertin (ed.) *Chronology, migration and drought in interlacustrine Africa.* London, Longmans, 1980.

1070. Weisbord, Robert G. *African Zion: the attempt to establish a Jewish colony in the East African Protectorate, 1903–1905.* Philadelphia, Jewish Publication Society of America, 1968.

History—Northeast Africa

1071. Doresse, Jean. *Histoire sommaire de la corne orientale de l'Afrique.* Second edition. Paris, Librairie Orientaliste Paul Geuthner, 1983.

1072. Johnson, Douglas H., and D. M. Anderson (eds.) *The ecology of survival: case studies from northeast African history.* London, Lester Crook, 1988.

1073. Moorehead, Alan. *The Blue Nile.* Revised edition. London, Hamish Hamilton, 1972.

1074. Saccone, Salvatore, et al. *Aspetti politici ed economici nell'esplorazione italiana dell'Africa, 1867–1900.* Bologna, Pàtron, 1976.

Ik—Ethnography

1075. Turnbull, Colin M. *The mountain people.* London, Cape, 1973.

Industry—East Africa

1076. Kisanga, Eliawony J. *Industrial and trade cooperation in eastern and southern Africa.* Aldershot, Avebury, 1991.

1077. Pearson, D. S. *Industrial development in East Africa*. Nairobi, Oxford University Press, 1969.

1078. Zajadacz, Paul (ed.) *Studies in production and trade in East Africa*. Munich, Weltforum-Verlag, 1970.

Infibulation—Northeast Africa

1079. Hicks, Esther K. *Infibulation: female genital mutilation in Islamic northeastern Africa*. New Brunswick, Transaction Publishers, 1993.

Ingessana—Language

1080. Crewe, W. J. *The phonological features of the Ingessana language*. Khartoum, University of Khartoum, Institute of African and Asian Studies, 1975.

Iraqw—Ethnography

1081. Thornton, Robert J. *Space, time and culture among the Iraqw of Tanzania*. New York, Academic Press, 1980.

Iraqw—Folktales

1082. Kamera, W. D. *Tales of Wairaqw of Tanzania*. Kampala, East African Literature Bureau, 1976.

1083. Wada, Shohei, et al. *Hadithi za mapokeo ya Wairaqw: Iraqw folktales in Tanzania*. Tokyo, Institute for the Study of Languages and Cultures of Asia and Africa, 1976.

Iraqw—Language

1084. Nordbustad, F. *Iraqw grammar: an analytical study of the Iraqw language*. Berlin, Dietrich Reimer, 1988.

1085. Wada, Shohei. *Iraqw basic vocabulary with Swahili equivalents*. Tokyo, Institute for the Study of Languages and Cultures of Asia and Africa, 1973.

Islam—East Africa

1086. Farsy, Abdallah Salih. *The Shafi'i ulama of East Africa, ca. 1830–1970: hagiographic account*. Edited by R. L. Pouwels. Madison, University of Wisconsin, African Studies Program, 1989.

1087. Pouwels, R. L. *Horn and crescent: cultural change and traditional Islam on the East African coast, 800–1900*. Cambridge, Cambridge University Press, 1987.

1088. Trimingham, John Spencer. *Islam in East Africa*. Oxford, Clarendon Press, 1964.

Islam—Northeast Africa

1089. Samatar, Said S. (ed.) *In the shadow of conquest: Islam in colonial northeast Africa*. Trenton, Red Sea Press, 1992.

Ja'aliyyin—Folktales

1090. Hurreiz, Sayyid Hamid. *Ja'aliyyin folktales*. Bloomington, Indiana University, 1977.

Jie—History

1091. Lamphear, John. *The traditional history of the Jie of Uganda*. Oxford, Clarendon Press, 1976.

Jinja—Social Conditions

1092. Gerken, E., et al. *The industrial town as a factor of economic and social development: the example of Jinja, Uganda*. Munich, Weltforum-Verlag, 1972.

Jonglei Canal

1093. Beshir, Mohamed El Mahdi. *The Jonglei canal project*. Uppsala, Scandinavian Institute of African Studies, 1979.

1094. Beshir, Mohamed El Mahdi. *The Jonglei canal and the Upper Nile swamps*. Wad Medani, Centre Region Press, 1985.

1095. Collins, Robert O. *The waters of the Nile: hydropolitics and the Jonglei Canal, 1900–1988*. Oxford, Clarendon Press, 1990.

1096. El Sammani, Mohamed Osman. *Jonglei canal: dynamics of planned change in the Twic area*. Khartoum, University of Khartoum, Graduate College, 1984.

1097. Howell, Paul, et al. (eds.) *The Jonglei canal: impact and opportunity*. Cambridge, Cambridge University Press, 1988.

1098. Tvedt, Terje. *Water and politics: a history of the Jonglei Project in the southern Sudan*. Fantoft, Chr. Michelsen Institute, Development Research Action Programme, 1986.

Juba—Population

1099. House, William J., and N. B. Cohen. *An extended socio-economic and demographic profile of the population of urban Juba*. Geneva, UNFPA/ILO Project SUD/79/PO6, 1986.

Juba—Social Conditions

1100. House, William J. *The state of human resources, conditions of employment and determinants of incomes and poverty in southern Sudan: evidence from Juba's enterprise economy.* Juba, UNFPA/ILO Project SUD/79/PO6, 1984.

1101. Mills, L. R. *People of Juba: demographic and socio-economic characteristics of the capital of southern Sudan.* Wad Medani, University of Gezira, Population Studies Centre, [n.d.] [based on material collected in 1979].

Kababish — Ethnography

1102. Asad, Talal. *The Kababish Arabs: power, authority and consent in a nomadic tribe.* London, Christopher Hurst, 1970.

Kadugli — Language

1103. Abdalla, A. I. *Kadugli language and language usage.* Khartoum, University of Khartoum, Institute of African and Asian Studies, 1973.

Kaguru — Ethnography

1104. Beidelman, Thomas O. *Moral imagination in Kaguru modes of thought.* Bloomington, Indiana University Press, 1986.

1105. Beidelman, Thomas O. *The Kaguru: a matrilineal people of East Africa.* New York, Holt, Rinehart and Winston, 1971.

Kalambo Falls

1106. Clark, John Desmond. *Kalambo Falls prehistoric site I: the geology, palaeoecology and detailed stratigraphy of the excavations.* Cambridge, Cambridge University Press, 1969.

1107. Clark, John Desmond. *Kalambo Falls prehistoric site II: the later prehistoric cultures.* Cambridge, Cambridge University Press, 1974.

Kalenjin — Bibliography

1108. Daniels, Robert E., et al. *A bibliography of the Kalenjin peoples of East Africa.* Madison, University of Wisconsin, African Studies Program, 1987.

Kalenjin — Language

1109. Creider, Chet A. *Studies in Kalenjin nominal tonology.* Berlin, Dietrich Reimer, 1982.

1110. Ng'elechei, C. C. *Tikshenari ne bo Kalenjin ak English koboto Tikshenari ne bo English ak Kelenjin: Kalenjin-English, English-Kalenjin dictionary.* Nairobi, Transafrica, 1979.

1111. Toweett, Taaitta. *A study of Kalenjin linguistics.* Nairobi, Kenya Literature Bureau, 1979.

1112. Toweett, Taaitta. *English-Swahili-Kalenjin nouns pocket dictionary.* Nairobi, Kenya Literature Bureau, 1979.

Kalenjin—Oral Literature

1113. Chesaina, Ciarunji. *Oral literature of the Kalenjin.* Nairobi, Heinemann Kenya, 1991.

Kamba—Colonial History

1114. Forbes Munro, J. *Colonial rule and the Kamba: social change in the Kenya highlands, 1889–1939.* Oxford, Clarendon Press, 1975.

Kamba—Education

1115. Hill, M. J. D. *The Harambee movement in Kenya: self-help, development and education among the Kamba of Kitui District.* London, Athlone Press, 1991.

Kamba—Ethnography

1116. Ndeti, Kivuto. *Elements of Akamba life.* Nairobi, East African Publishing House, 1972.

1117. O'Leary, Michael. *The Kitui Akamba: economic and social change in semi-arid Kenya.* Nairobi, Heinemann, 1984.

Kamba—Health

1118. Molvaer, Reidulf Knut. *Kibwezi survey: report on an investigation into health-related beliefs and practices in a Kamba district of Kenya.* Nairobi, AMREF, 1981.

Kamba—Music

1119. Kavyu, Paul Ndilya. *An introduction to Kamba music.* Kampala, East African Literature Bureau, 1977.

1120. Kavyu, Paul Ndilya. *Drum beats of the Akamba.* Hohenschäftlarn, Karl Renner, 1986.

Kamba—Oral Literature

1121. Kieti, Mwikali, and Peter Coughlin. *Barking you'll be eaten! The wisdom of Kamba oral literature.* Nairobi, Phoenix, 1990.

Kamba—Social Conditions

1122. Kabwegyere, Tarsis B., and J. Mbula. *A case of the Akamba of eastern Kenya.* Canberra, Australian National University, 1979.

Kambata—History

1123. Braukämper, Ulrich. *Die Kambata: Geschichte und Gesellschaft eines süd-äthiopischen Bauernvolkes.* Stuttgart, Franz Steiner, 1983.

Kampala — Agriculture

1124. Maxwell, Daniel. *Urban farming in Africa: the case of Kampala*. Nairobi, Acts Press, 1992.

Kampala — Prostitution

1125. Bakwesegha, Christopher James. *Profiles of urban prostitution: a case study from Uganda*. Nairobi, Kenya Literature Bureau, 1982.

Kampala — Social Conditions

1126. Gutkind, Peter C. W. *The royal capital of Buganda: a study of internal conflict and external ambiguity*. The Hague, Mouton, 1963.

1127. Mulumba, S. S. *Urbanization in developing countries, a case study: Kampala, Uganda. An elementary survey of land and dwelling environments*. Cambridge, Mass., MIT Education Research Program, 1974.

1128. Parkin, David. *Neighbours and nationals in an African city ward*. London, Routledge, 1969.

Kampala — Urban Development

1129. Scaff, Alvin H., et al. *Recommendations for urban development in Kampala and Mengo*. New York, United Nations, Commissioner for Technical Assistance, Department of Economic and Social Affairs, 1964.

Karagwe — History

1130. Katoke, Israel K. *The Karagwe kingdom: a history of the Abanyambo of northwestern Tanzania, c. 1400–1915*. Nairobi, East African Publishing House, 1975.

Karimojong — Description

1131. Farina, Felice. *Nel paese dei bevitore di sangue: genti nuove alla ribalta; il popolo Karimojong. Pagine vive di attualità*. Bologna, Editrice Nigrizia, 1965.

Karimojong — Ethnography

1132. Dyson-Hudson, Neville. *Karimojong politics*. Oxford, Clarendon Press, 1966.

1133. Novelli, Bruno. *Aspects of Karimojong ethnosociology*. Verona, n. publ., 1988.

1134. Pazzaglia, Augusto. *I karimojong: note storiche, migrazione, iniziazione (Asapan)*. Bologna, Editrice Nigrizia, 1973.

Karimojong—Language

1135. Novelli, Bruno. *A grammar of the Karimojong language*. Berlin, Dietrich Reimer, 1985.

1136. Novelli, Bruno. *Small grammar of the Karimojong language*. Verona, Verona Fathers, 1987.

Kawahla—Economy

1137. Beck, K. *Die Kawahla von Kordofan: ökologische und ökonomische Strategien arabischer Nomaden im Sudan*. Stuttgart, Franz Steiner, 1988.

Kenya—Administration

1138. Hyden, Goren, et al. (eds.) *Development administration: the Kenyan experience*. Nairobi, Oxford University Press, 1970.

1139. Leonard, David K. (ed.) *Rural administration in Kenya: a critical appraisal. Conference on Comparative Administration in East Africa, 1971, Arusha*. Nairobi, East African Literature Bureau, 1973.

Kenya—Agricultural Technology

1140. Anthony, C. G. *Mechanization and maize: agriculture and its politics of technology transfer in East Africa*. Irvington, Columbia University Press, 1987.

Kenya—Agriculture

1141. Aguilar, Renato. *Efficiency in production: theory and an application on Kenyan smallholders*. Göteborg, Universitas Regia Gothoburgensis, 1988.

1142. Bates, Robert H. *Beyond the miracle of the market: the political economy of agrarian development in Kenya*. Cambridge, Cambridge University Press, 1989.

1143. Bevan, David, et al. *Agriculture and the policy environment: Tanzania and Kenya*. Paris, OECD Development Centre, 1993.

1144. Clayton, Eric S. *Agrarian development in peasant economies: some lessons from Kenya*. Oxford, Pergamon Press, 1964.

1145. Cone, L. W., and J. F. Lipscomb. *The history of Kenya agriculture*. Nairobi, University Press of Africa, 1972.

1146. Flury, Manuel. *Rain-fed agriculture in Central Division, Laikipia District, Kenya*. Bern, Arbeitsgemeinschaft Geographica Bernensia, 1988.

1147. Frey, H. J. *Intensivierung kleinbäuerlicher Betriebe durch angepasste Agrartechnik: Arbeitszeitstudien im Bahati Settlement Scheme, Kenia*. München, Weltforum-Verlag, 1976.

1148. Glover, D., and K. Kusterer. *Small farmers, big business: contract farming and rural development.* Basingstoke, Macmillan, 1990.

1149. Hebinck, Paulus. *The agrarian structure in Kenya: state, farmers and commodity relations.* Saarbrücken, Breitenbach, 1990.

1150. Heyer, Judith, et al. (eds.) *Agricultural development in Kenya: an economic assessment.* Nairobi, Oxford University Press, 1976.

1151. Leonard, David K. *Reaching the peasant farmer: organization theory and practice in Kenya.* Chicago, University of Chicago Press, 1977.

1152. Linder, Harald. *Crop production improvement.* Uppsala, Swedish University of Agriculture, Forestry and Veterinary Medicine, 1976.

1153. Lofchie, Michael F. *The policy factor: agricultural performance in Kenya and Tanzania.* Boulder, Lynne Rienner, 1989.

1154. Maitha, J. K. *Coffee in the Kenyan economy: an econometric analysis.* Nairobi, East African Literature Bureau, 1974.

1155. Meyers, L. Richard. *A sociological approach to farming systems in Kenya.* Ithaca, Cornell University, College of Agriculture and Life Sciences, 1982.

1156. Odingo, Richard Samson. *The Kenya highlands: land use and agricultural development.* Nairobi, East African Publishing House, 1971.

1157. Oswald, K. F. *Agrarwirtschaft und sozialer Wandel in Baringo District, Kenya.* Frankfurt am Main, Im Selbstverlag des Instituts für Wirtschafts- und Sozialgeographie der Johann Wolfgang Goethe-Universität, 1980.

1158. Ruthenberg, Hans. *African agricultural production development policy in Kenya, 1952–1965.* Berlin, Springer, 1966.

1159. Sharpley, J. *Economic policies and agricultural performance: the case of Kenya.* Paris, OECD, 1986.

1160. Staudt, Kathleen A. *Agricultural policy implementation: a case study from western Kenya.* West Hartford, Kumarian Press, 1985.

1161. Talbott, I. D. *Agricultural innovation in colonial Africa: Kenya and the great depression.* Lewiston, Edwin Mellen Press, 1990.

1162. Thurston, Anne. *Smallholder agriculture in colonial Kenya: the official mind and the Swynnerton plan.* Cambridge, University of Cambridge, African Studies Centre, 1987.

1163. Thurston, Anne. *The intensification of smallholder agriculture in Kenya: the genesis and implementation of the Swynnerton plan.* Oxford, Rhodes House Library, 1984.

1164. Tibaijuka, Anna Kajumulo. *Kenya: a study of the agricultural sector.* Uppsala, Swedish University of Agricultural Sciences, 1981.

1165. Tod, W. H. W. *A comparison of smallholder agricultural development in Kenya and Malawi.* Edinburgh, University of Edinburgh, Centre of African Studies, 1984.

1166. Trapman, C. *Change in administrative structures: a case study of Kenyan agricultural development.* London, Overseas Development Institute, 1974.

1167. Uchendu, Victor Chikezie, and K. R. M. Anthony. *Agricultural change in Kisii District, Kenya: a study of economic, cultural and technical determinants of agricultural change in tropical Africa.* Nairobi, East African Literature Bureau, 1975.

1168. Vasthoff, Josef. *Small farm credit and development: some experiences in East Africa, with special reference to Kenya.* Munich, Weltforum-Verlag, 1968.

1169. Weber, A. *Energy use in Kenya's agricultural sector, 1960–1978: a statistical and economic analysis.* Nairobi, University of Nairobi, Housing Research Development Unit, 1983.

1170. Wegner, Gerhard. *Bauern, Kapital und Staat in Kenia: eine Einführung.* Hamburg, Argument, 1983.

1171. Wilde, John C. de. *Expériences de développement agricole en Afrique tropicale, 2: Kenya.* Paris, Maisonneuve & Larose, 1968.

1172. Zwanenberg, Roger M. van. *The agricultural history of Kenya to 1939.* Nairobi, East African Publishing House, 1972.

Kenya—Alcohol Consumption

1173. Partanen, J. *Sociability and intoxication: alcohol and drinking in Kenya, Africa and the modern world.* Helsinki, Finnish Foundation for Alcohol Studies, 1991.

Kenya—Archaeology

1174. Cornelissen, Els. *Site GnJh-17 and its implications for the archaeology of the middle Kapthurin formation, Baringo, Kenya.* Tervuren, Koninklijk Museum voor Midden Afrika, 1992.

1175. Foley, Robert. *Off-site archaeology and human adaptation in eastern Africa.* Oxford, British Archaeological Reports, 1981.

1176. Fort Jesus Museum. *Chinese porcelain from coastal sites in Kenya.* Oxford, British Archaeological Reports, 1978.

1177. Kirkman, James S. *Ungwana on the Tana.* The Hague, Mouton, 1966.

1178. Leakey, Richard E., and L. J. Slikkerveer (eds.) *Origins and development of agriculture in East Africa: the ethnosystems approach to the study of early food production in Kenya.* Ames, Iowa State University, Technology and Social Change Program, 1991.

1179. Robbins, L. H., et al. *Lopoy and Lothagam.* East Lansing, Michigan State University, 1980.

1180. Sassoon, Caroline. *Chinese porcelain marks from coastal sites in Kenya: aspects of trade in the Indian Ocean, XIV–XIX centuries.* Oxford, British Archaeological Reports, 1978.

1181. Sutton, J. E. G. *Archaeology of the western highlands of Kenya*. Nairobi, British Institute in Eastern Africa, 1973.

Kenya—Architecture

1182. Andersen, Kaj Blegvad. *African traditional architecture: a study of the housing and settlement patterns of rural Kenya*. Nairobi, Oxford University Press, 1977.

1183. Wilson, Thomas H. *The monumental architecture and archeology of the central and southern Kenya coast*. Nairobi, National Museums of Kenya, 1980.

Kenya—Art and Artists

1184. Maranga, J. S. *Schooling, cognition and work: a study of cognitive aspects of stone-carving*. Kisumu, Kenyatta University, Bureau of Educational Research, 1987.

1185. Sheikh-Dilthey, Helmtraud. *Kenia: Kunst, Kultur und Geschichte am Eingangstor zu Innerafrika*. Seventh edition. Köln, DuMont, 1991.

Kenya—Asians

1186. Dittmann, F. *Kultur und Leistung: zur Frage der Leistungsdispositionen bei Luo und Indern in Kenia*. Saarbrücken, Sozialwissenschaftlicher Studienkreis, 1973.

1187. Salvadori, Cynthia. *Through open doors: a view of Asian cultures in Kenya*. Second edition. Nairobi, Kenway Publications, 1989.

1188. Seidenberg, Dana April. *Uhuru and the Kenya Indians: the role of a minority community in Kenya politics, 1939–1963*. New Delhi, Vikas, 1983.

1189. Sheikh-Dilthey, Helmtraud. *Die Punjabi-Muslim in Kenya: Leistungen und Schicksal einer asiatischen Minorität in Afrika*. München, Weltforum-Verlag, 1974.

Kenya—Atlases

1190. Department of Resource Surveys and Remote Sensing. *Kenya from space: an aerial atlas*. Nairobi, East African Educational Publishers, 1992.

Kenya—Banking

1191. Frediani, Lorenzo. *The liquidity policy of deposit banks in Kenya*. Milano, Cassa di Risparmio delle Provincie Lombarde, 1975.

Kenya—Bibliography

1192. Collison, Robert L. *Kenya*. Oxford, Clio Press, 1982.

1193. Müller, Ties, and Anne Jansen. *Wirtschafts- Agrar- und Sozialpolitik in Ostafrika, Kenia, Tansania: ausgewählte neuere Literatur*. Hamburg, Deutsches Institut für Afrika-Forschung, 1974.

1194. Ng'ang'a, James Mwangi. *Kenya: a subject index, 1967–1976. A select bibliography of articles.* Nairobi, Africa Book Services, 1983.

1195. Ng'ang'a, James Mwangi. *Theses and dissertations on Kenya: an international bibliography.* Nairobi, Africa Book Services, 1983.

1196. Nørgaard, Ole. *Kenya in the social sciences: an annotated bibliography, 1867–1979.* Nairobi, Kenya Literature Bureau, 1980.

1197. Webster, John B., et al. *A bibliography on Kenya.* Syracuse, Syracuse University, Program of Eastern African Studies, 1967.

Kenya — Botany

1198. Dale, Ivan R., and P. J. Greenway. *Kenya trees and shrubs.* Nairobi, Buchanan, 1961.

1199. Moorjani, Shakuntala, and Barbara Simpson. *Seaweeds of the Kenya coast.* Nairobi, Oxford University Press, 1988.

1200. Ojiambo, J. A. *The trees of Kenya.* Nairobi, Kenya Literature Bureau, 1978.

Kenya — Child Welfare

1201. Dallape, Fabio. *An experience with street children.* Second edition. Nairobi, Undugu Society of Kenya, 1988.

1202. Ginneken, J. K. van, and A. S. Muller (eds.) *Maternal and child health in rural Kenya.* London, Croom Helm, 1984.

1203. K'Okul, Richard N. O. *Maternal and child health in Kenya: a study of poverty, disease and malnutrition in Samia.* Uppsala, Scandinavian Institute of African Studies, 1992.

1204. Kayongo-Male, Diane, and P. Walji. *Children at work in Kenya.* Nairobi, Oxford University Press, 1984.

Kenya — Christianity

1205. Barrett, D. B., et al. (eds.) *Kenya churches handbook: the development of Kenyan Christianity, 1498–1973.* Kisumu, Evangelical Publishing House, 1973.

1206. Bergmann, Jürgen. *Christentum und sozioökonomische Entwicklung: eine empirische Untersuchung im ruralen Kenia.* Aachen, Alano-Verlag, 1992.

1207. Burgman, H. *The way the Catholic Church started in western Kenya.* London, Mission Book Service, 1990.

1208. Chepkwony, Agnes. *The role of non-governmental organizations in development: a study of the National Christian Council of Kenya (NCCK), 1963–1978.* Uppsala, University of Uppsala, 1987.

1209. Gakobo, J. K. *History of Christianity in Kenya, 1844–1977: a select bibliography.* Nairobi, Kenyatta University College Library, 1979.

1210. Kariuki, Obadiah. *A bishop facing Mount Kenya: an autobiography, 1902–1978*. Nairobi, Uzima Press, 1985.

1211. Mbiti, John S. *New Testament eschatology in an African background*. London, Oxford University Press, 1971.

1212. Mbotela, James Juma. *Recollections of James Juma Mbotela*. Nairobi, East African Publishing House, 1977.

1213. Neckebrouck, Valeer. *Le onzième commandement: étiologie d'une église indépendante au pied du mont Kenya*. Immensee, Neue Zeitschrift für Missionswissenschaft, 1978.

1214. Wanyoike, E. N. *An African pastor*. Nairobi, East African Publishing House, 1974.

1215. Welbourn, F. B., and Bethwell A. Ogot. *A place to feel at home: a study of two independent churches in western Kenya*. London, Oxford University Press, 1966.

Kenya—Climate

1216. Berger, Peter. *Rainfall and agroclimatology of the Laikipia Plateau, Kenya*. Bern, Arbeitsgemeinschaft Geographica Bernensia, 1989.

1217. Ominde, Simeon H., and Calestous Juma (eds.) *A change in the weather: African perspectives on climatic change*. Revised edition. Nairobi, Acts Press, 1991.

Kenya—Colonial History

1218. Ambler, C. H. *Kenyan communities in the age of imperialism: the central region in the late nineteenth century*. New Haven, Yale University Press, 1988.

1219. Atieno Odhiambo, E. S. *The paradox of collaboration and other essays*. Nairobi, East African Literature Bureau, 1974.

1220. Bennett, George. *Kenya: a political history, the colonial period*. London, Oxford University Press, 1963.

1221. Berman, Bruce. *Control and crisis in colonial Kenya: the dialectic of domination*. London, James Currey, 1990.

1222. Berman, Bruce, and John Lonsdale. *Unhappy valley: clan, class and state in colonial Kenya*. London, James Currey, 1992.

1223. Blundell, Michael. *So rough a wind*. London, Weidenfeld and Nicolson, 1964.

1224. Bogonko, Sorobea Nyachieo. *Kenya 1945–1963: a study in African national movements*. Nairobi, Kenya Literature Bureau, 1980.

1225. Butter, John. *Uncivil servant*. Edinburgh, Pentland Press, 1989.

1226. Clough, M. S. *Fighting two sides: Kenyan chiefs and politicians, 1918–1940*. Niwot, University Press of Colorado, 1990.

1227. Dilley, M. R. *British policy in Kenya*. New York, Barnes and Noble, 1966.

1228. Douglas-Home, Charles. *Evelyn Baring: the last pro-consul*. London, Collins, 1978.

1229. Frost, Richard. *Enigmatic proconsul: Sir Philip Mitchell and the twilight of empire*. London, Radcliffe Press, 1992.

1230. Hansen, Eric. *The curse*. Tedburn St Mary, Hansen-Page, 1990.

1231. Kaggia, Bildad M. *Roots of freedom: the autobiography of Bildad Kaggia*. Nairobi, East African Publishing House, 1975.

1232. Kamoche, Jidlaph G. *Imperial trusteeship and political evolution in Kenya, 1923–1963: a study of the official views and the road to decolonization*. Washington, University Press of America, 1981.

1233. Kenyatta, Jomo. *Suffering without bitterness: the founding of the Kenya nation*. Nairobi, East African Publishing House, 1968.

1234. Kipkorir, Ben E. (ed.) *Biographical essays on imperialism and collaboration in colonial Kenya*. Nairobi, Kenya Literature Bureau, 1980.

1235. Maciel, M. *Bwana Karani*. Braunton, Merlin, 1985.

1236. Maxon, Robert M. *John Ainsworth and the making of Kenya*. Lanham, University Press of America, 1980.

1237. Maxon, Robert M. *Struggle for Kenya: the loss and reassertion of imperial initiative, 1912–1923*. Rutherford, Fairleigh Dickinson University Press, 1993.

1238. Mungeam, G. H. *British rule in Kenya, 1895–1912: the establishment of administration in the East African Protectorate*. Oxford, Clarendon Press, 1966.

1239. Mungeam, G. H. (comp.) *Kenya: select historical documents, 1884–1923*. Nairobi, East African Publishing House, 1978.

1240. Myrick, Bismark, et al. *Three aspects of crisis in colonial Kenya*. Syracuse, Syracuse University, Maxwell School of Citizenship and Public Affairs, 1975.

1241. Nazareth, John Maximian. *Brown man, black country: a peep into Kenya's freedom struggle*. New Delhi, Tidings, 1981.

1242. Ogot, Bethwell A. (ed.) *Politics and nationalism in colonial Kenya*. Nairobi, East African Publishing House, 1972.

1243. Perham, Margery. *East African journey: Kenya and Tanganyika, 1929–30*. London, Faber and Faber, 1976.

1244. Spencer, J. *James Beauttah: freedom fighter*. Nairobi, Stellascope, 1983.

1245. Thuku, Harry. *An autobiography*. Nairobi, Oxford University Press, 1970.

1246. Tignor, R. L. *The colonial transformation of Kenya: the Kamba, Kikuyu and Maasai from 1900–1939*. Princeton, Princeton University Press, 1976.

1247. Trench, Charles Pocklington Chenevix. *Men who ruled Kenya: the Kenya administration, 1892–1963*. London, Radcliffe Press, 1993.

1248. Wachanga, H. K. *The swords of Kirinyaga: the fight for land and freedom*. Nairobi, East African Literature Bureau, 1975.

1249. Watkins, Elizabeth. *Wouse: the life of Leslie Whitehouse*. Calais, Mulberry Books, 1993.

1250. Wolff, Richard D. *The economics of colonialism: Britain and Kenya, 1870–1930*. New Haven, Yale University Press, 1964.

Kenya—Communications

1251. Alot, Magaga. *People and communication in Kenya*. Nairobi, Kenya Literature Bureau, 1982.

1252. Mwaura, Peter. *Communications policies in Kenya*. Paris, UNESCO, 1980.

Kenya—Constitution

1253. Ojwang, J. B. *Constitutional development in Kenya: institutional adaptation and social change*. Nairobi, Acts Press, 1990.

Kenya—Cooperatives

1254. Bager, Torben. *Marketing cooperatives and peasants in Kenya*. Uppsala, Scandinavian Institute of African Studies, 1980.

1255. Gyllström, Björn. *State-administered rural change: agricultural cooperatives in Kenya*. London, Routledge, 1991.

1256. Hedlund, Hans. *Coffee, cooperatives and culture: an anthropological study of a coffee cooperative in Kenya*. Nairobi, Oxford University Press, 1992.

1257. Holmquist, Frank W. *Peasant organization, clientelism and dependency: a case study of an agricultural producers' cooperative in Kenya*. Bloomington, Indiana University Press, 1975.

1258. Maini, K. M. *Cooperatives and law, with emphasis on Kenya*. Nairobi, East African Literature Bureau, 1972.

1259. Ouma, Sylvester J. *Development in Kenya through cooperatives*. Nairobi, Shirikon, 1987.

1260. Ouma, Sylvester J. *A history of the cooperative movement in Kenya*. Nairobi, Bookwise, 1980.

1261. Ouma, Sylvester J. *The transformation of the informal sector: the cooperative perspective*. Nairobi, Shirikon, 1990.

1262. Ouma, Sylvester J. *21 essays on cooperation and development in Kenya*. Nairobi, Shirikon, 1990.

Kenya—Corporations

1263. Kaplinsky, Raphael (ed.) *Readings on the multinational corporation in Kenya.* Nairobi, Oxford University Press, 1978.

1264. Langdon, Steven W. *Multinational corporations in the political economy of Kenya.* London, Macmillan, 1981.

Kenya—Cotton

1265. Dijkstra, T. *Marketing policies and economic interests in the cotton sector of Kenya.* Leiden, African Studies Centre, 1990.

Kenya—Credit Unions

1266. Dublin, Jack, and Selma M. Dublin. *Credit unions in a changing world: the Tanzania-Kenya experience.* Detroit, Wayne State University Press, 1983.

Kenya—Criminology

1267. Gavron, Jeremy. *Darkness in Eden: the murder of Julie Ward.* London, Harper Collins, 1991.

1268. Kercher, Leonard C. *The Kenya penal system, past, present and prospect.* Washington, University Press of America, 1981.

1269. Muga, Erasto. *Crime and delinquency in Kenya.* Nairobi, East African Literature Bureau, 1975.

1270. Muga, Erasto. *Crime in a Kenyan town: a case study of Kisumu.* Kampala, East African Literature Bureau, 1977.

1271. Muga, Erasto. *Robbery with violence.* Nairobi, Kenya Literature Bureau, 1980.

Kenya—Cultural Policy

1272. Ndeti, Kivuto. *Cultural policy in Kenya.* Paris, UNESCO, 1975.

Kenya—Dairy Farming

1273. Blick, Paddy. *Dairy farming in Kenya.* Nairobi, Heinemann Kenya, 1986.

1274. Launonen, Riitta, et al. *Rural dairy development in Meru: a socio-economic study of smallholder milk production, consumption and marketing.* Helsinki, University of Helsinki, Institute of Development Studies, 1985.

1275. Leegwater, P., et al. *Dairy development and nutrition in Kilifi District, Kenya.* Leiden, African Studies Centre, 1991.

Kenya—Description and Travel

1276. Adamson, Joy. *Peoples of Kenya.* New York, Harcourt, Brace and World, 1967.

1277. Amin, Mohamed. *Cradle of mankind*. London, Chatto & Windus, 1981.

1278. Amin, Mohamed. *Journey through Kenya*. London, Bodley Head, 1982.

1279. Amin, Mohamed, et al. *Kenya, the magic land*. London, Bodley Head, 1988.

1280. Barbier, B. *Le Kenya*. Paris, Jeune Afrique, 1981.

1281. Berghe, Myriam vanden. *Le Kenya*. Paris, L'Harmattan, 1991.

1282. Cubitt, G., and E. Robins. *The book of Kenya*. London, Collins and Harvill, 1980.

1283. Fedders, Andrew, and Cynthia Salvadori. *Peoples and cultures of Kenya*. Nairobi, Transafrica, 1979.

1284. Hecklau, Hans. *Kenia*. München, Oscar Beck, 1993.

1285. Hillaby, John. *Journey to the jade sea*. St. Albans, Paladin, 1973.

1286. Maren, Michael. *The land and people of Kenya*. New York, Lippincott, 1989.

1287. Mollison, Simon. *Kenya's coast*. Nairobi, East African Publishing House, 1971.

1288. Naipaul, Shiva. *North of South: an African journey*. London, Deutsch, 1978.

1289. Pavitt, Nigel. *Kenya: the first explorers*. London, Aurum, 1989.

1290. Reece, Alys. *To my wife, fifty camels*. London, Harvill Press, 1963.

1291. Ruben, Hilary. *African harvest*. London, Harvill Press, 1972.

1292. Waugh, Daisy. *A small town in Africa*. London, Heinemann, 1994.

Kenya—Documentation

1293. Gregory, Robert G., and Richard E. Lewis. *A guide to secretariat circulars: Kenya National Archives microfilm*. Syracuse, Syracuse University, Maxwell School of Citizenship and Public Affairs, 1984.

1294. Gregory, Robert G. *A guide to the Kenya National Archives: to the microfilms of the provincial and district annual reports, record books, and handing-over reports; miscellaneous correspondence and intelligence reports*. Syracuse, Syracuse University, Program of Eastern African Studies, 1968.

1295. Howell, John Bruce. *Kenya: subject guide to official publications*. Washington, U.S. Government Printing Office, 1978.

1296. Kenya National Archives. *A guide to government monographs, reports and research works*. Nairobi, Kenya National Archives, 1984.

1297. Morton, Rodger F., and Harvey Soff. *Microfilms relating to eastern Africa. Pt 1: Kenya, miscellaneous. A guide to recent acquisitions of Syra-*

cuse University. Syracuse, Syracuse University, Maxwell School of Citizenship and Public Affairs, Program of Eastern African Studies, 1971.

1298. Robins, Kate. *Subject guide to information sources in Kenya.* Nairobi, Kenya Library Association and National Council for Science and Technology, 1984.

1299. Walker, Audrey. *Official publications of British East Africa. Part 3: Kenya and Zanzibar.* Washington, Library of Congress, 1962.

Kenya—Drought

1300. Downing, T. E., et al. (eds.) *Coping with drought in Kenya: national and local strategies.* Boulder, Lynne Rienner, 1989.

Kenya—Economy

1301. Barve, A. G. *The foreign trade of Kenya: a perspective.* Nairobi, Transafrica, 1984.

1302. Bigsten, Arne. *Regional inequality and development: a case study of Kenya.* Farnborough, Gower, 1980.

1303. Burrows, J. (ed.) *Kenya, into the second decade: report of a mission sent by the World Bank.* Baltimore, Johns Hopkins University Press, 1975.

1304. Child, Frank C., and Mary E. Kempe (eds.) *Small-scale enterprise: proceedings of a conference organized by the Institute for Development Studies, University of Nairobi, and held at Masai Lodge, Nairobi, 26 and 27 February, 1973.* Nairobi, University of Nairobi, Institute for Development Studies, 1973.

1305. Desai, P. M. (ed.) *Economic and political development of Kenya.* Bombay, Himalaya Publishing House, 1979.

1306. Edinburgh University. *Developmental trends in Kenya: proceedings of a seminar held in the Centre of African Studies, April, 1972.* Edinburgh, University of Edinburgh, Centre of African Studies, 1972.

1307. Fearn, Hugh. *An African economy: a study of the economic development of the Nyanza Province of Kenya, 1903–1953.* London, Oxford University Press, 1961.

1308. Gichira, R. N. *Commerce for Kenya.* Nairobi, Macmillan Kenya, 1982.

1309. Godfrey, M. *Kenya to 1990: prospects for growth.* London, Economist Intelligence Unit, 1986.

1310. Hazlewood, Arthur. *The economy of Kenya: the Kenyatta era.* London, Oxford University Press, 1979.

1311. Himbara, David. *Kenyan capitalists, the state and development.* Boulder, Lynne Rienner, 1994.

1312. International Monetary Fund. *The case of Kenya.* Washington, International Monetary Fund, 1981.

1313. Jansen, K. *State, policy and the economy, with case studies from Kenya and Sri Lanka.* The Hague, Institute of Social Studies, 1982.

1314. Killick, Tony, and F. M. Mwega. *Monetary policy in Kenya, 1967–1988.* London, Overseas Development Institute, 1990.

1315. Killick, Tony. *The IMF and economic management in Kenya.* London, Overseas Development Institute, 1981.

1316. Killick, Tony (ed.) *Papers on the Kenyan economy: performance, problems, policies.* London, Heinemann, 1981.

1317. King, J. R. *Stabilization policy in an African setting: Kenya, 1963–1973.* London, Heinemann, 1979.

1318. Leys, Colin. *Underdevelopment in Kenya: the political economy of neocolonialism, 1964–1971.* London, Heinemann, 1975.

1319. Marris, Peter, and Anthony Somerset. *African businessmen: a study of entrepreneurship and development in Kenya.* London, Routledge & Kegan Paul, 1971.

1320. Mutalik-Desai, Priya (ed.) *Economic and political development of Kenya.* Bombay, Himalaya Publishing, 1979.

1321. Ndegwa, Philip. *Africa's development crisis and related international issues.* Nairobi, Heinemann, 1985.

1322. Nyangira, N. *Relative modernization and public resource allocation in Kenya: a comparative analysis.* Nairobi, East African Literature Bureau, 1975.

1323. Oser, Jacob. *Promoting economic development, with illustrations from Kenya.* Evanston, Northwestern University Press, 1967.

1324. Roe, Alan R., and Shyamalendu Pal. *Adjustment to oil shock in Kenya, 1972–1982.* Coventry, University of Warwick, Department of Economics, Development Economics Research Centre, 1986.

1325. Rwegasira, Kami S. P., and Louis A. Kanneworff (eds.) *Inflation in Kenya: causes, effects and control.* Dar es Salaam, Institute of Finance Management, 1980.

1326. Scott, Maurice FitzGerald, et al. *Project appraisal in practice: the Little-Mirrlees method applied in Kenya.* London, Heinemann, 1976.

1327. Slater, C. C., et al. (eds.) *KENSIM: a systems simulation of the developing Kenyan economy, 1970–1978.* Boulder, Westview Press, 1977.

1328. Swainson, Nicola. *The development of corporate capitalism in Kenya, 1918–1977.* London, Heinemann, 1980.

1329. Tostensen, A., and J. G. Scott (eds.) *Kenya: country study and Norwegian aid review.* Fantoft, Chr. Michelsen Institute, Department of Social Science and Development, Development Research and Action Programme, 1987.

1330. World Bank. *Kenya: growth and structural change.* Washington, World Bank, 1983.

1331. World Bank. *Kenya: reinvesting in stabilization and growth through public sector adjustment.* Washington, World Bank, 1992.

Kenya—Education

1332. Abreu, S. *The role of self-help in the development of education in Kenya, 1900–1973.* Nairobi, Kenya Literature Bureau, 1982.

1333. Achola, Paul P. P. W., et al. (eds.) *Trends and the future of university education in Kenya: proceedings of the 6th PWPA Conference . . . 1989.* Nairobi, Professors World Peace Academy of Kenya, 1990.

1334. Anderson, John E. *Organization and financing of self-help education in Kenya.* Paris, UNESCO International Institute for Educational Planning, 1973.

1335. Anderson, John E. *The struggle for the school: the interaction of missionary, colonial government and nationalist enterprise in the development of formal education in Kenya.* London, Longmans, 1970.

1336. Bogonko, Sorobea Nyachieo. *A history of modern education in Kenya, 1895–1991.* Nairobi, Evans Brothers, 1992.

1337. Brownstein, Lewis. *Education and development in rural Kenya: a study in primary school graduates.* New York, Praeger, 1972.

1338. Court, D., and Dharam P. Ghai (eds.) *Education, society and development: new perspectives from Kenya.* Nairobi, Oxford University Press, 1974.

1339. Cowan, Laing Gray. *The cost of learning: the politics of primary education in Kenya.* New York, Teachers College Press, 1970.

1340. Cumming, C., et al. *Practical subjects in Kenyan academic secondary schools: background papers.* Stockholm, Swedish International Development Authority, 1985.

1341. Dave, R. H., et al. (eds.) *Learning strategies for post-literacy and continuing education in Kenya, Nigeria, Tanzania and United Kingdom.* Hamburg, UNESCO Institute for Education, 1985.

1342. Eisemon, Thomas O. *Benefiting from basic education: school quality and functional literacy in Kenya.* Oxford, Pergamon Press, 1988.

1343. Eshiwani, George S. *Education in Kenya since independence.* Nairobi, East African Educational Publishers, 1993.

1344. Greaves, L. B. *Carey Francis of Kenya.* London, Rex Collings, 1969.

1345. Harik, Elsa M., and Donald G. Schilling. *The politics of education in colonial Algeria and Kenya.* Athens, Ohio University, Center for International Studies, 1984.

1346. Indire, Filemona F., and John W. Hanson. *Secondary level teachers: supply and demand in Kenya.* East Lansing, Michigan State University, African Studies Center and Institute for International Studies in Education, 1971.

1347. King, Kenneth. *The African artisan: education and the informal sector in Kenya.* London, Heinemann, 1977.

1348. Krauter, Armin. *Abhängige Entwicklung und Veränderungen im Bildungswesen: das nonformale Bildungswesen in Kenya.* München, Minerva, 1981.

1349. Lauglo, J. *Practical subjects in Kenyan academic secondary schools: general report.* Stockholm, Swedish International Development Authority, 1985.

1350. Linne, O. *An evolution of the Kenya Science Teachers College, 1970–71.* Uppsala, Scandinavian Institute of African Studies, 1973.

1351. Martin, R. *Anthem of bugles: the story of Starehe Boys Centre and School.* Nairobi, Heinemann, 1978.

1352. Meck, Margarete. *Problems and prospects of social services in Kenya: a study with special reference to education and health in the light of regional needs and demographic trends.* Munich, Weltforum-Verlag, 1971.

1353. Mutava, Dominic Musyoka. *Motivational factors toward enrollment in literacy training classes in Machakos, Kenya.* Tübingen, Eberhard-Karls-Universität, 1980.

1354. Mutua, R. W. *Development of education in Kenya.* Nairobi, East African Literature Bureau, 1975.

1355. Narman, A. *Practical subjects in Kenyan academic secondary schools: tracer study.* Stockholm, Swedish International Development Authority, 1985.

1356. Odondo, Harrison H. *Manpower and educational planning in Kenya: the possibilities and limitations of the application of an integrated planning model.* Regensburg, Roderer und Welz, 1993.

1357. Olembo, J. O. *Financing primary school buildings in Kenya.* Nairobi, Transafrica, 1985.

1358. Otiende, J. E., et al. *Education and development in Kenya: a historical perspective.* Nairobi, Oxford University Press, 1991.

1359. Sheffield, James R. *Education in Kenya: an historical study.* New York, Teachers College Press, 1973.

1360. Sheffield, James R. (ed.) *Education, employment and rural development: the proceedings of a conference held at Kericho, Kenya, in September, 1966.* Nairobi, East African Publishing House, 1967.

1361. Sheffield, James R., et al. *Agriculture in African secondary schools: case studies of Botswana, Kenya and Tanzania.* New York, African-American Institute, 1976.

1362. Sifuna, D. N. *Development of education in Africa: the Kenyan experience.* Nairobi, Initiatives, 1990.

1363. Sifuna, D. N. *Short essays on education in Kenya.* Nairobi, Kenya Literature Bureau, 1980.

1364. Sifuna, D. N. *Vocational education in schools: a historical survey of Kenya and Tanzania.* Nairobi, East African Literature Bureau, 1976.

1365. Smith, J. S. *The history of the Alliance High School.* Nairobi, Heinemann, 1973.

1366. Stabler, Ernest. *Education since Uhuru: the schools of Kenya.* Middletown, Wesleyan University Press, 1969.

1367. Sturmann, Uwe. *Bildung, Berufsbildung . . . und was dann? Angepasste Handwerkerausbildung für den ländlichen Raum—die Youth Polytechnics in Kenia.* Saarbrücken, Breitenbach, 1990.

1368. Tanno, Y. *Education in Kenya: a bibliographical approach.* Tokyo, Institute of Developing Economies, 1990.

1369. Thias, Hans Heinrich, and Martin Carnoy. *Cost-benefit analysis in education: a case study of Kenya.* Washington, World Bank, 1972.

1370. Were, P. *The Kenyan we want: an approach to social education and ethics.* Nairobi, Heinemann Kenya, 1987.

Kenya—Elections

1371. Amidu, Assibi A. *Kimwondo: a Kiswahili electoral contest.* Vienna, Afro-Pub, 1990.

1372. Amin, Mohamed, and Peter Moll. *One man, one vote: a photo-record of Kenya's 1974 general elections.* Nairobi, East African Publishing House, 1975.

1373. Andreassen, Berd-Anders, et al. *A hobbled democracy: the Kenya general elections, 1992.* Bergen, Chr. Michelsen Institute, Department of Social Science and Development, 1993.

1374. Bennett, George, and Carl G. Rosberg. *The Kenyatta election: Kenya, 1960–61.* London, Oxford University Press, 1961.

1375. National Election Monitoring Unit. *The multi-party general elections in Kenya, 29 December, 1992: the report of the National Election Monitoring Unit.* Nairobi, NEMU, 1993.

Kenya—Employment

1376. Cheru, Fantu. *Dependence, underdevelopment and unemployment in Kenya: school leavers in a peripheral capitalist political economy.* Lanham, University Press of America, 1987.

1377. Child, Frank C. *Employment, technology and growth: the role of the intermediate sector in Kenya.* Nairobi, University of Nairobi, Institute for Development Studies, 1976.

1378. Ghai, Dharam P., and Martin Godfrey (eds.) *Essays on employment in Kenya.* Nairobi, Kenya Literature Bureau, 1979.

1379. Hunt, Diana. *Employment, peripheral activities and development.* Manchester, University of Manchester, Department of Administrative Studies, 1983.

1380. International Labour Office. *Employment, incomes and equality: a strategy for increasing productive employment in Kenya.* Geneva, International Labour Office, 1972.

1381. Kaplinsky, Raphael. *Employment effects of multinational enterprises: a case study of Kenya.* Geneva, International Labour Office, 1979.

1382. McFarquhar, A. M. M., and G. B. A. Evans. *Employment creation in primary production in less developed countries: case studies of employment potential in the coffee sectors of Brazil and Kenya.* Paris, OECD, Development Centre, 1972.

1383. Rempel, Henry, and W. J. House. *The Kenya employment problem: an analysis of the modern sector labour market.* Nairobi, Oxford University Press, 1978.

Kenya—Energy

1384. Barnes, Carolyn, et al. (eds.) *Wood, energy and households: perspectives on rural Kenya.* Uppsala, Scandinavian Institute of African Studies, 1984.

1385. Hosier, Richard H. *Energy use in rural Kenya: household demand and rural transformation.* Uppsala, Scandinavian Institute of African Studies, 1985.

1386. Mayer, Herwig. *Ein Energiemasterplan für Kenia bis zur Jahrtausendwende.* Regensburg, Transfer Regensburg, 1989.

1387. O'Keefe, Phil, et al. (eds.) *Energy and development in Kenya: opportunities and constraints.* Uppsala, Scandinavian Institute of African Studies, 1984.

1388. Vainio-Mattila, Arja. *Bura Fuelwood Project: domestic fuel economy.* Helsinki, University of Helsinki, Institute of Development Studies, 1987.

Kenya—Environment

1389. Bartelmus, Peter. *Economic development and the human environment: a study of impacts and repercussions with particular reference to Kenya.* Munich, Weltforum-Verlag, 1980.

1390. Gichuki, F. N. (ed.) *Environmental change and dryland management in Machakos District, Kenya, 1930–1990: conservation profile.* London, Overseas Development Institute, 1991.

1391. Groot, Peter de, et al. *Taking root: revegetation in semi-arid Kenya.* Nairobi, Acts Press, 1992.

1392. Haller, René, and Sabine Baer. *Von der Steinwüste zum Paradies: die faszinierende Geschichte eines einzartig erfolgreichen Experiments in Kenia.* München, Koschany, 1992.

1393. Khasiani, Shanyisa Anota (ed.) *Groundwork: African women as environmental managers.* Nairobi, Acts Press, 1992.

1394. Kilewe, A. M., and D. B. Thomas. *Land degradation in Kenya: a framework for policy and planning.* London, Commonwealth Secretariat, 1992.

1395. Mortimore, M. (ed.) *Environmental change and dryland management in Machakos District, Kenya: a profile of technological change.* London, Overseas Development Institute, 1991.

1396. Östberg, Wilhelm. *Ramblings on soil conservation: an essay from Kenya.* Stockholm, Swedish International Development Authority, 1987.

1397. Schmidt, Robert. *Ecology of a tropical lowland rain forest: plant communities, soil characteristics and nutrient relations of the forests in the Shimba Hills National Reserve, Kenya.* Stuttgart, Borntraeger, 1991.

1398. Schuhmann, Ralph. *Umweltschutz durch Strafrecht in Schwarzafrika: eine vergleichende Untersuchung anhand eine Fallstudie für Kenia.* Freiburg, Max-Planck-Institut für Ausländisches und Internationales Strafrecht, 1991.

1399. Tiffen, Mary. *Environmental change and dryland management in Machakos District, Kenya, 1930–1990: farming and income systems.* London, Overseas Development Institute, 1992.

1400. Tiffen, Mary. *Environmental change and dryland management in Machakos District, Kenya, 1930–1990: population profile.* London, Overseas Development Institute, 1991.

1401. Tiffen, Mary (ed.) *Environmental change and dryland management in Machakos District, Kenya: production profile.* London, Overseas Development Institute, 1991.

1402. Tiffen, Mary, et al. *More people, less erosion: environmental recovery in Kenya.* Chichester, Wiley, 1994.

Kenya—Ethnography

1403. Kyewalyanga, Francis-Xavier S. *Marriage customs in East Africa, with special reference to selected tribes of Kenya: Akamba, Bantu Kavirondo, Gusii, Kipsigis, Luo, Nandi, and Teita.* Hohenschäftlarn, Karl Renner, 1977.

1404. Middleton, John, and G. Kershaw. *The central tribes of the north-eastern Bantu.* Revised edition. London, International African Institute, 1965.

1405. Nagashima, Nobuhiro (ed.) *Themes in socio-cultural ideas and behaviour among the six ethnic groups of Kenya: the Visukha, the Iteso, the Gusii, the Kipsigis, the Luo and the Kamba.* Kunitachi, Hitotsubashi University, 1981.

1406. Schlee, Günther. *Identities on the move: clanship and pastoralism in northern Kenya.* Manchester, Manchester University Press, 1989.

Kenya—Exports

1407. Schluter, Michael. *Constraints on Kenya's food and beverage exports.* Washington, International Food Policy Research Institute, 1984.

Kenya—Family Planning

1408. Molnos, Angela. *Attitudes towards family planning in East Africa: an investigation in schools around Lake Victoria and in Nairobi.* Munich, Weltforum-Verlag, 1968.

Kenya—Fertility

1409. Ocholla-Ayayo, A. B. C. *The spirit of a nation: an analysis of policy, ethics and customary rules of conduct for regulating fertility levels in Kenya.* Nairobi, Shirikon, 1991.

Kenya—Finance

1410. Effros, Robert C. (ed.) *Emerging financial centers, legal and institutional framework: Bahamas, Hong Kong, Ivory Coast, Kenya, Kuwait, Panama, Singapore.* Washington, International Monetary Fund, 1982.

1411. Grosh, Barbara. *Performance of financial parastatals in Kenya, 1964–1984.* Nairobi, University of Nairobi, Institute for Development Studies, 1987.

1412. Makanda, D. W., et al. (eds.) *Kenya's industrial and financial policies.* Nairobi, Kenyan Economic Association, 1986.

Kenya—Flora

1413. Agnew, A. D. Q. *Upland Kenya wild flowers.* London, Oxford University Press, 1974.

1414. Blundell, Michael. *The wild flowers of Kenya.* London, Collins, 1982.

Kenya—Folk Music

1415. Senoga-Zake, George W. *Folk music of Kenya.* Nairobi, Uzima, 1986.

Kenya—Food and Nutrition

1416. Greer, J., and E. Thorbecke. *Food, poverty and consumption patterns in Kenya.* Geneva, International Labour Office, 1986.

1417. Hoorweg, Jan, and R. Niemeijer. *Intervention in child nutrition: evaluation studies in Kenya.* London, Kegan Paul International, 1989.

1418. Kennedy, Eileen T., and Bruce Cogill. *Income and nutritional effects of the commercialization of agriculture in southwestern Kenya*. Washington, International Food Policy Research Institute, 1987.

1419. Kennedy, Eileen T. *The effects of sugarcane production on food security, health, and nutrition in Kenya: a longitudinal analysis*. Washington, International Food Policy Research Institute, 1989.

1420. Peters, Caroline, and Rudo Niemeijer. *Protein-energy malnutrition and the home environment: a study among children in Coast Province, Kenya*. Nairobi, Food and Nutrition Planning Unit, 1987.

Kenya—Foreign Aid

1421. Holtham, Gerald, and Arthur Hazlewood. *Aid and inequality in Kenya: British development assistance to Kenya*. London, Croom Helm, 1976.

1422. Tomasevski, Katarina. *Foreign aid and human rights: case studies of Bangladesh and Kenya*. Copenhagen, Danish Center of Human Rights, 1988.

1423. Walter, Franz. *Aufrecht gehen*. Berschis, Alternativverlag Kaschmi, 1988.

Kenya—Foreign Relations

1424. Adar, K. *Kenyan foreign policy behavior towards Somalia, 1963–83*. Lanham, University Press of America, 1993.

1425. Attwood, W. *The reds and the blacks*. London, Hutchinson, 1967.

1426. Godfrey, P. *United States of America's foreign policy towards Kenya, 1952–1969*. Nairobi, Gideon S. Were Press, 1992.

Kenya—Genetic Resources

1427. Juma, Calestous. *Biological diversity and innovation: conserving and utilizing genetic resources in Kenya*. Nairobi, Acts Press, 1989.

Kenya—Geography

1428. Diesfeld, H. J., and H. K. Hecklau. *Kenya: a geomedical monograph*. Berlin, Springer-Verlag, 1978.

1429. Henkel, Reinhard. *Central places in western Kenya*. Heidelberg, Universität Heidelberg, Geographisches Institut, 1979.

1430. Mwagiru, W. *A modern geography of Kenya*. Nairobi, MWASSCO Publications, 1986.

1431. Obudho, Robert A., and D. R. F. Taylor (eds.) *The spatial structure of development: a study of Kenya*. Boulder, Westview Press, 1979.

1432. Ogendo, Reuben Benjamin. *Industrial geography of Kenya, with special emphasis on the agricultural processing and fabricating industries*. Nairobi, East African Publishing House, 1972.

1433. Ojany, Francis F., and Reuben B. Ogendo. *Kenya: a study in physical and human geography*. Nairobi, Longmans, 1973.

1434. Soja, Edward W. *The geography of modernization in Kenya: a spatial analysis of social, economic and political change*. Syracuse, Syracuse University Press, 1968.

1435. Vorlaufer, Karl. *Kenya*. Stuttgart, Klett-Cotta, 1990.

Kenya — Handbook

1436. Nelson, Harold D. (ed.) *Kenya: a country study*. Third edition. Washington, American University, 1983.

Kenya — Health and Medicine

1437. Beck, Ann. *Medicine, tradition, and development in Kenya and Tanzania, 1920–1970*. Waltham, Crossroads Press, 1981.

1438. Brainard, Jean M. *Health and development in a rural Kenyan community*. New York, Peter Lang, 1991.

1439. Carman, John Ambrose. *A medical history of the colony and protectorate of Kenya: a personal memoir*. London, Collings, 1976.

1440. Good, Charles M. *Ethnomedical systems in Africa: patterns of traditional medicine in rural and urban Kenya*. New York, Guilford Press, 1987.

1441. Howell, John Bruce. *Rural health in Kenya: a guide to the literature*. Iowa City, University of Iowa Libraries, 1989.

1442. Meck, Margarete. *Problems and prospects of social services in Kenya: a study with special reference to education and health in the light of regional needs and demographic trends*. Munich, Weltforum-Verlag, 1971.

1443. Ndirangu, S. *A history of nursing in Kenya*. Nairobi, Kenya Literature Bureau, 1982.

1444. Raikes, Alanagh. *Pregnancy, birthing and family planning in Kenya: changing patterns of behaviour. A health service utilization study in Kisii District*. Copenhagen, Centre for Development Research, 1990.

1445. Silberschmidt, Margrethe. *Women's position in the household and their use of family planning and antenatal services: a case study from Kisii District, Kenya*. Copenhagen, Centre for Development Research, 1991.

1446. Vogel, L. C., et al. *Health and disease in Kenya*. Oxford, Clarendon Press, 1974.

Kenya — History

1447. Abuor, C. Ojwando. *White Highlands no more*. Nairobi, Pan African Researchers, 1970.

1448. Atieno Odhiambo, E. S., and Peter Wanyande. *History and government of Kenya*. Nairobi, Longmans, 1988.

1449. Bailey, Jim. *Kenya, the national epic: from the pages of Drum.* Nairobi, Kenway, 1993.

1450. Boxer, Charles Ralph, and Carlos de Azevedo. *Fort Jesus and the Portuguese in Mombasa, 1593–1729.* London, Hollis and Carter, 1960.

1451. Freeman-Grenville, G. S. P. (ed.) *The Mombasa rising against the Portuguese, 1631.* London, Oxford University Press for the British Academy, 1980.

1452. Gatheru, Mugo. *Child of two worlds.* London, Routledge & Kegan Paul, 1964.

1453. Huxley, Elspeth (ed.) *Nine faces of Kenya.* London, Collins Harvill, 1990.

1454. King, Kenneth, and Ahmed Salim (eds.) *Kenya historical biographies.* Nairobi, East African Publishing House, 1971.

1455. Kipkorir, Ben E., et al. (eds.) *Kerio Valley: past, present and future.* Nairobi, Eleza Services, 1983.

1456. Kitching, Gavin N. *Class and economic change in Kenya: the making of an African petite bourgeoisie, 1905–1970.* New Haven, Yale University Press, 1980.

1457. Macgoye, M. O. *The story of Kenya: the making of a modern nation.* Nairobi, Oxford University Press, 1986.

1458. Malhotra, Veena. *Kenya under Kenyatta.* Delhi, Kalinga Publications, 1990.

1459. Miller, N. N., and Rodger Yeager. *Kenya: the quest for prosperity.* Second edition. Boulder, Westview Press, 1994.

1460. Mwangi wa Githumo. *Land and nationalism: the impact of land expropriation and land grievances upon the rise and development of nationalist movements in Kenya, 1885–1939.* Washington, University Press of America, 1981.

1461. Ochieng', William Robert, and Robert M. Maxon. *An economic history of Kenya.* Nairobi, East African Educational Publishers, 1992.

1462. Ochieng', William Robert. *An outline history of the Rift Valley of Kenya up to AD 1900.* Nairobi, East African Literature Bureau, 1975.

1463. Ochieng', William Robert. *Eastern Kenya and its invaders.* Nairobi, East African Literature Bureau, 1975.

1464. Ochieng', William Robert. *The first word: essays on Kenya history.* Nairobi, East African Literature Bureau, 1975.

1465. Ochieng', William Robert. *The second word: more essays on Kenya history.* Nairobi, East African Literature Bureau, 1977.

1466. Ochieng', William Robert. *The third word: essays on Kenyan history and society.* Nairobi, Kenya Literature Bureau, 1984.

1467. Ochieng', William Robert (ed.) *A modern history of Kenya, 1895–1980: in honour of B. A. Ogot*. London, Evans Brothers, 1989.

1468. Ochieng', William Robert (ed.) *Themes in Kenyan history*. London, James Currey, 1991.

1469. Ogot, Bethwell A., and William Robert Ochieng' (eds.) *Decolonization and independence in Kenya, 1940–88*. London, James Currey, 1993.

1470. Ogot, Bethwell A. *Historical dictionary of Kenya*. Metuchen, Scarecrow Press, 1981.

1471. Ogot, Bethwell A. *Kenya before 1900*. Nairobi, East African Publishing House, 1976.

1472. Ogot, Bethwell A. (ed.) *Kenya in the 19th century*. Nairobi, Bookwise, 1985.

1473. Roelker, Jack R. *Mathu of Kenya: a political study*. Stanford, Hoover Institution Press, 1976.

1474. Sobania, Neil. *A background history to the Mount Kulal region of northern Kenya*. Nairobi, UNESCO, 1979.

1475. Spear, Thomas. *Kenya's past*. London, Longmans, 1981.

1476. Wandibba, Simiyu (ed.) *History and culture in western Kenya: the people of Bungoma District through time*. Nairobi, Gideon S. Were Press, 1985.

1477. Were, Gideon S. *Western Kenya, historical texts: Abaluyia, Teso and Elgon Kalenjin*. Nairobi, East African Literature Bureau, 1967.

1478. Zwanenberg, Roger M. van. *An economic history of Kenya and Uganda, 1800–1970*. London, Macmillan, 1975.

Kenya—Housing

1479. Guido, A. *Space standards for urban low cost housing in Kenya*. Nairobi, University of Nairobi, Housing Research and Development Unit, 1979.

1480. Muller, M. S. *Local authority housing in Kenya*. Nairobi, University of Nairobi, Housing Research and Development Unit, 1978.

1481. Sterkenberg, J. J., et al. *Rural housing conditions in Kisumu District, Kenya*. Nairobi, University of Nairobi, Housing Research Development Unit, 1982.

1482. Sterkenberg, J. J., et al. *Rural housing conditions in Aisii District, Kenya*. Nairobi, University of Nairobi, Housing Research Development Unit, 1981.

Kenya—Human Rights

1483. Africa Watch. *Kenya: taking liberties*. New York, Africa Watch, 1991.

1484. Amnesty International. *Kenya: torture, political detention and unfair trials*. London, Amnesty International, 1987.

Kenya—Human Settlements

1485. Boalt, Carin, et al. *Bibliography on human settlements with emphasis on households and residential environment: Kenya*. Nairobi, University of Nairobi, Housing Research and Development Unit, 1982.

Kenya—Income Distribution

1486. Ahmed, Osman Sheikh. *The potential effects of income redistribution on selected growth constraints: a case study of Kenya*. Washington, University Press of America, 1982.

1487. Bigsten, Arne. *Education and income distribution in Kenya*. Aldershot, Gower, 1984.

Kenya—Industry

1488. Coughlin, Peter, and Gerrishon K. Ikiara (eds.) *Industrialization in Kenya: in search of a strategy*. London, James Currey, 1989.

1489. Coughlin, Peter, and Gerrishon K. Ikiara (eds.) *Kenya's industrialization dilemma*. Nairobi, Heinemann, 1991.

1490. Hermann, Peter. *Der Beitrag der Industrie zur ländlichen Entwicklung in Kenia*. Saarbrücken, Breitenbach, 1988.

1491. Luttrell, William L. *Post-capitalist industrialization: planning economic independence in Kenya*. Westport, Greenwood Press, 1986.

1492. Makanda, D. W., et al. (eds.) *Kenya's industrial and financial policies*. Nairobi, Kenyan Economic Association, 1986.

1493. UNIDO. *Kenya: sustaining industrial growth through restructuring and integration*. Vienna, UNIDO, 1988.

Kenya—Informal Economy

1494. Aboagye, A. A. *Informal sector employment in Kenya: a survey of informal sector activities in Nairobi, Kisumu and Mombasa*. Addis Ababa, International Labour Organisation, Jobs and Skills Programme for Africa, 1986.

1495. King, Kenneth, and C. Abuodha. *The building of an industrial society: change and development in Kenya's informal (Jua Kali) sector, 1972–1991. A summary report*. Edinburgh, University of Edinburgh, Centre of African Studies, 1991.

1496. Ng'ethe, J., et al. *The rural informal sector in Kenya: a study of micro-enterprises in Nyeri, Meru, Uasin Gishu and Siaya districts*. Nairobi, University of Nairobi, Institute for Development Studies, 1989.

1497. Westley, Sidney B. (ed.) *The informal sector in Kenya.* Nairobi, University of Nairobi, Institute for Development Studies, 1977.

Kenya—Information Systems

1498. Hütteman, L. (ed.) *Coordination of information systems and services in Kenya.* Bonn, Deutsche Stiftung für Internationale Entwicklung, 1990.

Kenya—Investment

1499. Birgegard, L.-E. *The project selection process in developing countries: a study of the public investment project selection process in Kenya, Zambia and Tanzania.* Stockholm, Stockholm School of Economics, Economic Research Institute, 1975.

1500. Hilbert, Roger. *Ausländische Direktinvestitionen als Entwicklungsdeterminante Kenias.* Frankfurt am Main, Haag + Herchen, 1981.

Kenya—Irrigation

1501. Chambers, Robert, and Jon Moris (eds.) *Mwea: an irrigated rice settlement in Kenya.* Munich, Weltforum-Verlag, 1973.

1502. Cullis, Adrian, and Arthur Pacey. *A development dialogue: rainwater harvesting in Turkana.* London, Intermediate Technology Publications, 1992.

1503. Golkowsky, Rudolf. *Bewässerungslandwirtschaft in Kenya: Darstellung grandsätzlicher Zusammenhänge am Beispiel des Mwea Irrigation Settlement.* München, Weltforum-Verlag, 1969.

1504. Olsen, Maria M., and Karel J. Lenselink. *Annotated bibliography on irrigation and drainage in Kenya.* Nairobi, University of Nairobi, Department of Agricultural Engineering, 1988.

1505. Ruigu, George M., and Mandivamba Rukuni (eds.) *Irrigation policy in Kenya and Zimbabwe: proceedings of the second intermediate seminar on irrigation farming in Kenya and Zimbabwe held in Harare 26–30th May, 1987.* Nairobi, University of Nairobi, Institute for Development Studies, 1990.

Kenya—Journalism

1506. Abuoga, John Baptist, and Absalom Aggrey Mutere. *The history of the press in Kenya.* Nairobi, African Council on Communication Education, 1988.

Kenya—Labor

1507. Amsden, Alice Hoffenberg. *International firms and labour in Kenya, 1945–70.* London, Frank Cass, 1971.

1508. Clayton, Anthony, and Donald C. Savage. *Government and labour in Kenya, 1895–1963.* London, Frank Cass, 1974.

1509. Collier, P., and D. Lal. *Labour and poverty in Kenya, 1900–1980*. Oxford, Clarendon Press, 1986.

1510. Cooper, F. J. *From slaves to squatters: plantation labor and agriculture in Zanzibar and coastal Kenya, 1890–1925*. New Haven, Yale University Press, 1980.

1511. Mikkelsen, B. *Formation of an industrial labour force in Kenya: experiences of labour training in the metal manufacturing industries*. Nairobi, University of Nairobi, Institute for Development Studies, 1987.

1512. Stichter, Sharon. *Migrant labour in Kenya: capitalism and African response, 1895–1975*. London, Longmans, 1982.

1513. Zwanenberg, Roger M. van. *Colonial capitalism and labour in Kenya, 1919–1939*. Nairobi, East African Literature Bureau, 1975.

Kenya—Land

1514. Leo, Christopher. *Land and class in Kenya*. Toronto, University of Toronto Press, 1984.

1515. Link, H. *Die Besitzreform von Grossfarmen im Hochland von Kenya: Analyse und Erfolgsbeurteilung*. München, Weltforum-Verlag, 1973.

1516. Okoth-Ogendo, H. W. C. *Tenants of the Crown: evolution of agrarian law and institutions in Kenya*. Nairobi, Acts Press, 1991.

1517. Simpson, S. Rowton, et al. *Land tenure and economic development: problems and policies in Papua New Guinea and Kenya*. Canberra, Australian National University, New Guinea Research Unit, 1971.

1518. Wanjala, Smokin C. *Land law and disputes in Kenya*. Nairobi, Oxford University Press, 1990.

1519. Wasserman, Gary. *Politics of decolonization: Kenya, Europeans and the land issue, 1960–1965*. Cambridge, Cambridge University Press, 1976.

Kenya—Land Reform

1520. Harbeson, John Willis. *Nation-building in Kenya: the role of land reform*. Evanston, Northwestern University Press, 1973.

1521. Herz, Barbara K. *Land reform in Kenya*. Washington, United States Agency for International Development, 1970.

1522. Hunt, Diana. *The impending crisis in Kenya: the case for land reform*. Aldershot, Gower, 1984.

Kenya—Land Use

1523. Bronner, Gerhard. *Vegetation and land use in the Matthews Range area, Samburu District, Kenya*. Stuttgart, Borntraeger, 1990.

1524. Bullock, R. A. *Ndeiya, Kikuyu frontier: the Kenya land problem in microcosm*. Waterloo, University of Waterloo, 1975.

1525. Kiriro, A., and Calestous Juma. *Gaining ground: institutional innovation in land-use management in Kenya.* Nairobi, Acts Press, 1991.

1526. Kohler, Thomas. *Land use in transition, aspects and problems of small scale farming in a new environment: the example of Laikipia District, Kenya.* Bern, Arbeitsgemeinschaft Geographica Bernensia, 1988.

1527. Runge, Freya, et al. *Landnutzung und Landschaftsdegradation im Tiefland von Kitui und in den Taita Hills, Kenia.* Paderborn, Universität-Gesamthochschule-Paderborn, 1992.

Kenya—Languages

1528. Gorman, Thomas Patrick (ed.) *A glossary in English, Kiswahili, Kikuyu and Dholuo, etc.* London, Cassell, 1972.

1529. Heine, Bernd, and Wilhelm J. G. Möhlig. *Language and dialect atlas of Kenya, I: geographical and historical introduction, language and society; selected bibliography.* Berlin, Dietrich Reimer, 1980.

1530. Heine, Bernd. *The non-Bantu languages of Kenya.* Berlin, Dietrich Reimer, 1980.

1531. Mutahi, E. K. *Sound change and the classification of the dialects of southern Mt. Kenya.* Berlin, Dietrich Reimer, 1983.

1532. Whiteley, W. H. (ed.) *Language in Kenya.* Nairobi, Oxford University Press, 1974.

Kenya—Law

1533. Cotran, Eugene. *Casebook on Kenya customary law.* Abingdon, Professional Books, 1987.

1534. Ghai, Yash P., and J. P. W. B. McAuslan. *Public law and political change in Kenya: a study of the legal framework of government from colonial times to the present.* Nairobi, Oxford University Press, 1970.

1535. Hussain, Ashiq. *A textbook of company law in Kenya.* Nairobi, Heinemann Educational Books, 1980.

1536. Jackson, Tudor. *The law of Kenya: an introduction.* Nairobi, East African Literature Bureau, 1970.

1537. Kibwana, Kivutha (ed.) *Law and the administration of justice in Kenya.* Nairobi, International Commission of Jurists, Kenya Section, 1992.

1538. Maini, K. M. *Land law in East Africa.* London, Oxford University Press, 1967.

1539. Mbaya, William. *Commercial law of Kenya.* Nairobi, Petrans, 1991.

1540. Mutungi, Onesmus Kimweh. *The legal aspects of witchcraft in East Africa, with particular reference to Kenya.* Nairobi, East African Literature Bureau, 1977.

1541. Mwalimu, Charles. *The Kenyan legal system: an overview.* Washington, Library of Congress, Law Library, 1988.

1542. Onalo, A. *Land law and conveyancing in Kenya.* Nairobi, Heinemann Kenya, 1986.

1543. Thompson, Dudley. *From Kingston to Kenya: the making of a pan-Africanist lawyer.* Dover, Md., The Majority Press, 1994.

1544. Wacker, U. *Der Konflikt verschiedener Rechtssysteme vor, während und nach der Kolonialzeit in Kenia.* Frankfurt am Main, Peter Lang, 1976.

Kenya—Literature

1545. Maughan-Brown, D. *Land, freedom and fiction: history and ideology in Kenya.* London, Zed Books, 1985.

Kenya—Local Government

1546. Akivaga, S. K., et al. *Local authorities in Kenya.* Nairobi, Heinemann Kenya, 1985.

Kenya—Maize

1547. Pinckney, Thomas C. *Storage, trade and price policy under production instability: maize in Kenya.* Washington, International Food Policy Research Institute, 1988.

1548. Rundquist, Franz-Michael. *Hybrid maize diffusion in Kenya: policies, diffusion patterns and consequences. Case studies from Central and South Nyanza Provinces.* Lund, Gleerup, 1984.

Kenya—Manpower

1549. Nzomo, Nzele. *Education for executive jobs: a study in occupational Kenyanization-indigenization.* Nairobi, Kenya Literature Bureau, 1978.

1550. Wa'Weru, Murathi. *Management of human resources in Kenya.* Nairobi, Kenya Literature Bureau, 1984.

1551. Würkner, Reinhard A. *Systemstabilisierung durch Afrikanisierung?* München, Weltforum-Verlag, 1982.

Kenya—Marriage

1552. Kirwen, Michael C. *African widows: an empirical study of the problems of adapting western Christian teachings on marriage to the leviratic customs for the care of widows in four rural African societies.* Maryknoll, Orbis Books, 1979.

Kenya—Military History

1553. Shiroya, O. J. E. *Kenya and World War II: African soldiers in the European war.* Nairobi, Kenya Literature Bureau, 1985.

Kenya — Missionaries

1554. Brock, Carolyn. *Asante Africa*. Independence, Herald, 1990.

1555. Cousins, P. *Ethelstan Cheese: saint of no fixed abode*. Worthing, Churchman Publishing, 1986.

1556. Gissel, Fritz, and Hanna Gissel. *Einhundert Jahre Neukirchener Mission am Tana, 1887–1987*. Saarbrücken, Homo et Religio, 1991.

1557. Maggione, Giuseppe. *Padre Peppino: la sua Africa*. Bologna, Editrice Missionaria Italiana, 1990.

1558. Strayer, Robert W. *The making of mission communities in East Africa: Anglicans and Africans in colonial Kenya, 1875–1935*. London, Heinemann, 1978.

1559. Temu, A. J. *British Protestant missions*. London, Longman, 1972.

1560. Trevisiol, Alberto. *I primi missionari della Consolata nel Kenya, 1902–1905*. Roma, Università Gregoriana, 1983.

Kenya — Musical Instruments

1561. Hyslop, Graham. *Musical instruments of East Africa. Vol. 1: Kenya*. Nairobi, Nelson Africa, 1975.

1562. Kavyu, Paul Ndilya. *Traditional musical instruments of Kenya*. Nairobi, Kenya Literature Bureau, 1980.

Kenya — National Parks

1563. Gore, Michael. *On Safari in Kenya: a pictorial guide to the national parks and reserves*. Nairobi, Kenway, 1984.

Kenya — Oral Literature

1564. Kabira, Wanjiku Mukabi. *The oral artist*. Nairobi, Heinemann, 1983.

1565. Odaga, Asenath Bole. *Yesterday's today: the study of oral literature*. Kisumu, Lake, 1984.

Kenya — Ornithology

1566. Moore, R. *Where to watch birds in Kenya*. Nairobi, Transafrica, 1984.

Kenya — Parliament

1567. Gicheru, H. B. Ndoria. *Parliamentary practice in Kenya*. Nairobi, Transafrica Publishers, 1976.

Kenya — Pastoral Production

1568. Evangelou, Phylo. *Livestock development in Kenya's Maasailand: pastoralists' transition to a market economy*. Boulder, Westview Press, 1984.

1569. Kerven, C. *Customary commerce: a historical reassessment of pastoral live-stock marketing in Africa.* London, Overseas Development Institute, 1992.

Kenya—Pastoralists

1570. Barthelme, John Webster. *Fisher-hunters and neolithic pastoralists in east Turkana, Kenya.* Oxford, British Archaeological Reports, 1985.

1571. Dietz, T. *Pastoralists in dire straits: survival strategies and external interventions in a semi-arid region at the Kenya/Uganda border, Western Pokot, 1900–1986.* Amsterdam, Universiteit van Amsterdam, 1987.

1572. Farah, Mohamed I. *From ethnic response to clan identity: a study of state penetration among the Somali nomadic pastoral society of northeastern Kenya.* Uppsala, Acta Universitatis Upsaliensis, 1993.

1573. Jones, David Keith. *Shepherds of the desert.* London, Elm Tree, 1984.

1574. Little, Peter D. *The elusive granary: herder, farmer and state in northern Kenya.* Cambridge, Cambridge University Press, 1992.

1575. Robertshaw, P., et al. *Early pastoralists of south-western Kenya.* Nairobi, British Institute in Eastern Africa, 1990.

1576. Walz, G. *Nomaden in Nationalstaat: zur Integration der Nomaden in Kenia.* Berlin, Dietrich Reimer, 1991.

Kenya—Planning

1577. Ghai, Dharam P., et al. *Planning for basic needs in Kenya: performance, policies and prospects.* Geneva, International Labour Office, 1979.

1578. Hoeven, Ralph van der. *Planning for basic needs: a soft option or a solid policy? A basic needs simulation model applied to Kenya.* Aldershot, Avebury, 1988.

1579. Norcliffe, Glen, and Tom Pinfold (eds.) *Planning African development.* Boulder, Westview Press, 1981.

1580. Pinfold, Tom, and Glen Norcliffe (eds.) *Development planning in Kenya: essays on the planning process and policy issues.* Downsview, York University, Atkinson College, Department of Geography, 1980.

1581. Stremplat, Axel V., and Petra Stremplat-Platte. *Kommentare zur Regionalplanung in Entwicklungsländern: Shinyanga Regional Integrated Development Plan, etc.* Saarbrücken, Breitenbach, 1981.

Kenya—Police

1582. Foran, Robert. *The Kenya police, 1887–1960.* London, Robert Hale, 1962.

Kenya—Politics

1583. Anon. *Independent Kenya.* London, Zed Press, 1982.

1584. Ballot, Frank. *Politische Herrschaft in Kenia: der neo-patrimoniale Staat, 1963–1978.* Rheinfelden, Schäuble Verlag, 1986.

1585. Barkan, Joel D. (ed.) *Politics and public policy in Kenya and Tanzania.* Revised edition. New York, Praeger, 1984.

1586. Bienen, Henry. *Kenya: the politics of participation and control.* Princeton, Princeton University Press, 1974.

1587. Bilger, Harald R. *Verführung und Last der Freiheit: Probleme der Entwicklungspolitik dargestellt an den Beispielen Kenia und Tansania.* Konstanz, Universitätsverlag Konstanz, 1972.

1588. Bourmaud, Daniel. *Histoire politique du Kenya: état et pouvoir local.* Paris, Karthala, 1988.

1589. Dauch, Gene, and Denis Martin. *L'héritage de Kenyatta: la transition politique au Kenya, 1975–1982.* Paris, L'Harmattan, 1985.

1590. Frost, Richard. *Race against time: human relations and politics in Kenya before independence.* London, Collins, 1978.

1591. Gertzel, Cherry J. *The politics of independent Kenya, 1963–1968.* Nairobi, East African Publishing House, 1970.

1592. Gertzel, Cherry J., et al. (eds.) *Government and politics in Kenya: a nation-building text.* Nairobi, East African Publishing House, 1969.

1593. Godia, George I. *Understanding Nyayo: principles and policies of contemporary Kenya.* Nairobi, Transafrica, 1984.

1594. Gordon, D. F. *Decolonization and the state in Kenya.* Boulder, Westview Press, 1986.

1595. Grignon, François. *Le multipartisme au Kenya? Reproduction autoritaire, légitimation, et culture politique en mutation, 1990–1992.* Nairobi, Institut Français de Recherche en Afrique, 1993.

1596. Gupta, Vijay. *Kenya: politics of (in)dependence.* New Delhi, People's Publishing House, 1981.

1597. Holmquist, Frank W., and Joel D. Barkan. *A comprehensive bibliography: politics and public policy in Kenya and Tanzania.* Iowa City, University of Iowa, Center for International and Comparative Studies, 1984.

1598. Jones, Norman Stewart Carey. *The anatomy of Uhuru: dynamics and problems of African independence in an age of conflict.* Manchester, Manchester University Press, 1966.

1599. Kenyatta, Jomo. *Harambee! The Prime Minister of Kenya's speeches, 1963–1964.* Nairobi, Oxford University Press, 1964.

1600. Koigi wa Wamwere. *Conscience on trial: why I was detained. Notes of a political prisoner in Kenya.* Trenton, Africa World Press, 1988.

1601. Maillu, David G. *Pragmatic leadership: evaluation of Kenya's cultural and political development, featuring Daniel arap Moi, President of Republic of Kenya.* Nairobi, Maillu, 1988.

1602. Maina, Kiongo, and Kaara wa Macharia. *Matiba: let the people decide.* Nairobi, Berisco, 1992.

1603. Matiba, Kenneth Stanley. *Kenya: return to reason.* Nairobi, Kalamka, 1993.

1604. Mboya, Thomas Joseph. *Freedom and after.* Nairobi, Heinemann Kenya, 1986.

1605. Mboya, Thomas Joseph. *The challenge of nationhood: a collection of speeches and writings.* London, Heinemann, 1970.

1606. Mohiddin, Ahmed. *African socialism in two countries.* London, Croom Helm, 1981.

1607. Moi, Daniel T. arap. *Continuity and consolidation in Kenya: selected and prefaced extracts from the public speeches ... made during the period December 1979 to July 1981.* Nairobi, East African Publishing House, 1982.

1608. Moi, Daniel T. arap. *Kenya African nationalism: Nyayo philosophy and principles.* London, Macmillan, 1986.

1609. Moi, Daniel T. arap. *Transition and continuity in Kenya: selected and prefaced extracts from the public speeches of His Excellency President Daniel T. arap Moi, President of the Republic of Kenya, made during the period August 1978–October 1979.* Nairobi, East African Publishing House, 1979.

1610. Mutiso, G. C. M. *Kenya: politics, policy and society.* Nairobi, East African Literature Bureau, 1975.

1611. Ngugi wa Thiong'o. *Barrel of a pen: resistance to oppression in neo-colonial Kenya.* Trenton, Africa World Press, 1983.

1612. Ngugi wa Thiong'o. *Detained: a writer's prison diary.* London, Heinemann, 1981.

1613. Ngugi wa Thiong'o. *Writers and politics: essays.* London, Heinemann, 1981.

1614. Nyamu, H. J. *Aspects of Kenya's development: a participant's view.* Nairobi, East African Publishing House, 1980.

1615. Ochieng', P., and J. Karimi. *The Kenyatta succession.* Nairobi, Transafrica, 1981.

1616. Odera Oruka, H. *Oginga Odinga: his philosophy and beliefs.* Nairobi, Initiatives, 1992.

1617. Odinga, Oginga Jaramogi. *Not yet Uhuru: an autobiography.* London, Heinemann, 1967.

1618. Ross, Marc Howard. *The political integration of urban squatters.* Evanston, Northwestern University Press, 1973.

1619. Rothchild, Donald S. *Racial bargaining in independent Kenya: a study of minorities and decolonization.* London, Oxford University Press, 1973.

1620. Schatzberg, M. (ed.) *The political economy of Kenya.* New York, Praeger, 1987.

1621. Shiroya, O. J. E. *Dimensions of nationalism: the African context.* Nairobi, Jomo Kenyatta Foundation, 1992.

1622. Spencer, J. *The Kenyan African Union.* London, Kegan Paul International, 1985.

1623. Teubert-Seiwert, Bärbel. *Parteipolitik in Kenya, 1960–1969.* Frankfurt am Main, Peter Lang, 1987.

1624. United Movement for Democracy in Kenya. *Struggle for democracy in Kenya.* London, UMOJA, 1988.

1625. Widner, Jennifer A. *The rise of a party-state in Kenya: from "Harambee!" to "Nyayo!"* Berkeley, University of California Press, 1992.

1626. Wood, Susan. *Kenya: the tensions of progress.* Second edition. London, Oxford University Press, 1962.

Kenya—Population

1627. Ahlberg, B. M. *Women, sexuality and the changing social order: the impact of government policies on reproductive behavior in Kenya.* Philadelphia, Gordon and Breach, 1991.

1628. Anker, R., and J. C. Knowles. *Population growth, employment and economic-demographic interactions in Kenya: Bachue-Kenya.* Aldershot, Gower, 1983.

1629. Bondestam, Lars. *Population growth in Kenya.* Uppsala, Scandinavian Institute of African Studies, 1972.

1630. Faruqee, Rashid, et al. *Kenya: population and development.* Washington, World Bank, 1980.

1631. Gil, B., and J. K. Ronohy. *The Kenya Civil Registration Demonstration Project (CRDP): a strategy for a rapidly developing country in Africa.* Nairobi, Department of the Registrar General, 1990.

1632. Gyepi-Garbrah, Benjamin. *Adolescent fertility in Kenya.* Boston, Pathfinder Fund, 1985.

1633. Kelley, Allen C., and Charles E. Nobbe. *Kenya at the demographic turning point: hypotheses and a proposed research agenda.* Washington, World Bank, 1990.

1634. Krystall, Abigail, and Anne Schneller. *A guide to population activities in Kenya.* Nairobi, National Council for Population and Development, 1987.

1635. Morgan, W. T. W., and N. Manfred Shaffer. *Population of Kenya: density and distribution. A geographical introduction to the Kenya Population Census, 1962.* Nairobi, Oxford University Press, 1966.

1636. Ndeti, Kivuto, and Cecilia Ndeti. *Cultural values and population policy in Kenya.* Nairobi, Kenya Literature Bureau, 1980.

1637. Ominde, Simeon H. *Land and population movements in Kenya.* Evanston, Northwestern University Press, 1968.

1638. Ominde, Simeon H. (ed.) *Kenya's population growth and development to the year 2000.* London, James Currey, 1989.

1639. Ominde, Simeon H. (ed.) *Population and development in Kenya.* Nairobi, Heinemann, 1984.

1640. World Bank. *Kenya: population and development.* Washington, World Bank, 1980.

Kenya—Ports

1641. Hoyle, Brian Stewart. *Seaports and development: the experience of Kenya and Tanzania.* New York, Gordon and Breach, 1983.

Kenya—Potato Production

1642. Mbogho, S. G. *The potato industry of Kenya.* Nairobi, University of Nairobi, Department of Agricultural Economics, 1977.

Kenya—Pottery

1643. Barbour, J., and S. Wandibba. *Kenyan pots and potters.* Nairobi, Oxford University Press, 1989.

Kenya—Prehistory

1644. Coppens, Yves, et al. (eds.) *Earliest man and environments in the Lake Rudolf Basin: stratigraphy, paleoecology and evolution.* Chicago, University of Chicago Press, 1976.

1645. Isaac, Glynn Llywelyn. *Olorgesailie: archeological studies of a Middle Pleistocene lake basin in Kenya.* Chicago, University of Chicago Press, 1977.

1646. Leakey, Richard E., and Roger Lewin. *People of the lake: man, his origins, nature and future.* London, Collins, 1979.

Kenya—Prisons

1647. Bundeh, B. G. *Birds of Kamiti.* Nairobi, Heinemann, 1991.

Kenya—Proverbs

1648. Knappert, Jan. *Proverbs from the Lamu archipelago and the central Kenya coast.* Berlin, Dietrich Reimer, 1986.

Kenya—Public Enterprise

1649. Grosh, Barbara. *Public enterprise in Kenya: what works, what doesn't and why.* Boulder, Lynne Rienner, 1991.

Kenya—Publishing

1650. Abukutsa, J. L. (ed.) *The role of books in development: proceedings of the fifth biennial conference, Nairobi, September 25th–29th, 1972*. Nairobi, Kenya Library Association, 1974.

Kenya—Refugees

1651. Harris, J. E. *Repatriates and refugees in a colonial society: the coast of Kenya*. Washington, Howard University Press, 1987.

Kenya—Religion

1652. Neckebrouck, Valeer. *Le peuple affligé: les déterminants de la fissiparité dans un nouveau mouvement religieux au Kenya central*. Immensee, Neue Zeitschrift für Missionswissenschaft, 1983.

1653. Were, Gideon S. *Essays on African religion in western Kenya*. Nairobi, Kenya Literature Bureau, 1979.

1654. Wortham, R. *Spatial developments and religious orientation in Kenya*. Lewiston, Edwin Mellen Press, 1990.

Kenya—Roads

1655. Veen, J. J. de. *The rural access roads programme: appropriate technology in Kenya*. Geneva, International Labour Office, 1980.

Kenya—Rural Conditions

1656. Bigsten, Arne, and P. Collier. *Education, innovation and income in rural Kenya*. Nairobi, University of Nairobi, Institute for Development Studies, 1980.

1657. Carlsen, John. *Economic and social transformation in rural Kenya*. Uppsala, Scandinavian Institute of African Studies, 1980.

1658. Child, Frank C. *Small-scale rural industry in Kenya*. Los Angeles, University of California, African Studies Center, 1977.

1659. Kempe, M. E., and L. D. Smith (eds.) *Strategies for improving rural welfare: proceedings of a workshop held in the Institute for Development Studies, University of Nairobi, May 31st–June 3rd, 1971*. Nairobi, University of Nairobi, Institute for Development Studies, 1971.

1660. Lavrijsen, Jan Simon Gerardus. *Rural poverty and impoverishment in western Kenya*. Utrecht, J. S. G. Lavrijsen, 1984.

1661. Silberfein, M. *Rural change in Machakos, Kenya: a historical geography perspective*. Lanham, University Press of America, 1989.

1662. Wallis, M. A. H. *Bureaucrats, politicians and rural communities in Kenya*. Manchester, University of Manchester, Department of Administrative Studies, 1982.

Kenya—Rural Development

1663. Borton, Raymond E., et al. *A development program for the Ada District, based on a socio-economic survey.* Menlo Park, Stanford Research Institute, 1969.

1664. Fordham, P. *Rural development in the Kenya highlands: a report of geographical field work carried out during August 1971.* Nottingham, University of Nottingham, Geography Field Group, 1973.

1665. Freeman, D. B., and G. B. Norcliffe. *Rural enterprise in Kenya: development and spatial organization of the non-farm sector.* Chicago, University of Chicago, Department of Geography, 1985.

1666. Heyer, Judith, et al. *Rural development in Kenya.* Nairobi, East African Publishing House, 1971.

1667. Kronenburg, J. B. M. *Empowerment of the poor: a comparative analysis of two development endeavours in Kenya.* Amsterdam, Koninklijk Instituut voor de Tropen, 1986.

1668. Lamb, Geoffrey. *Peasant politics: conflict and development in Murang'a.* London, Julian Friedmann, 1974.

1669. Leonard, David K. *African successes: four public managers of Kenyan rural development.* Berkeley, University of California Press, 1991.

1670. Livingstone, Ian. *Rural development, employment and incomes in Kenya.* Aldershot, Gower, 1986.

1671. Mbithi, P. M. *Rural sociology and rural development: its application in Kenya.* Nairobi, East African Literature Bureau, 1974.

1672. Mbithi, P. M., and Rasmus Rasmusson. *Self-reliance in Kenya: the case of Harambee.* Uppsala, Scandinavian Institute of African Studies, 1977.

1673. Porter, D., et al. *Development in practice: paved with good intentions.* London, Routledge, 1991.

1674. Rogers, J. D. *Patterns of rural development and impact on employment and incomes, a comparative sub-regional study: the case of Kenya.* Addis Ababa, International Labour Organisation, Jobs and Skills Programme for Africa, 1985.

1675. Thomas, B. P. *Politics, participation and poverty: development through self-help in Kenya.* Boulder, Westview Press, 1985.

Kenya—Rural Research

1676. Ackello-Ogutu, A. C. (ed.) *Kenya's rural research priorities: proceedings of a seminar held at Safariland Lodge, Naivasha, 28–30 April, 1988.* Nairobi, University of Nairobi, Institute for Development Studies, 1989.

Kenya — Seed Industry

1677. Ruigu, George M., et al. *The Kenyan seed industry: evolution, current status and future prospects*. Nairobi, University of Nairobi, Institute for Development Studies, 1989.

Kenya — Settlement Schemes

1678. Clayton, Eric S. *A comparative study of settlement schemes in Kenya*. Ashford, Wye College, University of London, 1978.

1679. Haugwitz, Hans Wilhelm von. *Some experiences with smallholder settlement in Kenya, 1963/64 to 1966/67*. Munich, Weltforum-Verlag, 1972.

1680. Hoorweg, Jan, et al. *Economic and nutritional conditions at settlement schemes in Coast Province*. Leiden, African Studies Centre, 1991.

Kenya — Settler Society

1681. Best, Nicholas. *Happy valley: the story of the English in Kenya*. London, Secker and Warburg, 1979.

1682. Cole, Eleanor. *Random recollections of a pioneer Kenya settler*. Woodbridge, Baron, 1975.

1683. Curtis, A. (ed.) *Memories of Kenya: stories from the pioneers*. London, Evans Brothers, 1986.

1684. Farrant, Leda. *The legendary Grogan: the only man to trek from Cape to Cairo. Kenya's controversial pioneer*. London, Hamish Hamilton, 1981.

1685. Fox, James. *White mischief: the murder of Lord Erroll*. Harmondsworth, Penguin, 1984.

1686. Hoyt, Alta Howard. *We were pioneers*. Wichita, Friends University, 1971.

1687. Huxley, Elspeth, and Arnold Curtis (eds.) *Pioneers' scrapbook: reminiscences of Kenya, 1890–1968*. London, Evans Brothers, 1980.

1688. Kennedy, Dane. *Islands of white: settler society and culture in Kenya and Southern Rhodesia, 1890–1939*. Durham, Duke University Press, 1987.

1689. Leys, Norman Maclean, and J. H. Oldham. *By Kenya possessed: the correspondence of Norman Leys and J. H. Oldham, 1918–1926*. Edited by John W. Cell. Chicago, University of Chicago Press, 1976.

1690. Mosley, Paul. *The settler economies: studies in the economic history of Kenya and Southern Rhodesia, 1900–1963*. Cambridge, Cambridge University Press, 1983.

1691. Sorrenson, M. P. K. *Origins of European settlement in Kenya*. Nairobi, Oxford University Press, 1968.

1692. Trzebinski, Errol. *Silence will speak: a study of the life of Denys Finch Hatton and his relationship with Karen Blixen*. London, Heinemann, 1977.

1693. Trzebinski, Errol. *The Kenyan pioneers*. London, Mandarin, 1991.

Kenya—Slavery

1694. Cooper, F. J. *Plantation slavery on the east coast of Africa*. New Haven, Yale University Press, 1977.

1695. Morton, Fred. *Children of Ham: freed slaves and fugitive slaves on the Kenya coast, 1873–1907*. Boulder, Westview Press, 1990.

Kenya—Social Conditions

1696. Arnold, Guy. *Modern Kenya*. London, Longmans, 1981.

1697. Berg-Schlosser, D. *Tradition and change in Kenya: a comparative analysis of seven major ethnic groups*. Paderborn, Ferdinand Schoningh, 1984.

1698. Cohen, David William, and E. S. Atieno Odhiambo. *Burying SM: the politics of knowledge and the sociology of power in Africa*. London, James Currey, 1992.

1699. Cohen, David William, and E. S. Atieno Odhiambo. *Siaya: the historical anthropology of an African landscape*. London, James Currey, 1989.

1700. Dutto, C. A. *Nyeri townsmen Kenya*. Nairobi, East African Literature Bureau, 1975.

1701. Forrester, Marion Wallace. *Kenya today: social prerequisites for economic development*. The Hague, Mouton, 1962.

1702. Goldschmidt, Armin M. *Social-psychological determinants of rural-urban migration in Kenya: an eco-psychological village study on social change in Meru District, Mt. Kenya*. Saarbrücken, Breitenbach, 1986.

1703. Hjort, Anders. *Savanna town: rural ties and urban opportunities in northern Kenya*. Stockholm, University of Stockholm, Department of Social Anthropology, 1979.

1704. House-Midamba, Bessie. *Class, development and gender inequality in Kenya, 1963–1990*. Lewiston, Edwin Mellen Press, 1990.

1705. Jules-Rosette, Bennetta. *Terminal signs: computers and social change in Africa*. Berlin, Mouton de Gruyter, 1990.

1706. Kipkorir, Ben E., and J. W. Ssennyongal (eds.) *A socio-cultural profile of Elgeyo-Marakwet District: a report of the District Socio-Cultural Profiles project*. Nairobi, University of Nairobi, Institute of African Studies and Ministry of Finance and Planning, 1984.

1707. Kipkorir, Ben E. (ed.) *South Nyanza District socio-cultural profile*. Nairobi, University of Nairobi, Institute of African Studies and Ministry of Planning and National Development, 1986.

1708. Kongstad, Per, and M. Mönsted. *Family, labour and trade in western Kenya*. Uppsala, Scandinavian Institute of African Studies, 1980.

1709. Lubeck, P. M. (ed.) *The African bourgeoisie: capitalist development in Nigeria, Kenya and Ivory Coast.* Boulder, Lynne Rienner, 1987.

1710. Mbithi, P. M., and C. Barnes. *The spontaneous settlement problem in Kenya.* Kampala, East African Literature Bureau, 1975.

1711. Meyerhoff, Elizabeth. *Taking stock: changing livelihoods in an agropastoral community.* Nairobi, Acts Press, 1991.

1712. Ojwang, J. B., and J. N. K. Mugambi. *The S. M. Otieno case: death and burial in modern Kenya.* Nairobi, Nairobi University Press, 1989.

1713. Sandbrook, R. *Proletarians and African capitalism: the Kenyan case, 1960–1972.* Cambridge, Cambridge University Press, 1975.

1714. Silberschmidt, Margrethe. *Rethinking men and gender relations: an investigation of men, their changing roles within the household, and the implications for gender relations in Kisii District, Kenya.* Copenhagen, Centre for Development Research, 1991.

1715. Visram, M. G. *On a plantation in Kenya.* Mombasa, M. G. Visram, 1987.

1716. Were, Gideon S. (ed.) *Baringo District socio-cultural profile.* Nairobi, University of Nairobi, Institute of African Studies and Ministry of Planning and National Development, 1986.

1717. Were, Gideon S. (ed.) *Kenya socio-cultural profile: Meru District.* Nairobi, University of Nairobi, Institute of African Studies and Ministry of Planning and National Development, 1986.

1718. Were, Gideon S. (ed.) *Kenya socio-cultural profile: Narok District.* Nairobi, University of Nairobi, Institute of African Studies and Ministry of Planning and National Development, 1986.

1719. Were, Gideon S. (ed.) *Kenya, Kisii District: socio-cultural profile.* Nairobi, University of Nairobi, Institute of African Studies and Ministry of Planning and National Development, 1986.

1720. Were, Gideon S. (ed.) *Marsabit District socio-cultural profile.* Nairobi, University of Nairobi, Institute of African Studies and Ministry of Planning and National Development, 1986.

Kenya—Social Welfare

1721. Fuchs, Maximilian. *Soziale Sicherheit in der dritten Welt, zugleich eine Fallstudie Kenia.* Baden-Baden, Nomos, 1985.

Kenya—Soil Conservation

1722. Thomas, D. B., and W. M. Senga (eds.) *Soil and water conservation in Kenya: proceedings of the second national workshop, Nairobi, 10–16 March, 1982.* Nairobi, University of Nairobi, Institute for Development Studies, 1983.

1723. Thomas, D. B., et al. (eds.) *Soil and water conservation in Kenya.* Nairobi, University of Nairobi, Department of Agricultural Engineering, 1989.

Kenya—Taxation

1724. Butt, Safdar Ali. *An introduction to taxation in Kenya.* London, Cassell, 1978.

Kenya—Tea Production

1725. Gyllström, Björn. *The organisation of production as a space-modelling mechanism in underdeveloped countries: the case of tea production in Kenya.* Lund, LiberLaromedel/Gleerup, 1977.

1726. Stern, Nicholas Herbert. *An appraisal of tea production on small holdings in Kenya: an experiment with the Little-Mirrlees method.* Paris, OECD Development Centre, 1972.

Kenya—Theatre

1727. Björkman, I. *"Mother, sing for me": people's theatre in Kenya.* London, Zed Books, 1989.

Kenya—Tourism

1728. Bachmann, Philipp. *Tourism in Kenya: a basic need for whom?* Berne, Peter Lang, 1988.

1729. Hemsing, Jan. *Ker and Downey Safaris Ltd: the inside story.* Nairobi, Sealpoint Publicity, 1989.

1730. Jommo, Rosemary B. *Indigenous enterprise in Kenya's tourism industry.* Geneva, Institut Universitaire d'Études du Développement, 1987.

1731. Migot-Adholla, S. E., et al. *Study of tourism in Kenya, with emphasis on the attitudes of residents of the Kenya coast.* Nairobi, University of Nairobi, Institute for Development Studies, 1982.

1732. Schurian-Bremecker, Christiane. *Kenia in der Sicht deutscher Touristen: eine Analyse von Denkmustern und Verhaltensweisen beim Urlaub in einem Entwicklungsland.* Münster, Lit-Verlag, 1989.

Kenya—Trade Unions

1733. Leitner, K. *Workers, trade unions and peripheral capitalism in Kenya after independence.* Berne, Peter Lang, 1977.

1734. Singh, Makhan. *History of Kenya's trade union movement to 1952.* Nairobi, East African Publishing House, 1969.

1735. Singh, Makhan. *Kenya's trade unions, 1952–1956.* Nairobi, Uzima Press, 1980.

Kenya—Training

1736. Godfrey, E. M., and G. C. M. Mutiso. *Politics, economics and technical training: a Kenyan case study.* Nairobi, Kenya Literature Bureau, 1979.

Kenya—Tsetse Control

1737. Engelskjn, K. *Tsetse fly control in a Maasai pastoralist society in Nguru-man, southwest Kenya.* Oslo, Noragric, 1990.

Kenya—Urbanization

1738. Obudho, Robert A. *Demography, urbanization and spatial planning in Kenya: a bibliographical survey.* Westport, Greenwood Press, 1985.

1739. Obudho, Robert A., and P. P. Waller. *Periodic markets, urbanization and regional planning: a case study from western Kenya.* Westport, Green-wood Press, 1976.

1740. Obudho, Robert A. *Urbanization in Kenya: a bottom-up approach to development planning.* Lanham, University Press of America, 1983.

1741. Obudho, Robert A. (ed.) *Urbanization and development planning in Kenya.* Nairobi, Kenya Literature Bureau, 1981.

Kenya—Water Supply

1742. Carruthers, I., and A. Weir. *Impact and economics of community water supply: a study of rural water investment in Kenya.* Ashford, Wye College, Agrarian Development Unit, 1973.

1743. Seppälä, Pekka. *Water supply as a medium of rural development in Kenya.* Helsinki, University of Helsinki, Institute of Development Studies, 1986.

Kenya—Wildlife

1744. Holman, D. *The elephant people.* London, Murray, 1967.

1745. Hughes, Ian Meredith. *Black moon, jade sea.* London, Clifford Frost, 1988.

1746. Yeager, P., and N. N. Miller. *Wildlife, wild death: land use and survival in eastern Africa.* Albany, State University of New York Press, 1986.

Kenya—Women

1747. Akerele, O. *Women workers in Ghana, Kenya, Zambia.* Addis Ababa, UN Economic Commission for Africa, Training and Research Centre for Women, 1979.

1748. Bülow, Dorthe van, and Anne Sorensen. *Gender dynamics in contract farming: women's role in smallholder tea production in Kericho District, Kenya.* Copenhagen, Centre for Development Research, 1988.

1749. Gutto, Shadrack B. O. *The status of women in Kenya: a study of paternalism, inequality and underprivilege.* Nairobi, University of Nairobi, Institute for Development Studies, 1976.

1750. Likimani, Muthoni. *Women of Kenya: 27 years of development.* Nairobi, Noni's Publicity, 1991.

1751. Mbeo, M. A., and O. Ooko-Ombaka (eds.) *Women and law in Kenya: perspectives and emerging issues.* Nairobi, Public Law Institute, 1989.

1752. Meyer-Mansour, Dorothee. *Frauen-Selbsthilfegruppen in Kenia.* Hamburg, Weltarchiv, 1985.

1753. Mickelwait, Donald R., et al. *Women in rural development: a survey of the roles of women in Ghana, Lesotho, Kenya, Nigeria, Bolivia, Paraguay, and Peru.* Boulder, Westview Press, 1976.

1754. Njau, E., and G. Mulaki. *Kenya women heroes and their mystical power.* Nairobi, Risk, 1984.

1755. Obura, Anna P. *Changing images: portrayal of girls and women in Kenyan textbooks.* Nairobi, Acts Press, 1991.

1756. Pala, Achola O., and Madina Ly. *La femme africaine dans la société précoloniale.* Paris, UNESCO, 1979.

1757. Pala, Achola O., et al. (eds.) *The participation of women in Kenya society.* Nairobi, Kenya Literature Bureau, 1983.

1758. Reining, Priscilla, et al. *Village women, their changing lives and fertility: studies in Kenya, Mexico and the Philippines.* Washington, American Association for the Advancement of Science, 1977.

1759. Were, Gideon S., et al. *Women and development in Kenya: Siaya District.* Nairobi, University of Nairobi, Institute for African Studies, 1991.

1760. World Bank. *Kenya: the role of women in economic development.* Washington, World Bank, 1989.

Kenyatta, Jomo

1761. Amin, Mohamed, and Peter Moll. *Mzee Jomo Kenyatta: a photobiography.* Nairobi, Marketing & Publishing, 1978.

1762. Arnold, Guy. *Kenyatta and the politics of Kenya.* London, Dent, 1974.

1763. Delf, George. *Jomo Kenyatta: towards truth about "the light of Kenya."* London, Gollancz, 1961.

1764. Friedmann, J. *Jomo Kenyatta.* London, Wayland Publishers, 1975.

1765. Macharia, R. *The truth about the trial of Jomo Kenyatta.* Nairobi, Longman, 1991.

1766. Murray-Brown, Jeremy. *Kenyatta.* Second edition. London, Allen and Unwin, 1979.

1767. Slater, Montagu. *The trial of Jomo Kenyatta.* London, Mercury Books, 1965.

1768. Wepman, Dennis. *Jomo Kenyatta.* New York, Chelsea House, 1985.

Kerebe—History

1769. Hartwig, Gerald W. *The art of survival in East Africa: the Kerebe and long distance trade, 1800–1895.* New York, Africana, 1976.

Kerma—Ethnography

1770. Gratien, B. *Les cultures kerma: essai de classification.* Villeneuve d'Ascq, Publications de l'Université de Lille III, 1978.

Khartoum—Geography

1771. Schwerthöffer, Rüdiger, and Horst Nusser. *Metropole in Entwicklungsland, die Stadt Khartoum: Zentralfunktion und Regionalplanung.* München, Horst Nusser, 1991.

Khartoum—Social Conditions

1772. Miller, Catherine, and Al-Amin Abu-Manga. *Language change and national integration: rural migrants in Khartoum.* London, Ithaca Press, 1993.

Kikuyu—Agriculture

1773. Fisher, J. M. *Anatomy of Kikuyu domesticity and husbandry.* London, Department of Technical Cooperation, 1964.

1774. Sottas, Beat. *Afrika entwickeln und modernisieren: Paradigmen Identitätsbildung und kleinbäuerliche Überlebensstrategien.* Freiburg, Universitätsverlag Freiburg Schweiz, 1992.

Kikuyu—Christianity

1775. Bottignole, S. *Kikuyu traditional culture and Christianity: self examination of an African church.* Nairobi, Heinemann Educational Books, 1984.

1776. Sandgren, David P. *Christianity and the Kikuyu: religious divisions and social conflict.* New York, Peter Lang, 1989.

Kikuyu—Documentation

1777. Pugliese, Cristiana. *Gikuyu political pamphlets and hymn books, 1945–1952.* Nairobi, Institut Français de Recherche en Afrique, 1993.

Kikuyu—Ethnobotany

1778. Gachathi, F. N. *Kikuyu botanical dictionary of plant names and uses.* Nairobi, AMREF, 1989.

Kikuyu—Ethnography

1779. Tietmeyer, E. *Gynaegamie im Wandel: die Agikuyu zwischen Tradition und Anpassung.* Münster, Lit-Verlag, 1991.

Kikuyu—History

1780. Leakey, L. S. B. *The southern Kikuyu before 1903.* London, Academic Press, 1977. 3 vols.

1781. Muriuki, G. *A history of the Kikuyu, 1500–1900.* Nairobi, Oxford University Press, 1974.

Kikuyu — Land Reform

1782. Fliedner, Hanfried. *Die Bodenrechtsreform in Kenya: Studie über die Änderung der Bodenrechtsverhältnisse im Zuge der Agrarreform, unter besonderer Berücksichtigung des Kikuyu-Stammesgebietes.* Berlin, Springer, 1965.

1783. Sorrenson, M. P. K. *Land reform in Kikuyu country: a study in government policy.* Nairobi, Oxford University Press, 1967.

Kikuyu — Language

1784. Barlow, A. R. *English-Kikuyu dictionary.* London, Oxford University Press, 1975.

1785. Bennett, Patrick R., et al. *Gikuyu ni Kioigire: a first course in Kikuyu.* Madison, University of Wisconsin, African Studies Program, 1985.

1786. Benson, T. G. (ed.) *Kikuyu-English dictionary.* Oxford, Clarendon Press, 1964.

1787. Pick, Vittoria Merlo. *Ndai na Gicandi: Kikuyu enigmas/enigmi Kikuyu.* Bologna, Editrice Missionaria Italiana, 1974.

Kikuyu — Oral Literature

1788. Kabira, Wanjiku Mukabi, and Karega Mutahi. *Gikuyu oral literature.* Nairobi, Heinemann Kenya, 1988.

Kikuyu — Social Conditions

1789. Cavicchi, E. *Problems of change in Kikuyu tribal society.* Bologna, EMI, 1977.

1790. Gecaga, Bethuel Mareka. *Kariuki na muthoni: a study of childhood and youth among the Kikuyu.* Nairobi, Kenya Literature Bureau, 1983.

1791. Krabbe, Günter, and Hans P. Mayer. *Die schwarze Familie. Wie Entwicklungshilfe die schwarzafrikanische Familie und die Rolle ihrer Mitglieder verändert hat: eine Untersuchung am Beispiel des kenianischen Volkes des Kikuyu.* Frankfurt am Main, Peter Lang, 1992.

1792. Naidu, Naiduayah. *Spatial aspects of social change.* Lund, Gleerup, 1975.

Kikuyu — Women

1793. Davison, J. *Voices from Mutira: lives of rural Gikuyu women.* Boulder, Lynne Rienner, 1989.

Kilwa

1794. Chittick, Neville. *Kilwa: an Islamic trading city on the East African coast.* Nairobi, British Institute in Eastern Africa, 1974.

1795. Freeman-Grenville, G. S. P. *The French at Kilwa Island: an episode in eighteenth-century East African history.* Oxford, Clarendon Press, 1965.

Kimathi, Dedan

1796. Durrani, Shiraz. *Kimaathi: Mau Mau's first prime minister of Kenya.* Wembley, Vita, 1986.

1797. Kahiga, S. *Dedan Kimathi: the real story.* Nairobi, Longman, 1990.

1798. Kimathi, Dedan. *Kimathi's letters: a profile of courage.* Edited by M. wa Kinyatti. Nairobi, Heinemann, 1986.

1799. Maina wa Kinyatti (ed.) *Kenya's freedom struggle: the Dedan Kimathi papers.* London, Zed Books, 1989.

1800. Wandai, Karuga. *Kimathi: a tribute to a national hero.* Thika, Mount Kilimanjaro Publishers, 1990.

1801. Watene, Kenneth. *Dedan Kimathi.* Nairobi, Transafrica Publishers, 1974.

Kimbu—History

1802. Shorter, Aylward. *Chiefship in western Tanzania: a political history of the Kimbu.* Oxford, Clarendon Press, 1972.

Kinga—Religion

1803. Triebl, Johannes. *Gottesglaube und Heroenkult in Afrika: Untersuchungen zum Lwembe-Kult der Wakinga in Südtanzania.* Erlangen, Verlag der Evangelisch-Lutherischen Mission, 1993.

Kipsigis—Ethnography

1804. Orchardson, I. Q. *The Kipsigis.* Nairobi, East African Literature Bureau, 1961.

Kipsigis—History

1805. Mwanzi, Henry A. *A history of the Kipsigis.* Nairobi, East African Literature Bureau, 1977.

Kisumu—Geography

1806. Oucho, John O. *The port of Kisumu in the Lake Victoria trade: a geographical study.* Nairobi, Kenya Literature Bureau, 1980.

Kisumu—Land Use

1807. Olima, Washington H. A. *The land use planning in provincial towns of Kenya: a case study of Kisumu and Eldoret towns.* Dortmund, Projekt Verlag, 1993.

Kitale—Social Conditions

1808. Muller, M. S. *Action and interaction: social relationships in a low-income housing estate in Kitale, Kenya.* Leiden, African Studies Centre, 1976.

Kiziba—History

1809. Ishumi, Abel G. M. *Kiziba: the cultural heritage of an old African kingdom*. Syracuse, Syracuse University, Maxwell School of Citizenship and Public Affairs, 1980.

Konso—Ethnography

1810. Hallpike, C. R. *The Konso of Ethiopia: a study of the values of a Cushitic people*. London, Oxford University Press, 1972.

Koobi Fora

1811. Harris, J. M. (ed.) *Koobi Fora Research Project, Vol. 3. The fossil ungulates: geology, fossil artiodactyls and palaeoenvironments*. Oxford, Clarendon Press, 1991.

1812. Harris, J. M. (ed.) *Koobi Fora Research Project, Vol. 2. The fossil ungulates: proboscidea, perssodactyla and suidae*. Oxford, Clarendon Press, 1983.

1813. Leakey, Meave G., and Richard E. Leakey (eds.) *Koobi Fora Research Project, Vol. 1. The fossil hominids and an introduction to their context, 1968–1974*. Oxford, Clarendon Press, 1978.

1814. Wood, Bernard (ed.) *Koobi Fora Research Project, Vol. 4. Hominid cranial remains*. Oxford, Clarendon Press, 1991.

Kora National Reserve

1815. Coe, Malcolm James. *Islands in the bush: Kora National Reserve, Kenya*. London, George Philip, 1985.

Kordofanian Languages

1816. Schadeberg, Thilo C. *A survey of Kordofanian*. Hamburg, Helmut Buske, 1981. 2 vols.

Kresh Languages

1817. Santandrea, Stefano. *The Kresh group, Aja and Baka languages, Sudan*. Napoli, Istituto Universitario Orientale, 1976.

Krongo—Language

1818. Reh, Mechthild. *Die Krongo-Sprache (nìnò mó-dì): Beschreibung, Texte, Wörterverzeichnis*. Berlin, Dietrich Reimer, 1985.

Kuliak Languages

1819. Heine, Bernd. *The Kuliak languages of eastern Uganda*. Nairobi, East African Publishing House, 1976.

1820. Lamberti, Marcello. *Kuliak and Cushitic: a comparative study*. Heidelberg, Carl Winter, 1988.

Kunama—Language

1821. Böhm, Gerhard. *Grammatik der Kunama-Sprache.* Wien, Institut für Afrikanistik und Ägyptologie der Universität Wien, 1984.

Kuria—Ethnography

1822. Rwezaura, Barthazar Aloys. *Traditional family law and change in Tanzania: a study of the Kuria social system.* Baden-Baden, Nomos, 1985.

1823. Tobisson, E. *Family dynamics among the Kuria, agro-pastoralists in northern Tanzania.* Göteborg, Acta Universitatis Gothoburgensis, 1986.

Kuria—History

1824. Abuso, Paul Asaka. *A traditonal history of the Abakuria, c. A.D. 1400–1914.* Nairobi, Kenya Literature Bureau, 1980.

Kwaya—Ethnography

1825. Huber, H. *Marriage and the family in rural Bukwaya.* Fribourg, University Press, 1973.

Lake Turkana

1826. Butzer, Karl. *Recent history of an Ethiopian delta: the Omo River and the level of Lake Turkana.* Chicago, University of Chicago, Department of Geography, 1971.

1827. Imperato, Pascal James. *Arthur Donaldson Smith and the exploration of Lake Rudolf.* Lake Success, Medical Society of the State of New York, 1987.

Lamu—History

1828. Ylvisaker, Marguerite. *Lamu in the nineteenth century: land, trade and politics.* Boston, Boston University, African Studies Center, 1979.

Lamu—Religion

1829. El Zein, Abdul Hamid M. *The sacred meadows: a structural analysis of religious symbolism in an East African town.* Evanston, Northwestern University Press, 1974.

Lamu—Social Conditions

1830. Ghaidan, Usam. *Lamu: a study of the Swahili town.* Nairobi, East African Literature Bureau, 1975.

1831. Prins, Adriaan Hendrik Johan. *Sailing from Lamu: a study of maritime culture in Islamic East Africa.* Assen, Van Gorcum, 1965.

Lamu—Women

1832. Le Guennec-Coppens, Françoise. *Femmes voilées de Lamu, Kenya: variations culturelles et dynamiques sociales.* Paris, Éditions Recherche sur les Civilisations, 1983.

Land—East Africa

1833. Obol-Ochola, James Yonason (ed.) *Land law reform in East Africa: papers delivered to a seminar organised by the Milton Obote Foundation, Adult Education Centre.* Kampala, Milton Obote Foundation, Adult Education Centre, 1969.

Lango—Ethnography

1834. Curley, Richard T. *Elders, shades and women: ceremonial change in Lango, Uganda.* Berkeley, University of California Press, 1973.

Lango—History

1835. Tosh, John. *Clan leaders and colonial chiefs in Lango: the political history of an East African stateless society, c. 1800–1939.* Oxford, Clarendon Press, 1978.

Lango—Language

1836. Noonan, Michael. *A grammar of Lango.* Berlin, Mouton de Gruyter, 1992.

Language—East Africa

1837. Brenzinger, Matthias. *Language death: factual and theoretical explorations with special reference to East Africa.* Berlin, Mouton de Gruyter, 1992.

1838. Molnos, Angela. *Language problems in Africa: a bibliography, 1946–67. A summary of the present situation with special reference to Kenya, Tanzania, and Uganda.* Nairobi, East African Research Information Centre, 1969.

1839. Whiteley, W. H. (ed.) *Language and social change: problems of multilingualism with special reference to eastern Africa.* London, Oxford University Press, 1971.

Language—Northeast Africa

1840. Tucker, Archibald Norman, and Margaret Arminel Bryan. *Linguistic analysis: the non-Bantu languages of north-eastern Africa.* London, Oxford University Press, 1966.

Law—East Africa

1841. Eze, Osita C. *The legal status of foreign investments in the East African Common Market.* Leiden, Sijthoff, 1975.

1842. Harvey, W. B. *Introduction to the legal system in East Africa.* Kampala, East African Literature Bureau, 1975.

1843. Hodgin, R. W. *Law of contract in East Africa.* Kampala, East African Literature Bureau, 1975.

1844. Kanyeihamba, George W., and J. P. W. B. McAuslan (eds.) *Urban legal problems in eastern Africa.* Uppsala, Scandinavian Institute of African Studies, 1978.

1845. Katende, J. W., et al. *The law of business organisations in East and Central Africa.* Nairobi, East African Literature Bureau, 1976.

1846. Morris, Henry Francis, and James S. Read. *Indirect rule and the search for justice: essays in East African legal history.* Oxford, Clarendon Press, 1972.

1847. Oluyede, Peter. *Administrative law in East Africa.* Nairobi, East African Literature Bureau, 1973.

1848. Sawyerr, G. F. A. *East African law and social change.* Nairobi, East African Publishing House, 1967.

1849. Spry, J. *The courts of appeal for eastern Africa.* London, Commonwealth Secretariat, 1991.

1850. Thomas, Philip Aneurin (ed.) *Private enterprise and the East African Company.* Dar es Salaam, Tanzania Publishing House, 1969.

Libraries—East Africa

1851. Kaungamno, Ezekiel E., and C. S. Ilomo. *Books build nations, Vol. 1: library services in West and East Africa.* Dar es Salaam, Tanzania Library Service, 1979.

1852. Wallenius, Anna-Britta (ed.) *Libraries in East Africa.* Uppsala, Scandinavian Institute of African Studies, 1971.

Literature—East Africa

1853. Gurr, Andrew, and Angus Calder (eds.) *Writers in East Africa.* Nairobi, East African Literature Bureau, 1974.

1854. Kariara, Jonathan, and Ellen Kitonga. *An introduction to East African poetry.* Nairobi, Oxford University Press, 1976.

1855. Killam, G. D. (ed.) *The writings of East and Central Africa.* Nairobi, Heinemann, 1984.

1856. Lindfors, Bernth (ed.) *Masungumzo: interviews with East African writers, publishers, editors and scholars.* Athens, Ohio University, Center for International Studies, 1980.

1857. Liyong, Taban lo. *Another last word.* Nairobi, Heinemann Kenya, 1990.

1858. Wanjala, Chris. *For home and freedom.* Nairobi, Kenya Literature Bureau, 1980.

1859. Wanjala, Chris. *The season of harvest: some notes on East African literature.* Nairobi, Kenya Literature Bureau, 1978.

Lotuho—Ethnography

1860. Grüb, Andreas. *The Lotuho of the southern Sudan: an ethnological monograph.* Stuttgart, Franz Steiner, 1992.

Lugbara—Bibliography

1861. Dalfovo, Albert Titus. *A bibliography of Lugbara studies and literature.* Revised and enlarged edition. Kampala, Makerere University, 1988.

Lugbara—Ethnography

1862. Middleton, John. *Lugbara religion: ritual and authority among an East African people.* London, Oxford University Press, 1960.

1863. Middleton, John. *The Lugbara of Uganda.* New York, Holt, Rinehart and Winston, 1965.

Lugbara—Language

1864. Barr, L. I. *A course in Lugbara.* Nairobi, East African Literature Bureau, 1965.

1865. Crazzolara, J. Pasquale. *A study of the Logbara (Ma'adi) language, grammar and vocabulary.* London, Oxford University Press, 1960.

Luguru—Land

1866. Young, Roland, and Henry A. Fosbrooke. *Land and politics among the Luguru of Tanganyika.* London, Routledge & Kegan Paul, 1960.

Lungu—Language

1867. Kagaya, Ryohei. *A classified vocabulary of the Lungu language.* Tokyo, Institute for the Study of Languages and Cultures of Asia and Africa, 1987.

Luo—Bibliography

1868. DuPre, Carole E. *The Luo of Kenya: an annotated bibliography.* Washington, Institute for Cross Cultural Research, 1968.

Luo—Ethics

1869. Ocholla-Ayayo, A. B. C. *Traditional ideology and ethics among the southern Luo.* Uppsala, Scandinavian Institute of African Studies, 1976.

Luo—Ethnobotany

1870. Kokwaro, J. O. *Luo-English botanical dictionary of plant names and uses.* Nairobi, East African Publishing House, 1972.

Luo—Ethnography

1871. Hauge, Hans-Egil. *Luo religion and folklore.* Oslo, Universitetsforlaget, 1974.

1872. Parker, Shipton. *Bitter money: cultural economy and some African meanings of forbidden commodities.* Washington, American Anthropological Association, 1989.

1873. Parkin, David. *The cultural definition of political response: lineal destiny among the Luo*. London, Academic Press, 1978.

Luo—History

1874. Ayot, Henry Okello. *A history of Luo-Abasuba of western Kenya from A.D. 1760–1940*. Nairobi, Kenya Literature Bureau, 1979.

1875. Ogot, Bethwell A. *History of the southern Luo. Vol. 1: migration and settlement, 1500–1900*. Nairobi, East African Publishing House, 1967.

1876. Onyango-ku-Odongo, J. M., and James Bertin Webster (eds.) *The central Lwo during the Aconya*. Nairobi, East African Literature Bureau, 1976.

1877. Wipper, Audrey. *Rural rebels: a study of Luo protest movements in Kenya*. Nairobi, Oxford University Press, 1977.

Luo—Language

1878. Jacobson, Leon Carl. *DhoLuo vowel harmony: a phonetic investigation*. Los Angeles, University of California, 1978.

1879. Okoth-Okombo, Duncan. *Dholuo morphophonemics in a generative framework*. Berlin, Dietrich Reimer, 1982.

1880. Omondi, Lucia Ndong'a. *The major syntactic structures of Dholuo*. Berlin, Dietrich Reimer, 1982.

Luo—Material Culture

1881. Ocholla-Ayayo, A. B. C. *The Luo culture: a reconstruction of the material culture patterns of a traditional African society*. Stuttgart, Franz Steiner, 1980.

Luo—Psychology

1882. Dittmann, F. *Kultur und Leistung: zur Frage der Leistungsdispositionen bei Luo und Indern in Kenia*. Saarbrücken, Sozialwissenschaftlicher Studienkreis, 1973.

Luo—Religion

1883. P'Bitek, O. *Religion of the central Luo*. Nairobi, East African Literature Bureau, 1971.

Luyia—Ethnography

1884. Malusu, Joseph. *The Luyia way of death, based on the Isukha people of Kakamega district*. Nairobi, Oxford University Press, 1978.

Luyia—History

1885. Osogo, John N. B. *A history of the Baluyia*. Nairobi, Oxford University Press, 1966.

129

1886. Were, Gideon S. *A history of the Abaluyia of western Kenya, c. 1500–1930.* Nairobi, East African Publishing House, 1967.

Luyia—Language

1887. Angogo Kanyoro, Rachel. *Unity in diversity: a linguistic survey of the Abaluyia of western Kenya.* Vienna, Institut für Afrikanistik und Ägyptologie der Universität Wien, 1983.

Maale—Ethnography

1888. Donham, Donald L. *History, power, ideology: central issues in Marxism and anthropology.* Cambridge, Cambridge University Press, 1990.

1889. Donham, Donald L. *Work and power in Maale, Ethiopia.* Ann Arbor, UMI Research Press, 1985.

Maasai—Art and Artists

1890. Turle, Gillies. *The art of the Maasai: 300 newly discovered objects and works of art.* New York, Knopf, 1992.

Maasai—Description

1891. Amin, Mohamed, et al. *The last of the Maasai.* London, Bodley Head, 1987.

1892. Bentsen, Cheryl. *Maasai days.* New York, Summit Books, 1989.

1893. Solomon ole Saibull and Rachel Carr. *Herd and spear.* London, Collins and Harvill Press, 1981.

1894. Tepilit ole Saitoti and Carol Beckwith. *Maasai.* London, Elm Tree Books, 1980.

Maasai—Ecology

1895. Århem, Kaj. *Pastoral man in the garden of Eden: the Maasai of the Ngorongoro conservation area, Tanzania.* Uppsala, Scandinavian Institute of African Studies, 1985.

Maasai—Ethnography

1896. Ahr, Christina. *Fruchtbarkeit und "Respekt": filmethnologische Untersuchungen eines Geschlechterkonflikts um ein Ritual bei den Maasai.* Göttingen, Re, 1991.

1897. Gulliver, Philip H. *Social control in an African society: a study of the Arusha, agricultural Masai of northern Tanganyika.* London, Routledge & Kegan Paul, 1963.

1898. Hauge, Hans-Egil. *Maasai religion and folklore.* Nairobi, City Printing Works, 1979.

1899. Hurskainen, A. *Cattle and culture: the structure of a pastoral Parakuyo society.* Helsinki, Finnish Oriental Society, 1984.

1900. Laube, R. *Maasai: Identität und sozialer Wandel bei den Maasai*. Basel, Social Strategies Publishers Cooperative, 1986.

1901. Rigby, Peter. *Cattle, capitalism and class: Ilparakuyo Maasai transformations*. Philadelphia, Temple University Press, 1992.

1902. Spear, Thomas, and Richard Waller (eds.) *Being Maasai: ethnicity and identity in East Africa*. London, James Currey, 1993.

1903. Spencer, Paul. *The Maasai of Matapato: a study of rituals of rebellion*. Manchester, Manchester University Press, 1988.

1904. Wagner-Glenn, Doris. *Searching for a baby's calabash: a study of Arusha Maasai fertility songs as crystallized expression of central cultural values*. Affalterbach, Philipp Verlag, 1992.

Maasai—History

1905. Tepilit ole Saitoti. *The worlds of a Maasai warrior: an autobiography*. London, Andre Deutsch, 1986.

Maasai—Land

1906. Rutten, M. M. *Selling wealth to buy poverty: the process of the individualization of landownership among the Maasai pastoralists of Kajiado District, Kenya, 1890–1990*. Saarbrücken, Breitenbach, 1992.

Maasai—Language

1907. Heine, Bernd, and U. Claudi. *On the rise of grammatical categories: some examples from Maa*. Berlin, Dietrich Reimer, 1986.

1908. Mol, F. *Maa: a dictionary of the Maasai language and folklore, English-Maasai*. Nairobi, Marketing and Publishing, 1978.

1909. Sim, Ronald J. *A sociolinguistic profile of Maasai-Samburu-Ilchamus languages, Kenya*. Dallas, Summer Institute of Linguistics, 1980.

1910. Vossen, Rainer. *Towards a comparative study of the Maa dialects of Kenya and Tanzania*. Hamburg, Helmut Buske, 1987.

Maasai—Material Culture

1911. Kalter, Johannes. *Die materielle Kultur der Maasai und ihr Wandel*. Bremen, Übersee-Museum, 1978.

Maasai—Missionaries

1912. Neckebrouck, Valeer. *Resistant peoples: the case of the pastoral Maasai of East Africa*. Roma, Editrice Pontificia Università Gregoriana, 1993.

Maasai—Oral Literature

1913. Kipury, Naomi N. Ole. *Oral literature of the Maasai*. London, Heinemann, 1983.

Maasai — Pastoral Production

1914. Fiocco, L., and G. Sivini. *Allevamento tradizionale et progetti di sviluppo in Africa: la riproduzione sociale dei maasai.* Roma, Asal, 1988.

1915. Ndagala, D. *Territory, pastoralists and livestock resource control among the Kisongo Maasai.* Uppsala, Acta Universitatis Upsaliensis, 1993.

1916. Solomon Bekure, et al. (eds.) *Maasai herding: an analysis of the livestock production system of Maasai pastoralists in eastern Kajiado District, Kenya.* Addis Ababa, International Livestock Centre for Africa, 1991.

Maasai — Religion

1917. Priest, Doug. *Doing theology with the Maasai.* Pasadena, William Carey Library, 1990.

Maasai — Social Conditions

1918. Gorham, Alex. *Education and social change in a pastoral society.* Stockholm, University of Stockholm, Institute of International Education, 1980.

1919. Holland, Killian. *On the horns of a dilemma: the future of the Maasai.* Montreal, McGill University, Centre for Developing-Area Studies, 1987.

1920. Kituyi, Mukhisa. *The state and the pastoralists: the marginalization of the Kenyan Maasai.* Bergen, Chr. Michelsen Institute, 1985.

1921. Kituyi, Mukhisa. *Becoming Kenyans: socio-economic transformation of the pastoral Maasai.* Nairobi, Acts Press, 1990.

1922. Sonnen-Wilke, Christa. *Probleme der Ansiedlung und Integration von afrikanischen Nomadenvölkern am Beispiel der Maasai in Tanzania.* Hamburg, Institut für Afrika-Kunde, 1981.

Maasai — Women

1923. Mitzlaff, Ulrike. *Maasai-Frauen: Leben in einer patriarchalischen Gesellschaft. Feldforschung bei den Parakuyo, Tansania.* München, Trickster Verlag, 1988.

1924. Talle, Aude. *Women at a loss: changes in Maasai pastoralism and their effects on gender relations.* Stockholm, University, Department of Social Anthropology, 1988.

Madi — Language

1925. Bilbao, O., and L. Moizi. *Ma'di-English dictionary.* Limone, Casa Comboni, 1984.

Majangir — Ethnography

1926. Stauder, Jack. *The Majangir: ecology and society of a southwest Ethiopian people.* Cambridge, Cambridge University Press, 1971.

Makonde—Art and Artists

1927. Korn, J. *Modern Makonde art*. London, Hamlyn, 1974.

1928. Mohl, Max. *Masterpieces of the Makonde: an East African documentation*. Heidelberg, Max Mohl, 1990. 2 vols.

1929. Stout, J. Anthony. *Modern Makonde sculpture*. London, Kegan Paul, 1966.

1930. Walloschek, P. Arnold. *Ebenholz und Elfenbein: Reichtum der Makonde-schnitzerei*. St. Ottilien, EOS Verlag, 1982.

Makonde—Colonial History

1931. Liebenow, J. Gus. *Colonial rule and political development in Tanzania: the case of the Makonde*. Evanston, Northwestern University Press, 1971.

Makonde—Ethnography

1932. Pollig, Hermann (ed.) *Makonde: eine ostafrikanische Dokumentation*. Stuttgart, Forum für Kulturaustausch, Institut für Auslandsbeziehungen, 1971.

Malindi—History

1933. Martin, Esmond Bradley. *The history of Malindi: a geographical analysis of an East African coastal town from the Portuguese period to the present*. Nairobi, East African Literature Bureau, 1973.

Manda Island

1934. Chittick, Neville. *Manda: excavations at an island port on the Kenya coast*. Nairobi, British Institute in Eastern Africa, 1984.

Mandara—History

1935. Barkindo, Bawuro Mubi. *The Sultanate of Mandara to 1902: history of the evolution, development and collapse of a central Sudanese kingdom*. Stuttgart, Franz Steiner, 1989.

Mandari—Ethnography

1936. Buxton, Jean C. *Chiefs and strangers: a study of political assimilation among the Mandari*. Oxford, Clarendon Press, 1963.

1937. Buxton, Jean C. *Religion and healing in Mandari*. Oxford, Clarendon Press, 1973.

Mande Languages

1938. Böhm, Gerhard. *Elemente des Satzbaus in den Mande-Sprachen und ihre Verbreitung im Sudan*. Wien, Afro-Pub, 1984.

Mapping—East Africa

1939. McGrath, Gerald. *The surveying and mapping of British East Africa, 1890 to 1946: origins, development and coordination.* Toronto, B. V. Gutsell, 1976.

Marakwet—Ethnography

1940. Kipkorir, Ben E. *The Marakwet of Kenya: a preliminary study.* Nairobi, East African Literature Bureau, 1973.

1941. Moore, Henrietta L. *Space, text and gender: an anthropological study of the Marakwet of Kenya.* Cambridge, Cambridge University Press, 1986.

Marine Resources—East Africa

1942. Okidi, Odidi C. (ed.) *Management of coastal and offshore resources in eastern Africa: papers presented at the workshop held at the Institute for Development Studies, University of Nairobi, April 26–29, 1977.* Nairobi, University of Nairobi, Institute for Development Studies, 1978.

Markets—East Africa

1943. Wood, L. J. *Market origins and development in East Africa.* Kampala, Makerere University, Department of Geography, 1974.

Marriage—East Africa

1944. Hastings, Adrian. *Christian marriage in Africa: being a report commissioned by the Archbishops of Cape Town, Central Africa, Kenya, Tanzania and Uganda.* London, S.P.C.K., 1973.

Masalit—History

1945. Kapteijns, Lidwien. *Mahdist faith and Sudanic tradition: the history of the Masalit Sultanate, 1870–1930.* London, KPI, 1985.

Masalit—Language

1946. Edgar, John. *A Masalit grammar with notes on other languages of Darfur and Wadai.* Berlin, Dietrich Reimer, 1989.

Massawa—History

1947. Talhami, Ghada Hashem. *Suakin and Massawa under Egyptian rule, 1865–1885.* Washington, University Press of America, 1979.

Mau Mau

1948. Barnett, Donald L., and Karari Njama. *Mau Mau from within: an analysis of Kenya's peasant revolt.* New York, Monthly Review Press, 1966.

1949. Buijtenhuijs, Robert. *Essays on Mau Mau: contributions to Mau Mau historiography*. Leiden, African Studies Centre, 1982.

1950. Buijtenhuijs, Robert. *Le mouvement "Mau Mau."* The Hague, Mouton, 1971.

1951. Buijtenhuijs, Robert. *Mau Mau, twenty years after: the myth and the survivors*. The Hague, Mouton, 1973.

1952. Clayton, Anthony. *Counter-insurgency in Kenya: a study of military operations against Mau Mau*. Nairobi, Transafrica Publishers, 1976.

1953. Corfield, F. D. *Historical survey of the origins and growth of Mau Mau*. London, H.M.S.O., 1960.

1954. Edgerton, Robert B. *Mau Mau: an African crucible*. London, I. B. Tauris, 1990.

1955. Furedi, F. *The Mau Mau war in perspective*. London, James Currey, 1989.

1956. Gakaara wa Wanjau. *Mau Mau author in detention*. Nairobi, Heinemann, 1988.

1957. Gikoyo, Gucu G. *We fought for freedom. Tulipigania uhuru*. Nairobi, East African Publishing House, 1979.

1958. Itote, Waruhiu. *Mau Mau in action*. Nairobi, Transafrica, 1979.

1959. Jackson, Kennell, and Marshall Clough. *A bibliography on Mau Mau*. Stanford, Stanford University Press, 1975.

1960. Kanogo, T. *Squatters and the roots of Mau Mau, 1905–63*. London, James Currey, 1987.

1961. Kariuki, Josiah Mwangi. *"Mau Mau" detainee: the account by a Kenya African of his experiences in detention camps, 1953–1960*. Nairobi, Oxford University Press, 1975.

1962. Kitson, Frank. *Gangs and counter-gangs*. London, Barrie and Rockliff, 1960.

1963. Maina wa Kinyatti (ed.) *Thunder from the mountains: Mau Mau patriotic songs*. London, Zed Books, 1980.

1964. Maina, P. *Six Maumau generals*. Nairobi, Gazelle Books, 1977.

1965. Majdalany, Fred. *State of emergency: the full story of Mau Mau*. London, Longmans, 1962.

1966. Maloba, W. O. *Mau Mau and Kenya: an analysis of a peasant revolt*. Bloomington, Indiana University Press, 1993.

1967. Muriithi, J. Kiboi. *War in the forest*. Nairobi, East African Publishing House, 1971.

1968. Njagi, David. *The last Mau Mau field marshals. Kenya's freedom war, 1952–63 and beyond: their own story*. Meru, Ngwataniro Self-Help Group, 1993.

1969. Presley, Cora Ann. *Kikuyu women, the "Mau Mau" rebellion and social change in Kenya.* Boulder, Westview Press, 1992.

1970. Rosberg, Carl G., and John Nottingham. *The myth of Mau Mau: nationalism in Kenya.* New York, Praeger, 1966.

1971. Throup, David. *Economic and social origins of Mau Mau, 1945–53.* London, James Currey, 1987.

1972. Vehys, L. *A history of the Mau Mau movement in Kenya.* Prague, Charles University, 1970.

Mbeere—Environment

1973. Riley, Bernard W., and David Brokensha. *The Mbeere in Kenya. Volume 1: changing rural ecology.* Lanham, University Press of America, 1989.

Mbeere—Ethnobotany

1974. Riley, Bernard W., and David Brokensha. *The Mbeere in Kenya. Volume 2: botanical identities and uses.* Lanham, University Press of America, 1989.

Mbeere—Land

1975. Glazier, J. *Land and the uses of tradition among the Mbeere of Kenya.* Lanham, University Press of America, 1985.

Mboya, Tom

1976. Goldsworthy, David. *Tom Mboya: the man Kenya wanted to forget.* London, Heinemann, 1982.

Medicinal Plants—East Africa

1977. Kokwaro, J. O. *Medicinal plants of East Africa.* Kampala, East African Literature Bureau, 1976.

Mengo—Urban Development

1978. Scaff, Alvin H., et al. *Recommendations for urban development in Kampala and Mengo.* New York, United Nations, Commissioner for Technical Assistance, Department of Economic and Social Affairs, 1964.

Meroe

1979. Adams, William Y. *Meroitic north and south: a study in cultural contrasts.* Berlin, Akademie-Verlag, 1976.

1980. Ahmed, Khidir Abdelkarim. *Meroitic settlement in the central Sudan: an analysis of sites in the Nile Valley and the western Butana.* Oxford, British Archaeological Reports, 1984.

1981. Donadoni, Sergio, and Steffen Wenig (eds.) *Studia Meroitica 1984: proceedings of the fifth international conference for Meroitic studies.* Berlin, Akademie-Verlag, 1989.

1982. El Zaki, O. H. *Amun: role and iconography in the Meroitic religion.* Khartoum, University of Khartoum, Graduate College, 1983.

1983. Hakem, A. M. A. *Meroitic architecture: a background of an African civilization.* Khartoum, Khartoum University Press, 1989.

1984. Hintze, Fritz. *Beiträge zur meroitischen Grammatik.* Berlin, Akademie-Verlag, 1979.

1985. Hofmann, Inge, and Herbert Tomandl. *Die Bedeutung des Tieres in der meroitischen Kultur vor dem Hintergrund der Fauna und ihrer Darstellung bis zum Ende der Napata-Zeit.* Wien, Institut für Afrikanistik und Ägyptologie der Universität Wien, 1987.

1986. Hofmann, Inge. *Beiträge zur meroitischen Chronologie.* Sankt Augustin, Anthropos Institut, 1978.

1987. Hofmann, Inge. *Material für eine meroitische Grammatik.* Wien, Institut für Afrikanistik und Ägyptologie der Universität Wien, 1981.

1988. Shinnie, P. L. *Meroe: a civilisation of the Sudan.* London, Thames and Hudson, 1967.

1989. Török, László. *Der meroitische Staat 1: Untersuchungen und Urkunden zur Geschichte des Sudan im Altertum.* Berlin, Akademie-Verlag, 1986.

Meru—Agriculture

1990. Bernard, Frank. *East of Mount Kenya: Meru agriculture in transition.* Munich, Weltforum-Verlag, 1972.

Meru—Ethnography

1991. Moore, Sally Falk. *The Chagga and Meru of Tanzania.* London, International African Institute, 1977.

Meru—History

1992. Fadiman, Jeffrey A. *An oral history of tribal warfare.* Athens, Ohio University Press, 1982.

1993. Fadiman, Jeffrey A. *Mountain warriors.* Athens, Ohio University, Center for International Studies, 1980.

1994. Fadiman, Jeffrey A. *The moment of conquest: Meru, Kenya, 1907.* Athens, Ohio University, Center for International Studies, 1979.

1995. Fadiman, Jeffrey A. *When we began there were witchmen: an oral history from Mount Kenya.* Berkeley, University of California Press, 1993.

1996. Nelson, Anton. *The freemen of Meru.* London, Oxford University Press, 1967.

Meru—Land

1997. Japhet, Kirilo, and Earle Seaton. *The Meru lands case.* Nairobi, East African Publishing House, 1967.

Mijikenda—Ethnography

1998. Slater, Mariam K. *African odyssey.* Bloomington, Indiana University Press, 1977.

Mijikenda—History

1999. Spear, Thomas. *The Kaya complex: a history of the Mijikenda peoples of the Kenya coast to 1900.* Nairobi, Kenya Literature Bureau, 1978.

2000. Spear, Thomas. *Traditions of origin and their interpretation: the Mijikenda of Kenya.* Athens, Ohio University, Center for International Studies, 1981.

2001. Willis, Justin. *Mombasa, the Swahili and the making of the Mijikenda.* Oxford, Clarendon Press, 1993.

Military History—East Africa

2002. Grahame, Iain. *Jambo effendi: seven years with the King's African Rifles.* London, J. A. Allen, 1968.

2003. Hodges, G. *The Carrier Corps: military labor in the East African campaign, 1914–1918.* New York, Greenwood Press, 1986.

Military History—Northeast Africa

2004. Misuraca, Pepita. *I miei racconti africani.* Palermo, Scuola Grafica Salesiana, 1977.

Miri—Social Conditions

2005. Baumann, G. *National integration and local integrity: the Miri of the Nuba mountains in the Sudan.* Oxford, Clarendon Press, 1987.

Missionaries—East Africa

2006. Eggert, J. *Missionsschule und sozialer Wandel in Ostafrika.* Gutersloh, Bertelsmann Universitäts Verlag, 1970.

2007. Kendall, R. Elliott. *Charles New and the East Africa mission.* Nairobi, Kenya Literature Bureau, 1978.

2008. Oliver, Roland. *The missionary factor in East Africa.* Second edition. London, Longmans, 1965.

Mogadishu—Architecture

2009. Inzerillo, Michelle. *Le moschée di Mogadiscio: contributo alla conoscenza dell'architettura islamica.* Palermo, Italo-Latino-Americana Palma, 1980.

Mogadishu—Informal Economy

2010. Aboagye, A. A. *The informal sector in Mogadishu: an analysis of a survey.* Addis Ababa, International Labour Organisation, 1988.

Mogadishu—Woodfuel

2011. Laux, Hubert. *Die Brennholz-und Holzkohleversorgung in Mogadishu, Somalia.* Hamburg, Institut für Afrika-Kunde, 1989.

Mohammed Abdalle Hassan

2012. Abdi Sheik Abdi. *Divine madness: Mohammed Abdalle Hassan of Somalia, 1865–1920.* London, Zed Books, 1992.

2013. Beachey, R. W. *The warrior mullah: the Horn aflame, 1892–1920.* London, Bellew, 1990.

2014. Samatar, Said S. *Oral poetry and Somali nationalism: the case of Sayyid Mahammad Abdille Hasan.* Cambridge, Cambridge University Press, 1982.

Mombasa—Architecture

2015. Sabini, Maurizio. *The architecture of Mombasa.* Vienna, n. publ., 1993. 2 vols.

Mombasa—Geography

2016. Blij, Harm J. de. *Mombasa: an African city.* Evanston, Northwestern University Press, 1968.

Mombasa—Housing

2017. Stren, R. E. *Housing the urban poor in Africa: policy, politics and bureaucracy in Mombasa.* Berkeley, University of California, 1978.

Mombasa—Labor

2018. Cooper, F. J. *On the African waterfront: urban disorder and the transformation of work in colonial Mombasa.* New Haven, Yale University Press, 1987.

Mombasa—Social Conditions

2019. Kindy, Hyder. *Life and politics in Mombasa.* Nairobi, East African Publishing House, 1972.

Mombasa—Women

2020. Strobel, M. *Muslim women in Mombasa, 1890–1975.* New Haven, Yale University Press, 1979.

Morogoro—Economy

2021. Lundqvist, Jan. *The economic structure of Morogoro town: some sectoral and regional characteristics of a medium-sized African town.* Uppsala, Scandinavian Institute of African Studies, 1973.

Mount Kenya

2022. Coe, Malcolm James. *The ecology of the alpine zone of Mount Kenya.* The Hague, W. Junk, 1967.

2023. Decurtins, Silvio. *Hydrological investigations in the Mount Kenya sub-catchment of the Ewaso Ng'iro river.* Bern, Arbeitsgemeinschaft Geographica Bernensia, 1988.

2024. Mackinder, H. J. *The first ascent of Mount Kenya.* London, Christopher Hurst, 1991.

2025. Mahaney, William C. *Ice on the Equator: quaternary geology of Mount Kenya, East Africa.* Sister Bay, William Caxton, 1990.

2026. Reader, John. *Mount Kenya.* London, Elm Tree Books, 1989.

2027. Winiger, M. (ed.) *Mount Kenya area: contributions to ecology and socio-economy.* Berne, University of Berne, Institute of Geography, 1986.

2028. Winiger, M., et al. (eds.) *Mount Kenya area: differentiation and dynamics of a tropical mountain ecosystem. Proceedings of the international workshop . . . held at Nanyuki . . . 1989.* Berne, Geographica Bernensia, 1990.

Mount Kilimanjaro

2029. Hutchinson, J. A. (ed.) *Kilimanjaro.* Revised edition. Dar es Salaam, Tanzania Society, 1974.

2030. Newmark, William D. *The conservation of Mount Kilimanjaro.* Gland, IUCN, 1991.

2031. Reader, John. *Kilimanjaro.* London, Elm Tree Books, 1982.

Mountains—East Africa

2032. Rheker, J. R., et al. *Bibliography of east African mountains, compiled on the occasion of the "workshop on ecology and socio-economy of Mount Kenya area" in Nanyuki, Kenya, March 5–12th 1989.* Berne, University of Berne, Institute of Geography, 1989.

Mundu—Language

2033. Santandrea, Stefano. *Note grammaticali e lessicali sul gruppo Feroge e sul Mundu, Sudan.* Napoli, Istituto Universitario Orientale, 1969.

Murle—Ethnography

2034. Klausberger, Friedrich. *Ruoni Murlen, Recht ohne Gesetz: eine rechtsethnologische Studie der Murle im Süd-Sudan.* Göttingen, Edition Re, 1989.

2035. Lewis, B. A. *The Murle: red chiefs and black commoners.* Oxford, Clarendon Press, 1972.

Murle—Language

2036. Arensen, Jonathan E. *A grammar of the Murle language.* Pibor, Summer Institute of Linguistics, 1979.

2037. Arensen, Jonathan E. *Mice are men: language and society among the Murle of Sudan.* Dallas, Summer Institute of Linguistics, 1992.

Music—East Africa

2038. Kubik, Gerhard. *Musikgeschichte in Bildern: Ostafrika.* Leipzig, VEB Deutscher Verlag für Musik, 1982.

Nairobi—Agriculture

2039. Freeman, D. B. *A city of farmers: informal urban agriculture in the open spaces of Nairobi, Kenya.* Montreal, McGill/Queens University Press, 1991.

Nairobi—Housing

2040. Mitullah, Winnie V. *State policy and urban housing in Kenya: the case of low income housing in Nairobi.* Nairobi, University of Nairobi, Institute for Development Studies, 1992.

Nairobi—Local Government

2041. Werlin, Herbert Holland. *Governing an African city: a study of Nairobi.* New York, Africana Publishing, 1974.

Nairobi—Politics

2042. Ross, Marc Howard. *Grass roots in an African city: political behavior in Nairobi.* Cambridge, Mass., MIT Press, 1975.

Nairobi—Population

2043. Etherton, D. (ed.) *Mathare valley: a case study of uncontrolled settlement in Nairobi.* Nairobi, University of Nairobi, Housing Research and Development Unit, 1973.

Nairobi—Prostitution

2044. White, Louise. *The comforts of home: prostitution in colonial Nairobi.* Chicago, University of Chicago Press, 1990.

Nairobi—Social Conditions

2045. Hake, Andrew. *African metropolis: Nairobi's self-help city.* London, Chatto and Windus for Sussex University Press, 1977.

2046. Morgan, W. T. W. (ed.) *Nairobi: city and region.* Nairobi, Oxford University Press, 1967.

Nairobi—Women Traders

2047. Adagala, K. *Self-employed women in the peri-urban setting: petty traders in Nairobi.* Nairobi, Derika Associates, 1985.

Nandi—Ethnography

2048. Langley, Myrtle S. *The Nandi of Kenya: life crisis rituals in a period of change.* London, Christopher Hurst, 1979.

Nandi—History

2049. Matson, A. T. *Nandi resistance to British rule, 1890–1906.* Nairobi, East African Publishing House, 1972.

2050. Walter, B. *Territorial expansion of the Nandi of Kenya, 1500–1905.* Athens, Ohio University, Center for International Studies, 1970.

Nandi—Language

2051. Creider, Chet A., and Jane Tapsubei Creider. *A grammar of Nandi.* Hamburg, Helmut Buske, 1989.

Nandi—Women

2052. Oboler, R. S. *Women, power, and economic change: the Nandi of Kenya.* Stanford, Stanford University Press, 1985.

National Parks—East Africa

2053. Williams, John George. *Field guide to the national parks of East Africa.* Revised edition. London, Collins, 1981.

Ndendeuli—Ethnography

2054. Gulliver, Philip H. *Neighbours and networks: the idiom of kinship in social action among the Ndendeuli of Tanzania.* Berkeley, University of California Press, 1974.

New Halfa Scheme

2055. Salem-Murdock, M. *Arabs and Nubians in New Halfa: a study of settlement and irrigation.* Salt Lake City, University of Utah Press, 1989.

2056. Sørbø, Gunnar M. *Tenants and nomads in eastern Sudan: a study of economic adaptations in the New Halfa Scheme.* Uppsala, Scandinavian Institute of African Studies, 1985.

Ngoni—Ethnography

2057. Moser, R. *Aspekte der Kulturgeschichte der Ngoni in der Mkoa wa Ruvuma, Tanzania: Materialien zum Kultur- und Sprachwandel.* Wien, Institut für Afrikanistik und Ägyptologie der Universität Wien, 1983.

Ngoni—Politics

2058. Redmond, Patrick M. *The politics of power in Songea Ngoni society, 1860–1962.* Chicago, Adams Press, 1985.

Ngorongoro Game Reserve

2059. Fosbrooke, Henry. *Ngorongoro: the eighth wonder.* London, Andre Deutsch, 1972.

2060. Homewood, K. M., and W. A. Rodgers. *Maasailand ecology: pastoralist development and wildlife conservation in Ngorongoro, Tanzania.* Cambridge, Cambridge University Press, 1991.

2061. Kunkel, Reinard. *Ngorongoro.* Milano, Rizzoli, 1992.

Ngugi wa Thiong'o

2062. Adagala, K. *Wanja of "Petals of Blood": the woman question and imperialism in Kenya.* Nairobi, Derika Associates, 1985.

2063. Bardolph, Jacqueline. *Ngugi wa Thiong'o: l'homme et l'oeuvre.* Paris, Présence Africaine, 1991.

2064. Cook, D., and M. Okenimpke. *Ngugi wa Thiong'o: an exploration of his writings.* London, Heinemann, 1983.

2065. Dramé, Kandioura. *The novel as transformation myth: a study of the novels of Mongo Beti and Ngugi wa Thiong'o.* Syracuse, Syracuse University, Maxwell School of Citizenship and Public Affairs, 1990.

2066. Killam, G. D. *An introduction to the writings of Ngugi.* London, Heinemann, 1980.

2067. Killam, G. D. (ed.) *Critical perspectives on Ngugi wa Thiong'o.* Washington, Three Continents Press, 1984.

2068. Meyer, Herta. *"Justice for the oppressed": the political dimension in the language use of Ngugi wa Thiong'o.* Essen, Die Blaue Eule, 1991.

2069. Robson, Clifford B. *Ngugi wa Thiong'o.* London, Macmillan, 1979.

2070. Sicherman, Carol. *Ngugi wa Thiong'o: a bibliography of primary and secondary sources, 1957–1987.* London, Hans Zell, 1989.

2071. Sicherman, Carol. *Ngugi wa Thiong'o: the making of a rebel. A source book in Kenyan literature and resistance.* London, Hans Zell, 1990.

Ngulu — Ethnography

2072. Grohs, Elisabeth. *Kisazi: Reiferriten der Mädchen bei den Zigua und Ngulu Ost-Tansanias.* Berlin, Dietrich Reimer, 1980.

Nile River

2073. Collins, Robert O. *The waters of the Nile: an annotated bibliography.* London, Hans Zell, 1991.

2074. Howell, Paul, and J. A. Allan. *The Nile: resource evaluation, resource management, hydropolitics and legal issues.* London, Royal Geographical Society and the School of Oriental and African Studies, 1990.

2075. Waterbury, John. *Hydropolitics of the Nile valley.* Syracuse, Syracuse University Press, 1979.

Nilo-Hamites — Ethnography

2076. Gulliver, Pamela, and Philip H. Gulliver. *The central Nilo-Hamites.* London, International African Institute, 1968.

Nilo-Hamitic Languages

2077. Hohenberger, Johannes. *Semitische und hamitische Wortstämme im Nilo-Hamitischen, mit phonetische Analysen.* Berlin, Dietrich Reimer, 1988.

2078. Hohenberger, Johannes. *The nominal and verbal afformatives of Nilo-Hamitic and Hamito-Semitic, with some phonetic observations and a new vocabulary.* Stuttgart, Franz Steiner, 1975.

Nilo-Saharan Languages

2079. Bender, Marvin Lionel (ed.) *Nilo-Saharan language studies.* East Lansing, Michigan State University, African Studies Center, 1983.

2080. Bender, Marvin Lionel (ed.) *Proceedings of the fourth Nilo-Saharan conference, Bayreuth, Aug. 30–Sept. 2, 1989.* Hamburg, Helmut Buske, 1989.

2081. Bender, Marvin Lionel (ed.) *Topics in Nilo-Saharan linguistics.* Hamburg, Helmut Buske, 1989.

2082. Rottland, Franz, and Lucia N. Omondo (eds.) *Proceedings of the third Nilo-Saharan linguistics colloquium, Kisumu, Kenya, August 4–9, 1986.* Hamburg, Helmut Buske, 1991.

2083. Schadeberg, Thilo C., and Marvin Lionel Bender (eds.) *Nilo-Saharan: proceedings of the first Nilo-Saharan linguistics colloquium, Leiden, September 8–10, 1980.* Dordrecht, Foris, 1981.

Nilotes—Ethnography

2084. Best, Günter. *Ehen der Südniloten: intra- und interethnische Heiratsformen im Vergleich*. Münster, Lit-Verlag, 1989.

2085. Lincoln, Bruce. *Priests, warriors and cattle: a study in the ecology of religions*. Berkeley, University of California Press, 1981.

Nilotes—History

2086. Vossen, Rainer, and Marianne Bechhaus-Gerst (eds.) *Nilotic studies: proceedings of the international symposium on languages and history of the Nilotic peoples, Cologne, January 4–6, 1982*. Berlin, Dietrich Reimer, 1983. 2 vols.

Nilotes—Politics

2087. Säfholm, Per. *The river-lake Nilotes: politics of an African tribal group*. Uppsala, Acta Universitatis Upsaliensis, 1973.

Nilotic Languages

2088. Creider, Chet A. *The syntax of the Nilotic languages: themes and variations*. Berlin, Dietrich Reimer, 1989.

2089. Vossen, Rainer, and Marianne Bechhaus-Gerst (eds.) *Nilotic studies: proceedings of the international symposium on languages and history of the Nilotic peoples, Cologne, January 4–6, 1982*. Berlin, Dietrich Reimer, 1983. 2 vols.

2090. Vossen, Rainer. *The eastern Nilotes: linguistic and historical reconstructions*. Berlin, Dietrich Reimer, 1982.

Nkore—History

2091. Karugire, Samwiri Rubaraza. *A history of the kingdom of Nkore in western Uganda to 1896*. Oxford, Clarendon Press, 1971.

Nuba Mountains—Research

2092. Dabitz, G. *Geschichte der Erforschung der Nuba-Berge*. Stuttgart, Franz Steiner, 1985.

Nuba—Art and Artists

2093. Faris, James Chester. *Nuba personal art*. London, Duckworth, 1972.

Nuba—Description

2094. Riefenstahl, Leni. *Die Nuba von Kau*. Berlin, Ullstein Sachbuch, 1991.

Nuba—Economy

2095. Iten, Oswald. *Economic pressures on traditional society: a case study of southeastern Nuba economy in the modern Sudan*. Bern, Peter Lang, 1979.

Nuba—Ethnography

2096. Dubois, Élaine. *Soudan, pays des Nouba*. Lausanne, Edita, 1980.

2097. Faris, James Chester. *Southeast Nuba social relations*. Aachen, Alano, 1989.

2098. Husmann, R. *Transkulturation bei den Nuba: ethnohistorische Aspekte des kulturellen Wandels im 19. und 20. Jahrhundert*. Göttingen, Herodot, 1984.

2099. Rottenburg, Richard. *Die Lemwareng-Nuba: ein Beispiel kultureller Akkresenz im heutigen Nil-Sudan*. Berlin, Das Arabische Buch, 1988.

2100. Rottenburg, Richard. *Ndemewareng: Wirtschaft und Gesellschaft in den Morobergen*. München, Trickster Verlag, 1991.

2101. Stevenson, R. C. *The Nuba people of Kordofan Province: an ethnographic survey*. Khartoum, Khartoum University, Graduate College, 1984.

Nuba—History

2102. Ibrahim, A. U. M. *The dilemma of British rule in the Nuba mountains, 1898–1947*. Khartoum, Khartoum University, Graduate College, 1985.

Nuba—Social Conditions

2103. Iten, Oswald. *Fungor: ein Nuba-Dorf wird ruiniert*. Frankfurt am Main, Ullstein, 1983.

2104. Manger, Leif O. *From the mountains to the plains: the integration of the Lalofa Nuba into Sudanese society*. Uppsala, Scandinavian Institute of African Studies, 1994.

Nubi—Language

2105. Heine, Bernd. *The Nubi language of Kibera: an Arabic creole*. Berlin, Dietrich Reimer, 1982.

Nubia—Archaeology

2106. Edwards, David N. *Archaeology and settlement in Upper Nubia in the 1st millennium A.D.* Oxford, British Archaeological Reports, 1989.

2107. Hinkel, Friedrich W. *Auszug nach Nubien*. Berlin, Akademie-Verlag, 1978.

2108. Hintze, Fritz, and Walter F. Reineke (eds.) *Felsinschriften aus dem sudanesischen Nubien*. Berlin, Akademie-Verlag, 1989. 2 vols.

2109. Keating, R. *Nubian rescue*. London, Robert Hale, 1975.

2110. Shinnie, P. L., and Margaret Shinnie. *Debeira West: a mediaeval Nubian town*. Warminster, Aris & Phillips, 1978.

2111. Török, László. *Late antique Nubia: history and archaeology of the southern neighbour of Egypt in the 4th–6th c. A.D.* Budapest, Archaeological Institute of the Hungarian Academy of Sciences, 1988.

2112. Trigger, Bruce. *History and settlement in lower Nubia*. New Haven, Yale University Publications in Anthropology, 1965.

2113. Trigger, Bruce. *Nubia under the Pharoahs*. Boulder, Westview Press, 1976.

2114. Vila, André. *Le cimetière Kémaïque d'Ukma: la prospection archéologique de la vallée du Nil en Nubie soudanaise*. Paris, Éditions du CNRS, 1987.

Nubia—Art and Artists

2115. Hintze, Fritz (ed.) *Africa in antiquity: the arts of ancient Nubia and the Sudan. Proceedings of the symposium held in conjunction with the exhibition, Brooklyn . . . 1978*. Berlin, Akademie-Verlag, 1979.

Nubia—Ethnography

2116. Hale, Sondra. *Nubians: a study in ethnic identity*. Khartoum, University of Khartoum, Institute of African and Asian Studies, 1971.

Nubia—History

2117. Adams, William Y. *Nubia: corridor to Africa*. Princeton, Princeton University Press, 1976.

Nubia—House Decoration

2118. Wenzel, Marian. *House decoration in Nubia*. London, Duckworth, 1972.

Nubia—Islam

2119. Cuoq, Joseph. *Islamisation de la Nubie chrétienne, VIIe–XVIe siècles*. Paris, Librairie Orientaliste Paul Geuthner, 1986.

Nubia—Prehistory

2120. El Amin, Yousif Mukhtar. *Later Pleistocene cultural adaptions in Sudanese Nubia*. Oxford, British Archaeological Reports, 1981.

Nubia—Rock Art

2121. Cervicek, Paul. *Rock pictures of Upper Egypt and Nubia*. Napoli, Istituto Universitario Orientale, 1986.

Nubia—Social Conditions

2122. Dafalla, H. *The Nubian exodus*. Khartoum, Khartoum University Press, 1975.

2123. Fahim, Hussein M. *Dams, people and development: the Aswan High Dam case*. New York, Pergamon, 1981.

2124. Kennedy, J. G. *Struggle for change in a Nubian community: an individual in society and history*. Palo Alto, Mayfield, 1977.

Nubia—Studies

2125. Hägg, Tomas (ed.) *Nubian culture past and present: main papers presented at the sixth international conference for Nubian studies, Uppsala, 11–16 August, 1986.* Stockholm, Kungl. Vitterhets Historie och Antikvitets Akademien, 1987.

2126. Plumley, J. M. (ed.) *Nubian studies: proceedings of the symposium for Nubian studies.* Warminster, Aris & Phillips, 1982.

Nubian Language

2127. Armbruster, Charles H. *Dongolese Nubian: lexicon.* Cambridge, Cambridge University Press, 1965.

2128. Hofmann, Inge, and Anton Vorbichler. *Das nubische Wörterverzeichnis des Arcangelo Carradori (O.F.M.) aus dem frühen 17. Jahrhundert.* Wien, Institut für Afrikanistik und Ägyptologie der Universität Wien, 1983.

2129. Hofmann, Inge. *Einführung in den nubischen Kenzi-Dialekt.* Wien, Institut für Afrikanistik und Ägyptologie der Universität Wien, 1983.

2130. Hofmann, Inge. *Nubisches Wörterverzeichnis: nubisch-deutsches und deutsch-nubisches Wörterverzeichnis nach dem Kenzi-Material des Samuel Ali Hisen, 1863–1927.* Berlin, Dietrich Reimer, 1986.

2131. Khalil, Mokhtar. *Studien zum Altnubischen: nubisch-ägyptische Beziehungen.* Frankfurt am Main, Peter Lang, 1988.

Nuer—Ethnography

2132. Aster Akalu. *Beyond morals? Experiences of living the life of the Ethiopian Nuer.* Lund, LiberForlag Malmo, 1985.

2133. Aster Akalu. *The Nuer view of biological life: nature and sexuality in the experience of the Ethiopian Nuer.* Stockholm, Almqvist & Wiksell, 1989.

2134. Coriat, Percy. *Governing the Nuer: documents in Nuer history and ethnography, 1922–1931.* Edited with introductions and notes by Douglas H. Johnson. Oxford, JASO, 1993.

2135. Kelly, R. C. *The Nuer conquest: the structure and development of an expansionist system.* Ann Arbor, University of Michigan Press, 1985.

Nuer—Song

2136. Svoboda, T. *Cleaned the crocodile's teeth: Nuer song.* Greenfield Centre, Greenfield Review Press, 1985.

Nyakyusa—Economy

2137. Konter, Jan Herman. *Facts and factors in the rural economy of the Nyakyusa.* Leiden, African Studies Centre, 1974.

Nyakyusa—Ethnography

2138. Charsley, Simon R. *The princes of Nyakyusa*. Nairobi, East African Publishing House, 1969.

2139. Hartmann, Werner. *Das politische System der Nyakyusa: Überlegungen zu einer Kontroverse*. Saarbrücken, Breitenbach, 1991.

2140. Meyer, Theodor. *Die Konde: ethnographische Aufzeichnungen, 1891– 1916 des Missionssuperintendenten Theodor Meyer von den Nyakyusa, Tanzania*. Hohenschäftlarn, Karl Renner, 1989.

2141. Wilson, Monica. *For men and elders: change in the relations of generations and of men and women among the Nyakyusa-Ngonde people, 1875–1971*. London, International African Institute, 1977.

Nyamwezi—Ethnography

2142. Abrahams, R. G. *The political organization of Unyamwezi*. Cambridge, Cambridge University Press, 1967.

2143. Tcherkézoff, Serge. *Dual classification reconsidered: Nyamwezi sacred kingship and other examples*. Cambridge, Cambridge University Press, 1987.

2144. Tcherkézoff, Serge. *Le roi nyamwezi, la droite et la gauche*. Cambridge, Cambridge University Press, 1983.

Nyamwezi—History

2145. Bennett, Norman R. *Mirambo of Tanzania, c. 1840–1884*. London, Oxford University Press, 1971.

2146. Rothlach, Roswitha. *Der Wandel der Wanjamwesi-Gesellschaft in vorkolonialer Zeit und die Ideen Nyereres über die traditionelle afrikanische Gesellschaft*. München, Karl Renner, 1975.

Nyamwezi—Language

2147. Maganga, Clement, and Thilo C. Schadeberg. *Kinyamwezi: grammar, texts, vocabulary*. Cologne, Rüdiger Küppe, 1992.

Nyamwezi—Social Conditions

2148. Abrahams, R. G. *The Nyamwezi today: a Tanzanian people in the 1970s*. Cambridge, Cambridge University Press, 1981.

Nyankore—Kiga Language

2149. Taylor, Charles. *Nkore-Kiga*. London, Croom Helm, 1985.

Nyanza—History

2150. Ochieng', William Robert. *An outline history of Nyanza up to 1914*. Kampala, East African Literature Bureau, 1974.

Nyaturu—Ethnography

2151. Schneider, Harold K. *The Wahi Wanyaturu: economics in an African society*. Chicago, Aldine, 1970.

Nyerere, Julius

2152. Hatch, John Charles. *Two African statesmen: Kaunda of Zambia and Nyerere of Tanzania*. London, Secker & Warburg, 1976.

2153. Mwenegoha, H. A. K. *Mwalimu Julius Kambarage Nyerere: a bio-bibliography*. Nairobi, Foundation Books, 1976.

2154. Smith, William Edgett. *Nyerere of Tanzania*. London, Gollancz, 1973.

Nyoro—Colonial History

2155. Pawlikova-Vilhanová, Viera. *History of anti-colonial resistance and protest in the kingdoms of Buganda and Bunyoro, 1890–1899*. Prague, Oriental Institute of the Czechoslovak Academy of Sciences, 1988.

Nyoro—Ethnography

2156. Beattie, John. *Bunyoro: an African kingdom*. New York, Holt, Rinehart and Winston, 1960.

2157. Beattie, John. *The Nyoro state*. Oxford, Clarendon Press, 1971.

2158. Beattie, John. *Understanding an African kingdom: Bunyoro*. New York, Holt, Rinehart and Winston, 1965.

Nyoro—History

2159. Dunbar, Archibald Ranulph. *A history of Bunyoro-Kitara*. Second edition. Nairobi, Oxford University Press, 1970.

2160. Kiwanuka, M. S. M. Semakula. *The empire of Bunyoro-Kitara: myth or reality?* Kampala, Longmans, 1968.

2161. Nyakatura, J. W. *Anatomy of an African kingdom: a history of Bunyoro-Kitara*. Garden City, Anchor Press, 1973.

Nyoro—Religion

2162. Byaruhanga-Akiiki, A. B. T. *Religion in Bunyoro*. Nairobi, Kenya Literature Bureau, 1982.

Obote, Milton

2163. Gingyera-Pinycwa, A. G. G. *Apolo Milton Obote and his times*. New York, NOK Publishers, 1978.

2164. Gupta, Vijay. *Obote: second liberation*. New Delhi, Vikas, 1983.

2165. Ingham, Kenneth. *Obote: a political biography*. London, Routledge, 1994.

Ochollo—Ethnography

2166. Abélès, Marc. *Le lieu du politique*. Paris, Société d'Ethnographie, 1983.

Olduvai Gorge

2167. Hay, Richard Le Roy. *The geology of Olduvai Gorge: a study of sedimentation in a semi-arid basin*. Berkeley, University of California Press, 1976.

2168. Leakey, L. S. B. *Olduvai Gorge: a preliminary report on the geology and fauna, 1951–61*. Cambridge, Cambridge University Press, 1965.

2169. Leakey, Mary D. *Olduvai Gorge*. London, Collins, 1979.

2170. Leakey, Mary D. *Olduvai Gorge: excavations in beds I and II, 1960–1963*. Cambridge, Cambridge University Press, 1971.

2171. Potts, R. *Early hominid activities at Olduvai*. New York, Aldine de Gruyter, 1988.

2172. Tobias, P. V. *Olduvai Gorge: the cranium and maxillary dentition of Australopithecus-Zinjanthropus-Boisei*. Cambridge, Cambridge University Press, 1967.

Omotic Languages

2173. Bechhaus-Gerst, Marianne, and Fritz Serzisko (eds.) *Cushitic-Omotic: papers from the international symposium on Cushitic and Omotic languages, Cologne, January 6–9, 1986*. Hamburg, Helmut Buske, 1989.

2174. Bender, Marvin Lionel. *Omotic: a new Afroasiatic language family*. Carbondale, Southern Illinois University, 1975.

2175. Hayward, Richard J. *Omotic language studies*. London, University of London, School of Oriental and African Studies, 1990.

Orig—Language

2176. Schadeberg, Thilo C., and Philip Elias. *A description of the Orig language, southern Kordofan, based on the notes of Fr. Carlo Muratori*. Tervuren, Musée Royale de l'Afrique Centrale, 1979.

Ornithology—East Africa

2177. Britton, P. L. (ed.) *Birds of East Africa: their habitat, status and distribution*. Nairobi, East Africa Natural History Society, 1980.

2178. Mackworth-Praed, Cyril Winthrop. *Birds of eastern and northeastern Africa*. Second edition. London, Longmans, 1980. 2 vols.

2179. Williams, John George, and Norman Arlott. *A field guide to the birds of East Africa*. London, Collins, 1980.

Oromo—Ethnobotany

2180. Heine, Bernd, and Matthias Brenzinger. *Plant concepts and plant use: an ethnobotanical survey of the semi-arid and arid lands of East Africa. Part IV: the Borana, Ethiopia and Kenya.* Saarbrücken, Breitenbach, 1988.

Oromo—Ethnography

2181. Asmarom Legesse. *Gada: three approaches to the study of African society.* New York, The Free Press, 1973.

2182. Dahl, Gudrun. *Suffering grass: subsistence and society of Waso Borana.* Stockholm, University of Stockholm, Department of Social Anthropology, 1979.

2183. Haberland, Eike. *Galla Süd-Äthiopiens.* Stuttgart, Kohlhammer, 1963.

2184. Hinnant, John. *The Guji of Ethiopia.* New Haven, Human Relations Area Files, 1972. 2 vols.

2185. Hultin, Jan. *The long journey: essays on history, descent and land among the Macha Oromo.* Uppsala, University, Department of Cultural Anthropology, 1987.

2186. Knutsson, K. E. *Authority and change: a study of the Kallu institution among the Macha Galla of Ethiopia.* Göteborg, Etnografiska Museet, 1963.

2187. Lewis, H. S. *A Galla monarchy: Jimma Abba Jifar, 1830–1932.* Madison, University of Wisconsin Press, 1965.

2188. Lonfernini, Bruno. *I gugi giamgiam, gente del ghirgia.* Bologna, EMI, 1984.

2189. Loo, Joseph van de. *Guji Oromo culture in southern Ethiopia: religious capabilities in rituals and songs.* Berlin, Dietrich Reimer, 1991.

Oromo—Health and Medicine

2190. Buschkens, Willem F. L., and L. J. Slikkerveer. *Health care in East Africa: illness behaviour of the eastern Oromo in Hararghe, Ethiopia.* Assen, Van Gorcum, 1982.

Oromo—History

2191. Asafa Jalata. *Oromia and Ethiopia: state formation and ethnonational conflict, 1868–1992.* Boulder, Lynne Rienner, 1993.

2192. Asma Giyorgis. *History of the Galla and the Kingdom of Sawa.* Stuttgart, Franz Steiner, 1987.

2193. Gadaa Melbaa. *Oromia: a brief introduction.* Addis Ababa, the Author, 1980.

2194. Hasselblatt, Gunnar. *Gespräch mit Gudina.* Stuttgart, Radius-Verlag, 1989.

2195. Hassen, Mohammed. *The Oromo of Ethiopia: a history, 1570–1860*. Cambridge, Cambridge University Press, 1990.

2196. Mekuria Bulcha. *The social and economic foundations of the Oromo states of the nineteenth century: social differentiation and state formation among the Macha Oromo, circ. 1700–1900*. Hanledare, Goran Ahrme, 1984.

Oromo—Language

2197. Ali, Mohammed, and Andrzej Zaborski. *Handbook of the Oromo language*. Stuttgart, Franz Steiner, 1990.

2198. Gragg, Gene B. *Oromo dictionary*. East Lansing, Michigan State University, African Studies Center, 1982.

2199. Heine, Bernd. *The Waata dialect of Oromo: grammatical sketch and vocabulary*. Berlin, Dietrich Reimer, 1981.

2200. Leus, T. *Boran-English dictionary*. Yabello, Catholic Church, Dadim, 1988.

2201. Owens, J. *A Grammar of Harar Oromo, northeastern Ethiopia*. Hamburg, Helmut Buske, 1985.

2202. Stroomer, H. *A comparative study of three southern Oromo dialects in Kenya: phonology, morphology and vocabulary*. Hamburg, Helmut Buske, 1987.

2203. Tilahun Gamta. *Oromo-English dictionary*. Addis Ababa, Addis Ababa University Printing Press, 1989.

2204. Venturino, B. *Dizionario borana-italiana*. Bologna, Editrice Missionaria Italiana, 1973.

2205. Venturino, B. *Dizionario italiano-borana*. Marsabit, Catholic Mission, 1976.

Oromo—Missionaries

2206. Massaia, Guglielmo. *Memorie storiche del vicariato apostolico dei Galla, 1845–1880*. Padova, Edizioni Messagero, 1984.

Oromo—Politics

2207. Hasselblatt, Gunnar. *Das geheime Lachen im Bambuswald: vom Freiheitskampf der Oromo in Äthiopien*. Stuttgart, Radius-Verlag, 1990.

2208. Hasselblatt, Gunnar. *Nächtes Jahr in Oromoland*. Stuttgart, Radius-Verlag, 1982.

Oromo—Proverbs

2209. Cotter, George. *Proverbs and sayings of the Oromo people of Ethiopia and Kenya with English translations*. Lewiston, Edwin Mellen Press, 1992.

Oromo—Religion

2210. Bartels, Lambert. *Oromo religion. Myths and rites of the western Oromo of Ethiopia: an attempt to understand.* Berlin, Dietrich Reimer, 1983.

Pangwa—Ethnography

2211. Stirnimann, Hans. *Die Pangwa von SW.-Tansania: soziale organisation und riten des Lebens.* Freiburg, Universitätsverlag Freiburg Schweiz, 1979.

2212. Stirnimann, Hans. *Existenzgrundlagen und traditionelles Handwerk der Pangwa von SW.-Tansania.* Freiburg, Universitätsverlag Freiburg Schweiz, 1976.

Pangwa—Language

2213. Stirnimann, Hans. *Praktische Grammatik der Pangwa-Sprache, SW.-Tansania.* Freiburg, Universitätsverlag Freiburg Schweiz, 1983.

Pare—History

2214. Kimambo, Isaria N. *A political history of the Pare of Tanzania, ca. 1500–1900.* Nairobi, East African Publishing House, 1969.

2215. Kimambo, Isaria N. *Penetration and protest in Tanzania: the impact of the world economy on the Pare, 1860–1960.* London, James Currey, 1991.

Pare—Language

2216. Kagaya, Ryohei. *A classified vocabulary of the Pare language.* Tokyo, Institute for the Study of Languages and Cultures of Asia and Africa, 1989.

Pari—Language

2217. Simeoni, Antonio. *Päri: a Luo language of southern Sudan.* Bologna, Editrice Missionaria Italiana, 1978.

Pastoral Production—East Africa

2218. Bennett, John W. *Political ecology and development projects affecting pastoralist peoples in East Africa.* Madison, University of Wisconsin-Madison, Land Tenure Center, 1984.

2219. Jahnke, H. E. *Tsetse flies and livestock development in East Africa: a study in environmental economics.* Munich, Weltforum-Verlag, 1976.

2220. Murmann, C. *Change and development in East African cattle husbandry: a study of four societies during the colonial period.* Copenhagen, Akademisk, 1974.

2221. Raikes, Philip. *Livestock development and policy in East Africa.* Uppsala, Scandinavian Institute of African Studies, 1981.

Pastoralists — East Africa

2222. Englebert, Victor. *Wind, sand and silence: travels with Africa's last nomads*. San Francisco, Chronicle Books, 1992.

2223. Fukui, Katsuyoshi, and David Turton (eds.) *Warfare among East African herders*. Osaka, National Museum of Ethnology, 1979.

2224. Meeker, M. E. *The pastoral son and the spirit of patriarchy: religion, society and person among East African stock keepers*. Madison, University of Wisconsin Press, 1989.

2225. Rigby, Peter. *Persistent pastoralists: nomadic societies in transition*. London, Zed Books, 1985.

2226. Schneider, Harold K. *Livestock and equality in East Africa*. Bloomington, Indiana University Press, 1979.

Pastoralists — Northeast Africa

2227. Englebert, Victor. *Wind, sand and silence: travels with Africa's last nomads*. San Francisco, Chronicle Books, 1992.

2228. Markakis, John (ed.) *Conflict and the decline of pastoralism in the Horn of Africa*. Basingstoke, Macmillan, 1992.

Pastureland — East Africa

2229. Strange, L. R. N. *African pastureland ecology, with particular reference to the pastoral environment of eastern Africa*. Rome, Food and Agriculture Organization, 1980.

2230. Strange, L. R. N. *An introduction to African pastureland production: with special reference to farm and rangeland environments of eastern Africa*. Rome, Food and Agriculture Organization, 1980.

2231. Strange, L. R. N. *Human influences in African pastureland environments: with special reference to the arid and semiarid pastoral regions of eastern Africa*. Rome, Food and Agriculture Organization, 1980.

Planning — East Africa

2232. Clark, Paul G. *Development planning in East Africa*. Nairobi, East African Publishing House, 1965.

2233. Molnos, Angela. *Development in Africa: planning and implementation. A bibliography, 1946–1969 and outline, with some emphasis on Kenya, Tanzania and Uganda*. Dar es Salaam, East African Academy, Research Information Centre, 1970.

2234. Safier, Michael (ed.) *The role of urban and regional planning in national development for East Africa: papers and proceedings of a seminar organised by the Milton Obote Foundation*. Kampala, Milton Obote Foundation, Adult Education Centre, 1967.

2235. Vente, Rolf E. *Planning processes: the East African case.* Munich, Welt-forum-Verlag, 1970.

Pogoro — Ethnography

2236. Schoenaker, Sidonius. *Die ideologischen Hintergründe im Gemeinschafts-sleben der Pogoro.* Wien, Verlag Österreichische Ethnologische Gesell-schaft, 1965.

Pokomo — Folktales

2237. Geider, Thomas. *Die Figur des Oger in der traditionellen Literatur und Lebenswelt der Pokomo in Ost-Kenya.* Köln, Rüdiger Küppe, 1990.

Pokomo — Islam

2238. Bunger, R. L. *Islamization among the upper Pokomo.* Syracuse, Syracuse University, Maxwell School of Citizenship and Public Affairs, 1973.

Pokot — Environment

2239. Reckers, Ute. *Nomadische Viehhalter in Kenya: die Ost-Pokot aus hu-man-ökologischer Sicht.* Hamburg, Institut für Afrika-Kunde, 1992.

Pokot — Ethnography

2240. Bollig, Michael. *Die Krieger der gelben Gewehre: Intra- und intereth-nische Konfliktsaustragung bei den Pokot Nordwestkenias.* Münster, Lit-Verlag, 1992.

Pokot — Language

2241. Crazzolara, J. Pasquale. *A study of the Pokot (Suk) language: grammar, and vocabulary.* Bologna, Editrice Missionaria Italiana, 1978.

2242. Herreros Boroja, Tomás, et al. *Analytical grammar of the Pokot language.* Trieste, Università di Trieste and Missionari Comboniani, 1989.

Pokot — Religion

2243. Visser, Johannes Jacobus. *Pokoot religion.* Oegstgeest, Hendrik Kraemer Instituut, 1989.

Politics — East Africa

2244. Bennett, Norman R. (ed.) *Leadership in eastern Africa: six political bi-ographies.* Boston, Boston University Press, 1968.

2245. Berg-Schlosser, D., and R. Siegler. *Political stability and development: a comparative study of Kenya, Tanzania and Uganda.* Boulder, Lynne Ri-enner, 1990.

2246. Diamond, Stanley, and Fred G. Burke (eds.) *The transformation of East Africa: studies in political anthropology.* New York, Basic Books, 1966.

2247. Fallers, Lloyd A. *The social anthropology of the nation-state*. Chicago, Aldine, 1974.

2248. Lytton, Noel Anthony Scawen. *The stolen desert: a study of uhuru in North East Africa*. London, Macdonald, 1966.

2249. Mazrui, Ali A. *Cultural engineering and nation-building in East Africa*. Evanston, Northwestern University Press, 1972.

2250. Mazrui, Ali A. *Violence and thought: essays on social tensions in Africa*. Harlow, Longmans, 1969.

2251. Richards, Audrey I. *The multiracial states of East Africa*. Montreal, McGill-Queens University Press, 1969.

2252. Salim, A. I. (ed.) *State formation in eastern Africa*. Nairobi, Heinemann Educational, 1984.

2253. Saul, John S. *The state and revolution in eastern Africa*. London, Heinemann, 1979.

2254. Yilma Makonnen. *The Nyerere doctrine of state succession and the new states of East Africa*. Arusha, Eastern Africa Publications, 1984.

Politics—Northeast Africa

2255. Aquarone, Marie-Christine. *Les frontières du refus: six séparatismes africains*. Paris, Éditions Nationales de la Recherche Scientifique, 1987.

2256. Ayoob, Mohammed. *The Horn of Africa: regional conflict and super-power involvement*. Canberra, Australian National University, 1978.

2257. Bhardwaj, Raman G. *The dilemma of the Horn of Africa*. New Delhi, Sterling, 1979.

2258. Brüne, Stefan, and V. Matthies. *Krisenregion Horn von Afrika*. Hamburg, Institut für Afrika-Kunde, 1990.

2259. Doornbos, Martin R., et al. (eds.) *Beyond conflict in the Horn: the prospects for peace, recovery and development in Ethiopia, Somalia, Eritrea and Sudan*. Trenton, Red Sea Press, 1992.

2260. Farer, Tom J. *War clouds on the Horn of Africa: the widening storm*. New York, Carnegie Endowment for International Peace, 1979.

2261. Fukui, Katsuyoshi, and John Markakis (eds.) *Ethnicity and conflict in the Horn of Africa*. London, James Currey, 1994.

2262. Gorman, Robert F. *Political conflict on the Horn of Africa*. New York, Praeger, 1981.

2263. Henze, Paul B. *The Horn of Africa: from war to peace*. Basingstoke, Macmillan, 1991.

2264. Legum, Colin, and Bill Lee. *Conflict in the Horn of Africa*. London, Rex Collings, 1977.

2265. Legum, Colin, and Bill Lee. *The Horn of Africa in continuing crisis*. New York, Africana Publishing, 1979.

2266. Lewis, I. M. (ed.) *Nationalism and self-determination in the Horn of Africa*. London, Ithaca Press, 1983.

2267. Markakis, John. *National conflict and class conflict in the Horn of Africa*. Cambridge, Cambridge University Press, 1987.

2268. Matthies, Volker. *Äthiopien, Eritrea, Somalia, Djibouti: das Horn von Afrika*. München, C. H. Beck, 1992.

2269. Nzongola-Ntajala, G. (ed.) *Conflict in the Horn of Africa*. Atlanta, African Studies Association, 1991.

2270. Sinclair, M. R. *The strategic significance of the Horn of Africa*. Pretoria, University of Pretoria, Institute for Strategic Studies, 1980.

Population — East Africa

2271. Clark University: Program for International Development. *Eastern Africa regional studies: trends and interrelationships in food, population, and energy in eastern Africa. A preliminary analysis*. Worcester, Clark University, Program for International Development, 1980. 3 vols.

2272. Molnos, Angela (ed.) *Cultural source materials for population planning in East Africa*. Nairobi, East African Publishing House, 1972–73. 4 vols.

2273. Mönsted, Mette, and Parveen Walji. *A demographic analysis of East Africa: a sociological interpretation*. Uppsala, Scandinavian Institute of African Studies, 1978.

2274. Ominde, Simeon H. *The population of Kenya-Uganda-Tanzania*. Nairobi, Heinemann, 1975.

Port Sudan — History

2275. Perkins, Kenneth J. *Port Sudan: the evolution of a colonial city*. Boulder, Westview Press, 1993.

Ports — East Africa

2276. Datoo, B. A. *Port development in East Africa: spatial patterns from the ninth to the sixteenth centuries*. Nairobi, East African Literature Bureau, 1975.

2277. Hoyle, Brian Stewart. *The seaports of East Africa: a geographical study*. Nairobi, East African Publishing House, 1967.

Prehistory — East Africa

2278. Cole, Sonia. *Leakey's luck: the life of Louis Seymour Bazett Leakey, 1903–1972*. London, Collins, 1975.

2279. Cole, Sonia. *The prehistory of East Africa*. Second edition. London, Weidenfeld and Nicolson, 1964.

2280. Isaac, Glynn Llywelyn, and Elizabeth McCown (eds.) *Human origins: Louis Leakey and the East African evidence.* Menlo Park, W. A. Benjamin, 1976.

2281. Leakey, L. S. B. *By the evidence: memoirs, 1932–1951.* New York, Harcourt, Brace, Jovanovich, 1974.

2282. Leakey, Mary D. *Disclosing the past.* London, Weidenfeld and Nicolson, 1984.

2283. Phillipson, David W. *The later prehistory of eastern and southern Africa.* London, Heinemann, 1977.

2284. Phillipson, Laurel, and David Phillipson. *East Africa's prehistoric past.* Nairobi, Longmans, 1978.

Prehistory—Northeast Africa

2285. Klees, Frank, and Rudolph Kuper (eds.) *New light on the Northeast African past: current prehistoric research.* Cologne, Heinrich-Barth-Institut, 1992.

Qemant—Ethnography

2286. Gamst, F. C. *The Qemant: a pagan-hebraic peasantry of Ethiopia.* New York, Holt, Rinehart and Winston, 1969.

Rahad Irrigation Project

2287. Benedict, P., et al. *Sudan: the Rahad irrigation project.* Washington, United States Agency for International Development, 1982.

Railways—East Africa

2288. Amin, Mohamed. *Railway across the equator: the story of the East African line.* London, Bodley Head, 1986.

2289. Beckenham, Arthur F. *Wagons of smoke: an informal history of the East African Railways and Harbours Administration, 1948–1961.* London, Cadogan Publications, 1987.

2290. Miller, Charles. *The lunatic express: an entertainment in imperialism.* London, Macdonald, 1971.

2291. Patience, K. *Steam in East Africa: a pictorial history of the railways in East Africa, 1893–1976.* Nairobi, Heinemann, 1976.

Rangi—Ethnography

2292. Kesby, John D. *The Rangi of Tanzania: an introduction to their culture.* New Haven, Human Relations Area Files, 1981.

Refugees—Northeast Africa

2293. Ruiz, H. A. *Beyond the headlines: refugees in the Horn of Africa.* Washington, U.S. Committee for Refugees, 1988.

Regional Integration—East Africa

2294. Aliboni, Roberto (ed.) *Integrazione in Africa orientale*. Bologna, Il Mulino, 1970.

2295. Assefa Mehretu. *Regional integration for economic development of greater East Africa: a quantified analysis of possibilities*. Kampala, Uganda Publishing House, 1973.

2296. Baumhögger, Goswin. *Dominanz oder Kooperation: die Entwicklung der regionalen Integration in Ostafrika*. Hamburg, Institut für Afrika-Kunde, 1978.

2297. Collignon, Stefan. *Regionale Integration und Entwicklung in Ostafrika*. Hamburg, Institut für Afrika-Kunde, 1990.

2298. Delupis, Ingrid D. di. *The East African Community and Common Market*. London, Longmans, 1970.

2299. East African Community. *The East African Community: a handbook*. Nairobi, East African Community, Information Division, 1972.

2300. Franck, Thomas M. *East African unity through law*. New Haven, Yale University Press, 1964.

2301. Hammond, R. C. *Fiscal harmonization in the East African Community*. Amsterdam, International Bureau of Fiscal Documentation, 1975.

2302. Hazlewood, Arthur. *Economic integration: the East African experience*. London, Heinemann, 1975.

2303. Howell, John Bruce. *East African Community: subject guide to official publications*. Washington, Library of Congress, 1976.

2304. Hughes, A. J. *East Africa, the search for unity: Kenya, Tanganyika, Uganda and Zanzibar*. Revised edition. Harmondsworth, Penguin, 1969.

2305. Leys, Colin, and Peter Robson. *Federation in East Africa: opportunities and problems*. Nairobi, Oxford University Press, 1965.

2306. Nabudere, D. Wadada. *Imperialism in East Africa*. London, Zed Press, 1982.

2307. Ndegwa, Philip. *The common market and development in East Africa*. Nairobi, East African Publishing House, 1965.

2308. Nixson, Frederick Ian. *Economic integration and industrial location: an East African case study*. London, Longmans, 1973.

2309. Nsibambi, Apolo, and Timothy Wangusa (eds.) *Regional cooperation for African development: proceedings of the first conference of the East African PWPA, Kampala, Uganda*. New York, Professors World Peace Academy, 1987.

2310. Nye, Joseph S. *Pan Africanism and East African integration*. Cambridge, Mass., Harvard University Press, 1965.

2311. Potholm, Christian P., and Richard A. Fredland (eds.) *Integration and disintegration in East Africa.* Washington, University Press of America, 1980.

2312. Rothchild, Donald S. (ed.) *Politics of integration: an East African documentary.* Nairobi, East African Publishing House, 1968.

2313. Sircar, Parbati Kumar. *Development through integration: lessons from East Africa.* Delhi, Kalinga Publications, 1990.

2314. Umbricht, Victor H. *Multilateral mediation: practical experiences and lessons.* Dordrecht, Nijhoff, 1989.

Religion—East Africa

2315. Barrett, D. B. (ed.) *African initiatives in religion: 21 studies from eastern and central Africa.* Nairobi, East African Publishing House, 1971.

2316. Ranger, Terence O., and Isaria N. Kimambo (eds.) *The historical study of African religion, with special reference to East and Central Africa.* London, Heinemann, 1972.

Rendille—Ethnobotany

2317. Heine, Bernd, and I. Heine. *Plant concepts and plant use: an ethnobotanical survey of the semi-arid and arid lands of East Africa. Part III: Rendille plants, Kenya.* Saarbrücken, Breitenbach, 1988.

Rendille—Ethnography

2318. Schlee, Günther. *Das Glaubens- und Sozialsystem der Rendille, Kamelnomaden Nord-Kenias.* Berlin, Dietrich Reimer, 1979.

2319. Spencer, Paul. *Nomads in alliance: symbiosis and growth among Rendille and Samburu of Kenya.* London, Oxford University Press, 1973.

Rendille—Language

2320. Schlee, Günther. *Sprachliche Studien zum Rendille: Grammatik, Texte, Glossar, with English summary of Rendille.* Hamburg, Helmut Buske, 1978.

Reptiles—East Africa

2321. Hedges, Norman G. *Reptiles and amphibians of East Africa.* Nairobi, Kenya Literature Bureau, 1983.

Rural Conditions—East Africa

2322. Barghouti, Shawki M., et al. *Rural diversification: lessons from East Africa.* Washington, World Bank, 1990.

2323. Chrétien, Jean-Pierre. *Histoire rurale de l'Afrique des Grands Lacs: guide de recherches, bibliographie et textes.* Paris, AFERA, 1983.

Rural Development—East Africa

2324. Apthorpe, Raymond J. (ed.) *Land settlement and rural development in eastern Africa*. Kampala, Nkanga Editions, 1971.

2325. Chambers, Robert. *Managing rural development: ideas and experience from East Africa*. Uppsala, Scandinavian Institute of African Studies, 1974.

2326. Cliffe, Lionel, et al. (eds.) *Government and rural development in East Africa: essays on political penetration*. The Hague, Nijhoff, 1977.

2327. Fassil Gebre Kiros (ed.) *Challenging rural poverty: experiences in institution building and popular participation for rural development in eastern Africa*. Trenton, Africa World Press, 1985.

2328. Fassil Gebre Kiros (ed.) *The development problems and prospects of semi-arid areas in eastern Africa: proceedings of a workshop, April 9–13, 1980, Nazareth, Ethiopia*. Addis Ababa, Organization for Social Science Research in Eastern Africa, 1980.

2329. Mbilinyi, Simon M. (ed.) *Agricultural research for rural development: how do we use what we know? Proceedings of the 6th annual symposium of the East African Academy*. Nairobi, East African Literature Bureau, 1973.

Safwa—Ethnography

2330. Harwood, Alan. *Witchcraft, sorcery and social categories among the Safwa*. London, Oxford University Press, 1970.

Samburu—Description

2331. Pavitt, Nigel. *Samburu*. London, Kyle Cathie, 1991.

Samburu—Ethnobotany

2332. Heine, Bernd, and I. Heine. *Plant concepts and plant use: an ethnobotanical survey of the semi-arid and arid lands of East Africa. Part V: plants of the Samburu, Kenya*. Saarbrücken, Breitenbach, 1988.

Samburu—Ethnography

2333. Parducci, Francesco. *Samburu: vita e dramma di un popolo africano*. Firenze, Nardini Press, 1989.

2334. Spencer, Paul. *Nomads in alliance: symbiosis and growth among the Rendille and Samburu of Kenya*. London, Oxford University Press, 1973.

2335. Spencer, Paul. *The Samburu: a study of gerontocracy in a nomadic tribe*. London, Routledge & Kegan Paul, 1965.

Samburu—Language

2336. Sim, Ronald J. *A sociolinguistic profile of Maasai-Samburu-Ilchamus languages, Kenya*. Dallas, Summer Institute of Linguistics, 1980.

Samburu—Weapons

2337. Larick, Roy R. *Sedentary makers and nomadic owners: the circulation of steel weapons in Samburu District*. Nairobi, University of Nairobi, Institute of African Studies, 1984. 2 vols.

Science and Technology—East Africa

2338. Jumba-Masagazi, A. H. K. *Science and technology in East Africa: a bibliography and short commentaries*. Nairobi, East African Academy, 1973.

2339. Seyoum, B. *Technology licensing in eastern Africa: a critical exposition and analysis*. Aldershot, Avebury, 1990.

Sebei—Ethnography

2340. Goldschmidt, Walter. *Culture and behavior of the Sebei: a study in continuity and adaptation*. Berkeley, University of California Press, 1976.

2341. Goldschmidt, Walter. *Kambuya's cattle: the legacy of an African herdsman*. Berkeley, University of California Press, 1969.

2342. Goldschmidt, Walter. *The Sebei: a study in adaptation*. New York, Holt, Rinehart and Winston, 1986.

Sebei—Language

2343. O'Brien, Richard J., and Wim A. M. Cuypers. *A descriptive sketch of the grammar of Sebei*. Washington, Georgetown University Press, 1975.

Selous Game Reserve

2344. Robins, Eric. *Secret Eden*. London, Elm Tree Books, 1980.

Semitic Languages

2345. Leslau, Wolf. *An annotated bibliography of the Semitic languages of Ethiopia*. The Hague, Mouton, 1965.

2346. Leslau, Wolf. *Arabic loan words in Ethiopian Semitic*. Wiesbaden, Otto Harrassowitz, 1990.

2347. Leslau, Wolf. *Fifty years of research: selection of articles on Semitic, Ethiopian Semitic and Cushitic*. Wiesbaden, Otto Harrassowitz, 1988.

Sennar—History

2348. Spaulding, Jay. *The heroic age in Sinnar*. East Lansing, Michigan State University, African Studies Center, 1985.

Sennar—Women

2349. Kenyon, Susan M. *Five women of Sennar*. Oxford, Clarendon Press, 1991.

Serengeti National Park

2350. Sinclair, A. R. E., and M. Norton-Griffiths (eds.) *Serengeti: dynamics of an ecosystem*. Chicago, University of Chicago Press, 1979.

2351. Turner, Myles. *My Serengeti years: the memoirs of an African game warden*. London, Elm Tree, 1987.

Shaiqiya—Ethnography

2352. Al-Shahi, Ahmed. *Themes from northern Sudan*. London, Ithaca Press, 1986.

2353. Ibrahim, Hayder. *The Shaiqiya: the cultural and social change of a northern Sudanese riverain people*. Stuttgart, Franz Steiner, 1979.

Shambala—Ethnography

2354. Winans, Edgar V. *Shambala: the constitution of a traditional state*. Berkeley, University of California Press, 1962.

Shambala—History

2355. Feierman, Steven. *Peasant intellectuals: anthropology and history in Tanzania*. Madison, University of Wisconsin Press, 1990.

2356. Feierman, Steven. *The Shambala kingdom: a history*. Madison, University of Wisconsin Press, 1974.

Shambala—Language

2357. Besha, R. M. *A study of tense and aspect in Shambala*. Berlin, Dietrich Reimer, 1989.

Shilluk—Language

2358. Gilley, Leoma G. *An autosegmental approach to Shilluk phonology*. Dallas, Summer Institute of Linguistics, 1992.

Sidamo—Ethnography

2359. Brøgger, Jan. *Belief and experience among the Sidamo: a case study towards an anthropology of knowledge*. Oslo, Norwegian University Press, 1986.

Sidamo—Language

2360. Gasparini, Armido. *Sidamo-English dictionary*. Bologna, EMI, 1983.

Sidamo—Social Conditions

2361. Hamer, J. H. *Humane development: participation and change among the Sadama of Ethiopia*. Tuscaloosa, University of Alabama Press, 1987.

Slave Trade and Slavery—East Africa

2362. Alpers, Edward A. *The East African slave trade.* Nairobi, East African Publishing House, 1967.

2363. Beachey, R. W. *A collection of documents on the slave trade of eastern Africa.* London, Collings, 1976.

2364. Beachey, R. W. *The slave trade of eastern Africa.* London, Collings, 1976.

2365. Clarence-Smith, W. G. (ed.) *The economics of the Indian Ocean slave trade in the nineteenth century.* London, Frank Cass, 1989.

2366. Collister, Peter. *The Sulivans and the slave trade.* London, Rex Collings, 1988.

2367. Collister, Peter. *The last days of slavery: England and the East African slave trade, 1870–1900.* Dar es Salaam, East African Literature Bureau, 1961.

2368. Harris, J. E. *The African presence in Asia: consequences of the East African slave trade.* Evanston, Northwestern University Press, 1971.

2369. Howell, Raymond. *The Royal Navy and the slave trade.* New York, St. Martin's Press, 1987.

2370. Nwulia, Moses D. E. *Britain and slavery in East Africa.* Washington, Three Continents Press, 1975.

2371. Wright, Marcia. *Strategies of slaves and women: life stories from East/ Central Africa.* London, James Currey, 1993.

So—Ethnobotany

2372. Heine, Bernd, and C. König. *Plant concepts and plant use: an ethnobotanical survey of the semi-arid and arid lands of East Africa. Part II: plants of the So, Uganda.* Saarbrücken, Breitenbach, 1988.

So—Ethnography

2373. Laughlin, Charles D., and Elizabeth R. Algeier. *An ethnography of the So of northeastern Uganda.* New Haven, Human Relations Area Files, 1979.

Soba—Archaeology

2374. Welsby, Derek A., and Charles M. Daniels. *Soba: archaeological research at a medieval capital on the Blue Nile.* Nairobi, British Institute in Eastern Africa, 1991.

Social Conditions—East Africa

2375. Apthorpe, Raymond J., and Peter Rigby (eds.) *Society and social change in eastern Africa.* Kampala, Makerere Institute for Social Research, 1969.

2376. Brokensha, David W., and P. D. Little (eds.) *Anthropology of development and change in East Africa.* Boulder, Westview Press, 1988.

2377. Edgerton, Robert B. *The individual in cultural adaptation: a study of four East African peoples*. Berkeley, University of California Press, 1971.

2378. Gleiss, Fritz (ed.) *Ostafrika: Kenya, Burundi, Uganda, Rwanda, Tanzania. Gesellschaft, Politik, Wirtschaft*. Leer, Mundo, 1991.

2379. Graebner, Werner (ed.) *Sokomoko: popular culture in East Africa*. Amsterdam, Rodolphi, 1992.

2380. Gulliver, Philip H. (ed.) *Tradition and transition in East Africa: studies of the tribal element in the modern era*. London, Routledge and Kegan Paul, 1969.

2381. Hutton, John (ed.) *Urban challenge in East Africa*. Nairobi, East African Publishing House, 1972.

2382. Kilbride, P. L., and J. C. Kilbride. *Changing family life in East Africa: women and children at risk*. University Park, Pennsylvania State University Press, 1990.

2383. Kitching, Gavin N. *Economic and social inequality in rural East Africa: the present as a clue to the past*. Swansea, University College of Swansea, Centre for Development Studies, 1977.

2384. Knappert, Jan. *East Africa: Kenya Tanzania & Uganda*. London, Sangam Books, 1987.

2385. Kuria, L., and John B. Webster. *A bibliography on anthropology and sociology in Tanzania and East Africa*. Syracuse, Syracuse University, Maxwell Graduate School, 1966.

2386. Kyewalyanga, Francis-Xavier S. *Einige Aspekte des Kulturwandels in Ostafrika: die Veränderungen der traditionellen Wirtschaftsformen bei ausgewählten Ethnien und die Rolle der Schulerziehung*. Hohenschäftlarn, Karl Renner, 1982.

2387. Linnebuhr, E. (ed.) *Transition and continuity of identity in East Africa and beyond: in memoriam David Miller*. Bayreuth, Eckhard Breitinger, 1989.

2388. Neuloh, Otto (ed.) *Der ostafrikanische Industriearbeiter zwischen Shamba und Maschine: Untersuchungen über den sozialen und personalen Wandel in Ostafrika*. München, Weltforum-Verlag, 1969.

2389. Omari, C. K., and L. P. Shaidi. *Social problems in eastern Africa*. Dar es Salaam, Dar es Salaam University Press, 1991.

2390. Parkin, David (ed.) *Town and country in central and eastern Africa*. London, Oxford University Press, 1975.

2391. Ranger, Terence O. *Dance and society in eastern Africa, 1890–1970: the Beni Ngoma*. London, Heinemann, 1975.

Social Conditions—Northeast Africa

2392. Tvedt, Terje (ed.) *Conflicts in the Horn of Africa: human and ecological consequences of war*. Uppsala, Uppsala University, Department of Social and Economic Geography, Research Programme on Environmental Policy and Society, 1993.

Soga—Christianity

2393. Tom Tuma, A. D. *Building a Ugandan church: African participation in church growth and expansion in Busoga, 1891–1940*. Nairobi, Kenya Literature Bureau, 1980.

Soga—Ethnography

2394. Fallers, Margaret Chave. *The eastern lacustrine Bantu: Ganda and Soga*. London, International African Institute, 1960.

Soga—History

2395. Cohen, David William. *The historical tradition of Busoga: Mukama and Kintu*. Oxford, Clarendon Press, 1972.

2396. Cohen, David William (ed.) *Towards a reconstructed past: historical texts from Busoga, Uganda*. Oxford, Oxford University Press for the British Academy, 1986.

Soga—Law

2397. Fallers, Lloyd A. *Law without precedent: legal ideas in action in the courts of colonial Busoga*. Chicago, University of Chicago Press, 1969.

Soga—Politics

2398. Fallers, Lloyd A. *Bantu bureaucracy: a century of political evolution among the Basoga of Uganda*. Chicago, University of Chicago Press, 1965.

Soga—Social Conditions

2399. Marvin, Richard. *Land or wages: the evaluation of occupational and residential alternatives by rural Basoga*. Munich, Weltforum-Verlag, 1978.

Somali—Ethnography

2400. Battista, Piero. *La Somalia: nelle sue genti e nella sua vita. Storia, folklore, tradizioni*. Roma, Signorelli, 1969.

2401. Farah, Mohamed I. *From ethnic response to clan identity: a study of state penetration among the Somali nomadic pastoral society of northeastern Kenya*. Uppsala, Acta Universitatis Upsaliensis, 1993.

2402. Helander, Bernhard. *Gender and gender characteristics as a folk model in southern Somali social classification and symbolism*. Uppsala, University of Uppsala, 1987.

2403. Lewis, I. M. *A pastoral democracy: a study of pastoralism and politics among the northern Somali of the Horn of Africa*. London, Oxford University Press, 1961.

2404. Lewis, I. M. *Marriage and the family in northern Somaliland*. Kampala, East African Institute of Social Research, 1962.

2405. Mohamed Abdi, Mohamed. *Anthropologie somalienne: actes du IIe colloque des études somaliennes, Besançon 8/11 octobre, 1990*. Paris, Les Belles Lettres, 1993.

2406. Puccioni, Nello. *Anthropology and ethnography of the peoples of Somalia*. New Haven, Human Relations Area Files, 1960.

Somali—Language

2407. Abdi-Asis, Muhumed Qani, et al. *Omimee's English-Somali dictionary: qaamuuska af-Ingiriis - af-Soomaali*. Cologne, Omimee, 1992.

2408. Adam, Hussein Mohamed, and Charles L. Geshekter. *The revolutionary development of the Somali language*. Los Angeles, University of California Press, 1980.

2409. Agostini, Francesco, et al. *Dizionario somalo-italiano*. Roma, Gangemi, 1985.

2410. Andrzejewski, B. W. *The case system in Somali*. London, University of London, School of Oriental and African Studies, 1979.

2411. Andrzejewski, B. W. *The declensions of Somali nouns*. London, University of London, School of Oriental and African Studies, 1964.

2412. Caney, John Charles. *The modernisation of Somali vocabulary, with particular reference to the period from 1972 to the present*. Hamburg, Helmut Buske, 1984.

2413. Cardona, Giorgio R. (ed.) *Studi somali I: fonologia e lessico*. Roma, Ministero degli Affari Esteri, Dipartimento per la Cooperazione allo Sviluppo, 1981.

2414. El Solamo-Mewis, Catherine. *Lehrbuch des Somali*. Leipzig, VEB Verlag Enzyklopädie, 1987.

2415. Farah, Mohammed Ali, and Dietmar Heck. *Somali Wörterbuch: Deutsch-Somali/Somali-Englisch-Deutsch*. Second edition. Hamburg, Helmut Buske, 1993.

2416. Labahn, Thomas. *Sprache und Staat: Sprachpolitik in Somalia*. Hamburg, Helmut Buske, 1982.

2417. Laitin, David D. *Politics, language, and thought: the Somali experience*. Chicago, University of Chicago Press, 1977.

2418. Lamberti, Marcello. *Die Nordsomali-Dialekte: eine synchronische Beschreibung*. Heidelberg, Carl Winter, 1988.

2419. Lamberti, Marcello. *Die Somali-Dialekte: eine vergleichende Untersuchung mit 35 Karten und zahlreichen Tabellen*. Hamburg, Helmut Buske, 1986.

2420. Lamberti, Marcello. *Map of Somali dialects in the Somali Democratic Republic.* Hamburg, Helmut Buske, 1986.

2421. Lamberti, Marcello. *Somali language and literature* [Bibliography]. Hamburg, Helmut Buske, 1986.

2422. Luling, Virginia. *Somali-English dictionary.* Wheaton, Dunwoody Press, 1987.

2423. Puglielli, Annarita (ed.) *Studi somali II: sintassi della lingua somala.* Roma, Ministero degli Affari Esteri, Dipartimento per la Cooperazione allo Sviluppo, 1981.

2424. Saeed, John Ibrahim. *Somali reference grammar.* Wheaton, Dunwoody Press, 1987.

2425. Saeed, John Ibrahim. *The syntax of focus and topic in Somali.* Hamburg, Helmut Buske, 1984.

2426. Serzisko, Fritz. *Der Ausdruck der Possessivität im Somali.* Tübingen, Gunter Narr, 1984.

2427. Zorc, R. David, and Abdullahi A. Issa. *Somali textbook.* Wheaton, Dunwoody Press, 1990.

Somali—Literature

2428. Andrzejewski, B. W., and I. M. Lewis. *Somali poetry: an introduction.* Oxford, Clarendon Press, 1964.

2429. Johnson, John William. *Heellooy heelleellooy: the development of the genre heello in modern Somali poetry.* Bloomington, Indiana University Press, 1974.

2430. Lamberti, Marcello. *Somali language and literature* [Bibliography]. Hamburg, Helmut Buske, 1986.

Somali—Oral Traditions

2431. Axmed Cali Abokor. *The camel in Somali oral traditions.* Mogadisho, Somali Academy of Sciences and Arts, 1987.

Somalia—Administration

2432. Mohamed, O. O. *Administrative efficiency and administrative language in Somalia.* Mogadishu, Somali Institute of Development Administration, 1976.

Somalia—Agriculture

2433. Conze, P., and Thomas Labahn (eds.) *Somalia: agriculture in the winds of change.* Saarbrücken-Schafbrücke, EPI Verlag, 1986.

2434. Massey, G. *Subsistence and change: lessons of agropastoralism in Somalia.* Boulder, Westview Press, 1987.

2435. Querini, Giulio. *Agricoltura e sviluppo economico: il caso della Somalia.* Roma, Edizioni Ricerche, 1969.

2436. Società Agricola Italo-Somala. *L'opera della Società agricola italo-somala in Somalia. Significato e valore delle realizzazioni delle esperienze e degli studi compiuti dalla S.A.I.S. nei suoi 44 anni di vita.* Milano, Coppini, 1970.

Somalia—Art and Artists

2437. Loughran, Katheryne S., et al. (eds.) *Somalia in word and image.* Bloomington, Indiana University Press for the Foundation for Cross Cultural Understanding, 1986.

2438. Manca, Clara. *Somalia: monili ed ornamenti tradizionali.* Roma, Istituto Italo-Africano, 1989.

Somalia—Bibliography

2439. Carbani, Fabio (ed.) *Bibliografia Somalia.* Roma, Ministero degli Affari Esteri, 1983.

2440. Conover, Helen F. *Official publications of Somaliland, 1941–1959: a guide.* Washington, Library of Congress, Reference Department, General Reference and Bibliography Division, 1960.

2441. DeLancey, M. W., et al. *Somalia.* Oxford, Clio Press, 1988.

2442. Salad, Mohamed Khalief. *Somalia: a bibliographical survey.* Westport, Greenwood Press, 1977.

Somalia—Boundaries

2443. Drysdale, John. *The Somali dispute.* London, Pall Mall Press, 1964.

2444. Matthies, Volker. *Der Grenzkonflikt Somalias mit Äthiopien und Kenya.* Hamburg, Institut für Afrika-Kunde, 1977.

Somalia—Camels

2445. Hjort af Ornäs, Anders (ed.) *The multi-purpose camel: interdisciplinary studies on pastoral production in Somalia.* Uppsala, University, Research Programme on Environmental Policy and Society, 1993.

2446. Hussein, Mohamed Ali (ed.) *Camel forum: camel pastoralism in Somalia. Proceedings from a workshop held in Baydhabo, April 8–13, 1984.* Stockholm, Somali Camel Research Project, Department of Social Anthropology, University of Stockholm, 1984.

Somalia—Colonial History

2447. Finazzo, Giuseppina. *L'Italia nel Benadir: l'azione di Vicenzo Filonardi 1884–1896.* Roma, Ateneo, 1966.

2448. Grassi, Fabio. *Le origini dell'imperialismo italiano: il caso somalo, 1896–1915.* Lecce, Milella, 1980.

2449. Hess, Robert L. *Italian colonialism in Somalia*. Chicago, University of Chicago Press, 1966.

2450. Novati, Giampaolo Calchi. *L'annessione dell'Oltregiuba nella politica coloniale italiana*. Roma, Istituto Italo-Africano, 1985.

Somalia—Constitution

2451. Muhammad, Haji N. A. Noor. *The development of the constitution of the Somali Republic*. Mogadishu, Ministry of Grace and Justice, 1969.

Somalia—Description and Travel

2452. Balsan, François. *À pied au nord somali: grenier d'aromates des pharaons*. Paris, La Palatine, 1965.

2453. Ghisellini, Giuseppe. *Un anno in Somalia*. Cosenza, LPE, 1978.

2454. Hanghe, Ahmed A. *The sons of Somal*. Cologne, Omimee, 1993.

2455. Manara Gaburro, Annalisa. *Cara Somalia: pensieri, parole, opere*. Padova, Rebellato, 1975.

2456. Mantovani, Agostino. *In Somalia*. Bornato, Centro Studi Arti Grafiche Sardini, 1977.

2457. Tutino, Saverio. *Viaggio in Somalia*. Milano, Mazzotta, 1975.

Somalia—Drought

2458. Abbas, A. S. *The health and nutrition aspect of the drought in Somalia*. Mogadishu, Ministry of Health, Community Health Department Nutrition Unit, 1978.

2459. Lewis, I. M. (ed.) *Abaar: the Somali drought*. London, International African Institute, 1975.

Somalia—Economy

2460. International Labour Office. *Economic transformation in a socialist framework: an employment and basic needs oriented development strategy for Somalia*. Addis Ababa, International Labour Office, Jobs and Skills Programme for Africa, 1977.

2461. Noor, Mohamed H. *Ursachen der Arbeitslosigkeit, Inflation und Marktspaltung und ihre Auswirkungen auf die somalische Wirtschaft: eine kritische Analyse*. München, Marino Verlag, 1991.

Somalia—Education

2462. Schwöbel, Hans P. *Erziehung zur Überwindung von Unterentwicklung: Curriculumentwicklung emanzipatorischer Alphabetisierung und Grundziehung zwischen Tradition und Moderne. Das Beispiel Somalia*. Frankfurt am Main, dipa-Verlag, 1982.

Somalia—Employment

2463. International Labour Office. *Generating employment and incomes in Somalia*. Geneva, International Labour Office, 1989.

Somalia—Energy

2464. UNDP. *Somalia: issues and options in the energy sector*. New York, United Nations, 1985.

Somalia—Famine

2465. Omaar, Rakiya, and Alex de Waal. *Somalia: crimes and blunders*. London, James Currey, 1993.

Somalia—Folktales

2466. Hanghe, Ahmed A. *Folktales from Somalia*. Collected and translated by A. A. Hanghe. Uppsala, Scandinavian Institute of African Studies, 1988.

Somalia—Food and Nutrition

2467. Abbas, A. S. (ed.) *Food and nutrition in Somalia*. Mogadishu, Ministry of Health, 1982.

Somalia—Foreign Relations

2468. Lefebvre, Jeffrey A. *Arms for the Horn: U.S. security policy in Ethiopia and Somalia, 1953–1991*. Pittsburgh, University of Pittsburgh Press, 1991.

2469. Touval, Saadia. *Somali nationalism: international politics and the drive for unity in the Horn of Africa*. Cambridge, Mass., Harvard University Press, 1963.

Somalia—Forestry

2470. Bowen, M. Roderick. *A bibliography of forestry in Somalia and Djibouti*. Mogadishu, British Forestry Project Somalia, Overseas Development Administration, 1990.

2471. Bowen, M. Roderick, and Neil M. Bird. *A partially annotated bibliography of forestry in Somalia, with additional background information*. Second edition. Mogadishu, British Forestry Project Somalia, Overseas Development Administration, 1988.

Somalia—Frankincense

2472. Farah, Ahmed Yusuf. *The milk of the Boswellia forests: frankincense production among the pastoral Somali*. Uppsala, University, Department of Social and Economic Geography, Research Programme on Environmental Policy and Society, 1994.

Somalia—Handbook

2473. Nelson, Harold D. (ed.) *Somalia: a country study*. Third edition. Washington, American University, 1982.

Somalia—Health and Medicine

2474. Buschkens, Willem F. L. *Community health in the developing world: the case of Somalia*. Assen, Van Gorcum, 1990.

2475. Cahill, Kevin M. *Somalia: a perspective*. Albany, State University of New York Press, 1980.

2476. Serkkola, Ari. *Organizational diversity of health services in Mogadishu, Somalia*. Helsinki, University of Helsinki, Institute of Development Studies, 1992.

Somalia—History

2477. Cassanelli, L. V. *The shaping of Somali society: reconstructing the history of a pastoral people, 1600–1900*. Philadelphia, University of Pennsylvania Press, 1982.

2478. Castagno, Margaret. *Historical dictionary of Somalia*. Metuchen, Scarecrow Press, 1975.

2479. Cremascoli, Bruno. *Il paese di Punt: viaggio nella storia della Somalia*. Milano, Unicopli, 1987.

2480. Fitzgibbon, Louis. *The betrayal of the Somalis*. London, Rex Collings, 1982.

2481. Fitzgibbon, Louis. *The evaded duty*. London, Rex Collings, 1985.

2482. Karp, Mark. *The economics of trusteeship in Somalia*. Boston, Boston University Press, 1960.

2483. Lewis, I. M. *A modern history of Somalia: nation and state in the Horn of Africa*. Revised, updated, and expanded edition. Boulder, Westview Press, 1988.

2484. Lewis, I. M. *Understanding Somalia: guide to culture, history and social institutions*. Second edition. London, HAAN Associates, 1993.

Somalia—Human Rights

2485. Africa Watch. *Somalia: a government at war with its own people. Testimonies about the killings and the conflict in the North*. New York, Africa Watch, 1990.

Somalia—Industry

2486. Hummen, Wilhelm, et al. *The private manufacturing sector in Somalia*. Berlin, German Development Institute, 1984.

Somalia—Law

2487. Angeloni, Renato. *Codice penale somalo: commentato ed annotato in base ai lavori preparatori.* Milano, Giuffrè, 1965.

2488. Angeloni, Renato. *Diritto constituzionale somalo.* Milano, Giuffrè, 1964.

2489. Angeloni, Renato, and Mario S. Rugiu. *Principi di diritto amministrativo somalo.* Milano, Giuffrè, 1965.

2490. Contini, Paolo. *The Somali republic: an experiment in legal integration.* London, Frank Cass, 1969.

2491. Ganzglass, Martin R. *The penal code of the Somali Democratic Republic.* New Brunswick, Rutgers University Press, 1971.

2492. Guadagni, Marco. *Xeerka beeraha: diritto fondiario somalo. Le terre agricole dal regime consuetudinario e coloniale verso la riforma socialista.* Milano, Giuffrè, 1981.

2493. Mellana, V. (ed.) *L'amministrazione della giustizia in Eritrea e Somalia.* Roma, Istituto Poligrafico dello Stato, 1971.

2494. Muhammad, Haji N. A. Noor. *The legal system of the Somali Democratic Republic.* Charlottesville, Michie, 1972.

2495. Sacco, Rodolfo. *Le grandi linee del sistema giuridico somalo.* Milano, Giuffrè, 1985.

Somalia—Maize

2496. Varotti, Adriano. *Il ciclo del mais nella economia somala.* Roma, Gangemi, 1989.

Somalia—Manpower

2497. Nigam, Shyam Behari Lal. *The manpower situation in Somalia: report submitted to the Government of Somalia.* Mogadiscio, Ministry of Health and Labour, Department of Labour, 1965.

Somalia—Pastoral Production

2498. Abdullahi, Ahmed Mohamed. *Pastoral production systems in Africa: a study of nomadic household economy and livestock marketing in central Somalia.* Kiel, Wissenschaftsverlag Vauk, 1990.

2499. Baas, Stephan. *Weidenpotential und Tragfähigkeit in Zentralsomalia.* Berlin, Dietrich Reimer, 1994.

2500. Baumann, M. P. O., et al. (eds.) *Pastoral production in central Somalia.* Rossdorf, TZ-Verlags-Gesellschaft, 1993.

Somalia—Pastoralists

2501. Mirreh, Abdi Gaileh. *Die sozialökonomischen Verhältnisse der nomadischen Bevölkerung im Nordern der Demokratischen Republik Somalia.* Berlin, Akademie-Verlag, 1978.

2502. Mohamed, Ahmed Farah, and Jasmin Touati. *Sedentarisierung von Nomaden: Chancen und Gefahren einer Entwicklungsstrategie am Beispiel Somalias.* Saarbrücken, Breitenbach, 1991.

Somalia—Politics

2503. Adam, Hussein Mohamed (ed.) *Somalia and the world: proceedings of an international symposium, held in Mogadishu, on the tenth anniversary of the Somali revolution, October 15–21, 1979.* Mogadishu, State Printing Press, 1980.

2504. Aidid, Mohammed Farah, and Satya Pal Ruhela (eds.) *The preferred future development in Somalia.* New Delhi, Vikas Publishing House, 1993.

2505. Bayne, E. A. *Four ways of politics: state and nation in Italy, Somalia, Israel, and Iran.* New York, American Universities Fieldstaff, 1965.

2506. Becker, E., and C. Mitchell. *Chronology of conflict resolution initiatives in Somalia.* Fairfax, George Mason University, Institute for Conflict Analysis and Resolution, 1991.

2507. Decraene, Philip. *L'expérience socialiste somalienne.* Paris, Berger-Levrault, 1977.

2508. Gebreyesus, E. G. *Somalia in difficulties.* Utrecht, Federatie van Vluchtelingen-Organisaties in Nederlands, 1992.

2509. Haakonsen, J. M. *Scientific socialism and self-reliance: the case of Somalia's "instant" fishermen.* Bergen, University of Bergen, Department of Social Anthropology, 1984.

2510. Laitin, David D., and S. S. Samatar. *Somalia: nation in search of a state.* Boulder, Westview Press, 1987.

2511. Mesfin Wolde Mariam. *Somalia: the problem child of Africa.* Addis Ababa, Addis Ababa University, 1977.

2512. Michler, Walter. *Somalia: ein Volk sterbt. Der Bürgerkrieg und das Versagen des Auslands.* Bonn, Ditez/Libri F, 1993.

2513. Ministry of Information and National Guidance. *Somalia under the revolution: two years of progress.* Mogadishu, Ministry of Information and National Guidance, 1971.

2514. Omar, Mohamed Osman. *The road to zero: Somalia's self destruction. Personal reminiscences.* London, HAAN Associates, 1992.

2515. Pestalozza, Luigi. *The Somalian revolution.* Paris, Éditions Afrique, Asie, Amérique Latine, 1973.

2516. Pillitteri, Paolo (ed.) *Somalia '81: intervista con Siad Barre*. Milano, SugarCo, 1981.

2517. Potholm, Christian P. *Four African political systems*. Englewood Cliffs, Prentice-Hall, 1970.

2518. Samatar, A. I. *Socialist Somalia: rhetoric and reality*. London, Zed Books, 1988.

2519. Siyad Barre, Mohamed. *My country and my people: selected speeches of the SRSP Secretary-General and the Somali Democratic Republic President, Jaalle Mohamed Siad Barre*. Mogadishu, Ministry of Information and National Guidance, 1979.

2520. Smith, Stephen. *Somalie: la guerre perdue de l'humanitaire*. Paris, Calmann-Levy, 1993.

2521. Torrenzano, Antonio. *Somalia: bilancio di un regime*. Firenze, L'Autore Libri Firenze, 1991.

Somalia—Postal Services

2522. Bianchi, P. *Storia dei servizi postali della Somalia italiana dalle origini al 1941*. Vignola, Edizione Vaccari, 1992.

Somalia—Public Sector

2523. Derlye, Abdulkadir H. *Somalia: the role of the public sector in developing countries*. Ljubljana, International Center for Public Enterprises in Developing Countries, 1983.

Somalia—Range Management

2524. Iannelli, Pierino. *The principles of pasture improvement and range management and their application in Somalia*. Rome, Food and Agriculture Organization, 1984.

Somalia—Refugees

2525. Elander, G. *Refugees in Somalia*. Uppsala, Scandinavian Institute of African Studies, 1980.

2526. Ministry of National Planning. *Short and long-term programme for refugees in the Somali Democratic Republic*. Mogadishu, Ministry of National Planning, 1981.

Somalia—Religion

2527. Mohamed-Abdi, Mohamed. *Histoire des croyances en Somalie: religions traditionelles et religions du livre*. Paris, Centre de Recherches d'Histoire Ancienne, 1992.

Somalia—Rural Conditions

2528. Leser, H. *Landwirtschaftsbewertungen und Landwirtschaftsplanung in afrikanischen Entwicklungsländern: Beispiel Somalia.* Basle, Basler Afrika Bibliographen, 1990.

2529. Samatar, A. I. *The state and rural transformation in northern Somalia, 1884–1986.* Madison, University of Wisconsin Press, 1989.

Somalia—Social Conditions

2530. Battista, Piero. *Introduzione alla cultura somala. Dal tribalismo alla nuova realtà socio-politica.* Napoli, Conte, 1979.

2531. Hicks, Norman. *Poverty and basic needs in Somalia.* Washington, World Bank, 1978.

2532. Makinda, Samuel M. *Seeking peace from chaos: humanitarian intervention in Somalia.* Boulder, Lynne Rienner, 1993.

Somalia—Studies

2533. Labahn, Thomas (ed.) *Proceedings of the second International Congress of Somali Studies, University of Hamburg, August 1–6, 1983.* Hamburg, Helmut Buske, 1984. 4 vols.

2534. Puglielli, Annarita (ed.) *Proceedings of the Third International Congress of Somali Studies.* Rome, Il Pensiero Scientifico, 1988.

Somalia—Trees

2535. Mahony, D. *Trees of Somalia: a fieldguide for development workers.* Oxford, OXFAM, 1990.

Somalia—Women

2536. Forni, E. *Una nuova vita in Somalia: note sulla condizione femminile e su un'esperienza di sedentarizzazione dei nomadi nella Somalia socialista.* Milano, Angeli, 1984.

2537. Grassivaro, Gallo P. *La circoncisione femminile in Somalia: una ricerca sul campo.* Milano, Giuffrè, 1986.

Sonjo—Ethnography

2538. Gray, Beverly Ann. *Beyond the Serengeti plains: adventures of an anthropologist's wife among the Sonjo.* New York, Vantage Press, 1971.

2539. Gray, Robert F. *The Sonjo of Tanganyika: an anthropological study of an irrigation-based society.* London, Oxford University Press, 1963.

Southern Nilotic Languages

2540. Rottland, Franz. *Die südnilotischen Sprachen: Beschreibung, Vergleichung und Rekonstruktion.* Berlin, Dietrich Reimer, 1982.

Suakin—Architecture

2541. Greenlaw, Jean-Pierre. *The coral buildings of Suakin.* Stocksfield, Oriel, 1976.

Suakin—History

2542. Talhami, Ghada Hashem. *Suakin and Massawa under Egyptian rule, 1865–1885.* Washington, University Press of America, 1979.

Sudan—Administration

2543. Ahmed, Rafia Hassan. *Critical appraisal to the role of the Public Service Commission in the Sudan, 1954–1969.* Khartoum, Tamaddon Printing Press, 1974.

2544. James, Eric. *Perspectives in public administration in Sudan: proceedings of the fourth round table, March 10–19, 1962.* Khartoum, Institute of Public Administration, 1966.

2545. Moharir, V. V., and S. Kagwe. *Administrative reform and development planning in the Sudan, 1956–1975.* Khartoum, University of Khartoum, Development Studies and Research Centre, 1987.

Sudan—Agriculture

2546. Abdel Ati, H. A. *The problems of the agricultural sector in Sudan: an account of policy gaps.* Khartoum, University of Khartoum, Department of Geography, 1986.

2547. Abu Sin, M. E., et al. *Problems of agricultural development in the Sudan: selected papers of a seminar.* Aachen, Alano, 1982.

2548. Anhuf, Dieter. *Klima und Ernteertrag: eine statistische Analyse an ausgewählten Beispielen nord- und südsaharischer Trockenräume, Senegal, Sudan, Tunesien.* Bonn, Dümmler's, 1989.

2549. Craig, G. M. (ed.) *The agriculture of the Sudan.* Oxford, Oxford University Press, 1991.

2550. Heinritz, Günter (ed.) *Problems of agricultural development in the Sudan: selected papers of a seminar.* Göttingen, Edition Herodot, 1982.

2551. Mamoun, Izz Eldin. *Bibliography of agricultural and veterinary research in Sudan up to 1974.* Khartoum, National Council for Research, Agricultural Research Council, 1978.

2552. Mohamed-Salih, Mohamed A. (ed.) *Agrarian change in the central rainlands, Sudan: a socio-economic analysis.* Uppsala, Scandinavian Institute of African Studies, 1987.

2553. Nigam, Shyam Behari Lal. *The labour requirement and supply situation in agriculture in the Sudan, 1973–1985.* Addis Ababa, International Labour Organisation, Jobs and Skills Programme for Africa, 1980.

2554. Oesterdiekhoff, Peter. *Agrarpolitische Orientierungen: Phasen, Tendenzen und Alternativen.* Bremen, Universität Bremen, 1979.

2555. Sakamoto, K. (ed.) *Agriculture and land utilization in the eastern Zaire and the southern Sudan.* Kyoto, Kyoto University, 1984.

2556. Shaaeldin, Elfatih (ed.) *The evolution of agrarian relations in the Sudan: a reader.* The Hague, Institute of Social Studies, 1987.

2557. Shaw, D. J. *Agricultural development in the Sudan: 13th annual conference, Dec. 3–6, 1965, Khartoum.* Khartoum, Philosophical Society of the Sudan, 1966.

2558. Simpson, I. G., and M. C. Simpson. *Alternative strategies for agricultural development in the central rainlands of the Sudan, with special reference to the Damazine area.* Leeds, University of Leeds, Department of Agricultural Economics, 1978.

2559. Zahlan, A. B. *Agricultural bibliography of Sudan, 1974–1983: selected, classified and annotated.* London, Ithaca Press, 1984.

2560. Zahlan, A. B. (ed.) *The agricultural sector of Sudan: policy and systems studies.* London, Ithaca Press, 1986.

Sudan—Arabic Language

2561. Kaye, Alan S. *Chadian and Sudanese Arabic in the light of comparative Arabic dialectology.* The Hague, Mouton, 1976.

Sudan—Archaeology

2562. Bradley, Rebecca J. *Nomads in the archaeological record: case studies in the northern provinces of the Sudan.* Berlin, Akademie-Verlag, 1992.

2563. Caneva, Isabella (ed.) *El Geili: the history of a Middle Nile environment, 7000 B.C.–A.D. 1500.* Oxford, British Archaeological Reports, 1988.

2564. Hinkel, Friedrich W. *The archaeological map of the Sudan.* Berlin, Akademie-Verlag, 1979.

2565. Hintze, Fritz, and Ursula Hintze. *Civilizations of the old Sudan: Kerma, Kush, Christian Nubia.* Leipzig, Edition Leipzig, 1968.

2566. Hintze, Fritz, et al. *Musawwarat es Sufa. Bd. 1: der Löwentempel.* Berlin, Akademie-Verlag, 1993. 2 vols.

2567. Hofmann, Inge, et al. *Der antike Sudan heute.* Wien, Afro-Pub, 1985.

2568. Mack, John, and Peter Robertshaw (eds.) *Culture history of the southern Sudan: archaeology, linguistics and ethnohistory.* Nairobi, British Institute in Eastern Africa, 1982.

2569. Simpson, William Kelly, and Whitney M. Davis (eds.) *Studies in ancient Egypt, the Aegean and the Sudan: essays in honor of Dows Dunham on the occasion of his 90th birthday, June 1, 1980.* Boston, Museum of Fine Arts, Department of Egyptian and Ancient Near Eastern Art, 1981.

2570. Török, László. *The royal crowns of Kush: a study in Middle Nile Valley regalia and iconography in the 1st millennia B.C. and A.D.* Oxford, British Archaeological Reports, 1987.

Sudan—Art and Artists

2571. Martens-Czarnecka, Malgorzata. *Les éléments décoratifs sur les peintures de la Cathédrale de Faras.* Varsovie, Éditions Scientifiques de Pologne, 1982.

Sudan—Banking

2572. Saeed, Osman Hassan. *The Industrial Bank of Sudan, 1962–1968: an experiment in development banking.* Khartoum, Khartoum University Press, 1971.

2573. Staab, Christian H. *Die Bedeutung islamischer Banken für die wirtschaftliche Entwicklung im Sudan.* Meckenheim, Dieter Falk, 1989.

Sudan—Bibliography

2574. Dagher, Joseph A. *A Sudanese bibliography: Arabic sources, 1875–1967.* London, Luzac, 1968.

2575. Daly, M. W. *Sudan.* Revised edition. Oxford, Clio Press, 1992.

2576. El Nasri, Abdel Rahman. *A bibliography of the Sudan, 1938–1958.* London, Oxford University Press, 1962.

2577. Geddes, C. L. *An analytical guide to the bibliographies on modern Egypt and the Sudan.* Denver, American Institute of Islamic Studies, 1972.

2578. Wawa, Yosa H., et al. *Southern Sudan: a select bibliography.* Khartoum, University of Khartoum, Institute of African and Asian Studies, Library and Documentation, 1988.

Sudan—Boat Building

2579. Kirscht, Holger. *Bootsbau in Omdurman, Sudan.* Stuttgart, Franz Steiner, 1990.

Sudan—Child Welfare

2580. Dodge, Cole P., and Magne Raundalen. *Reaching children in war: Sudan, Uganda and Mozambique.* Bergen, Sigma Forlag, 1991.

Sudan—Christianity

2581. Vantini, Giovanni. *Christianity in the Sudan.* Bologna, Editrice Missionaria Italiana, 1981.

Sudan—Climate

2582. El Tom, M. A. *The rains of the Sudan: mechanism and distribution.* Khartoum, Khartoum University Press, 1975.

2583. Hulme, Michael. *An annotated bibliography of the climate of Sudan.* Cambridge, African Studies Centre, 1987.

2584. Kuba, G. K. *Climate of the Sudan.* Khartoum, University of Khartoum, National Building Research Station, 1968.

Sudan—Cooperatives

2585. Bardeleben, Manfred. *The cooperative system in the Sudan: development, characteristics and importance in the socio-economic development process.* Munich, Weltforum-Verlag, 1973.

2586. Mann, Wirsa Singh. *Cooperative movement in the Democratic Republic of Sudan.* Khartoum, Khartoum University Press, 1978.

Sudan—Description and Travel

2587. Asher, Michael. *In search of the forty days road.* Harlow, Longmans, 1984.

2588. Bonn, Gisela. *Das doppelte Gesicht des Sudan.* Wiesbaden, Brockhaus, 1961.

2589. Daly, M. W., and L. E. Forbes. *Sudan in original photographs.* London, Kegan Paul International, 1988.

2590. Dominguez, Z., and A. Pena. *Sudan.* Havana, Ciencias Sociales, 1990.

2591. Dumoulin, S. *Soudan.* Paris, Seuil, 1979.

2592. Hoagland, Edward. *African Calliope: a journey to the Sudan.* New York, Random House, 1979.

2593. Lightfoot-Klein, Hanny. *A woman's odyssey into Africa: tracks across a life.* New York, Haworth Press, 1992.

Sudan—Drought

2594. Cole, R. (ed.) *Measuring drought and drought impacts in Red Sea Province, Sudan.* Oxford, OXFAM, 1990.

Sudan—Economy

2595. Abdelkarim, Abbas. *Primitive capital accumulation in the Sudan.* London, Frank Cass, 1992.

2596. Al-Hassan, Ali Mohammed (ed.) *An introduction to the Sudan economy.* Khartoum, Khartoum University Press, 1971.

2597. Ali, Ali Abdel Gadir (ed.) *The Sudan economy in disarray: essays on the IMF model.* Khartoum, Ali Abdel Gadir Ali, 1985.

2598. Ali, Mohamed Abdel Rahman. *Fluctuations and impact of government expenditure in the Sudan, 1966–1967.* Khartoum, Khartoum University Press, 1974.

2599. Ali, Mohamed Abdel Rahman. *Government expenditure and economic development: a case study of the Sudan.* Khartoum, Khartoum University Press, 1974.

2600. Ayokev, Kunijwok G. *State and development in the black Sudan.* Khartoum, Khartoum University Press, 1983.

2601. Ayoub, Amal, et al. *Economics: a bibliography of studies on the Sudan.* Khartoum, National Council for Research, 1974.

2602. Beshai, Adel Amin. *Export performance and economic development in Sudan, 1900–1967.* London, Ithaca Press, 1976.

2603. Brown, Richard P. C. *Public debt and private wealth: debt, capital flight and the IMF in Sudan.* Basingstoke, Macmillan, 1992.

2604. El Hassan, Ali M. (ed.) *An introduction to the Sudan economy.* Khartoum, Khartoum University Press, 1976.

2605. El Hassan, Ali M. (ed.) *Essays on the economy and society of the Sudan.* Khartoum, Economic and Social Research Council, 1977.

2606. International Labour Office. *Growth, employment and equity: a comprehensive strategy for the Sudan.* Geneva, International Labour Office, 1976.

2607. Lees, Francis A., and Hugh C. Brooks. *The economic and political development of the Sudan.* London, Macmillan, 1977.

2608. Mamoun, Izz Eldin. *Bibliography of social sciences of the Sudan. Vol. 1: economics and sociology up to 1977.* Khartoum, National Council for Research, 1978.

2609. Messaoud, Jir. *Soudan: trente ans d'indépendence: mutations et obstacles au développement socio-économique.* Paris, Présence Africaine, 1987.

2610. Nimeiri, Sayed. *Taxation and economic development: a case study of the Sudan.* Khartoum, Khartoum University Press, 1974.

2611. Oesterdiekhoff, Peter, and Karl Wohlmuth (eds.) *The development perspectives of the Democratic Republic of Sudan: the limits of the breadbasket strategy.* Munich, Weltforum-Verlag, 1983.

2612. Stucken, Rudolf. *Entwicklungsbedingungen und Entwicklungschancen der Republik Sudan.* Berlin, Duncker & Humblot, 1963.

2613. Sulayman, Ali Ahmed. *Issues in the economic development of the Sudan.* Khartoum, Khartoum University Press, 1975.

2614. Taha, Elhafiz Attaelmannan, et al. *Towards alternative economic policies for Sudan.* Bremen, University of Bremen, Sudan Economy Research Group, 1990.

2615. Tetzlaff, Rainer, and Karl Wohlmuth (eds.) *Der Sudan: Probleme und Perspektiven der Entwicklung.* Frankfurt am Main, Alfred Metzner, 1980.

2616. Umbadda, Siddig. *Import policy in Sudan, 1966–76.* Khartoum, Khartoum University Press, 1984.

2617. Van der Wel, Paul, and Abdel Ghaffar Muhammad Ahmad (eds.) *Perspectives on development in the Sudan: selected papers from a research workshop in The Hague, July, 1984.* The Hague, Institute of Social Studies, 1986.

2618. Wohlmuth, Karl. *Internationale Ressourcen im Sudan: Auslandsverschuldung und Auslandskapital.* Bremen, Universität Bremen, 1979.

2619. Yongo-Bure, B. *Economic development of the southern Sudan: an overview and a strategy.* Bremen, University of Bremen, Sudan Economy Research Group, 1989.

Sudan—Education

2620. Beasley, Ina. *Before the wind changed: people, places and education in the Sudan.* Oxford, Oxford University Press, 1992.

2621. Beshir, Mohamed Omer. *Educational development in the Sudan, 1898–1956.* London, Oxford University Press, 1969.

2622. Beshir, Mohamed Omer. *Educational policy and the employment problem in the Sudan.* Khartoum, University of Khartoum, Faculty of Economic and Social Studies, Development Studies and Research Centre, 1977.

2623. Griffiths, V. L. *Teacher-centred: quality in Sudan primary education, 1930 to 1970.* London, Longmans, 1975.

2624. Ibrahim, Abdel Mageed A. *Health and academic achievement of Khartoum University students.* Khartoum, Khartoum University Press, 1988.

2625. Rashid, Sadig, and Terry Sandell (eds.) *Non-formal education in the Sudan: proceedings of a workshop . . . 1978.* Khartoum, University of Khartoum, Development Studies and Research Centre, 1980.

2626. Sanderson, Lilian Passmore, and G. N. Sanderson. *Education, religion and politics in southern Sudan, 1899–1964.* London, Ithaca Press, 1981.

2627. Sanyal, Bikas C., and El Sammani A. Yacoub. *Higher education and employment in the Sudan.* Paris, UNESCO International Institute for Educational Planning, 1975.

2628. Sanyal, Bikas C., et al. *From college to work: the case of Sudan.* Paris, UNESCO International Institute for Educational Planning, 1987.

Sudan—Employment

2629. El Hassan, Ali M. (ed.) *Growth, employment and equity: a selection of papers presented to the ILO Comprehensive Employment Strategy Mission to the Sudan, 1974–1975.* Khartoum, International Labour Office, 1977.

Sudan—Energy

2630. Digernes, Turi Hammer. *Wood for fuel: energy crisis implying desertification. The case of Bara, the Sudan.* Bergen, Geografisk Institutt, Universitetet i Bergen, 1977.

Sudan—Environment

2631. Ahlcrona, Eva. *The impact of climate and man on land transformation in central Sudan: applications of remote sensing.* Lund, University of Lund Press, 1988.

2632. El Khalifa, M. D., et al. *Sudan's southern stock route: an environmental impact assessment.* Khartoum, University of Khartoum, Institute of Environmental Studies, 1985.

2633. El Mangouri, Hassan Abdalla. *Environmental management in the Sudan: Umm Kaddada District, Northern Darfur Province. Final report.* Khartoum, University of Khartoum, Institute of Environmental Studies, 1985.

2634. El Sammani, Mohamed Osman, and H. O. Abdel Nour. *Northern Kordofan: a collection of papers on desertification, drought-impact and related issues.* Khartoum, University of Khartoum, Institute of Environmental Studies, 1986.

2635. Miehe, Sabine. *Vegetation ecology of the Jebel Marra massif in the semiarid Sudan.* Stuttgart, Borntraeger, 1988.

2636. Olsson, Lennart. *An integrated study of desertification: applications of remote sensing, GIS and spatial models in semi-arid Sudan.* Malmo, Gleerup, 1985.

2637. Olsson, Lennart. *Desertification of climate? Investigation regarding the relationship between land degradation and climate in the central Sudan.* Lund, University of Lund Press, 1983.

2638. Osman, Mohamed T. *Verwüstung: die Zerstörung von Kulturland am Beispiel des Südsudan.* Bremen, CON Literaturvertrieb, 1989.

Sudan—Ethics

2639. Nordenstam, Tore. *Sudanese ethics.* Uppsala, Scandinavian Institute of African Studies, 1968.

Sudan—Ethnography

2640. Boddy, J. *Wombs and alien spirits: women, men and the zar cult in northern Sudan.* Madison, University of Wisconsin Press, 1989.

2641. Cunnison, Ian, and Wendy James (eds.) *Essays in Sudan ethnography presented to Sir Edward Evans-Pritchard.* London, Hurst, 1972.

2642. Deng, Francis Mading. *The man called Deng Majok: a biography of power, polygyny, and change.* New Haven, Yale University Press, 1986.

2643. Giorgi, Liliani de. *Culto dei gemelli nel Sudan meridionale.* Bologna, Editrice Missionaria Italiana, 1964.

2644. Iten, Oswald. *Schwarzer Sudan: die Stamme der Nuba, Ingessana, Schilluk, Dinka, Nuer, Azande und Latuka.* Kreuzlingen, Neptune Verlag, 1978.

2645. Kramer, Fritz, and Bernhard Streck (eds.) *Sudanesische Marginalien: eine ethnographische Programm.* München, Trickster-Verlag, 1991.

2646. Mohammed, Abbas Ahmed. *White Nile Arabs: political leadership and economic change.* London, Athlone Press, 1980.

2647. Simonse, S. *Kings of disaster: dualism, centralism and the scapegoat king in the southeastern Sudan.* Leiden, E. J. Brill, 1992.

2648. Soeffing, Helmut. *Veränderungen in der Siedlungsweise bei den For im Jebel Marra.* Bremen, Übersee-Museum, 1979.

2649. Streck, Bernhard (ed.) *Tradition, Migration, Notstand: Themen heutiger Sudanethnographie.* Göttingen, Edition Re, 1990.

Sudan—Famine

2650. Article 19. *Starving in silence: a report on famine and censorship.* London, Article 19, 1990.

2651. Banga, Luther (ed.) *Reducing people's vulnerability to famine: an evaluation of Band Aid and Live Aid financed projects in Africa. Vol. 6: Sudan, country annexe and case studies.* London, Band Aid, 1991.

2652. Deng, Francis Mading, and Larry Minear. *The challenges of famine relief: emergency operations in the Sudan.* Washington, Brookings Institution, 1992.

2653. Heiden, David. *Dust to dust: a doctor's view of famine in Africa.* Philadelphia, Temple University Press, 1992.

2654. Hutchinson, B. *Famine mitigation bibliography, with special emphasis on Ethiopia, Sudan and Angola.* Tucson, University of Arizona, Arid Lands Information Center, 1992.

2655. International Labour Office. *After the famine: a programme of action to strengthen the survival strategies of affected populations.* Geneva, International Labour Office, 1986.

2656. Minear, Larry. *Humanitarianism under siege: a critical review of Operation Lifeline Sudan.* Trenton, Red Sea Press, 1991.

2657. Tesfaye Teklu, et al. *Drought and famine relationships in Sudan: policy implications.* Washington, International Food Policy Research Institute, 1991.

Sudan—Female Circumcision

2658. El Dareer, Asma. *Woman, why do you weep? Circumcision and its consequences.* London, Zed Press, 1982.

2659. Lightfoot-Klein, Hanny. *Prisoners of ritual: an odyssey into female genital circumcision in Africa.* New York, Haworth Press, 1989.

2660. Sanderson, Lilian Passmore. *Against the mutilation of women: the struggle to end unnecessary suffering.* London, Ithaca, 1981.

Sudan—Flora

2661. Wickens, G. E. *The flora of Jebel Marra (Sudan Republic) and its geographical affinities.* London, H.M.S.O., 1976.

Sudan—Folktales

2662. Al-Shahi, Ahmed, and F. C. T. Moore (eds.) *Wisdom from the Nile: a collection of folk-stories from northern and central Sudan.* Oxford, Clarendon Press, 1978.

2663. Hurreiz, Sayyid Hamid, and Herman Bell (eds.) *Directions in Sudanese linguistics and folklore.* Khartoum, Khartoum University Press, 1975.

2664. Mitchnik, Helen. *Egyptian and Sudanese folk-tales.* Oxford, Oxford University Press, 1978.

2665. Nasr, A. A. (ed.) *Folklore and development in the Sudan.* Khartoum, Khartoum University, Institute of African Studies, 1985.

Sudan—Food and Nutrition

2666. Dirar, Hamid A. *The indigenous fermented foods of the Sudan: a study in African food and nutrition.* Wallingford, CAB International, 1993.

2667. Maxwell, Simon. *Food insecurity in north Sudan.* Brighton, University of Sussex, Institute of Development Studies, 1989.

2668. Maxwell, Simon (ed.) *To cure all hunger: food policy and food security in Sudan.* London, Intermediate Technology Publishers, 1991.

2669. Ogbe, Gebregiorgis. *Ernährungssicherungpolitik in Schwarzafrika: ökonomische Analyse und Entwicklungsstrategie am Beispiel des Sudans.* Stuttgart, Peter Lang, 1991.

2670. Sharp, Kay, and Wayne Foord. *Food policy in the Sudan: an annotated bibliography.* Brighton, University of Sussex, Institute of Development Studies, 1989.

2671. Taha, S. A. *Society, food and nutrition in the Gezira: a social and medical study.* Khartoum, Khartoum University Press, 1977.

Sudan—Foreign Aid

2672. Le Masson, Hugues. *Faut-il, encore, aider les pays en développement? Histoire d'un cas exemplaire.* Paris, Éditions du Félin, 1992.

Sudan—Foreign Relations

2673. Beshir, Mohamed Omer (ed.) *Sudan, aid and external relations: selected essays.* London, Ithaca Press, 1984.

2674. Issa, Abdelmonein I. *Die entwicklungspolitischen Beziehungen zwischen dem Sudan und der Bundesrepublik Deutschland, 1956–1979.* Frankfurt am Main, Haag + Herchen, 1980.

2675. Sabry, Hussein Zulfakar. *Sovereignty for Sudan.* London, Ithaca Press, 1982.

2676. Salah El-Din, Z. *Die Süd-Süd Kooperation als Entwicklungsstrategie: Beispiel der ägyptische-sudanesischen Integrationsbestrebungen, 1974– 1984.* Berlin, Arlt und Schiller, 1986.

Sudan—Forestry

2677. Al-Tayeb, G. D. *Forestry and land use in the Sudan.* Khartoum, Khartoum University Press, 1972.

2678. Bayoumi, A. A. *A forest bibliography of the Sudan to 1973.* Khartoum, National Council for Research, Agricultural Research Council, 1974.

2679. Gamser, Matthew S. *Power from the people: innovation, user participation, and forest energy development.* London, Intermediate Technology Publications, 1988.

2680. Kapp, Gerald B. *Agroforstliche Landnutzung in der Sahel-Sudanzone: traditionelle Bewirtschaftung, Nutzungsprobleme, Lösungsansätze durch Projekte und Forschung.* München, Weltforum-Verlag, 1987.

Sudan—Geography

2681. Barbour, K. M. *The Republic of Sudan: a regional geography.* London, University of London Press, 1961.

2682. Gurdon, Charles (ed.) *Field studies in Abu Gubeiha, Sudan, 1978.* London, University of London, School of Oriental and African Studies, 1978.

2683. Schultze, Joachim Heinrich. *Der Ost-Sudan: Entwicklungsland zwischen Wüste und Regenwald.* Berlin, Dietrich Reimer, 1963.

Sudan—Geology

2684. Ahmed, Adly Abdel Mageed. *General outlines of the geology and mineral occurrence of the Red Sea Hills.* Khartoum, Geological and Mineral Resources Department, 1979.

2685. Omer, M. K. *Genesis and diagenesis of the Nubian sandstone formation in Khartoum Province.* Khartoum, Geological and Mineral Resources Department, 1975.

2686. Saeed, M. T. *Hydrogeology of Khartoum Province and northern Gezira area.* Khartoum, Geological and Mineral Resources Department, 1975.

2687. Tahir Hussein, M. *Hydrogeological investigation of Khor Arbaat basin.* Khartoum, Geological and Mineral Resources Department, 1975.

2688. Vail, J. R. *Outline of the geology and mineral deposits of the Democratic Republic of the Sudan and adjacent areas.* London, H.M.S.O., 1978.

2689. Whiteman, A. J. *The geology of the Sudan Republic.* Oxford, Clarendon Press, 1971.

2690. Williams, M. A. J., and D. A. Adamson (eds.) *A land between two Niles: quaternary geology and biology of the central Sudan.* Rotterdam, Balkema, 1982.

Sudan—Handbook

2691. Nelson, Harold D. (ed.) *Sudan: a country study.* Third edition. Washington, American University, 1982.

Sudan—Health and Medicine

2692. Bayoumi, Ahmed. *The history of Sudan health services.* Nairobi, Kenya Literature Bureau, 1979.

2693. Cruickshank, Alexander. *The kindling fire: medical adventures in the southern Sudan.* London, Heinemann, 1962.

2694. El Safi, A. *Native medicine in the Sudan: sources, concepts and methods.* Khartoum, Sudan Research Unit, 1970.

2695. Hartwig, Gerald W., and Karl David Patterson. *Cerebrospinal meningitis in West Africa and the Sudan in the twentieth century.* Los Angeles, Crossroads Press, 1984.

2696. Hartwig, Gerald W., and Karl David Patterson. *Schistosomiasis in twentieth-century Africa: historical studies on West Africa and Sudan.* Los Angeles, Crossroads Press, 1984.

Sudan—History

2697. Abdel-Rahim, Muddathir. *Imperialism and nationalism in the Sudan: a study in constitutional and political development, 1899–1956.* Khartoum, Khartoum University Press, 1986.

2698. Abu Hasabu, Afaf Abdel Majid. *Factional conflict in the Sudanese nationalist movement, 1918–1948.* Khartoum, University of Khartoum, Graduate College, 1985.

2699. Arkell, A. J. *A history of the Sudan from the earliest times to 1821.* Second edition. London, Athlone Press, 1961.

2700. Badal, Raphael Koba. *Origins of the underdevelopment of the southern Sudan: British administrative neglect.* Khartoum, Khartoum University Press, 1983.

2701. Bakheit, Jaafar M. A. *Communist activities in the Middle East between 1919–1927, with special reference to Egypt and the Sudan.* Khartoum, Khartoum University Press, 1968.

2702. Balfour-Paul, Glen. *The end of Empire in the Middle East: Britain's relinquishment of power in her last three Arab dependencies.* Cambridge, Cambridge University Press, 1991.

2703. Bano, L. *Mezzo secolo di storia Sudanese, 1842–1898, dall'archivio parrochiale di Khartum.* Bologna, Editrice Missionaria Italiana, 1977.

2704. Barthorp, Michael. *War on the Nile: Britain, Egypt and the Sudan, 1882–1898*. Poole, Blandford, 1984.

2705. Bates, Darrell. *The Fashoda incident of 1898: encounter on the Nile*. Oxford, Oxford University Press, 1984.

2706. Bedri, Babikr. *The memoirs of Babikr Bedri*. Vol. 1: London, Oxford University Press, 1969. Vol. 2: London, Ithaca Press, 1980.

2707. Bell, Gawain. *Shadows on the sand: the memoirs of Sir Gawain Bell*. London, Hurst, 1983.

2708. Bjørkelo, Anders. *Prelude to the Mahdiyya: peasants and traders in the Shendi region, 1821–1885*. Cambridge, Cambridge University Press, 1989.

2709. Bleuchot, H., et al. *Sudan: history, identity, ideology*. London, Ithaca Press, 1991.

2710. Brook-Shepherd, Gordon. *Between two flags: the life of Baron Sir Rudolph von Slatin Pasha*. London, Weidenfeld and Nicolson, 1972.

2711. Collins, Robert O., and Francis Mading Deng (eds.) *The British in the Sudan, 1898–1956: the sweetness and the sorrow*. London, Macmillan, 1984.

2712. Collins, Robert O., and Robert L. Tignor. *Egypt and the Sudan*. Englewood Cliffs, Prentice-Hall, 1967.

2713. Collins, Robert O. *King Leopold, England and the Upper Nile, 1899–1909*. New Haven, Yale University Press, 1968.

2714. Collins, Robert O. *Land beyond the rivers: the southern Sudan, 1898–1918*. New Haven, Yale University Press, 1971.

2715. Collins, Robert O. *Shadows in the grass: Britain in the southern Sudan, 1918–1956*. New Haven, Yale University Press, 1983.

2716. Collins, Robert O. *The southern Sudan in historical perspective*. Tel Aviv, University of Tel Aviv, Shiloah Centre, 1975.

2717. Collins, Robert O. *The southern Sudan, 1883–1898: a struggle for control*. New Haven, Yale University Press, 1962.

2718. Daly, M. W. *British administration and the northern Sudan, 1917–1924: the Governor-Generalship of Sir Lee Stack in the Sudan*. Leiden, Nederlands Historisch-Archaeologisch Instituut te Istanbul, 1980.

2719. Daly, M. W. *Empire on the Nile: the Anglo-Egyptian Sudan, 1898–1934*. Cambridge, Cambridge University Press, 1986.

2720. Daly, M. W. *Imperial Sudan: the Anglo-Egyptian condominium, 1934–1956*. Cambridge, Cambridge University Press, 1991.

2721. Daly, M. W. (ed.) *Modernization in the Sudan: essays in honor of Richard Hill*. New York, Lilian Barber, 1985.

2722. Deng, Francis Mading, and M. W. Daly. *Bonds of silk: the human factor in the British administration of the Sudan.* East Lansing, Michigan State University Press, 1989.

2723. El Amin, Mohammed Nuri. *The emergence and development of the leftist movement in the Sudan during the 1930's and 1940's.* Khartoum, University of Khartoum, Institute of African and Asian Studies, 1984.

2724. El Mahdi, Mandour. *A short history of the Sudan.* London, Oxford University Press, 1965.

2725. Ewald, J. J. *Soldiers, traders and slaves: state formation and economic transformation in the greater Nile Valley, 1700–1885.* Madison, University of Wisconsin Press, 1990.

2726. Fabunmi, L. A. *The Sudan in Anglo-Egyptian relations: a case study of power politics, 1800–1956.* London, Longmans, 1960.

2727. Fauzy-Rossano, Didar D. *Le Soudan.* Paris, L'Harmattan, 1982.

2728. Fawzi, Saad ed-Din. *The labour movement in the Sudan, 1946–1955.* London, Oxford University Press, 1957.

2729. Fawzy, Didar. *La République du Soudan, 1956–1966.* Alger, Société Nationale d'Édition et de Diffusion, 1975.

2730. Fluehr-Lobban, Carolyn, et al. *Historical dictionary of the Sudan.* Second edition. Metuchen, Scarecrow Press, 1992.

2731. Foley, Helen. *Letters to her mother: war time Sudan, 1938–1945.* Castle Cary, Castle Cary Press, 1992.

2732. Giegler, Carl Christian. *The Sudan memoirs of Carl Christian Giegler Pasha, 1873–1883.* Edited by Richard Hill. London, Oxford University Press, 1984.

2733. Grandin, Nicole. *The Soudan nilotique et l'administration britannique, 1898–1956.* Leiden, E. J. Brill, 1982.

2734. Gray, R. *A history of the southern Sudan, 1839–1889.* London, Oxford University Press, 1961.

2735. Hassan, Yusuf Fadl. *The Arabs and the Sudan, from the seventh to the early sixteenth century.* Edinburgh, Edinburgh University Press, 1969.

2736. Henderson, K. D. D. *Set under authority: being a portrait of the life of the British District Officer in the Sudan under the Anglo-Egyptian Condominium, 1898–1955.* Castle Cary, Castle Cary Press, 1987.

2737. Henderson, K. D. D. *Sudan Republic.* New York, Praeger, 1965.

2738. Hicks, William. *The road to Shaykan: letters of General William Hicks Pasha written during the Sennar and Kordofan campaigns, 1883.* Edited by M. W. Daly. Durham, University of Durham, Centre for Middle Eastern and Islamic Studies, 1983.

2739. Hill, Richard. *A biographical dictionary of the Sudan*. Second edition. London, Frank Cass, 1967.

2740. Hill, Richard (ed.) *On the frontiers of Islam: two manuscripts concerning the Sudan under Turco-Egyptian rule, 1822–45*. Oxford, Clarendon Press, 1970.

2741. Hill, Richard. *Slatin Pasha*. London, Oxford University Press, 1965.

2742. Holt, Peter Malcolm, and M. W. Daly. *A history of the Sudan: from the coming of Islam to the present day*. Fourth edition. London, Longmans, 1988.

2743. Holt, Peter Malcolm. *The Mahdist state in the Sudan, 1881–1898*. Second edition. Oxford, Clarendon Press, 1970.

2744. Holt, Peter Malcolm. *Studies in the history of the Near East*. London, Frank Cass, 1973.

2745. Ibrahim, Hassan Ahmed. *The 1936 Anglo-Egyptian treaty: an historical study with special reference to the contemporary situation in Egypt and Sudan*. Khartoum, Khartoum University Press, 1976.

2746. Inglis, K. S. *The rehearsal: Australians at war in the Sudan, 1885*. Adelaide, Rigby Publishers, 1985.

2747. Kenrick, Rosemary. *Sudan tales: recollections of some Sudan Political Service wives, 1926–1956*. Cambridge, Oleander Press, 1987.

2748. Lavergne, Marc (ed.) *Le Soudan contemporaine de l'invasion turco-égyptienne à la rébellion africaine, 1821–1989*. Paris, Karthala, 1989.

2749. Lavin, Deborah (ed.) *The condominium remembered: proceedings of the Durham Sudan historical records conference, 1982. Vol. 1: the making of the Sudanese state*. Durham, University of Durham, Centre for Middle Eastern and Islamic Studies, 1991.

2750. Lea, C. A. E. *On trek in Kordofan: diaries of a British District Officer in the Sudan, 1931–33*. Edited by M. W. Daly. Oxford, Oxford University Press, 1994.

2751. MacLaren, Roy. *Canadians on the Nile, 1882–1898, being the adventures of the voyagers on the Khartoum Relief Expedition and other exploits*. Vancouver, University of British Columbia Press, 1978.

2752. Michel, Marc. *La mission Marchand, 1895–1899*. Paris, Mouton, 1972.

2753. Nimir, Babo. *Recollections of Babo Nimir*. London, Ithaca Press, 1982.

2754. O'Fahey, Rex S., and J. L. Spaulding. *Kingdoms of the Sudan*. London, Methuen, 1974.

2755. O'Fahey, Rex S. *States and state formation in the eastern Sudan*. Khartoum, Sudan Research Unit, 1970.

2756. Potter, M., and A. Potter. *Everything is possible: our Sudan years*. Gloucester, Alan Sutton, 1984.

2757. Robertson, James. *Transition in Africa: from direct rule to independence.* London, Christopher Hurst, 1974.

2758. Robson, Brian. *Fuzzy-wuzzy: the campaigns in the eastern Sudan, 1884– 1885.* Tunbridge Wells, Spellmount, 1993.

2759. Said, M. B. *The Sudan: crossroads of Africa.* Chester Springs, Dufour, 1965.

2760. Santi, Paul, and Richard Hill (eds.) *The Europeans in the Sudan, 1834– 1878: some manuscripts, mostly unpublished, written by traders, Christian missionaries, officials, and others.* Oxford, Clarendon Press, 1980.

2761. Shaked, Haim. *The life of the Sudanese Mahdi: an historical study of Kitab sa'adat al-mustahdi bi-sirat al-Imam al-Mahdi.* New Brunswick, Transaction Books, 1976.

2762. Sikainga, A. A. *The western Bahr al-Ghazal under British rule, 1898–1956.* Athens, Ohio University Press, 1991.

2763. Thomas, Graham F. *Sudan, 1950–85: death of a dream.* London, Darf, 1990.

2764. Toniolo, Elias, and Richard Hill (eds.) *The opening of the Nile basin: writings of the Catholic Mission to Central Africa on the geography and ethnography of the Sudan, 1842–1881.* New York, Barnes & Noble, 1975.

2765. Vogelsberger, Hartwig A. *Slatin Pascha: zwischen Wüstensand und Königskronen.* Graz, Styria, 1992.

2766. Voll, John Obert, and Sarah Potts Voll. *The Sudan: unity and diversity in a multicultural state.* Boulder, Westview Press, 1985.

2767. Warburg, Gabriel R. *Egypt and the Sudan: studies in history and politics.* London, Frank Cass, 1985.

2768. Warburg, Gabriel R. *Historical discord in the Nile Valley.* London, Hurst, 1992.

2769. Warburg, Gabriel R. *The Sudan under Wingate: administration in the Anglo-Egyptian Sudan, 1899–1916.* London, Frank Cass, 1971.

2770. Warner, Philip. *Dervish: the rise and fall of an African Empire.* London, Macdonald, 1973.

2771. Woodward, Peter. *Condominium and Sudanese nationalism.* London, Rex Collings, 1979.

2772. Woodward, Peter. *Sudan, 1898–1989: the unstable state.* Boulder, Lynne Rienner, 1990.

2773. Wright, P. *Conflict on the Nile: the Fashoda incident of 1898.* London, Heinemann, 1972.

2774. Zach, Michael. *Österreicher im Sudan, 1820 bis 1914.* Wien, Afro-Pub, 1985.

2775. Ziegler, P. *Omdurman*. London, Collins, 1973.

2776. Zulfo, Ismat Hasan. *Karari: the Sudanese account of the battle of Omdurman*. London, Frederick Warne, 1980.

Sudan—Human Rights

2777. Africa Watch. *Denying the "honor of living": Sudan, a human rights disaster*. New York, Africa Watch, 1990.

Sudan—Industry

2778. Affan, B. O. A. *Industrial policies and industrialization in the Sudan*. Khartoum, University of Khartoum, Graduate College, 1985.

2779. Hammeed, K. A. *Enterprise: industrial entrepreneurship in development, based on case studies from the Sudan*. London, Sage, 1974.

2780. Hansohm, Dirk. *Small industry development in Africa: lessons from Sudan*. Hamburg, Lit-Verlag, 1992.

2781. Imam, Faisal Bashir (ed.) *Industry in the Sudan: papers presented to the first Erkowit Conference, Erkowit, September, 1966*. Khartoum, University of Khartoum, School of Extra-Mural Studies, 1973.

2782. Massow, Heinrich von. *Die Industrie der Republik Sudan*. Hamburg, Afrika-Verein, Technisch-wirtschaftlicher Dienst, 1964.

2783. Oesterdiekhoff, Peter. *Industrieentwicklung und -struktur im Sudan*. Bremen, Universität Bremen, 1979.

2784. UNIDO. *The Sudan: towards industrial revitalization*. Vienna, UNIDO, 1989.

2785. Yongo-Bure, B. *The role of small scale industries in the recovery and development of the southern Sudan*. Bremen, University of Bremen, Sudan Economy Research Group, 1991.

Sudan—Informal Economy

2786. Trenk, Marin. *Der Schatten der Verschuldung: komplexe Kreditbeziehungen des informellen Finanzsecktors*. Saarbrücken, Breitenbach, 1991.

Sudan—Investment

2787. El Sheikh, Fath el Rahman Abdalla. *The legal regime of foreign private investment in Sudan and Saudi Arabia: a case study of developing countries*. Cambridge, Cambridge University Press, 1984.

Sudan—Islam

2788. Daly, M. W. (ed.) *Al Majdhubiyya and al Mikashfiyy: two Sufi tariqas in the Sudan*. Khartoum, University of Khartoum, Graduate College, 1985.

2789. Fluehr-Lobban, Carolyn. *Islamic law and society in the Sudan*. London, Frank Cass, 1987.

2790. Karrar, Ali Salih. *The Sufi brotherhoods in the Sudan*. London, Hurst, 1992.

2791. McHugh, Neil. *Holymen of the Blue Nile: the making of an Arab Islamic community in the Nilotic Sudan, 1500–1850*. Evanston, Northwestern University Press, 1993.

2792. Oevermann, Annette. *Die "Republikanischen Brüder" im Sudan: eine islamische Reformbewegung im zwanzigsten Jahrhundert*. Stuttgart, Peter Lang, 1993.

Sudan—Jewelry

2793. Semple, Clara. *Traditional jewellery and ornament of Sudan*. London, Kegan Paul International, 1993.

Sudan—Journalism

2794. Babiker, M. A. *Press and politics in the Sudan*. Khartoum, University of Khartoum, Graduate College, 1985.

Sudan—Labor

2795. El Bagir, I., et al. *Labour markets in the Sudan: a study carried out within the framework of the ILO/UNHCR project on income-generating activities for refugees in eastern and central Sudan*. Geneva, International Labour Office, 1984.

2796. Manger, Leif O. (ed.) *Communal labour in the Sudan*. Bergen, University of Bergen, Department of Social Anthropology, 1987.

Sudan—Land Use

2797. Lebon, John Harold George. *Land use in Sudan*. Bude, Geographical Publications, 1965.

Sudan—Language

2798. Abdalla, Abdelgadir Magmoud (ed.) *Studies in ancient languages of the Sudan: papers presented at the second international conference on language and literature in the Sudan*. Khartoum, Khartoum University Press, 1974.

2799. Abu-Manga, Al-Amin. *Fulfulde in the Sudan: process of adaptation to Arabic*. Berlin, Dietrich Reimer, 1986.

2800. Jernudd, Björn. *The language survey of the Sudan*. Umeå, Umeå Universitetsbiblioteket, 1979.

2801. Sandell, Lisa. *English language in Sudan: a history of its teachings and politics*. London, Ithaca Press, 1982.

2802. Thelwall, Robin (ed.) *Aspects of language in the Sudan*. Coleraine, New University of Ulster, 1978.

Sudan—Law

2803. Bruce, John W. *A bibliographical guide to the customary law of the Sudan*. Khartoum, University of Khartoum, Faculty of Law, 1979.

2804. El Mahdi, Saeed Mohamad Ahmed. *Introduction to the land law of the Sudan*. Khartoum, Khartoum University Press, 1979.

2805. Farran, Charles d'Olivier. *Matrimonial laws of the Sudan, being a study of the divergent religious and civil laws in African society*. London, Butterworths, 1963.

2806. Kongden, Olaf. *Das islamisierte Strafrecht des Sudan: von seiner Einführung 1983 bis Juli 1992*. Hamburg, Deutsches Orient-Institut, 1992.

2807. Mustafa, Zaki. *The common law in the Sudan: an account of the "justice, equity, and good conscience" provision*. Oxford, Clarendon Press, 1971.

2808. Vasdev, Krishna. *The law of evidence in the Sudan*. London, Butterworths, 1981.

2809. Vasdev, Krishna. *The law of homicide in the Sudan*. London, Butterworths, 1978.

Sudan—Local Government

2810. Al-Teraifi, Al-Agab Ahmed (ed.) *Decentralization in Sudan*. Khartoum, University of Khartoum, Graduate College, 1987.

2811. Howell, John (ed.) *Local government and politics in the Sudan*. Khartoum, Khartoum University Press, 1974.

Sudan—Manpower

2812. Berhanu Abegaz. *Manpower development planning: theory and an African case study*. Aldershot, Avebury, 1994.

Sudan—Migration

2813. Balamoan, G. Ayoub. *Migration policies in the Anglo-Egyptian Sudan, 1884–1956*. Cambridge, Mass., Harvard University, Center for Population Studies, 1976.

2814. Birks, J. S., and C. A. Sinclair. *Human capital on the Nile: development and emigration in the Arab Republic of Egypt and the Democratic Republic of the Sudan*. Geneva, International Labour Office, 1978.

2815. Gabal, Ahmed Abu. *Migration of Sudanese: causes and effects on Sudan economy*. Khartoum, Khartoum University Press, 1984.

2816. Ibrahim, Fouad N., and Helmut Ruppert (eds.) *Rural-urban migration and identity change: case studies from the Sudan*. Bayreuth, Druckhaus Bayreuth Verlagsgesellschaft, 1988.

2817. Kameir, El-Wathig Mohamed. *The political economy of labour migration in the Sudan: a comparative case study of migrant workers in an urban situation.* Hamburg, Institut für Afrika-Kunde, 1988.

Sudan — Missionaries

2818. Anderson, William B. *Ambassadors by the Nile.* London, Lutterworth Press, 1963.

2819. Bonfanti, Adriano. *Espulsi dal Sudan.* Second edition. Bologna, Editrice Nigrizia, 1964.

2820. Gaiga, Lorenzo. *Padre Lorenzo Violini: un cuore per l'Africa.* Bologna, Editrice Missionaria Italiana, 1990.

2821. Lonfernini, Bruno. *Nelle vecchie e nuove vigne africane.* Bologna, Editrice Missionaria Italiana, 1990.

2822. McEwan, Dorothy. *A Catholic Sudan: dream, mission, reality. A study of the Roman Catholic mission to Central Africa and its protection by the Hapsburg Empire from 1846–1900.* Roma, Stabilimento Tipografico Julia, 1988.

2823. Morlang, Francesco. *Missione in Africa Centrale: diario, 1855–1863.* Bologna, Editrice Nigrizia, 1973.

2824. Werner, Roland, et al. *Die Wüste sol blühen: Anfänge in Nordsudan.* Moers, Brendow, 1989.

Sudan — North/South Relations

2825. Abdel Ghaffar, Abdel Gadir Ahmed. *Politische Integration und Desintegration in einem Entwicklungsland: dargestellt am Beispiel des regionalen Konflikts in der Republik Sudan zwischen 1946–1969.* Frankfurt am Main, Haag + Herchen, 1979.

2826. Ahmad, Abdel Ghaffar Muhammad, and Gunnar M. Sørbø (eds.) *Management of the crisis in the Sudan.* Bergen, University, Centre for Development Studies, 1989.

2827. Albino, Oliver. *The Sudan: a southern viewpoint.* London, Oxford University Press, 1970.

2828. Alier, A. *Southern Sudan: too many agreements dishonoured.* Exeter, Ithaca Press, 1990.

2829. Arou, Mom K. N., and B. Yongo-Bure (eds.) *North-South relations in the Sudan since the Addis Ababa agreement.* Khartoum, University of Khartoum, Institute of African and Asian Studies, 1988.

2830. Beshir, Mohamed Omer. *The southern Sudan: background to conflict.* London, Hurst, 1968.

2831. Beshir, Mohamed Omer. *The southern Sudan: from conflict to peace.* London, Hurst, 1975.

2832. Beshir, Mohamed Omer (ed.) *Southern Sudan, regionalism and religion: selected essays*. Khartoum, University of Khartoum, Graduate College, 1984.

2833. Betts, T. *The southern Sudan: the ceasefire and after. Report prepared for the Africa Publications Trust*. London, Africa Publications Trust, 1974.

2834. Burr, J. Millard, and Robert O. Collins. *Requiem for the Sudan: war, drought and disaster relief on the Nile*. Boulder, Westview, 1995.

2835. Daly, M. W., and Ahmad Alawad Sikainga (eds.) *Civil war in the Sudan*. London, Academic Press, 1992.

2836. Deng, Francis Mading, and P. Gifford (eds.) *The search for peace and unity in the Sudan*. Washington, Wilson Center Press, 1987.

2837. Eprile, Cecil. *War and peace in the Sudan, 1955–1972*. Newton Abbot, David & Charles, 1974.

2838. Hizkias Assefa. *Mediation of civil wars, approaches and strategies: the Sudan conflict*. Boulder, Westview Press, 1987.

2839. Malwal, Bona, and Peter Nyot Kok (eds.) *Drift to separation in the Sudan*. London, Hurst, 1993.

2840. Mawut, Lazarus Leek. *The southern Sudan: why back to arms?* Khartoum, St. George Printing Press, 1986.

2841. Nyibil, Thaan. *Experiences in the resistance movement against Arab colonial rule in Sudan*. New York, Vantage Press, 1990.

2842. O'Ballance, Edgar. *The secret war in the Sudan, 1955–1972*. London, Faber and Faber, 1977.

2843. O'Fahey, Rex S. *The southern Sudan: symposium on conflicts in the middle African region*. London, International Institute of Strategic Studies, 1971.

2844. Oduho, J., and William Deng. *The problem of the southern Sudan*. London, Oxford University Press, 1963.

2845. Sidari, Francesco. *Il problema del Sudan meridionale*. Padova, CEDAM, 1979.

2846. Twose, Nigel, and B. Pogrund (eds.) *War wounds: development costs of conflict in southern Sudan*. London, Panos Institute, 1988.

2847. Wai, Dunstan M. *The African-Arab conflict in the Sudan*. New York, Africana Publishing, 1980.

2848. Wai, Dunstan M. *The southern Sudan: the problem of national integration*. London, Frank Cass, 1981.

2849. Wirz, Albert. *Krieg in Afrika*. Stuttgart, Franz Steiner, 1982.

2850. Yangu, Alexis Mbali. *The Nile turns red: Azanians chose freedom against Arab bondage*. New York, Pageant Press, 1966.

Sudan—Ornithology

2851. Nikolaus, Gerhard. *Distribution atlas of Sudan's birds, with notes on habitat and status.* Bonn, Zoologisches Forschungsinstitut und Museum Alexander Koenig, 1987.

Sudan—Pastoralists

2852. Ahmad, Abdel Ghaffar Muhammad (ed.) *Some aspects of pastoral nomadism in the Sudan.* Khartoum, Sudan National Population Committee and the Economic and Social Research Council, 1976.

2853. Amin, Nsr El Din Osman. *Nomadism versus sedentarization: an environmental choice in western Sudan. The case of Gerih el-Sarha.* Khartoum, University of Khartoum, Institute of Environmental Studies, 1986.

Sudan—Planning

2854. Güsten, Rolf. *Problems of economic growth and planning: the Sudan example. Some aspects and implications of the current ten-year plan.* Berlin, Springer-Verlag, 1966.

2855. Mirghani, Abdel R. *Development planning in the Sudan in the sixties.* Khartoum, Khartoum University Press, 1983.

Sudan—Politics

2856. Abdel-Rahim, Muddathir, et al. (eds.) *Sudan since independence: studies of the political development since 1986.* Aldershot, Gower, 1986.

2857. Ahmad, Abdel Ghaffar Muhammad. *Shaykhs and followers: political struggle in the Rufa'a al-Hoi Nazirate in the Sudan.* Khartoum, Khartoum University Press, 1974.

2858. Ahmed, Hassan Makki Mohamed. *Sudan: the Christian design.* Leicester, The Islamic Foundation, 1989.

2859. Al-Safi, Mahasin Abdelgadir (ed.) *The nationalist movement in the Sudan.* Khartoum, University of Khartoum, Institute of African and Asian Studies, 1989.

2860. Barnett, Tony, and Abbas Abdelkarim (eds.) *Sudan: state, capital and transformation.* London, Croom Helm, 1988.

2861. Bechtold, Peter. *Politics in the Sudan: parliamentary and military rule in an emerging African nation.* New York, Praeger, 1976.

2862. Becker, E., and C. Mitchell. *Chronology of conflict resolution initiatives in Sudan.* Fairfax, George Mason University, Institute for Conflict Analysis and Resolution, 1991.

2863. Beshir, Mohamed Omer. *Revolution and nationalism in Sudan.* London, Rex Collings, 1974.

2864. Conte, Carmelo. *The Sudan as a nation.* Milan, Giuffrè, 1976.

2865. Deng, Francis Mading. *Dynamics of identification: a basis for national integration in the Sudan*. Khartoum, Khartoum University Press, 1973.

2866. Edinburgh University. *Post-independence Sudan: proceedings of a seminar held in the Centre of African Studies, University of Edinburgh, 21st and 22nd November, 1980*. Edinburgh, University of Edinburgh, Centre of African Studies, 1980.

2867. El Affendi, Abdelwahab. *Turabi's revolution: Islam and power in Sudan*. London, Grey Seal, 1991.

2868. El Tayeb, Salah el-Din el-Zein. *The students' movement in the Sudan, 1940–1970*. Khartoum, Khartoum University Press, 1971.

2869. Garang, John. *The call for democracy in Sudan*. Revised edition. London, Kegan Paul International, 1992.

2870. Giovannini, Peter. *Der Sudan zwischen Krieg und Frieden*. Wien, Afro-Pub, 1988.

2871. Gurdon, Charles. *Sudan at the crossroads*. Outwell, Middle East and North African Studies Press, 1984.

2872. Gurdon, Charles. *Sudan in transition: a political risk analysis*. London, Economist Intelligence Unit, 1986.

2873. Haddad, George M. *Revolution and military rule in the Middle East. Volume 3: the Arab states: Egypt, the Sudan, Yemen, and Libya*. New York, Speller, 1973.

2874. Hurreiz, Sayyid Hamid, and Elfatih A. Abdel Salam (eds.) *Ethnicity, conflict and national integration in the Sudan*. Khartoum, University of Khartoum, Institute of African and Asian Studies, 1989.

2875. Kameir, El-Wathig Mohamed, and I. Kursany. *Corruption as a "fifth" factor of production in the Sudan*. Uppsala, Scandinavian Institute of African Studies, 1985.

2876. Khalid, Mansur. *Nimeiri and the revolution of dis-may*. London, Kegan Paul International, 1985.

2877. Khalid, Mansur. *The government they deserve: the role of the elite in Sudan's political evolution*. London, Kegan Paul International, 1990.

2878. Mahjub, Muhamed Ahmad. *Democracy on trial: reflections on Arab and African politics*. London, André Deutsch, 1974.

2879. Mahmoud, Fatima Babiker (ed.) *Calamity in the Sudan: civilian versus military rule*. London, Institute for African Alternatives, 1988.

2880. Malwal, Bona. *People and power in the Sudan*. London, Ithaca Press, 1981.

2881. Malwal, Bona. *The Sudan: a second challenge to nationhood*. New York, Thornton Books, 1985.

2882. Niblock, T. *Class and power in Sudan: the dynamics of Sudanese politics, 1898–1985*. Basingstoke, Macmillan, 1987.

2883. Sylvester, Anthony. *Sudan under Nimeiri*. London, Bodley Head, 1977.

2884. Tetzlaff, Rainer. *Der Sudan im Spannungsfeld von Islam, Tradition und Verwestlichung: ein politischer Entwicklungskonflikt um Staat und Nation*. Münster, Lit-Verlag, 1993.

2885. Thomas, Graham F. *Sudan: struggle for survival*. London, Darf, 1993.

2886. Voll, John Obert (ed.) *Sudan: state and society in crisis*. Bloomington, Indiana University Press, 1991.

2887. Warburg, Gabriel R. *Islam, nationalism and communism in a traditional society: the case of Sudan*. London, Frank Cass, 1978.

2888. Warburg, Gabriel R., and U. M. Kupferschmidt (eds.) *Islam, nationalism, and radicalism in Egypt and the Sudan*. New York, Praeger, 1983.

2889. Woodward, Peter (ed.) *Sudan after Nimeiri*. London, Routledge, 1991.

2890. Woodward, Peter (ed.) *Sudan since Nimeiri*. London, University of London, School of Oriental and African Studies, 1986.

Sudan—Population

2891. Balamoan, G. Ayoub. *Peoples and economics in the Sudan, 1884 to 1956*. Revised and enlarged edition. Cambridge, Mass., Harvard University, Center for Population Studies, 1981.

2892. El Mangouri, Hassan Abdalla. *The mechanization of agriculture as a factor influencing population mobility in the developing countries: experiences in the Democratic Republic of Sudan*. Berlin, Dietrich Reimer, 1983.

Sudan—Prehistory

2893. El Mahi, A. T. *Zooarchaeology in the Middle Nile Valley: a study of four Neolithic sites near Khartoum*. Oxford, British Archaeological Reports, 1988.

2894. Haaland, R. *Socio-economic differentiation in the Neolithic Sudan*. Oxford, British Archaeological Reports, 1987.

2895. Marks, Anthony E., and Abbas S. Mohammed-Ali (eds.) *The late prehistory of the eastern Sahel: the mesolithic and neolithic of Shagadud, Sudan*. Dallas, Southern Methodist University Press, 1991.

2896. Mohammed-Ali, Abbas S. *The Neolithic period in the Sudan, 6600–2500 B.C.* Oxford, British Archaeological Reports, 1982.

Sudan—Refugees

2897. Berar-Awad, Azita (ed.) *Towards self-reliance: a programme of action for refugees in eastern and central Sudan*. Geneva, International Labour Organisation and UN High Commission for Refugees, 1984.

2898. Gaim Kibreab. *The Sudan: from subsistence to wage labor. Refugee settlements in the central and eastern regions*. Trenton, Red Sea Press, 1990.

2899. Harrell-Bond, Barbara E. *Imposing aid: emergency assistance to refugees.* Oxford, Oxford University Press, 1986.

2900. Khalil, S. *The socio-economic and political implications of the environmental refugees in the vicinity of Omdurman.* Khartoum, University of Khartoum, Institute of Environmental Studies, 1987.

2901. Kuhlman, T. *Burden or boon? Eritrean refugees in the Sudan.* London, Zed Books, 1989.

2902. Pezaro, Angelika. *Normenwandel und Normkonflikte im Akkulturationsprozess: zur Orientierung in einer fremden Kultur am Beispiel eritreischer Flüchtlingsfrauen im Sudan.* Saarbrücken, Breitenbach, 1991.

2903. Rogge, J. R. *Too many, too long: Sudan's twenty-year refugee dilemma.* Totowa, Rowman & Allanheld, 1985.

2904. Sendker, Lisa. *Eritreischer Flüchtlinge im Sudan: zwischen Assimilation und Segregation.* Hamburg, Institut für Afrika-Kunde, 1990.

2905. Tieleman, H. J. *Enduring crisis: refugee problems in eastern Sudan.* Leiden, African Studies Centre, 1990.

Sudan—Religion

2906. Ahanotu, Austin Metumara (ed.) *Religion, state and society in contemporary Africa: Nigeria, Sudan, South Africa, Zaire and Mozambique.* New York, Peter Lang, 1992.

2907. Hunwick, John O. (ed.) *Religion and national integration in Africa: Islam, Christianity, politics in the Sudan and Nigeria.* Evanston, Northwestern University Press, 1992.

Sudan—Rural Conditions

2908. Bernal, V. *Cultivating workers: peasants and capitalism in a Sudanese village.* New York, Columbia University Press, 1990.

2909. Duffield, Mark. *Maiurno: capitalism and rural life in Sudan.* London, Ithaca Press, 1981.

2910. Reeves, Edward B. *An indigenous rural marketing system in North Kordofan, Sudan.* Lexington, University of Kentucky, 1984.

Sudan—Rural Development

2911. Davies, H. R. J. (ed.) *Natural resources and rural development in arid lands: case studies from Sudan.* Tokyo, United Nations University, 1985.

2912. Davies, H. R. J. (ed.) *Rural development in White Nile Province, Sudan: a case study of interaction between man and natural resources.* Tokyo, United Nations University, 1986.

2913. Fruzzetti, L., and A. Ostor. *Culture and change along the Blue Nile: courts, markets and strategies for development.* Boulder, Westview Press, 1990.

2914. Haaland, Gunnar (ed.) *Problems of savannah development: the Sudan case.* Bergen, University of Bergen, Department of Social Anthropology, 1980.

2915. Kalb, Detlev. *Fernsehen und ländliche Entwicklung: der Fall Sudan.* Hamburg, Institut für Afrika-Kunde, 1986.

2916. Keddeman, Willem, and Ali Abdel Gadir Ali (eds.) *Employment, productivity and incomes in rural Sudan.* Khartoum, Economic and Social Research Council, 1978.

2917. Klennert, Klaus (ed.) *Rural development and careful utilization of resources: the cases of Pakistan, Peru and Sudan.* Baden-Baden, Nomos, 1986.

2918. Salah-el-Din el-Shazali, Ibrahim. *Beyond underdevelopment: structural constraints on the development of productive forces among the Jok Gor in the Sudan.* Bergen, University of Bergen, Department of Social Anthropology, 1980.

2919. Thimm, Heinz Ulrich. *Development projects in the Sudan: an analysis of their reports with implications for research and training in arid land management.* Tokyo, United Nations University, 1979.

Sudan—Settlement Schemes

2920. Blackenburg, Peter, and Hubert Klemens. *The Khashm el-Girba settlement scheme in Sudan: an appraisal for the World Food Program.* Berlin, Institut für Ausländische Wirtschaft der Technischen Universität, 1969.

2921. Sørbø, Gunnar M. *Economic adaptations in Khashm el-Girba: a study of settlement problems in the Sudan.* Khartoum, Sudan Research Unit, 1971.

Sudan—Slavery and Slave Trade

2922. Ali, Abbas Ibrahim Muhammad. *The British, the slave trade and slavery in the Sudan, 1820–1881.* Khartoum, Khartoum University Press, 1972.

2923. Elbashir, A. E. *The United States, slavery and the slave trade in the Nile Valley.* London, University Press of Africa, 1983.

2924. Mowafi, Reda. *Slavery, slave trade and abolition attempts in Egypt and the Sudan, 1820–1882.* Stockholm, Esselte Studium, 1981.

Sudan—Social Conditions

2925. Awad, Mohamed Hashim (ed.) *Socio-economic change in the Sudan.* Khartoum, University of Khartoum, Graduate College, 1983.

2926. Ayoub, Amal, and Abbas Ahmed. *Anthropology and sociology: bibliography of studies in the Sudan.* Khartoum, National Council for Research, Economic and Social Research Council, 1974.

2927. Barclay, Harold B. *Buuri al Lamaab: a suburban village in the Sudan.* Ithaca, Cornell University Press, 1964.

2928. Harir, Sharif. *Old-timers and new-comers: politics and ethnicity in a Sudanese community.* Bergen, University of Bergen, Department of Social Anthropology, 1983.

2929. Ismail, Ellen T. *Bukra insha Allah: a look into Sudanese culture.* Cologne, Ellen Ismail, 1988.

2930. Mahmoud, Fatima Babiker. *The Sudanese bourgeoisie: vanguard of development?* London, Zed Books, 1984.

2931. Mamoun, Izz Eldin. *Bibliography of social sciences of the Sudan. Vol. 1: economics and sociology up to 1977.* Khartoum, National Council for Research, 1978.

2932. Manger, Leif O. *The sand swallows our land: overexploitation of productive resources and the problem of household viability in the Kheiran, a Sudanese oasis.* Bergen, University of Bergen, Department of Social Anthropology, 1981.

2933. Manger, Leif O. (ed.) *Trade and traders in the Sudan.* Bergen, University of Bergen, Department of Social Anthropology, 1984.

2934. McLoughlin, Peter F. M. *Language-switching as an index of socialization in the Republic of the Sudan.* Berkeley, University of California Press, 1964.

2935. Mohamed-Salih, Mohamed A., and Margaret A. Mohamed-Salih. *Family life in Sudan.* Khartoum, Khartoum University, Graduate College, 1987.

2936. O'Neill, Norman, and Jay O'Brien (eds.) *Economy and class in Sudan.* Aldershot, Avebury, 1988.

2937. Tully, D. *Culture and context in Sudan: the process of market incorporation in Dar Masalit.* Albany, State University of New York Press, 1988.

Sudan—Sorghum

2938. Hassan, Hassan Abbas. *Organization and performance of the marketing system of sorghum in the Sudan.* Berlin, Küster, 1993.

Sudan—Studies

2939. Abdalla, Ismail H., and David Sconyers (eds.) *Perspectives and challenges in the development of Sudanese studies.* Lewiston, Edwin Mellen Press, 1993.

2940. Hassan, Yusuf Fadl (ed.) *Sudan in Africa: studies presented to the first international conference sponsored by the Sudan Research Unit, 7–12 February, 1968.* Second edition. Khartoum, Khartoum University Press, 1985.

2941. Henn, Alexander. *Reisen in vergangene Gegenwart: Geschichte und Geschichtlichkeit der Nicht-Europäer im Denken des 19. Jahrhunderts. Die Erforschung des Sudan.* Berlin, Dietrich Reimer, 1988.

2942. Sudan Studies Society of the United Kingdom. *Sudan: environment and people. Second international Sudan studies conference papers, 8–11 April 1991, held at University of Durham*. Durham, Sudan Studies Society of the United Kingdom, 1991.

Sudan—Transport

2943. Hill, Richard. *Sudan transport: a history of railway, marine and river services in the Republic of Sudan*. London, Oxford University Press, 1965.

2944. Williams, C. R. *Wheels and paddles in the Sudan, 1923–1946*. Edinburgh, Pentland Press, 1986.

Sudan—Urbanization

2945. El Bushra, El Sayed (ed.) *Urbanization in the Sudan: proceedings of the 17th annual conference, 2d–4th August, 1972*. Khartoum, Philosophical Society of the Sudan, 1973.

2946. Pons, Valdo (ed.) *Urbanisation and urban life in Sudan*. Hull, University of Hull, Department of Sociology and Social Anthropology, 1980.

Sudan—Water Supply

2947. Shepherd, A., et al. *Water planning in arid Sudan*. London, Ithaca Press, 1987.

Sudan—Women

2948. Cloudsley, A. *Women of Omdurman: life, love and the cult of virginity*. London, Ethnographica, 1983.

2949. Hall, Marjorie, and Bakhita Amin Ismail. *Sisters under the sun: the story of Sudanese women*. London, Longmans, 1981.

2950. Ismail, Ellen T., and Maureen Makki. *Frauen im Sudan*. Wuppertal, Peter Hammer Verlag, 1990.

2951. Ismail, Ellen T. *Social environment and daily routine of Sudanese women: a case study of urban middle class housewives*. Berlin, Dietrich Reimer, 1982.

2952. Kenyon, Susan M. (ed.) *The Sudanese woman*. Khartoum, University of Khartoum, Graduate College, 1987.

2953. Shami, S., et al. *Women in Arab society: work patterns and gender relations in Egypt, Jordan and Sudan*. Oxford, Berg, 1990.

Sudan—Zoology

2954. Sweeney, R. Charles H. *Background of baobabs*. London, Constable, 1973.

Sukriyya—Arabic Dialect

2955. Reichmuth, Stefan. *Der arabische Dialekt der Sukriyya im Ostsudan*. Hildesheim, Olms, 1983.

Sukuma—Children

2956. Varkevisser, C. M. *Socialization in a changing society: Sukuma childhood in rural and urban Mwanza, Tanzania.* The Hague, CESO, 1973.

2957. Wanitzek, Ulrike. *Kindschaftsrecht in Tansania, unter besonderer Berücksichtigung des Rechts der Sukuma.* Hohenschäftlarn, Karl Renner, 1986.

Sukuma—Ethnography

2958. Schanne-Raab, Gertrud. *Social stratification and the diffusion of innovations among the Sukuma of Tanzania.* Frankfurt am Main, Peter Lang, 1977.

2959. Tanner, Ralph E. S. *Witch murders in Sukumaland.* Uppsala, Scandinavian Institute of African Studies, 1970.

Sukuma—Language

2960. Batibo, Herman M. *Le kesukuma, langue bantu de Tanzanie: phonologie, morphologie.* Paris, Éditions Recherche sur les Civilisations, 1985.

Sukuma—Religion

2961. Tanner, Ralph E. S. *Transition in African beliefs: traditional religion and Christian change. A study in Sukumaland, Tanzania, East Africa.* New York, Maryknoll Publications, 1967.

Swahili—Ethnography

2962. Allen, J. W. T. (ed.) *The customs of the Swahili people: the Desturi za Waswahili of Mtoro bin Mwinyi Bakari and other Swahili persons.* Berkeley, University of California Press, 1982.

2963. Allen, James de Vere. *Swahili origins, Swahili culture and the Shungwaya phenomenon.* London, James Currey, 1992.

2964. Caplan, Patricia. *Choice and constraint in a Swahili community: property, hierarchy and cognatic descent on the East African coast.* London, Oxford University Press, 1975.

2965. Le Guennec-Coppens, Françoise, and Patricia Caplan (eds.) *Les swahili entre Afrique et Arabie.* Paris, Karthala, 1991.

2966. Maw, Joan, and David Parkin (eds.) *Swahili language and society.* Vienna, Universität, Institut für Afrikanistik und Ägyptologie, 1984.

2967. Middleton, John. *The world of the Swahili: an African mercantile civilization.* New Haven, Yale University Press, 1992.

2968. Prins, Adriaan Hendrik Johan. *The Swahili-speaking peoples of Zanzibar and the East African coast, Arabs, Shirazi and Swahili.* London, International African Institute, 1961.

2969. Swartz, Marc Jerome. *The way the world is: cultural processes and social relations among the Mombasa Swahili.* Berkeley, University of California Press, 1991.

Swahili—History

2970. Nurse, Derek, and Thomas Spear. *The Swahili: reconstructing the history and language of an African society, 800–1500.* Philadelphia, University of Pennsylvania Press, 1985.

2971. Salim, A. I. *The Swahili-speaking peoples of Kenya's coast, 1895–1965.* Nairobi, East African Publishing House, 1973.

Swahili—Islam

2972. Hock, Klaus. *Gott und Magie in Swahili-Islam: zur Transformation religiöser Inhalte am Beispiel von Gottesvorstellung und magischen Praktiken.* Köln, Böhlau, 1987.

Swahili—Language

2973. Bakari, M. *The morphophonology of the Kenyan Swahili dialects.* Berlin, Dietrich Reimer, 1985.

2974. Barrett-Keach, Camilla. *The syntax and interpretation of the relative clause construction in Swahili.* New York, Garland, 1985.

2975. Blommaert, Jan (ed.) *Swahili studies: essays in honour of Marcel van Spaandonck.* Ghent, Academia Press, 1991.

2976. Contini-Morava, Ellen. *Discourse pragmatics and semantic categorization: the case of negation and tense-aspect, with special reference to Swahili.* Berlin, Mouton de Gruyter, 1989.

2977. Driever, D. *Aspects of a case grammar of Mombasa Swahili, with special reference to the relationship between informant variation and some sociological features.* Hamburg, Helmut Buske, 1976.

2978. Fabian, Johannes. *Language on the road: notes on Swahili in two nineteenth century travelogues.* Hamburg, Helmut Buske, 1985.

2979. Hinnebusch, Thomas J., and Sarah M. Mirza. *Swahili: a foundation for speaking, reading, and writing.* Washington, University Press of America, 1979.

2980. Khalid, Abdallah. *The liberation of Swahili from European appropriation.* Nairobi, Kenya Literature Bureau, 1977.

2981. Krifka, Manfred. *Zur semantischen und pragmatischen Motivation syntaktischer Regularitäten: eine Studie zur Wortstellung und Wortstellungsveränderung im Swahili.* München, Wilhelm Fink, 1983.

2982. Legère, Karsten (ed.) *The role of language in literacy programmes, with special reference to Kiswahili in eastern Africa: a contribution to the international literacy year, 1990.* Bonn, German Foundation for International Development, 1991.

2983. Legère, Karsten (ed.) *The role of language in primary education in eastern Africa, with special reference to Kiswahili: a reader prepared for the*

International Kiswahili Workshop, Dar es Salaam, September 2–11, 1991. Bonn, Deutsche Stiftung für Internationale Entwicklung, Zentralstelle für Erziehung, Wissenschaft und Dokumentation, 1991.

2984. Loogman, Alfons. *Swahili grammar and syntax.* Pittsburgh, Duquesne University Press, 1965.

2985. Maw, Joan, and John Kelly. *Intonation in Swahili.* London, University of London, School of Oriental and African Studies, 1975.

2986. Maw, Joan, and David Parkin (eds.) *Swahili language and society.* Vienna, Universität, Institut für Afrikanistik und Ägyptologie, 1984.

2987. Maw, Joan. *Twende! A practical Swahili course.* Oxford, Oxford University Press, 1985.

2988. Miehe, Gudrun. *Die Sprache der älteren Swahili-Dichtung: Phonologie und Morphologie.* Berlin, Dietrich Reimer, 1979.

2989. Nurse, Derek, and Thomas Spear. *The Swahili: reconstructing the history and language of an African society, 800–1500.* Philadelphia, University of Pennsylvania Press, 1985.

2990. Rhoades, J. *Linguistic diversity and language belief in Kenya: the special position of Swahili.* Syracuse, Syracuse University, Maxwell School of Citizenship and Public Affairs, 1977.

2991. Rombi, Marie-Françoise (ed.) *Le Swahili et ses limites: ambiguité des notions reçues. Table ronde internationale du CNRS, Sèvres, 20–22 avril, 1983.* Paris, Éditions CNRS, 1989.

2992. Russell, Joan. *Communicative competence in a minority group: a sociolinguistic study of the Swahili-speaking community in the Old Town, Mombasa.* Leiden, E. J. Brill, 1981.

2993. Vitale, Anthony J. *Swahili syntax.* Dordrecht, Foris, 1981.

2994. Whiteley, W. H. *Swahili: the rise of a national language.* London, Methuen, 1969.

2995. Zawawi, Sharifa M. *Loan words and their effect on the classification of Swahili nominals.* Leiden, E. J. Brill, 1979.

Swahili—Literature

2996. Abdulaziz, M. H. *Muyaka: 19th century Swahili popular poetry.* Nairobi, Kenya Literature Bureau, 1979.

2997. Amidu, Assibi A. *Kimwondo: a Kiswahili electoral contest.* Vienna, Afro-Pub, 1990.

2998. Bertoncini, Elena Zubkova. *Outline of Swahili literature: prose, fiction and drama.* Leiden, E. J. Brill, 1989.

2999. Knappert, Jan. *Four centuries of Swahili verse: a literary history and anthology.* London, Heinemann, 1979.

3000. Ohly, R. *Aggressive prose: a case study in Kiswahili prose of the seventies*. Dar es Salaam, University of Dar es Salaam, Institute of Kiswahili Studies, 1981.

3001. Rollins, Jack Drake. *A history of Swahili prose. Part 1: from earliest times to the end of the nineteenth century*. Leiden, E. J. Brill, 1983.

3002. Schild, Ulla (ed.) *The East African experience: essays on English and Swahili literature*. Berlin, Dietrich Reimer, 1980.

Swahili—Proverbs

3003. Farsi, S. S. *Swahili sayings from Zanzibar, Book I: proverbs*. Nairobi, East African Literature Bureau, 1973.

3004. Kalugila, Leonidas, and Abdulaziz Y. Lodhi. *More Swahili proverbs from East Africa*. Uppsala, Scandinavian Institute of African Studies, 1980.

3005. Scheven, Albert. *Swahili proverbs: nia zikiwa moja, kilicho mbali huja*. Washington, University Press of America, 1981.

Swahili—Riddles

3006. Farsi, S. S. *Swahili sayings from Zanzibar, Book II: riddles and superstitions*. Nairobi, East African Literature Bureau, 1973.

Swahili—Women

3007. Mirza, S., and M. Strobel (eds.) *Three Swahili women: life histories from Mombasa, Kenya*. Bloomington, Indiana University Press, 1989.

Taita—Ethnography

3008. Harris, Grace. *Casting out anger: religion among the Taita of Kenya*. Cambridge, Cambridge University Press, 1978.

Taita—Land Reform

3009. Mkangi, George C. *The social cost of small families and land reform: a case study of the Wataita of Kenya*. Oxford, Pergamon Press, 1983.

TANU

3010. Howell, John Bruce. *Tanganyika African National Union: a guide to publications by or about TANU*. Washington, Library of Congress, 1976.

3011. Hyden, Goren. *TANU yajenga nchi: political development in rural Tanzania*. Lund, Uniskol, 1968.

3012. Msekwa, Pius. *Towards party supremacy*. Nairobi, East African Literature Bureau, 1977.

3013. Muzo, C. R. S., et al. *The Party: essays on TANU*. Dar es Salaam, Tanzania Publishing House, 1976.

3014. O'Barr, Jean, and Joel Samoff (eds.) *TANU cell leaders: agents of order and change?* Nairobi, East African Publishing House, 1977.

3015. Proctor, J. H. (ed.) *The cell system of the Tanganyika African National Union.* Dar es Salaam, Tanzania Publishing House, 1971.

3016. Ruhumbika, Gabriel (ed.) *Towards ujamaa: twenty years of TANU leadership. A contribution of the University of Dar-es-Salaam to the 20th anniversary of TANU.* Kampala, East African Literature Bureau, 1974.

Tanzania — Administration

3017. Martin, Robert. *Personal freedom and the law in Tanzania: a study of socialist state administration.* Nairobi, Oxford University Press, 1974.

3018. Sperber, Klaus W. von. *Public administration in Tanzania.* Munich, Weltforum-Verlag, 1970.

Tanzania — Agricultural Equipment

3019. Mothander, Björn, et al. *Farm implements for small-scale farmers in Tanzania.* Uppsala, Scandinavian Institute of African Studies, 1989.

Tanzania — Agricultural Research

3020. Bhargava, S. C. *Bibliography on crop production research in East Africa, with particular reference to crop research in Tanzania.* Dar es Salaam, Ministry of Agriculture, Crop Development Division, 1975.

3021. Foote, R. J., and D. Rosjo. *A survey of five agricultural research institutes in Tanzania with emphasis on ways to improve management of the research system.* Morogoro, University of Dar es Salaam, Faculty of Agriculture and Forestry, Department of Rural Economy, 1978.

3022. Tanzania National Scientific Research Council. *Bibliography of agricultural research in Tanzania.* Uppsala, SAREC, 1990.

Tanzania — Agricultural Training

3023. Francke, A. *Kibaha Farmers' Training Centre impact study, 1965–1968, Coast Region, Tanzania.* Uppsala, Scandinavian Institute of African Studies, 1974.

Tanzania — Agriculture

3024. Anthony, Kenneth R. M. *Agricultural change in Geita district, Tanzania.* Nairobi, East African Literature Bureau, 1976.

3025. Bevan, David, et al. *Agriculture and the policy environment: Tanzania and Kenya.* Paris, OECD Development Centre, 1993.

3026. Butterman, L. *Peasant motivation towards Ujamaa production: a preliminary report.* Morogoro, University of Dar es Salaam, Department of Agricultural Education and Extension, 1980.

3027. Conyers, D. *Agro-economic zones of Tanzania.* Dar es Salaam, Dar es Salaam University, 1973.

3028. Dumont, Rene. *Tanzanian agriculture after the Arusha Declaration.* Dar es Salaam, Ministry of Economic Affairs and Economic Development, 1969.

3029. Eriksson, Gun. *Peasant response to price incentives in Tanzania: a theoretical and empirical investigation.* Uppsala, Scandinavian Institute of African Studies, 1993.

3030. Fuggles-Couchman, N. R. *Agricultural change in Tanganyika, 1945–1960.* Stanford, Stanford University, Food Research Institute, 1964.

3031. Glaeser, Bernhard. *Ecodevelopment in Tanzania: an empirical contribution on needs, self-sufficiency and environmentally-sound agriculture on peasant farms.* Berlin, Mouton, 1984.

3032. Glaeser, Bernhard (ed.) *Factors affecting land use and food production: a contribution to ecodevelopment in Tanzania.* Saarbrücken, Breitenbach, 1980.

3033. Graf, D. *Produktivkräfte in der Landwirtschaft und der nichtkapitalistische Weg Tansanias.* Berlin, Akademie-Verlag, 1973.

3034. Kjaerby, Finn. *Problems and contradictions in the development of ox cultivation in Tanzania.* Uppsala, Scandinavian Institute of African Studies, 1983.

3035. Kriesel, Herbert C., et al. *Agricultural marketing in Tanzania: background research and policy proposals.* East Lansing, Michigan State University, Department of Agricultural Economics, 1970.

3036. Lofchie, Michael F. *The policy factor: agricultural performance in Kenya and Tanzania.* Boulder, Lynne Rienner, 1989.

3037. Mackenzie, William. *The livestock economy of Tanzania: a study of beef industry.* Kampala, East African Literature Bureau, 1977.

3038. Ruthenberg, Hans. *Agricultural development in Tanganyika.* Berlin, Springer-Verlag, 1964.

3039. Ruthenberg, Hans (ed.) *Smallholder farming and smallholder development in Tanzania: ten case studies.* Munich, Weltforum-Verlag, 1968.

3040. Schmied, Doris. *Subsistence cultivation, market production and agricultural development in Ruvuma region, southern Tanzania.* Bayreuth, Eckhard Breitinger, 1989.

3041. Smith, Hadley E. (ed.) *Agricultural development in Tanzania.* London, Oxford University Press, 1965.

3042. Wood, Alan. *The groundnut affair.* London, The Bradley House, 1976.

Tanzania—Archaeology

3043. Schmidt, Peter R. *Historical archaeology: a structural approach in an African culture.* Westport, Greenwood Press, 1978.

Tanzania — Architecture

3044. Garlake, Peter S. *The early Islamic architecture of the East African coast.* London, Oxford University Press, 1966.

Tanzania — Banking

3045. Caselli, Clara. *The banking system of Tanzania.* Milan, Cassa di Risparmio delle Provincie Lombarde, 1975.

Tanzania — Bibliography

3046. Darch, Colin. *Tanzania.* Oxford, Clio Press, 1985.

3047. Müller, Ties, and Anne Jansen. *Wirtschafts- Agrar- und Sozialpolitik in Ostafrika, Kenia, Tansania: ausgewählte neuere Literatur.* Hamburg, Deutsches Institut für Afrika-Forschung, 1974.

Tanzania — Blacksmiths

3048. Müller, Jens. *Liquidation or consolidation of indigenous technology: a study of the changing conditions of production of village blacksmiths in Tanzania.* Aalborg, Aalborg University Press, 1980.

Tanzania — Christianity

3049. Bahendwa, L. F. *Christian religious education in the Lutheran diocese of northwestern Tanzania.* Helsinki, Finnish Society for Missiology and Ecumenics, 1990.

3050. Fiedler, Klaus. *Christentum und afrikanische Kultur.* Gütersloh, Mohn, 1983.

3051. Frostin, Per. *Liberation theology in Tanzania and South Africa: a first world interpretation.* Lund, Lund University Press, 1988.

3052. Henschel, Johannes. *Alles begann in Bagamoyo: 100 Jahre Kirche in Ostafrika.* Aachen, Missio Aktuell, 1983.

3053. Hertlein, Siegfried. *Die Kirche in Tansania: ein kurzer Überblick über Geschichte und Gegenwart.* Münsterschwarzach, Vier Türme Verlag, 1971.

3054. Hertlein, Siegfried (ed.) *Wege christlicher Verkündigung: eine pastoralgeschichtliche Untersuchung aus dem Bereich der katholischen Kirche Tansanias.* Münsterschwarzach, Vier Türme Verlag, 1983. 3 pts.

3055. Jaeschke, Ernst. *Gemeindeaufbau in Afrika.* Stuttgart, Calwer, 1981.

3056. Mellinghoff, Gerhard. *Lutherische Kirche Tanzania: ein Handbuch.* Erlangen, Verlag der Evangelisch-Lutherischen Mission, 1990.

3057. Niwagila, Wilson B. *From the catacomb to a self-governing church: a case study of the African initiative and the participation of the foreign missions in the mission history of the North-Western Diocese of the Evangel-*

ical Lutheran Church in Tanzania, 1890–1965. Hamburg, Verlag an der Lottbeck, 1991.

3058. Smedjebacka, Henrik. *Lutheran church autonomy in northern Tanzania, 1940–1963*. Åbo, Åbo Akademi, 1973.

3059. Sundkler, Bengt. *Bara Bukoba: church and community in Tanzania*. London, Hurst, 1980.

Tanzania — Civil Service

3060. Adedeji, A. *The Tanzanian civil service a decade after independence*. Ile-Ife, Ife University Press, 1974.

3061. Mamuya, I. *Structural adjustment and retrenchment in the civil service: the case of Tanzania*. Geneva, International Labour Office, 1991.

Tanzania — Coffee

3062. Mbilinyi, Simon M. *The economics of peasant coffee production*. Nairobi, Kenya Literature Bureau, 1976.

Tanzania — Colonial History

3063. Aas, Norbert. *Koloniale Entwicklung im Bezirkamt Lindi, Deutsch-Ostafrika: deutsche Erwartungen und regionale Wirklichkeit*. Bayreuth, Boomerang Press, 1989.

3064. Austen, Ralph A. *Northwest Tanzania under German and British rule: colonial policy and tribal politics, 1889–1939*. New Haven, Yale University Press, 1968.

3065. Bald, Detlev. *Deutsch-Ostafrika, 1900–1914: eine Studie über Verwaltung, Interessengruppen und wirtschaftliche Erschliessung*. München, Weltforum-Verlag, 1970.

3066. Bates, Darrell. *A fly-switch from the Sultan*. London, Rupert Hart-Davis, 1961.

3067. Bates, Darrell. *A gust of plumes: a biography of Lord Twining of Godalming and Tanganyika*. London, Hodder and Stoughton, 1972.

3068. Biermann, Werner. *Kolonie und City: britische Wirtschaftsstrategie und -politik in Tanganyika, 1920–1955*. Saarbrücken, Breitenbach, 1991.

3069. Chidzero, B. T. G. *Tanganyika and international trusteeship*. London, Oxford University Press, 1961.

3070. Gailey, Harry A. *Sir Donald Cameron, colonial governor*. Stanford, Hoover Institution Press, 1974.

3071. Gann, L. H., and Peter Duignan. *The rulers of German Africa, 1884–1914*. Stanford, Stanford University Press, 1977.

3072. Gründer, Horst. *Christliche Mission und deutscher Imperialismus, 1884–1914: eine politische Geschichte ihrer Beziehungen wahrend der deutschen*

Kolonialzeit (1884–1914) unter besonderer Berücksichtigung Afrikas und Chinas. Paderborn, Ferdinand Schöningh, 1982.

3073. Gwassa, G. C. K., and John Iliffe (eds.) *Records of the Maji-Maji rising.* Nairobi, East African Publishing House, 1967.

3074. Harris, Tim. *Donkey's gratitude: twenty two years in the growth of a new African nation, Tanzania.* Edinburgh, Pentland Press, 1992.

3075. Henderson, W. O. *The German colonial empire, 1884–1919.* London, Frank Cass, 1993.

3076. Heussler, Robert. *British Tanganyika: an essay and documents on district administration.* Durham, N.C., Duke University Press, 1971.

3077. Hoyt, E. P. *Guerilla: Colonel van Lettow-Vorbeck and Germany's East African empire.* London, Macmillan, 1981.

3078. Iliffe, John. *Tanganyika under German rule, 1905–1912.* Cambridge, Cambridge University Press, 1969.

3079. Kaniki, Martin H. Y. (ed.) *Tanzania under colonial rule.* London, Longmans, 1980.

3080. Kimambo, Isaria N. *Popular protest in colonial Tanzania.* Nairobi, East African Publishing House, 1971.

3081. Larsson, Birgitta. *Conversion to greater freedom? Women, church and social change in north-western Tanzania under colonial rule.* Uppsala, Acta Universitatis Upsaliensis, 1991.

3082. Lewis-Barned, John. *A fanfare of trumpets.* Witney, the Author, 1993.

3083. Loth, H. *Griff nach Ostafrika. Politik des deutschen Imperialismus und antikolonialer Kampf: Legende und Wirklichkeit.* Berlin, VEB Deutscher Verlag der Wissenschaften, 1968.

3084. Lumley, E. K. *Forgotten mandate: a British District Officer in Tanganyika.* London, Hurst, 1976.

3085. Mang'enya, Erasto A. M. *Discipline and tears: reminiscences of an African civil servant in colonial Tanganyika.* Dar es Salaam, Dar es Salaam University Press, 1984.

3086. Mapunda, O. B., and G. B. Mpangara. *The Maji Maji war in Ungoni.* Dar es Salaam, East African Publishing House, 1968.

3087. McCarthy, D. M. P. *Colonial bureaucracy and creating underdevelopment: Tanganyika, 1919–1940.* Ames, Iowa State University Press, 1982.

3088. Menzel, Gustav. *C. G. Büttner: Missionar, Sprachforscher und Politiker in der deutschen Kolonialbewegung.* Wuppertal, Vereinigte Evangelische Mission, 1992.

3089. Morris-Hale, W. *British administration in Tanganyika from 1920 to 1925.* Geneva, Imprimo, 1969.

3090. Perham, Margery. *East African journey: Kenya and Tanganyika, 1929–30.* London, Faber and Faber, 1976.

3091. Pipping-Van Hulten, Ida. *An episode of colonial history: the German press in Tanzania, 1901–1914.* Uppsala, Scandinavian Institute of African Studies, 1974.

3092. Seeberg, Karl-Martin. *Der Maji-Maji-Krieg gegen die deutsche Kolonialherrschaft.* Berlin, Dietrich Reimer, 1989.

3093. Smith, Charles D. *Did colonialism capture the peasantry? A case study of the Kagera District, Tanzania.* Uppsala, Scandinavian Institute of African Studies, 1989.

3094. Smith, Daniel R. *The influence of the Fabian Colonial Bureau on the independence movement in Tanganyika.* Athens, Ohio University, Center for International Studies, 1985.

3095. Stephens, Hugh W. *The political transformation of Tanganyika, 1920–67.* New York, Praeger, 1968.

3096. Stoecker, Helmut (ed.) *Drang nach Afrika.* Berlin, Akademie-Verlag, 1977.

3097. Tetzlaff, Rainer. *Koloniale Entwicklung und Ausbeutung: Wirtschafts- und Sozialegeschichte Deutsch-Ostafrikas, 1885–1914.* Berlin, Duncker & Humblot, 1970.

Tanzania—Communications

3098. Ng'wanakilala, Nkwabi. *Mass communication and development in Tanzania.* Dar es Salaam, Tanzania Publishing House, 1981.

Tanzania—Cooperatives

3099. Baldus, R. D. *Zur operationalen Effizienz der Ujamaa Kooperative Tansanias.* Göttingen, Vandenhoeck & Ruprecht, 1976.

3100. Cliffe, Lionel, et al. (eds.) *Rural cooperation in Tanzania.* Dar es Salaam, Tanzania Publishing House, 1975.

3101. Cranenberg, O. van. *The widening gyre: the Tanzanian one-party state and policy towards rural co-operatives.* Delft, Eburon, 1990.

3102. Mutaha, A. Z. *Cooperatives in Tanzania: problems of organisation building.* Dar es Salaam, Tanzania Publishing House, 1976.

Tanzania—Cotton

3103. Magoti, Charles K. *Peasant participation and rural productivity in Tanzania: the case of Mara cotton producers, 1955–1977.* Hamburg, Institut für Afrika-Kunde, 1984.

Tanzania—Credit Unions

3104. Dublin, Jack, and Selma M. Dublin. *Credit unions in a changing world: the Tanzania-Kenya experience.* Detroit, Wayne State University Press, 1983.

214 Bibliography

Tanzania—Cultural Policy

3105. Mbughuni, L. A. *The cultural policy of the United Republic of Tanzania.* Paris, UNESCO, 1974.

Tanzania—Description and Travel

3106. Amin, Mohamed. *Journey through Tanzania.* London, Bodley Head, 1984.

3107. Bennett, Norman R. (ed.) *From Zanzibar to Ujiji: the journal of Arthur W. Didgshun, 1877–1879.* Boston, Boston University, African Studies Center, 1969.

3108. Johnston, Erika. *The other side of Kilimanjaro.* London, Johnston, 1971.

3109. Kaula, Edna Mason. *The land and people of Tanganyika.* Philadelphia, Lippincott, 1963.

3110. McCulla, Patricia E. *Tanzania.* New York, Chelsea House, 1989.

3111. Naipaul, Shiva. *North of south: an African journey.* London, Deutsch, 1978.

Tanzania—Documentation

3112. Franz, E. G., and P. Geisslet. *Das Deutsch-Ostafrika-Archiv, Inventar der Abteilung "German Records" im Nationalarchiv der Vereinigten Republik Tanzania, Dar-es-Salaam.* Marburg, Archivschule, Institut für Archivwissenschaft, 1973.

Tanzania—Economy

3113. Bukuku, Enos S. *The Tanzanian economy: income distribution and economic growth.* Westport, Praeger, 1993.

3114. Campbell, Horace, and Howard Stein (eds.) *Tanzania and the IMF: the dynamics of liberalization.* Boulder, Westview, 1992.

3115. Chachage, C. S. L., et al. *Mining and structural adjustment: studies on Zimbabwe and Tanzania.* Uppsala, Scandinavian Institute of African Studies, 1993.

3116. Chandrasekhar, S. *Third world development experience: Tanzania.* Delhi, Daya, 1990.

3117. Due, Jean M. *Costs, returns and repayment experience of ujamaa villages in Tanzania, 1973–1976.* Washington, University Press of America, 1980.

3118. Green, R. H., et al. *Economic shocks and national policy making: Tanzania in the 1970s.* The Hague, Institute of Social Studies, 1980.

3119. Hartmann, Jeannette (ed.) *Rethinking the Arusha Declaration.* Copenhagen, Centre for Development Research, 1991.

3120. Havnevik, Kjell J. *Tanzania: the limits to development from above.* Uppsala, Scandinavian Institute of African Studies, 1993.

3121. Havnevik, Kjell J., et al. *Tanzania: country study and Norwegian aid review*. Bergen, University of Bergen, Centre for Development Studies, 1988.

3122. Hedlund, Stefan, and Mats Lundahl. *Ideology as a determinant of economic systems: Nyerere and ujamaa in Tanzania*. Uppsala, Scandinavian Institute of African Studies, 1989.

3123. International Labour Office. *Basic needs in danger: a basic needs oriented strategy for Tanzania*. Addis Ababa, International Labour Office, 1982.

3124. Joinet, Bernard. *Tanzanie: manger d'abord*. Paris, Karthala, 1981.

3125. Kahama, C. G., et al. *The challenge for Tanzania's economy*. London, James Currey, 1986.

3126. Kaya, Hassan Omari. *Problems of regional development in Tanzania: a case study of the Tanga region*. Saarbrücken, Breitenbach, 1985.

3127. Kim, Kwan S., et al. (eds.) *Papers on the political economy of Tanzania*. London, Heinemann, 1979.

3128. Kimble, Helen. *Price control in Tanzania*. Nairobi, East African Publishing House, 1970.

3129. Lipumba, N. I., and L. A. Msambichaka. *Stabilization policies in Tanzania*. Dar es Salaam, University of Dar es Salaam, Economic Research Bureau, 1983.

3130. O'Neill, Norman, and K. Mustafa (eds.) *Capitalism, socialism and the development crisis in Tanzania*. Aldershot, Avebury, 1990.

3131. Othman, Haroub, and Ernest Maganya (eds.) *Tanzania's debt problem and the world economy*. Dar es Salaam, Dar es Salaam University Press, 1990.

3132. Peiffer, Stephan. *Der IWF und Tansania: die Konditionalität der Bereitschaftskreditvereinbarung des Internationalen Währungsfonds mit Tansania von September 1980*. Hamburg, Institut für Afrika-Kunde, 1990.

3133. Pfennig, Werner, et al. (eds.) *Entwicklungsmodell Tansania: Sozialismus in Afrika. Geschichte, Ökonomie, Politik, Erziehung*. Frankfurt am Main, Campus Verlag, 1980.

3134. Rutman, Gilbert Lionel. *The economy of Tanzania*. New York, Praeger, 1968.

3135. Sarris, Alexander, and Rogier van den Brink. *Economic policy and household welfare during the crisis and adjustment in Tanzania*. New York, New York University Press, 1993.

3136. Smith, Hadley E. (ed.) *Readings on economic development and administration in Tanzania*. Dar es Salaam, Oxford University Press, 1966.

3137. Svendsen, Knud Erik (ed.) *The economy of Tanzania*. Dar es Salaam, Tanzania Publishing House, 1974.

216   Bibliography

3138. Taube, Günther. *Wirtschaftliche Stabilisierung und Strukturanpassung in Tansania: die Auswirkungen des Economic Recovery Programme, 1986–1989 im ländlichen Bereich. Fallstudie West-Usambara-Berge, Distrikt Lushoto.* Hamburg, Institut für Afrika-Kunde, 1992.

3139. Treuner, Peter, and Francos Halla (eds.) *Mechanisms of vertical and horizontal financial balance for the promotion of decentralized development, with a special reference to Tanzania.* Stuttgart, Universität Stuttgart, Institut für Raumordnung und Entwicklungsplanung, 1982.

3140. Wenzel, H.-D., and R. Wiedenmann. *Tanzania's economic performance in the eighties.* Saarbrücken, Breitenbach, 1989.

3141. Yaffey, Michael J. H. *Balance of payments problems of a developing country: Tanzania.* Munich, Weltforum-Verlag, 1970.

Tanzania — Education

3142. Auger, George A. *Tanzania education since Uhuru: a bibliography, 1961–1971 incorporating a study of Tanzania past and present and a guide to further sources of information on education in Tanzania.* Nairobi, East African Academy for the Institute of Education, University of Dar es Salaam, 1973.

3143. Bikes, C. S., and M. T. Kinunda. *Higher education for self-reliance: the Tanzanian experience.* Paris, UNESCO International Institute for Educational Planning, 1977.

3144. Buchert, Lene. *Education in the development of Tanzania.* London, James Currey, 1994.

3145. Cameron, John, and W. A. Dodd. *Society, schools and progress in Tanzania.* Oxford, Pergamon Press, 1970.

3146. Dave, R. H., et al. (eds.) *Learning strategies for post-literacy and continuing education in Kenya, Nigeria, Tanzania and United Kingdom.* Hamburg, UNESCO Institute for Education, 1985.

3147. Desselberger, H. *Schule und Ujamaa: Untersuchungen zur Wirtschaftsentwicklung und zum Ausbau der Primarschulen in der Tanga Region, Tansania.* Giessen, Geographisches Institut der Justus Liebig Universität, 1975.

3148. Dodd, William A. *Education for self reliance in Tanzania: a study of its vocational aspect.* New York, Columbia University Press, 1969.

3149. Dubbeldam, L. F. B. *The primary school and the community in Mwanza district, Tanzania.* Groningen, Wolters-Noordhoff, 1970.

3150. Elborgh, K. (ed.) *Rückkehr ohne Aussicht auf Erfolg.* Saarbrücken, Breitenbach, 1991.

3151. Gillette, Arthur Lavery. *Beyond the non-formal fashion: towards educational revolution in Tanzania.* Amherst, University of Massachusetts, Center for International Education, 1977.

3152. Gottneid, Allan J. (ed.) *Church and education in Tanzania, etc.* Nairobi, East African Publishing House, 1976.

3153. Grenholm, L. H. *Radio study group campaigns in the United Republic of Tanzania.* Paris, UNESCO, 1975.

3154. Hall, B. L. *Adult education and the development of socialism in Tanzania.* Nairobi, East African Literature Bureau, 1976.

3155. Hall, B. L., and K. Remtulla. *Adult education and national development in Tanzania.* Nairobi, East African Literature Bureau, 1973.

3156. Hinzen, H., and Volkhard H. Hundsdörfer. *The Tanzanian experience: education for liberation and development.* Second edition. Hamburg, UNESCO Institute for Education, 1982.

3157. Hundsdörfer, Volkhard H. *Die politische Aufgabe des Bildungswesens in Tanzania: Entwicklungen von den Arusha-Deklaration, 1967 zur Musoma-Deklaration, 1975.* Saarbrücken, Verlag der SSIP-Schriften Breitenbach, 1977.

3158. Ishumi, Abel G. M. *Community education and development: a study in the problems of harnessing community education and development efforts among rural and peri-urban communities in Tanzania.* Nairobi, Kenya Literature Bureau, 1981.

3159. Kaayk, J. *Education, estrangement and adjustment: a study among pupils and school leavers in Bukumbi, a rural community in Tanzania.* The Hague, Mouton, 1976.

3160. Kalugula, C., et al. (eds.) *The development of special education in Tanzania.* Dar es Salaam, University of Dar es Salaam, Institute of Education, 1984.

3161. Kassam, Y. O. *The adult education revolution in Tanzania.* Nairobi, Shungwaya, 1978.

3162. Kassam, Y. O. *Illiterate no more: voices of new literates from Tanzania.* Dar es Salaam, Tanzania Publishing House, 1979.

3163. Kröger, Werner. *Die Implementierung der "Education for Self-reliance" in einer tanzanischen Sekundarschule.* Saarbrücken, Breitenbach, 1987.

3164. Kurtz, Laura S. *An African education: the social revolution in Tanzania.* New York, Pageant-Poseidon Press, 1972.

3165. Laubjerg, Kristian. *Development and literacy education in Jamaica and Tanzania.* Birkerød, Kr. Laubjerg, 1979.

3166. Malya, Simoni. *Creating literacy surroundings in Tanzania.* Nairobi, Kenya Literature Bureau, 1978.

3167. Millonzi, J. C. *Citizenship in Africa: the role of adult education in the political socialization of Tanganyikans, 1891–1961.* Syracuse, Syracuse University, Maxwell School of Citizenship and Public Affairs, 1975.

3168. Morrison, David R. *Education and politics in Africa: the Tanzanian case.* London, Hurst, 1976.

3169. Msekwa, Pius, and T. L. Maliyamkono. *The experiments: education policy formation before and after the Arusha Declaration.* Dar es Salaam, Black Star Agencies, 1979.

3170. Mwingira, A. C., and Simon Pratt. *The process of educational planning in Tanzania.* Paris, UNESCO International Institute for Educational Planning, 1967.

3171. Omari, I. M. *Psychology and education in changing societies: new perspectives from Tanzania.* Dar es Salaam, Dar es Salaam University Press, 1983.

3172. Psacharopoulos, G., and W. Loxley. *Diversified secondary education and development: evidence from Colombia and Tanzania.* Baltimore, Johns Hopkins University Press for the World Bank, 1985.

3173. Renes, P. B. *Teacher training at Butimba: a case-study in Tanzania.* Groningen, Wolters-Noordhoff, 1970.

3174. Resnick, Idrian N. (ed.) *Tanzania: revolution by education.* Arusha, Longmans of Tanzania, 1968.

3175. Robertson, K. A. *Educational development in pre-independent Tanganyika.* Oxford, Rhodes House Library, 1983.

3176. Rubagumya, C. (ed.) *Language in education in Africa: a Tanzanian perspective.* Clevedon, Multilingual Matters, 1990.

3177. Sheffield, James R., et al. *Agriculture in African secondary schools: case studies of Botswana, Kenya and Tanzania.* New York, African-American Institute, 1976.

3178. Sifuna, D. N. *Vocational education in schools: a historical survey of Kenya and Tanzania.* Nairobi, East African Literature Bureau, 1976.

3179. Ta Ngoc Chau and F. Caillods. *Educational policy and its financial implications in Tanzania.* Paris, UNESCO, 1975.

3180. Tungaraza, F., et al. *The development of special education in Tanzania.* Dar es Salaam, University of Dar es Salaam, Institute of Education, 1984.

3181. Zanolli, N. V. *Education toward development in Tanzania: a study of the educative process in a rural area.* Basel, Pharos-Verlag, 1971.

Tanzania — Elections

3182. Cliffe, Lionel (ed.) *One party democracy: the 1965 Tanzania general election.* Second edition. Dar es Salaam, East African Publishing House, 1973.

3183. Kjekshus, Helge. *The elected elite: a socio-economic profile of candidates in Tanzania's parliamentary election 1970.* Uppsala, Scandinavian Institute of African Studies, 1975.

3184. University of Dar es Salaam Election Study Committee. *Socialism and participation: Tanzania's 1970 national elections*. Dar es Salaam, Tanzania Publishing House, 1974.

Tanzania—Employment

3185. International Labour Office. *Towards self-reliance development: employment and equity issues in Tanzania. Report to the government of Tanzania*. Addis Ababa, International Labour Office, Jobs and Skills Programme for Africa, 1978.

3186. Leonor, M. D. (ed.) *Unemployment, schooling and training in developing countries: Tanzania, Egypt, the Philippines and Indonesia*. London, Croom Helm, 1985.

Tanzania—Energy

3187. Mwandosya, M. J., and M. L. P. Luhanga. *Energy resources flows and end users in Tanzania*. Dar es Salaam, Dar es Salaam University Press, 1983.

Tanzania—English Language

3188. Schmied, Josef J. *Englisch in Tansania: sozio- und interlinguistische Probleme*. Heidelberg, Julius Groos, 1985.

Tanzania—Environment

3189. Christiansson, Carl. *Soil erosion and sedimentation in semi-arid Tanzania: studies of environmental change and ecological imbalance*. Uppsala, Scandinavian Institute of African Studies, 1981.

3190. Kjekshus, Helge. *Ecology control and economic development in East African history: the case of Tanganyika, 1850–1950*. London, Heinemann, 1977.

3191. Östberg, Wilhelm. *The Kondoa transformation: coming to grips with soil erosion in central Tanzania*. Uppsala, Scandinavian Institute of African Studies, 1986.

3192. Rapp, Anders (ed.) *Studies of soil erosion and sedimentation in Tanzania*. Dar es Salaam, University of Dar es Salaam, Bureau of Resources Assessment and Land Use Planning, 1973.

Tanzania—Ethnography

3193. Beidelman, Thomas O. *The matrilineal peoples of eastern Tanzania*. London, International African Institute, 1967.

3194. Lutahoire, Sebastian Kompaan. *The human life cycle among the Bantu, with special reference to the people of the west lake region, Tanzania*. Arusha, Evangelical Lutheran Church of Tanzania, 1974.

3195. Richards, Audrey I. (ed.) *East African chiefs: a study of political development in some Uganda and Tanganyika tribes*. London, Faber and Faber, 1960.

3196. Wembah-Rashid, J. A. R. *The ethno-history of the matrilineal peoples of southeast Tanzania.* Vienna, Institut für Völkerkunde der Universität Wien, 1975.

Tanzania — Family Planning

3197. Omari, C. K. *Socio-cultural factors in modern family planning methods in Tanzania.* Lewiston, Edwin Mellen Press, 1989.

Tanzania — Finance

3198. Binhammer, H. H. *The development of a financial infrastructure in Tanzania.* Kampala, East African Literature Bureau, 1975.

3199. Kimei, C. S. *Tanzania's financial experience in the post-war period.* Uppsala, Acta Universitatis Upsaliensis, 1987.

3200. Rwegasira, Kami S. P. *Financial analysis and institutional lending operations management in a developing country: a critical perspective of Tanzania banks and DFIs.* Dar es Salaam, Dar es Salaam University Press, 1991.

3201. Rwegasira, Kami S. P. *Problems of financial analysis in institutional lending operations: some lessons from Tanzania.* Aldershot, Avebury, 1992.

Tanzania — Folktales

3202. Seitel, Peter. *See so that we may see: performances and interpretations of traditional tales from Tanzania; from performances tape-recorded by S. Dauer and P. Seitel.* Bloomington, Indiana University Press, 1980.

Tanzania — Food and Nutrition

3203. Bryceson, Deborah Fahy. *Food insecurity and the social division of labour in Tanzania, 1919–85.* Basingstoke, Macmillan, 1990.

3204. Bryceson, Deborah Fahy. *Liberalizing Tanzania's food trade: public and private faces of urban marketing policy.* London, James Currey, 1992.

3205. Geier, Gabriele. *Nahrungssicherungspolitik in Afrika zwischen Katastrophenhilfe und Strukturanpassung: Überlegungen zur Konzeption und Wirksamkeit von Politiken, illustriert am Beispiel Tansania.* Berlin, Deutsches Institut für Entwicklungspolitik, 1992.

3206. Lappé, Frances Moore, and Adele Beccar-Varela. *Mozambique and Tanzania: asking the big questions.* San Francisco, Institute for Food and Development Policy, 1980.

3207. Latham, M. C., et al. *Thoughts for food: an evaluation of the Tanzania Food and Nutrition Centre.* Stockholm, Swedish International Development Authority, 1992.

3208. Mutesa, Fredrick. *Structural adjustment and food security in sub-Saharan Africa in the 1980s, with case studies of Tanzania and Zambia.* Konstanz, Hartung-Gorre, 1993.

Tanzania—Foreign Aid

3209. Elgstrom, Ole. *Foreign aid negotiations: Swedish-Tanzanian aid dialogue.* Aldershot, Avebury, 1992.

3210. Forss, Kim. *Planning and evaluation in aid organizations.* Stockholm, Economic Research Institute, Stockholm School of Economics, 1985.

3211. Gitelson, Susan Aurelia. *Multilateral aid for national development and self reliance: a case study of the UNDP in Uganda and Tanzania.* Nairobi, East African Literature Bureau, 1975.

3212. Gordenker, L. *International aid and national decisions: development programs in Malawi, Tanzania and Zambia.* Princeton, Princeton University Press, 1976.

3213. Mushi, Samuel S., and Helge Kjekshus (eds.) *Aid and development.* Oslo, Norwegian Institute of International Affairs, 1982.

3214. Young, Roger. *Canadian development assistance to Tanzania: an independent study.* Ottawa, North-South Institute, 1983.

Tanzania—Foreign Relations

3215. Crouch, S. C. *Western responses to Tanzanian socialism.* Aldershot, Avebury, 1987.

3216. Lüders, Klaus. *Tansania in der Sicht der Sowjetunion: eine Studie zur sowjetischen Schwarzafrika-Politik.* Hamburg, Institut für Afrika-Kunde, 1978.

3217. Mathews, K., and Samuel S. Mushi (eds.) *Foreign policy of Tanzania, 1961–1981: a reader.* Dar es Salaam, Tanzania Publishing House, 1981.

3218. Mwamba, Zuberi. *Tanzania: foreign policy and international politics.* Washington, University Press of America, 1978.

3219. Nnoli, Okwudiba. *Self reliance and foreign policy in Tanzania: the dynamics of the diplomacy of a new state, 1961 to 1971.* New York, NOK, 1978.

3220. Wilson, Amrit. *US foreign policy and revolution: the creation of Tanzania.* London, Pluto Press, 1989.

3221. Yu, George T. *China and Tanzania: a study in cooperative interaction.* Berkeley, University of California, Center for Chinese Studies, 1970.

3222. Yu, George T. *China's Africa policy: a study of Tanzania.* New York, Praeger, 1975.

Tanzania—Forestry

3223. Hamilton, A. C., and R. Bensted-Smith (eds.) *Forest conservation in the east Usambara mountains, Tanzania.* Gland, IUCN, 1989.

Tanzania—Geography

3224. Engelhard, Karl. *Tansania.* Gotha, Justus Perthes Verlag, 1993.

3225. Hoyle, Brian Stewart. *Gillman of Tanganyika, 1882–1946, the life and work of a pioneer geographer.* Aldershot, Avebury, 1987.

3226. Jätzold, Ralph. *Die wirtschaftsgeographische Struktur von Süd-tanzania.* Tübingen, Im Selbstverlag des Geographischen Instituts der Universität, 1970.

3227. Jätzold, Ralph. *The Kilombero valley, Tanzania: characteristic features of the economic geography of a semihumid East African flood plain and its margins, etc.* Munich, Weltforum-Verlag, 1968.

3228. Maro, Paul S., and Valery P. Maro. *The geography of Tanzania's development: a bibliography.* Dar es Salaam, Geographical Association of Tanzania, 1982.

3229. Schulze, Christa. *Räumliche Disparitäten in Tanzania: Karten und Kommentare.* Kaltenburg-Lindau, Informationszentrum Dritte Welt, 1981.

Tanzania—Handbook

3230. Kaplan, Irving (ed.) *Tanzania: a country study.* Second edition. Washington, U.S. Government Printing Office, 1978.

Tanzania—Handicrafts

3231. Kiyenze, Bernard K. S. *The transformation of Tanzanian handicrafts into co-operatives and rural small-scale industrialisation.* Helsinki, Finnish Anthropological Society, 1985.

Tanzania—Health and Medicine

3232. Beck, Ann. *Medicine, tradition and development in Kenya and Tanzania, 1920–1970.* Waltham, Crossroads Press, 1981.

3233. Clyde, D. F. *Malaria in Tanzania.* London, Oxford University Press, 1967.

3234. Etten, G. M. van. *Rural health development in Tanzania: a case study of medical sociology in a developing country.* Assen, Van Gorcum, 1976.

3235. Fritsch, Martin. *Environmental management for schistosomiasis control. River flushing: a case study in Namwawala, Kilombero District, Tanzania.* Berlin, vde-Verlag, 1993.

3236. Gish, Oscar. *Planning the health sector: the Tanzanian experience.* London, Croom Helm, 1975.

3237. Gottlieb, M. *Health care financing in mainland Tanzania.* Syracuse, Syracuse University, Maxwell School of Citizenship and Public Affairs, 1975.

3238. Harjula, Raimo. *Mirau and his practice: a study of the ethno-medical repertoire of a Tanzanian herbalist.* London, Tri-med, 1980.

3239. Holden, P. *Doctors and other medical personnel in the public health services in Africa, 1930–1965: Uganda, Tanganyika/Tanzania, Nigeria.* Oxford, Rhodes House Library, 1984.

3240. Holden, P. *Nursing sisters in Nigeria, Uganda, Tanganyika/Tanzania, 1929–1978: a report on the memoirs collected by Alison Smith for the Oxford Development Records Project on public health in Africa.* Oxford, Rhodes House Library, 1984.

3241. Jilek-Aall, Louise. *Call Mama Doctor: African notes of a young woman doctor.* London, Allen & Unwin, 1980.

3242. Kimati, V. P. *Childhood protein-energy malnutrition (PEM) and measles in Tanzania.* Dar es Salaam, Tanzania Publishing House, 1978.

3243. Nsekela, Amon James, and Aloysius M. Nhonoli. *The development of health services and society in mainland Tanzania: a historical overview. Tumetoka mbali.* Kampala, East African Literature Bureau, 1976.

3244. Stirling, Leader. *Tanzanian doctor.* London, Hurst, 1977.

3245. Turshen, Meredeth. *The political ecology of disease in Tanzania.* New Brunswick, Rutgers University Press, 1984.

Tanzania—History

3246. Bailey, Martin. *The union of Tanganyika and Zanzibar: a study in political integration.* Syracuse, Syracuse University, Maxwell Graduate School of Citizenship and Public Affairs, 1973.

3247. Clarke, Philip Henry Cecil. *A short history of Tanganyika.* London, Longmans, 1960.

3248. Freeman-Grenville, G. S. P. *The medieval history of the coast of Tanganyika, with special reference to recent archaeological discoveries.* London, Oxford University Press, 1962.

3249. Hatch, John Charles. *Tanzania: a profile.* London, Pall Mall, 1971.

3250. Herzog, Jurgen. *Geschichte Tansanias vom Beginn des 19. Jahrhunderts bis zur Gegenwart.* Berlin, Deutscher Verlag der Wissenschaften, 1986.

3251. Iliffe, John. *A modern history of Tanganyika.* Cambridge, Cambridge University Press, 1979.

3252. Iliffe, John (ed.) *Modern Tanzanians: a volume of biographies.* Nairobi, East African Publishing House, 1973.

3253. Kimambo, Isaria N., and A. Temu (eds.) *A history of Tanzania.* Nairobi, East African Publishing House, 1969.

3254. Kleine, Ekkehard. *Die Eigentums- und Agrarverfassungen im vorkolonialen Tanganyika.* München, Karl Renner, 1972.

3255. Koponen, Juhani. *People and production in late precolonial Tanzania.* Uppsala, Scandinavian Institute of African Studies, 1989.

3256. Kurtz, Laura S. *Historical dictionary of Tanzania.* Metuchen, Scarecrow Press, 1978.

3257. Listowel, Judith Hare. *The making of Tanganyika.* London, Chatto & Windus, 1965.

3258. Pratt, Cranford. *The critical phase in Tanzania, 1945–1968: Nyerere and the emergence of a socialist strategy.* Cambridge, Cambridge University Press, 1976.

3259. Roberts, Andrew (ed.) *Tanzania before 1900: seven area histories.* Nairobi, East African Publishing House, 1968.

Tanzania—Housing

3260. Stren, R. E. *Urban inequality and housing policy in Tanzania: the problem of squatting.* Berkeley, University of California, Institute of International Studies, 1975.

Tanzania—Industry

3261. Aere, A. *Rethinking industrialisation from a national to a local perspective: a case study of the industrialisation process in Tanzania, with particular emphasis on the construction industry.* Copenhagen, Centre for Development Research, 1992.

3262. Barker, C. E., et al. *African industrialisation: technology and change in Tanzania.* Aldershot, Gower, 1986.

3263. Jones, J. V. S. *Resources and industry in Tanzania: use, misuse and abuse.* Dar es Salaam, Tanzania Publishing House, 1981.

3264. Mbelle, Ammon. *Foreign exchange and industrial development: a study of Tanzania.* Göteborg, Nationalekonomiska Institutionen, Göteborgs Universitet, 1988.

3265. Rweyemamu, Justinian F. *The historical and institutional setting of Tanzanian industry.* Dar es Salaam, University of Dar es Salaam, Economic Research Bureau, 1971.

3266. Rweyemamu, Justinian F. *Underdevelopment and industrialisation in Tanzania: a study of perverse capitalist industrial development.* Nairobi, Oxford University Press, 1973.

3267. Schädler, Karl. *Crafts, small-scale industries, and industrial education in Tanzania.* Munich, Weltforum-Verlag, 1968.

3268. Silver, M. S. *The growth of manufacturing industry in Tanzania: an economic history.* Boulder, Westview Press, 1984.

3269. Skarstein, R., and S. M. Wangwe. *Industrial development in Tanzania: some critical issues.* Uppsala, Scandinavian Institute of African Studies, 1986.

3270. Zell, Helmut. *Die Kapitalgüterindustrie in Tanzania: Entwicklungsbedingungen und Entwicklungsmöglichkeiten.* Hamburg, Institut für Afrika-Kunde, 1990.

Tanzania—Informal Economy

3271. Maliyamkono, T. L., and M. S. D. Bagachwa. *The second economy in Tanzania.* London, James Currey, 1990.

Tanzania—Investment

3272. Birgegard, L.-E. *The project selection process in developing countries: a study of the public investment project selection in Kenya, Zambia and Tanzania.* Stockholm, Stockholm School of Economics, Economic Research Institute, 1975.

3273. Clark, W. Edmund. *Socialist development and public investment in Tanzania, 1964–1973.* Toronto, University of Toronto Press, 1978.

3274. Peter, C. M. *Promotion and protection of foreign investments in Tanzania: a comment on the new investment code.* Dar es Salaam, Friedrich Ebert Foundation, 1990.

Tanzania—Irrigation

3275. Hazlewood, Arthur, and Ian Livingstone. *Irrigation economics in poor countries, illustrated by the Usango plains of Tanzania.* Oxford, Pergamon Press, 1982.

3276. Martens, B. *Economic development that lasts: labour-intensive irrigation projects in Nepal and the United Republic of Tanzania.* Geneva, International Labour Office, 1989.

Tanzania—Islam

3277. Herterich-Akimpelu, Ilse. *Ethnizität und Stratifikation am Beispiel islamischer Organisationen und ihren Praktiken in Tansania, Ostafrika.* Würzburg, Ergon Verlag, 1991.

3278. Nimtz, August H. *Islam and politics in East Africa: the Sufi order in Tanzania.* Minneapolis, University of Minnesota Press, 1980.

Tanzania—Journalism

3279. Konde, Hadji S. *Press freedom in Tanzania.* Arusha, Eastern Africa Publications, 1984.

3280. Lederbogen, Utz. *Watchdog or missionary? A portrait of African news people and their work. A case study in Tanzania.* Stuttgart, Peter Lang, 1992.

Tanzania—Labor

3281. Barnum, H. N., and R. H. Sabot. *Migration, education and urban surplus labour: the case of Tanzania.* Paris, OECD Development Centre, 1976.

3282. Bienefeld, M. *Structural adjustment and rural labour markets in Tanzania.* Geneva, International Labour Office, 1991.

3283. Mapolu, Henry (ed.) *Workers and management.* Dar es Salaam, Tanzania Publishing House, 1976.

3284. Mihyo, Paschal B. *Industrial conflict and change in Tanzania.* Dar es Salaam, Tanzania Publishing House, 1983.

3285. Olle, W., and Wolfgang Schoeller. *World market, state and national average conditions of labour.* Dar es Salaam, University of Dar es Salaam, Economic Research Bureau, 1977.

3286. Tumbo, N. S. K., et al. *Labour in Tanzania.* Dar es Salaam, Tanzania Publishing House, 1977.

Tanzania—Land

3287. Friis-Hansen, E. *Changes in land tenure and land use since villagization and their impact on peasant agricultural production in Tanzania.* Copenhagen, Centre for Development Research, 1987.

3288. James, Rudolph William. *Land tenure and policy in Tanzania.* Toronto, University of Toronto Press, 1971.

3289. King, R. B. *Remote sensing manual of Tanzania.* Surbiton, Land Resources Development Centre, Overseas Development Administration, 1984.

3290. Pipping, Knut, et al. *Land holding in the Usangu plain: a survey of two villages in the southern highlands of Tanzania.* Uppsala, Scandinavian Institute of African Studies, 1976.

Tanzania—Land Use

3291. Ludwig, Heinz Dieter. *Ukara: ein Sonderfall tropischer Bodennutzung im Raum des Victoria-Sees: eine wirtschaftsgeographische Entwicklungsstudie.* München, Weltforum-Verlag, 1967.

3292. Mersmann, Christian. *Umweltwissen und Landnutzung im afrikanischen Dorf: zur Frage des bäuerlichen Engagements in der Gestaltung der Kulturlandschaft der Usambara-Berge, Tansanias.* Hamburg, Institut für Afrika-Kunde, 1993.

3293. Pitblado, J. Roger. *The North Mkata Plain, Tanzania.* Toronto, University of Toronto Press for the Department of Geography, University of Toronto, 1981.

3294. Rotenhan, Dietrich. *Bodennutzung und Viehhaltung in Sukumaland, Tanzania: die Organisation der Landbewirtschaftung in afrikanischen Bauernbetrieben.* Berlin, Springer-Verlag, 1966.

Tanzania—Language

3295. Nurse, Derek. *Description of sample Bantu languages of Tanzania.* London, International African Institute and OAU Inter-African Bureau of Languages, 1979.

3296. Polomé, Edgar C., and C. P. Hill (eds.) *Language in Tanzania.* Oxford, Oxford University Press, 1980.

3297. Polomé, Edgar C. *Language, society and paleoculture: essays.* Stanford, Stanford University Press, 1982.

Tanzania—Law

3298. Aguda, T. Akinola, et al. *African and western legal systems in contact.* Eckersdorf, Eckhard Breitinger, 1989.

3299. Cole, J. S. R., and W. N. Denison. *Tanganyika: the development of its laws and constitution.* London, Stevens, 1964.

3300. Fimbo, G. M. *Essays in land law Tanzania.* Dar es Salaam, Dar es Salaam University Press, 1992.

3301. James, Rudolph William, and G. M. Fimbo. *Customary land law of Tanzania: a source book.* Nairobi, East African Literature Bureau, 1973.

3302. James, Rudolph William, and F. M. Kassim. *Law and its administrators in a one-party state.* Nairobi, East African Literature Bureau, 1973.

3303. Shivji, Issa G. *Tanzania: the legal foundations of the Union.* Dar es Salaam, Dar es Salaam University Press, 1990.

Tanzania—Libraries

3304. Kaungamno, Ezekiel E., and C. S. Ilomo. *Books build nations, Vol. 2: library services in Tanzania.* Dar es Salaam, Tanzania Library Service, 1979.

3305. Mwinyimvua, E. A. *Directory of libraries in Tanzania.* New edition. Dar es Salaam, Tanzania Library Service, 1984.

Tanzania—Local Government

3306. Dryden, Stanley. *Local administration in Tanzania.* Nairobi, East African Publishing House, 1968.

3307. Haule, Martin, and Suleiman Ngware. *The forgotten level: village government in Tanzania.* Hamburg, Institut für Afrika-Kunde, 1993.

3308. Lee, Eugene. *Local taxation in Tanganyika.* Berkeley, University of California Press, 1965.

3309. Penner, Rudolph Gerhard. *Financing local government in Tanzania.* Nairobi, East African Publishing House, 1970.

3310. Samoff, Joel. *Tanzania: local politics and the structure of power.* Madison, University of Wisconsin Press, 1974.

3311. Semboja, Joseph. *Handbook on district level administration in Tanzania.* Dar es Salaam, Educational Publishers and Distributors, 1991.

3312. Semboja, Joseph, and Ole Therkildsen (eds.) *Recurrent cost financing at district level in Tanzania.* Copenhagen, Centre for Development Research, 1989.

Tanzania—Maize

3313. Temu, Peter Eliezer. *Marketing board pricing and storage policy with particular reference to maize in Tanzania.* New York, Vantage, 1984.

Tanzania—Manpower

3314. Khamis, Ishaw Abdulla. *Labour economics and manpower planning in Tanzania.* Nairobi, Kenya Literature Bureau, 1978.

Tanzania—Maps

3315. Berry, Leonard (ed.) *Tanzania in maps: graphic perspectives of a developing country.* London, University of London Press, 1971.

Tanzania—Migration

3316. Rodney, W., et al. *Migrant labour in Tanzania during the colonial period.* Hamburg, Institut für Afrika-Kunde, 1983.

3317. Sabot, Richard H. *Economic development and urban migration: Tanzania, 1900–1971.* Oxford, Clarendon Press, 1979.

Tanzania—Military History

3318. Miller, Charles. *Battle for the bundu: the first world war in East Africa.* London, Macdonald and Jane's, 1974.

3319. Mmbando, S. I. *The Tanzania-Uganda war in pictures.* Dar es Salaam, Longman Tanzania, 1980.

Tanzania—Minerals

3320. Kimambo, R. H. *Mining and mineral prospects in Tanzania.* Arusha, Eastern Africa Publications, 1984.

3321. Nilsen, O. *A bibliography of the mineral resources of Tanzania.* Uppsala, Scandinavian Institute of African Studies, 1980.

Tanzania—Missionaries

3322. Beidelman, Thomas O. *Colonial evangelism: a socio-historical study of an East African mission at the grassroots.* Bloomington, Indiana University Press, 1982.

3323. Heyden, Ulrich van der, and Winfried Brose (eds.) *Mit Kreuz und deutscher Flagge: 100 Jahre Evangelium im Süden Tanzanias. Zum Wirken der Berliner Mission in Ostafrika.* Münster, Lit-Verlag, 1993.

3324. Lindqvist, Ingmar. *Partners in mission.* Åbo, Åbo Akademi, 1982.

3325. Menzel, Gustav. *Die Bethel-Mission: aus 100 Jahren Missionsgeschichte.* Wuppertal, Vereinigte Evangelische Mission, 1986.

3326. Mirtschink, Bernhard. *Zur Rolle christlicher Mission in kolonialen Gesellschaften: Katholische Missionerziehung in "Deutsch Ostafrika."* Frankfurt am Main, Haag + Herchen, 1980.

3327. Shorter, Aylward. *Priest in the village: experiences of African community.* London, Geoffrey Chapman, 1979.

3328. Smedjebacka, Henrik. *Tjugofem år i Tanzania.* Åbo, Åbo Akademi, Kyrkohistoriska Arkivet, 1976.

3329. Sundkler, Bengt, and Per-Ake Wahlstrüm (eds.) *Vision and service: papers in honour of Barbro Johansson.* Uppsala, Scandinavian Institute of African Studies, 1977.

3330. Ühlein, Polykarp. *Damit in Allem Gott verherrlicht werde: Kirche und Mission in Tansania.* Münsterschwarzach, Vier Türme Verlag, 1980.

3331. White, Paul. *Jungle doctor's lion hunter: an African love story.* Exeter, Paternoster, 1983.

3332. Wright, Marcia. *German missions in Tanganyika, 1891–1941: Lutherans and Moravians in the southern highlands.* Oxford, Clarendon Press, 1971.

Tanzania—Music

3333. Brandel, Rose. *The music of central Africa, an ethnomusicological study: former French Equatorial Africa, the former Belgian Congo, Ruanda-Urundi, Uganda, Tanganyika.* The Hague, Nijhoff, 1961.

Tanzania—National Parks

3334. Matthiessen, Peter. *Sand rivers.* London, Aurum, 1981.

Tanzania—Planning

3335. Burke, Fred George. *Tanganyika: preplanning.* Syracuse, Syracuse University, 1965.

3336. Khakee, Abdul. *Development and planning in Tanzania.* Lund, Studentlitteratur, 1971.

3337. Rweyemamu, Anthony Hubert, and B. U. Mwansasu (eds.) *Planning in Tanzania: the background to decentralisation. Conference on Comparative Administration in East Africa, Arusha, 1971.* Nairobi, East African Literature Bureau, 1974.

3338. Rweyemamu, Justinian F., et al. *Towards socialist planning.* Dar es Salaam, Tanzania Publishing House, 1974.

Tanzania—Politics

3339. Bank of Tanzania. *Tanzania: twenty years of independence, 1961–1981. A review of political and economic performance.* Dar es Salaam, Bank of Tanzania, 1982.

3340. Barkan, Joel D. *An African dilemma: university students, development and politics in Ghana, Tanzania and Uganda.* Nairobi, Oxford University Press, 1975.

3341. Barkan, Joel D. (ed.) *Politics and public policy in Kenya and Tanzania.* Revised edition. New York, Praeger, 1984.

3342. Bienen, Henry. *Tanzania: party transformation and economic development.* Princeton, Princeton University Press, 1967.

3343. Bilger, Harald R. *Verführung und Last der Freiheit: Probleme der Entwicklungspolitik dargestellt an den Beispielen Kenia und Tansania.* Konstanz, Universitätsverlag Konstanz, 1972.

3344. Boesen, Jannik, et al. *Ujamaa: socialism from above.* Uppsala, Scandinavian Institute of African Studies, 1977.

3345. Bolton, D. *Nationalization, a road to socialism? The lessons of Tanzania.* London, Zed Books, 1985.

3346. Centro Studi Terzo Mondo. *La Tanzania verso il socialismo: realtà, problemi e prospettive della più viva e originale esperienza di socialismo africano.* Milano, Centro Studi Terzo Mondo, 1974.

3347. Cerasi, Giusto Lucio. *Socialismo africano: i casi della Tanzania e dello Zambia.* Roma, Coines, 1975.

3348. Cliffe, Lionel, and John S. Saul (eds.) *Socialism in Tanzania: an interdisciplinary reader.* Nairobi, East African Publishing House, 1972–73. 2 vols.

3349. Constantin, François, and Denis Martin (eds.) *Arusha (Tanzanie) vingt ans après: journées d'études du 22–23 octobre, 1987.* Pau, Université de Pau et des Pays de l'Adour, 1988.

3350. Coulson, Andrew. *Tanzania: a political economy.* Oxford, Clarendon Press, 1982.

3351. Coulson, Andrew (ed.) *African socialism in practice: the Tanzanian experience.* Nottingham, Spokesman, 1979.

3352. Duggan, William, and John Civille. *Tanzania and Nyerere: a study of ujamaa and nationhood.* Maryknoll, Orbis Books, 1976.

3353. Herzog, Jurgen. *Traditionelle Institutionen und nationale Befreiungsrevolution in Tansania: zum Problem der revolutionären Überwindung vorkapitalistischer gesellschaftlicher Verhältnisse im heutigen Afrika.* Berlin, Akademie-Verlag, 1975.

3354. Hodd, M. (ed.) *Tanzania after Nyerere.* London, Pinter, 1988.

3355. Holmquist, Frank W., and Joel D. Barkan. *A comprehensive bibliography: politics and public policy in Kenya and Tanzania.* Iowa City, University of Iowa, Center for International and Comparative Studies, 1984.

3356. Hopkins, Raymond F. *Political roles in a new state: Tanzania's first decade.* New Haven, Yale University Press, 1971.

3357. Kürschner, F. *Wie sozialistisch ist Tansania? Ein Informationsbuch.* Nürnberg, Laetare, 1977.

3358. Karioki, James N. *Tanzania's human revolution.* University Park, Pennsylvania State University Press, 1979.

3359. Laaser, W. *Afrikanischer Sozialismus und Genossenschaftspolitik in Tanzania.* Bamberg, M. Schadel, 1977.

3360. Macdonald, Alexander. *Tanzania: young nation in a hurry.* New York, Hawthorn Books, 1966.

3361. Maguire, G. Andrew. *Toward Uhuru in Tanzania: the politics of participation.* Cambridge, Cambridge University Press, 1969.

3362. McGowan, Patrick Jude, and Patrick Bolland. *The political and social elite of Tanzania: an analysis of social background factors.* Syracuse, Program for East African Studies, Syracuse University, 1971.

3363. Mittelman, James H. *Underdevelopment and the transition to socialism: Mozambique and Tanzania.* New York, Academic Press, 1981.

3364. Mmuya, Max, and Amon Chaligha. *Towards multiparty politics in Tanzania.* Dar es Salaam, Dar es Salaam University Press, 1992.

3365. Mohiddin, Ahmed. *African socialism in two countries.* London, Croom Helm, 1981.

3366. Mwansasu, Bismarck U., and Cranford Pratt (eds.) *Towards socialism in Tanzania.* Toronto, Toronto University Press, 1979.

3367. Nellis, John R. *A theory of ideology: the Tanzanian example.* London, Oxford University Press, 1972.

3368. Nsekela, Amon James. *A time to act: liberation and development in a Tanzanian context.* Dar es Salaam, Dar es Salaam University Press, 1984.

3369. Nsekela, Amon James. *Socialism and social accountability in a developing nation: problems in the transformation of the Tanzanian economy and society.* Nairobi, Kenya Literature Bureau, 1978.

3370. Nyerere, Julius K. *The Arusha declaration ten years after.* Dar es Salaam, Government Printer, 1977.

3371. Nyerere, Julius K. *Freedom and development: Uhuru na maendeleo.* London, Oxford University Press, 1973.

3372. Nyerere, Julius K. *Freedom and socialism.* London, Oxford University Press, 1968.

3373. Nyerere, Julius K. *Ujamaa: essays on socialism.* London, Oxford University Press, 1971.

3374. Okoko, K. A. B. *Socialism and self-reliance in Tanzania.* London, Kegan Paul International, 1987.

3375. Othman, Haroub (ed.) *The state in Tanzania: a selection of articles.* Dar es Salaam, Dar es Salaam University Press, 1980.

3376. Othman, Haroub (ed.) *The state in Tanzania: who controls it and whose interest does it serve?* Dar es Salaam, Dar es Salaam University Press, 1983.

3377. Othman, Haroub, et al. (eds.) *Tanzania: democracy in transition.* Dar es Salaam, Dar es Salaam University Press, 1990.

3378. Paech, Norman, and Manfred O. Hinz (eds.) *Der verdeckte Klassenkampf.* Bremen, Übersee-Museum, 1980.

3379. Potholm, Christian P. *Four African political systems.* Englewood Cliffs, Prentice-Hall, 1970.

3380. Resnick, Idrian N. *The long transition: building socialism in Tanzania.* New York, Monthly Review Press, 1981.

3381. Rweyemamu, Anthony Hubert (ed.) *Nation-building in Tanzania: problems and issues.* Nairobi, East African Publishing House, 1970.

3382. Shivji, Issa G. *Class struggles in Tanzania.* London, Heinemann, 1976.

3383. Shivji, Issa G. *Law, state and the working class in Tanzania, c. 1920–1964.* London, James Currey, 1986.

3384. Shivji, Issa G. (ed.) *The state and the working people in Tanzania.* Dakar, Codesria, 1986.

3385. Tandon, Y. (ed.) *The University of Dar es Salaam debate on class, state and imperialism.* Dar es Salaam, Tanzania Publishing House, 1983.

3386. Taylor, J. Clagett. *The political development of Tanganyika.* Stanford, Stanford University Press, 1963.

3387. Tordoff, William. *Government and politics in Tanzania: a collection of essays covering the period from September 1960 to July 1966.* Nairobi, East African Publishing House, 1967.

3388. Urfer, Sylvain. *La République Unie de Tanzanie.* Paris, Berger-Levrault, 1973.

3389. Urfer, Sylvain. *Socialisme et église en Tanzanie.* Paris, IDOC-France, 1975.

3390. Urfer, Sylvain. *Ujamaa: espoir du socialisme africain en Tanzanie.* Paris, Aubier Montaigne, 1971.

3391. Yeager, Rodger. *Tanzania: an African experiment.* Second edition. Boulder, Westview Press, 1991.

Tanzania — Population

3392. Economic Commission for Africa. *Final report on the national seminar on population and development in the United Republic of Tanzania.* Addis Ababa, Economic Commission for Africa, 1981.

3393. Hirst, M. A., et al. *Studies in the population geography of Uganda and Tanzania*. Kampala, Makerere University, 1970.

Tanzania—Ports

3394. Hoyle, Brian Stewart. *Seaports and development: the experience of Kenya and Tanzania*. New York, Gordon and Breach, 1983.

Tanzania—Psychiatry

3395. Diefenbacher, Albert. *Psychiatrie und Kolonialismus: zur "Irrenfürsorge" in der Kolonie Deutsch-Ostafrika*. Frankfurt, Campus-Verlag, 1985.

Tanzania—Public Enterprise

3396. El Namaki, M. S. S. *Problems of management in a developing environment, the case of Tanzania: state enterprises between 1967 and 1975*. Amsterdam, North-Holland, 1979.

3397. Mihyo, Paschal B. *Non-market controls and the accountability of public enterprises in Tanzania*. Basingstoke, Macmillan, 1994.

3398. Moshi, H. P. B. *Zum Entwicklungsbeitrag staatlicher Unternehmen in den Entwicklungsländern, dargestellt am Beispiel Tansania*. Baden-Baden, Nomos, 1992.

Tanzania—Publishing

3399. Kaungamno, Ezekiel E. *The book industry in Tanzania*. Dar es Salaam, National Central Library, 1980.

Tanzania—Race Relations

3400. UNESCO. *Two studies on ethnic group relations in Africa: Senegal, the United Republic of Tanzania*. Paris, UNESCO, 1974.

Tanzania—Railways

3401. Bailey, Martin. *Freedom railway: China and the Tanzania-Zambia link*. London, Rex Collings, 1976.

3402. Hall, Richard, and Hugh Peyman. *The great Uhuru railway: China's showpiece in Africa*. London, Victor Gollancz, 1976.

3403. Mutukwa, Kasuka S. *Politics of the Tanzania-Zambia rail project: a study of Tanzania-China-Zambia relations*. Washington, University Press of America, 1977.

3404. Schroeter, H., and R. Ramaer. *Die Eisenbahnen in den einst deutschen Schutzgebieten German Colonial Railways*. Krefeld, Röhr-Verlag, 1992.

Tanzania—Refugees

3405. Gasarasi, Charles P. *The tripartite approach to the resettlement and integration of rural refugees in Tanzania*. Uppsala, Scandinavian Institute of African Studies, 1984.

Tanzania — Religion

3406. Westerlund, David. *Ujamaa na dini: a study of some aspects of society and religion in Tanzania, 1961–1977.* Stockholm, Almqvist & Wiksell, 1980.

Tanzania — Rock Paintings

3407. Leakey, Mary D. *Africa's vanishing art: the rock paintings of Tanzania.* London, Hamish Hamilton, 1983.

3408. Masao, Fidelis Taliwawa. *The later stone age and the rock paintings of central Tanzania.* Stuttgart, Franz Steiner, 1979.

Tanzania — Rural Conditions

3409. Abrahams, R. G. (ed.) *Villagers, villages and the state in modern Tanzania.* Cambridge, African Studies Centre, 1985.

3410. Attems, Manfred. *Bauernbetriebe in tropischen Höhenlagen Ostafrikas: die Usambara-Berge im Übergang von der Subsistenz- zur Marktwirtschaft.* München, Weltforum-Verlag, 1967.

3411. Donner-Reichle, Carola. *Ujamaadörfer in Tanzania: Politik und Reaktionen der Bäuerinnen.* Hamburg, Institut für Afrika-Kunde, 1988.

3412. Forster, Peter G., and Sam Maghimbi (eds.) *The Tanzanian peasantry: economy in crisis.* Aldershot, Avebury, 1992.

3413. Hekken, R. M., and H. U. G. Thoden van Velzen. *Land scarcity and rural inequality in Tanzania: some case studies in Mbungwe District.* The Hague, Mouton, 1972.

3414. Kaya, Hassan Omari. *People's participation programmes and the dilemma of rural leadership in Tanzania.* Berlin, Schreiber-Kaya, 1989.

3415. Mshana, Rogate R. *Insisting upon people's knowledge to resist developmentalism: peasant communities as producers of knowledge for social transformation in Tansania.* Frankfurt am Main, Verlag für Interkulturelle Kommunikation, 1992.

3416. Putterman, L. *Peasants, collectives, and choice: economic theory and Tanzania's villages.* Greenwich, JAI Press, 1986.

3417. Rald, Jørgen, and Karen Rald. *Rural organisation in Bukoba district, Tanzania.* Uppsala, Scandinavian Institute of African Studies, 1975.

3418. Rudengren, Jan. *Peasants by preference?* Stockholm, Stockholm School of Economics, Economic Research Institute, 1981.

Tanzania — Rural Development

3419. Berg, Liv, et al. *Towards village industry: a strategy for development.* London, Intermediate Technology Publications, 1978.

3420. Collier, P., et al. *Labour and poverty in rural Tanzania: ujamaa and rural development in the United Republic of Tanzania.* Oxford, Clarendon Press, 1986.

3421. Eckhardt, Wolfgang, et al. (eds.) *Raumplanung und ländliche Entwicklung in Tanzania.* Dortmund, Informationskreis für Raumplanung, 1982.

3422. Finucane, James R. *Rural development and bureaucracy in Tanzania: the case of Mwanza region.* Uppsala, Scandinavian Institute of African Studies, 1974.

3423. Fortmann, Louise. *Peasants, officials and participation in rural Tanzania: experience with villagization and decentralization.* Ithaca, Cornell University, Center for International Studies, Rural Development Committee, 1980.

3424. Freyhold, Michaela von. *Ujamaa villages in Tanzania: analysis of a social experiment.* London, Heinemann, 1979.

3425. Groeneveld, Sigmar. *Probleme der landwirtschaftlichen Entwicklung im Küsengebiet Ostafrikas, am Beispiel der Kokospalmen-Rindviehprojecte in der Tanga-Region in Tanzania.* München, Weltforum-Verlag, 1967.

3426. Hyden, Goren. *Beyond ujamaa in Tanzania: underdevelopment and an uncaptured peasantry.* London, Heinemann, 1980.

3427. Ingle, Clyde R. *From village to state in Tanzania: the politics of rural development.* Ithaca, Cornell University Press, 1972.

3428. Macpherson, George A. *First steps in village mechanisation.* Dar es Salaam, Tanzania Publishing House, 1975.

3429. Matango, R. R. *The role of agencies for rural development in Tanzania: a case study of the Lushoto Integrated Development Project.* Dar es Salaam, University of Dar es Salaam, Economic Research Bureau, 1976.

3430. McHenry, Dean E. *Tanzania's ujamaa villages: the implementation of a rural development strategy.* Berkeley, University of California, Institute of International Studies, 1979.

3431. McHenry, Dean E. *Ujamaa villages in Tanzania: a bibliography.* Uppsala, Scandinavian Institute of African Studies, 1981.

3432. Omari, C. K. *The strategy for rural development: Tanzania experience.* Kampala, East African Literature Bureau, 1976.

3433. Omari, C. K. *Towards rural development in Tanzania.* Arusha, Eastern Africa Publications, 1984.

3434. Proctor, J. H. (ed.) *Building ujamaa villages in Tanzania.* Dar es Salaam, Tanzania Publishing House, 1971.

3435. Ruhumbika, Gabriel (ed.) *Towards ujamaa.* Nairobi, East African Literature Bureau, 1974.

3436. Schmale, Matthias. *The role of local organizations in Third World development: Tanzania, Zimbabwe and Ethiopia*. Aldershot, Avebury, 1993.

3437. Schultz, Jürgen. *Agrarlandschaftliche Veränderungen in Tanzania: Ursachen, Formen und Problematik landwirtschaftlicher Entwicklung am Beispiel des Iraqw-Hochlandes und seiner Randlandschaften*. München, Weltforum-Verlag, 1971.

3438. Serkkola, A. *Rural development in Tanzania: a bibliography*. Helsinki, University of Helsinki, Institute of Development Studies, 1987.

Tanzania—Science and Technology

3439. Bagachwa, M. S. D. *Choice of technology in industry: the economics of grain-milling in Tanzania*. Ottawa, International Development Research Centre, 1991.

3440. Mitschke-Collande, Peter von. *Transfer and development of technology: industrialization and engineering education in Tanzania*. Hamburg, Institut für Afrika-Kunde, 1980.

3441. Troil, Margaretha von. *Exchange of knowledge in technology transfer from Finland to Tanzania: case studies of Finnish technical assistance*. Helsinki, University of Helsinki, Institute of Development Studies, 1986.

3442. Vitta, P. B. *Dominance: the influence of circumstances on science in Tanzania*. Dar es Salaam, Dar es Salaam University Press, 1983.

Tanzania—Settlement Schemes

3443. Gagern, Axel von. *Die afrikanischen Siedler im Projekt Urambo/Tanzania: Probleme der Lebensgestaltung*. München, Weltforum-Verlag, 1969.

Tanzania—Sisal

3444. Guillebaud, Claude William. *An economic survey of the sisal industry of Tanganyika*. Third edition. Welwyn, Nisbet, 1966.

3445. Kaya, Hassan Omari. *Disarticulation and poor incentive programmes in African economies: the case of the sisal industry in Tanzania*. Berlin, Schreiber-Kaya, 1989.

3446. Lock, G. W. *Sisal: thirty year's sisal research in Tanzania*. Second edition. New York, Humanities Press, 1970.

Tanzania—Social Conditions

3447. Arens, William. *On the frontier of change, Mto wa Mbu, Tanzania*. Ann Arbor, University of Michigan Press, 1979.

3448. Boesen, Jannik, et al. (eds.) *Tanzania: crisis and struggle for survival*. Uppsala, Scandinavian Institute of African Studies, 1986.

3449. Campbell, John, and Valdo Pons. *Urbanization, urban planning and urban life in Tanzania: an annotated bibliography*. Hull, University of Hull, Department of Sociology and Social Anthropology, 1987.

3450. Hundsdörfer, Volkhard H., and Wolfgang Küper. *Bibliographie zur sozialwissenschaftlichen Erforschung Tanzanias: bibliography of social science research on Tanzania.* München, Weltforum-Verlag, 1974.

3451. Jellicoe, Marguerite. *The long path: a case study of social change in Wahi, Singida District, Tanzania.* Nairobi, East African Publishing House, 1978.

3452. Knight, Chester Gregory. *Ecology and change: rural modernization in an African community.* New York, Academic Press, 1974.

3453. Satzinger, W. *Stadt und Land im Entwicklungsland: ein Beitrag zur Diskussion über die urbane Befangenheit von Entwicklungsplanung und Entwicklungsprozess am Beispiel Tansanias.* Saarbrücken, Breitenbach, 1990.

3454. Sender, John, and Sheila Smith. *Poverty, class and gender in rural Africa: a Tanzanian case study.* London, Routledge, 1990.

3455. Wenner, Kate. *Shamba Letu.* Boston, Houghton & Mifflin, 1970.

Tanzania—Soils

3456. Hathout, S. A. *Soil atlas of Tanzania.* Dar es Salaam, Tanzania Publishing House, 1983.

3457. Hathout, S. A. *Soil resources of Tanzania.* Dar es Salaam, Tanzania Publishing House, 1983.

3458. Schaffer, Hannes, et al. *Soil conservation in Tanzania: the role of students in the management of global environmental dilemmas.* Vienna, MECCA, 1989.

3459. Woytek, Reinhard (ed.) *Soil erosion control and agroforestry in the west Usambara mountains.* Weikersheim, Josef Margraf, 1987.

Tanzania—Studies

3460. Svendsen, Knud Erik, and Merete Teisen (eds.) *Self-reliant Tanzania.* Dar es Salaam, Tanzania Publishing House, 1969.

Tanzania—Tobacco

3461. Boesen, Jannik, and A. T. Mohele. *The "success story" of peasant tobacco production in Tanzania.* Uppsala, Scandivanian Institute of African Studies, 1979.

3462. Scheffler, Walter. *Bäuerliche Produktion unter Aufsicht am Beispiel des Tabakanbaus in Tanzania.* München, Weltforum-Verlag, 1968.

Tanzania—Tourism

3463. Scherrer, Christian. *Tourismus und selbstbestimmte Entwicklung: ein Widerspruch. Das Fallbeispiel Tanzania.* Berlin, Dietrich Reimer, 1988.

3464. Shivji, Issa G. (ed.) *Tourism and socialist development.* Dar es Salaam, Tanzania Publishing House, 1973.

Tanzania — Trade

3465. Hawkins, H. C. G. *Wholesale and retail trade in Tanganyika.* New York, Praeger, 1965.

3466. Kainzbauer, Werner. *Der Handel in Tanzania.* Berlin, Springer-Verlag, 1968.

Tanzania — Trade Unions

3467. Friedland, William H. *Vuta kamba: the development of trade unions in Tanganyika.* Stanford, Hoover Institution Press, 1969.

Tanzania — Transport

3468. Chiteji, Frank M. *The development and socio-economic impact of transportation in Tanzania, 1884–present.* Washington, University Press of America, 1980.

3469. Hofmeier, Rolf. *Transport and economic development in Tanzania, with particular reference to roads and road transport.* Munich, Weltforum-Verlag, 1973.

3470. Mkama, J. *Transport planning in Tanzania: an assessment.* Dar es Salaam, University College, 1969.

Tanzania — Treaties

3471. Seaton, Earle, and Sostenes T. Maliti. *Tanzania treaty practice.* Nairobi, Oxford University Press, 1973.

Tanzania — Water Supply

3472. Heuvel, Kick van den. *Wood and bamboo for rural water supply: a Tanzanian initiative for self-reliance.* Delft, Delft University Press, 1981.

3473. Therkildsen, Ole. *Watering white elephants? Lessons from donor funded planning and implementation of rural water supplies in Tanzania.* Uppsala, Scandinavian Institute of African Studies, 1988.

3474. Tschannerl, G. (ed.) *Water supply: conference proceedings, 1971.* Dar es Salaam, Dar es Salaam University, 1971.

Tanzania — Wildlife

3475. Yeager, P., and N. N. Miller. *Wildlife, wild death: land use and survival in eastern Africa.* Albany, State University of New York Press, 1986.

Tanzania — Women

3476. Fiedler, Irene. *Wandel der Mädchenerziehung in Tanzania: der Einfluss von Mission, kolonialer Schulpolitik und nationalem Sozialismus.* Saarbrücken, Breitenbach, 1983.

3477. Kikopa, J. R. K. *Law and the status of women in Tanzania.* Addis Ababa, African Training and Research Centre for Women, ECA, 1982.

3478. Madsen, Birgit. *Women's mobilization and integration in development: a village case study from Tanzania.* Copenhagen, Centre for Development Research, 1984.

3479. Mascarenhas, Ophelia, and Marjorie Mbilinyi. *Women in Tanzania: an analytical bibliography.* Uppsala, Scandinavian Institute of African Studies, 1983.

3480. Mbilinyi, Marjorie. *Big slavery: agribusiness and the crisis in women's employment in Tanzania.* Dar es Salaam, University of Dar es Salaam Press, 1991.

3481. Mukurasi, Laeticia. *Post abolished: one woman's struggle for employment rights in Tanzania.* London, Women's Press, 1991.

3482. Ngaiza, Magdalene K., and Bertha Koda (eds.) *The unsung heroines: women's life histories from Tanzania.* Dar es Salaam, WRDP Publications, 1991.

3483. Shields, Nwanganga. *Women in the urban labor markets of Africa: the case of Tanzania.* Washington, World Bank, 1980.

3484. Swantz, Marja-Liisa. *Women in development, a creative role denied: the case of Tanzania.* London, Christopher Hurst, 1985.

3485. Vuorela, Ulla. *The women's question and the modes of human reproduction: an analysis of a Tanzanian village.* Uppsala, Scandinavian Institute of African Studies, 1987.

Taveta—History

3486. Frontera, A. E. *Persistence and change: a history of Taveta.* Los Angeles, Crossroads Press, 1978.

Taxation—East Africa

3487. Davey, K. J. *Taxing a peasant society: the example of graduated taxes in East Africa.* London, Charles Knight, 1974.

Terik—Language

3488. Roeder, Hilke. *Sprachlicher Wandel und Gruppenbewußtsein bei den Terik.* Hamburg, Helmut Buske, 1986.

Teso—Ethnography

3489. Karp, Ivan. *Fields of change among the Iteso of Kenya.* London, Routledge & Kegan Paul, 1978.

Teso—Folktales

3490. Akello, Grace. *Iteso thought patterns in tales.* Dar es Salaam, Dar es Salaam University Press, 1981.

Teso—History

3491. Webster, James Bertin (ed.) *The Iteso during the Asonya.* Nairobi, East African Publishing House, 1978.

Teso—Psychology

3492. Otaala, Barnabas. *The development of operational thinking in primary school children: an examination of Piaget's theory among the Iteso children of Uganda.* New York, Teachers College Press, 1973.

Tharaka—Ethnography

3493. Volpini, Domenico. *Il seme del ricino: iniziazione tribale et mutamento culturale fra i Tharaka del Kenya.* Roma, Officina, 1978.

Tigray—Architecture

3494. Plant, Ruth. *Architecture of the Tigre, Ethiopia.* Worcester, Ravens Educational and Development Services, 1985.

Tigray—History

3495. Peberdy, Max. *Tigray: Ethiopia's untold story.* London, Relief Society of Tigray UK Support Committee, 1985.

Tigray—Language

3496. Aressi, Tuquabo. *Concise English-Tigrinya dictionary.* Asmara, Ethiopian Studies Centre, 1987.

3497. Ullendorff, Edward. *A Tigrinya chrestomathy.* Stuttgart, Franz Steiner, 1985.

3498. Voigt, Rainer Maria. *Das tigrinische Verbalsystem.* Berlin, Dietrich Reimer, 1977.

Tigray—Social Conditions

3499. Bauer, Dan Franz. *Household and society in Ethiopia: an economic and social analysis of Tigray social principles and household organization.* Second edition. East Lansing, Michigan State University, African Studies Center, 1985.

Tigray—Women

3500. Druce, Nell, and Jenny Hammond (eds.) *Sweeter than honey: Ethiopian women and revolution. Testimonies of Tigrayan women.* Trenton, Red Sea Press, 1990.

Tigre—Language

3501. Nakano, Aki'o, and Yoichi Tsuge. *A vocabulary of Beni Amer dialect of Tigré*. Tokyo, Institute for the Study of Languages and Cultures of Asia and Africa, 1982.

3502. Raz, Shlomo. *Tigre grammar and texts*. Malibu, Undena, 1983.

Tippu Tip

3503. Farrant, Leda. *Tippu Tip and the East African slave trade*. London, Hamish Hamilton, 1975.

3504. Hahner-Hertzog, Iris. *Tippu Tip und der Elfenbeinhandel in Ost- und Zentralafrika im 19. Jahrhundert*. München, Tuduv-Verlagsgesellschaft, 1990.

3505. Kimena Kekwakwa Kinenge. *Tippo Tip: traitant et Sultan du Manyema*. Kinshasa, Centre de Recherches Pédagogiques, 1979.

3506. Renault, François. *Tippo Tip: un potentat arabe en Afrique centrale au XIXe siècle*. Paris, Société Française d'Outre-Mer, 1987.

Tiriki—Ethnography

3507. Sangree, Walter. *Age, prayer and politics in Tiriki*. London, Oxford University Press, 1966.

Toposa—Ethnography

3508. Müller, H. K. *Changing generations: dynamics of generation and age-sets in southeastern Sudan (Toposa) and northwestern Kenya (Turkana)*. Saarbrücken, Breitenbach, 1989.

Toro—History

3509. Ingham, Kenneth. *The kingdom of Toro in Uganda*. London, Methuen, 1975.

Tourism—East Africa

3510. Cameron, Kenneth M. *Into Africa: the story of the East African safari*. London, Constable, 1990.

3511. Ouma, Joseph P. B. M. *Evolution of tourism in East Africa, 1900–2000*. Nairobi, East African Literature Bureau, 1970.

3512. Popovic, Vojislav. *Tourism in eastern Africa*. Munich, Weltforum-Verlag, 1972.

Trade—East Africa

3513. Alpers, Edward A. *Ivory and slaves in East Central Africa: changing patterns of international trade to the later nineteenth century*. London, Heinemann, 1975.

3514. Anjaria, S. J., et al. *Payments arrangements and the expansion of trade in eastern and southern Africa.* Washington, International Monetary Fund, 1982.

3515. Gray, Richard, and David Birmingham (eds.) *Pre-colonial African trade: essays on trade in central and eastern Africa before 1900.* London, Oxford University Press, 1970.

Training—East Africa

3516. Maliyamkono, T. L., et al. *Training and productivity in eastern Africa: an Eastern African Universities Project.* London, Heinemann, 1982.

Transport—East Africa

3517. Hazlewood, Arthur. *Rail and road in East Africa: transport coordination in underdeveloped countries.* Oxford, Blackwell, 1967.

Tugen—Religion

3518. Behrend, H. *Die Zeit geht krumme Wege: Raum, Zeit und Ritual bei den Tugen in Kenia.* Frankfurt am Main, Campus-Verlag, 1987.

Turkana—Economy

3519. Henriksen, Georg. *Economic growth and ecological balance: problems of development in Turkana.* Bergen, University of Bergen, 1974.

Turkana—Ethnography

3520. Best, Günter. *Culture and language of the Turkana, NW Kenya.* Heidelberg, Carl Winter Universitätsverlag, 1983.

3521. Dyson-Hudson, Rada, and J. Terrence McCabe. *South Turkana nomads: coping with an unpredictable, varying environment.* New Haven, Human Relations Area Files, 1985. 2 vols.

3522. Hauge, Hans-Egil. *Turkana religion and folklore.* Stockholm, Universitet Stockholm, 1986.

3523. Müller, H. K. *Changing generations: dynamics of generation and age-sets in southeastern Sudan (Toposa) and northwestern Kenya (Turkana).* Saarbrücken, Breitenbach, 1989.

Turkana—History

3524. Lamphear, John. *The scattering of time: Turkana responses to the imposition of colonial rule.* Oxford, Clarendon Press, 1992.

Turkana—Language

3525. Barrett, Anthony J. *English-Turkana dictionary.* Nairobi, Macmillan Kenya, 1988.

3526. Barrett, Anthony J. *Turkana-English dictionary*. London, Macmillan, 1991.

3527. Dimmendaal, Gerrit Jan. *The Turkana language*. Dordrecht, Foris, 1983.

Turkana—Religion

3528. Jagt, K. A. van der. *De religie van de Turkana van Kenia*. Utrecht, K. A. van der Jagt, 1983.

Turkana—Social Conditions

3529. Best, Günter. *Nomaden und Bewasserungsprojekte: eine Studie zum rezenten Wandlungsprozess der Eheform und Familienstruktur bei den Turkana am oberen Turkwell, NW-Kenia*. Berlin, Dietrich Reimer, 1984.

3530. Best, Günter. *Vom Rindernomadismus zum Fischfang: der sozio-kulturelle Wandel bei den Turkana am Rodolfsee, Kenia*. Stuttgart, Franz Steiner, 1978.

3531. Odegi-Awuondo, Caspar. *Life in the balance: ecological sociology of Turkana nomads*. Nairobi, Acts Press, 1990.

3532. Soper, R. C. (ed.) *A socio-cultural profile of Turkana District: a report of the District Socio-Cultural Profiles Project*. Nairobi, University of Nairobi, Institute of African Studies and Ministry of Finance and Planning, 1985.

Uduk—Ethnography

3533. James, Wendy. *Kwanim Pa: the making of the Uduk people. An ethnographic study of survival in the Sudan-Ethiopian borderlands*. Oxford, Clarendon Press, 1979.

3534. James, Wendy. *The listening ebony: moral knowledge, religion, and power among the Uduk of Sudan*. Oxford, Clarendon Press, 1988.

Uganda—Agricultural Research

3535. Opio-Odongo, J. M. A. *Designs on the land: agricultural research in Uganda, 1890–1990*. Nairobi, Acts Press, 1992.

Uganda—Agriculture

3536. Hunt, Diana. *Credit for agricultural development: a case study of Uganda*. Nairobi, East African Publishing House, 1975.

3537. Jameson, J. D. *Agriculture in Uganda*. Second edition. London, Oxford University Press, 1970.

3538. Mettrick, Hal. *Aid in Uganda: agriculture*. London, Overseas Development Institute, 1967.

3539. Nsereko, Joseph. *Selected causes of agricultural problems in a peasant society, with examples from Uganda*. Nairobi, Kenya Literature Bureau, 1979.

3540. Uchendu, Victor Chikezie, and K. R. M. Anthony. *Agricultural change in Teso District, Uganda: a study of economic, cultural and technical determinants of rural development.* Nairobi, East African Literature Bureau, 1975.

3541. Vail, D. J. *A history of agricultural innovation and development in Teso District, Uganda.* Syracuse, Syracuse University, Maxwell School of Citizenship and Public Affairs, 1972.

3542. Wrigley, Christopher Crompton. *Crops and wealth in Uganda: a short agrarian history.* Nairobi, Oxford University Press, 1970.

Uganda—Asians

3543. Halbach, Axel J. *Die Ausweisung der Asiaten aus Uganda: sieben Monate Amin'scher Politik in Dokumenten.* München, Weltforum-Verlag, 1973.

3544. Mamdani, Mahmood. *From citizen to refugee: Uganda Asians come to Britain.* London, Pinter, 1973.

3545. Melady, Thomas P., and Margaret B. Melady. *Uganda: the Asian exiles.* Maryknoll, Orbis, 1976.

3546. Morris, H. S. *The Indians in Uganda: caste and sect in a plural society.* London, Weidenfeld and Nicolson, 1968.

3547. Patel, H. H. *Power, race, class and citizenship: towards a conceptual integration for the study of Indian political activity in Uganda.* Salisbury, University of Zimbabwe Library, 1979.

3548. Prunier, G. *L'Ouganda et la question indienne, 1896–1972.* Paris, Éditions Recherche sur les Civilisations, 1990.

3549. Ramchandani, R. R. *Uganda Asians: the end of an enterprise.* Bombay, United Asia Publications, 1976.

3550. Twaddle, Michael (ed.) *Expulsion of a minority: essays on Ugandan Asians.* London, Athlone Press, 1975.

Uganda—Bibliography

3551. Collison, Robert L. *Uganda.* Oxford, Clio Press, 1981.

3552. Gertzel, Cherry J. *Uganda: an annotated bibliography of source materials.* Oxford, Hans Zell, 1991.

Uganda—Botany

3553. Haines, Richard Wheeler, and Kere Arnstein Lye. *The sedges and rushes of East Africa: a flora of the families Juncaceae and Cyperaceae in East Africa, with particular reference to Uganda.* Nairobi, East African Natural History Society, 1983.

Uganda—Boundaries

3554. Kibulya, H. M., and B. W. Langlands. *The political geography of the Uganda-Congo boundary.* Kampala, Makerere University College, Department of Geography, 1967.

Uganda—Child Welfare

3555. Ainsworth, Mary D. Salter. *Infancy in Uganda: infant care and the growth of love.* Baltimore, Johns Hopkins Press, 1967.

3556. Dodge, Cole P., and Magne Raundalen. *Reaching children in war: Sudan, Uganda and Mozambique.* Bergen, Sigma Forlag, 1991.

3557. Dodge, Cole P., and Magne Raundalen (eds.) *War, violence and children in Uganda.* Oslo, Norwegian University Press, 1987.

Uganda—Christianity

3558. Bosa, Domenico. *La fontana dalle molte sorgenti: cento anni di cristianesimo in Uganda.* Bologna, Editrice Missionaria Italiana, 1979.

3559. Byabazaire, Deogratias M. *The contribution of the Christian churches to the development of western Uganda, 1894–1974.* Frankfurt am Main, Peter Lang, 1979.

3560. Faupel, John Francis. *African holocaust: the story of the Uganda martyrs.* Second edition. London, Geoffrey Chapman, 1965.

3561. Gaiga, Lorenzo. *Martiri comboniani in Uganda.* Bologna, Editrice Missionaria Italiana, 1990.

3562. Gingyera-Pinycwa, A. G. G. *Issues in pre-independence politics in Uganda: a case study on the contribution of religion to political debate in Uganda in the decade 1952–62.* Nairobi, East African Literature Bureau, 1976.

3563. Kavulu, David. *The Uganda martyrs.* Kampala, Longmans, 1969.

3564. Ladenius, Fred. *Ventidue croci in Uganda: i primi martiri della chiesa in Uganda.* Roma, Città Nuova, 1985.

3565. Luck, Anne. *African saint: the study of Apolo Kivebulaya.* London, SCM Press, 1963.

3566. Pirouet, Louise. *Black evangelists: the spread of Christianity in Uganda, 1891–1914.* London, Rex Collings, 1978.

3567. Pirouet, Louise (ed.) *A dictionary of Christianity in Uganda.* Kampala, Makerere University College, 1969.

3568. Sempangi, Kefa. *Reign of terror, reign of love.* Tring, Lion Publishing, 1979.

3569. Ssemakula, P. *They obeyed the true King: the story of the Uganda martyrs.* Kisubi, St. Paul Publications, 1983.

3570. Tom Tuma, A. D., and Phares Mutibwa (eds.) *A century of Christianity in Uganda, 1877–1977: a historical appraisal of the development of the Uganda Church over the last one hundred years.* Nairobi, Uzima Press, 1978.

3571. Tourigny, Yves. *So abundant a harvest: the Catholic church in Uganda, 1879–1979.* London, Darton, Longman and Todd, 1979.

3572. Van Rheeman, G. *Church planting in Uganda.* South Pasadena, William Carey Library, 1976.

3573. Welbourn, F. B. *East African rebels.* Liverpool, SCM Press, 1961.

3574. Welbourn, F. B. *Religion and politics in Uganda, 1952–1962.* Nairobi, East African Publishing House, 1965.

3575. Wooding, Dan, and Ray Barnett. *Uganda holocaust.* London, Pickering and Inglis, 1980.

Uganda — Civil Service

3576. Motani, Nizar A. *On His Majesty's Service in Uganda: the origins of Uganda's African civil service, 1912–1940.* Syracuse, Syracuse University, Maxwell School of Citizenship and Public Affairs, 1977.

Uganda — Colonial History

3577. Balezin, A. S. *African rulers and chiefs in Uganda: evolution of traditional power under colonialism, 1862–1962.* Moscow, Nauka, 1986.

3578. Barber, James. *Imperial frontier: a study of relations between the British and the pastoral tribes of northeast Uganda.* Nairobi, East African Publishing House, 1968.

3579. Bere, Rennie. *A cuckoo's parting cry: a personal account of life and work in Uganda between 1930 and 1960.* Cheltenham, Cedar Publishing, 1990.

3580. Kabwegyere, Tarsis B. *The politics of state formation: the nature and effects of colonialism in Uganda.* Nairobi, East African Literature Bureau, 1974.

3581. Osmaston, Anna. *Uganda before Amin: our family life in Uganda, 1949–1962.* Bristol, Henry Osmaston, 1991.

3582. Rowe, J. *Lugard at Kampala.* Kampala, Longmans, 1969.

3583. Steinhart, Edward I. *Conflict and collaboration: the kingdoms of western Uganda, 1890–1907.* Princeton, Princeton University Press, 1977.

3584. Vincent, Joan. *Teso in transformation: peasantry and class in colonial Uganda, 1890–1927.* Berkeley, University of California Press, 1982.

Uganda — Constitution

3585. Ibingira, G. S. *The forging of an African nation: the political and constitutional evolution of Uganda from colonial rule to independence, 1894–1962.* New York, Viking, 1973.

3586. Kanyeihamba, George W. *Constitutional law and government in Uganda: the theory and practice of constitutionalism in Uganda including the government and local administrations, the citizen and the state, administrative law, the East African Community and the Commonwealth.* Nairobi, East African Literature Bureau, 1975.

3587. Odongo, Onyango. *Why Uganda independence constitution failed.* Gulu District, Lapare General Agency, 1993.

Uganda—Cooperatives

3588. Mwaka, Victoria Miriam. *Agricultural marketing cooperatives in Uganda.* Kampala, Makerere University, Department of Geography, 1978.

3589. Okereke, Okoro. *The economic impact of Uganda cooperatives.* Nairobi, East African Literature Bureau, 1974.

3590. Young, Crawford, et al. *Co-operatives and development: agricultural politics in Ghana and Uganda.* Madison, Wisconsin University Press, 1981.

Uganda—Criminology

3591. Clinard, Marshall B., and Daniel J. Abbott. *Crime in developing countries: a comparative perspective.* New York, Wiley, 1973.

3592. Tanner, Ralph E. S. *Homicide in Uganda.* Uppsala, Scandinavian Institute of African Studies, 1964.

3593. Tibamanya mwene Mushanga. *Criminal homicide in Uganda: a sociological study of violent deaths in Ankole, Kigezi and Toro districts of western Uganda.* Nairobi, East African Literature Bureau, 1974.

Uganda—Deforestation

3594. Hamilton, A. C. *Deforestation in Uganda.* Nairobi, Oxford University Press, 1984.

Uganda—Description and Travel

3595. Bär-Stockburger, Elisabeth. *Abenteuer Uganda.* Neuhausen, Hänssler, 1991.

3596. Creed, Alexander. *Uganda.* New York, Chelsea House, 1988.

3597. Falaschi, Nermin. *La gru coronata.* Roma, Zephyr, 1976.

3598. Hanmer, Trudy J. *Uganda.* New York, Franklin Watts, 1989.

3599. Petteruti, Alfredo. *Il cuore dell'Africa: viaggio nel Karamogia nero.* Roma, Beta, 1988.

3600. Preston, John. *Touching the moon.* London, Heinemann, 1990.

3601. Yeoman, Guy. *Africa's Mountains of the Moon: journeys to the snowy sources of the Nile.* London, Elm Tree Books, 1989.

Uganda—Documentation

3602. Gray, Beverly Ann. *Uganda: subject guide to official publications.* Washington, Library of Congress, 1977.

Uganda—Economy

3603. Baird, M. *Uganda: country economic study.* Washington, World Bank, Eastern Africa Regional Office, 1982.

3604. Commonwealth Secretariat. *The rehabilitation of the economy of Uganda: a report by a Commonwealth team of experts.* London, Commonwealth Secretariat, 1979. 2 vols.

3605. Elkan, Walter. *The economic development of Uganda.* London, Oxford University Press, 1961.

3606. Fischer, Wolfgang E. *Die Entwicklungsbedingungen Ugandas: ein Beispiel für die Probleme afrikanischer Binnenstaaten.* München, Weltforum-Verlag, 1969.

3607. Ghai, Dharam P. *Taxation for development: a case study of Uganda.* Nairobi, East African Publishing House, 1966.

3608. Hansen, Holger Bernt, and Michael Twaddle (eds.) *Changing Uganda: the dilemmas of structural adjustment and revolutionary change.* London, James Currey, 1991.

3609. Hieber, Hans. *Wirtschaftsstatistik in Entwicklungsländern, dargestellt am Beispiel Ugandas.* München, Weltforum-Verlag, 1969.

3610. Kaberuka, Will. *The political economy of Uganda, 1890–1979: a case study of colonialism and underdevelopment.* New York, Vantage Press, 1990.

3611. Mamdani, Mahmood. *Contradictions of the IMF programme and perspective in Uganda.* Kampala, Centre for Basic Research, 1989.

3612. Nabudere, D. Wadada. *The IMF-World Bank's economic stabilisation and structural adjustment policies and the Uganda economy, 1981–1990.* Leiden, African Studies Centre, 1990.

3613. Seers, Dudley, et al. *The rehabilitation of the economy of Uganda.* London, Commonwealth Secretariat, Commonwealth Fund for Technical Cooperation, 1979.

3614. Tumusiime-Mutebile, E. *A critique of Professor Mamdani's "Uganda: contradictions of the IMF programme and perspective."* Kampala, Ministry of Planning and Economic Development, 1990.

3615. Wiebe, Paul D., and Cole P. Dodge. *Beyond crisis: development issues in Uganda.* Kampala, Makerere University, Institute of Social Research, 1987.

3616. World Bank. *The economic development of Uganda.* Baltimore, Johns Hopkins University Press, 1962.

3617. World Bank. *Uganda: progress towards recovery and prospects for development.* Washington, World Bank, 1985.

3618. World Bank. *Uganda: toward stabilization and economic recovery.* Washington, World Bank, 1988.

Uganda—Education

3619. Bagunywa, A. M. K. *Critical issues in African education: a case study of Uganda.* Nairobi, East African Publishing House, 1980.

3620. Bell, C. R. V. *Education in Uganda before independence.* Oxford, Rhodes House Library, n.d.

3621. Chesswas, John D. *Educational planning and development in Uganda.* Paris, UNESCO International Institute for Educational Planning, 1966.

3622. Eisemon, Thomas O. *Strengthening Uganda's policy environment for investing in university development.* Washington, World Bank, Population and Human Resources Department, 1993.

3623. Evans, David Russell. *Teachers as agents of national development: a case study of Uganda.* New York, Praeger, 1971.

3624. Goldthorpe, J. E. *An African elite: Makerere College students, 1922–1960.* London, Oxford University Press, 1966.

3625. Hanson, John W., and John P. Henderson. *Secondary level teachers: supply and demand in Uganda.* East Lansing, Michigan State University, Institute for International Education and African Studies Center, 1970.

3626. Heyneman, Stephen P., and Janice K. Currie. *Schooling, academic peformance and occupational attainment in a non-industrialized society.* Washington, University Press of America, 1979.

3627. Jolly, Richard. *Planning education for African development: economic and manpower perspectives.* Nairobi, East African Publishing House, 1969.

3628. Kasozi, Abdu B. K. *The crisis of secondary school education in Uganda, 1960–1970.* Kampala, Longmans, 1979.

3629. Katorobo, J. *Education for public service in Uganda.* New York, Vantage Press, 1982.

3630. Macpherson, Margaret. *They built for the future: a chronicle of Makerere University College, 1922–1962.* Cambridge, Cambridge University Press, 1964.

3631. Marshall, James. *A school in Uganda.* London, Gollancz, 1976.

3632. McGregor, G. *King's College Budo: the first sixty years.* London, Oxford University Press, 1967.

3633. Okech, John B. *Special education in Uganda.* Kampala, Ministry of Education and Sports, 1993.

3634. Omoding-Okwalinga, James. *Planning at Makerere University: a study of staff and student views on planning models in education*. Kampala, Makerere University Printer, 1976.

3635. Scanlon, D. G. *Education in Uganda*. Washington, United States Office of Education, 1964.

3636. Sekamwa, J. C., and S. M. E. Lugumba. *Educational development and administration in Uganda, 1900–1970: selected topics*. Kampala, Longman Uganda, 1973.

3637. Wandira, Asavia. *Early missionary education in Uganda*. Kampala, Makerere University, Department of Education, 1972.

3638. Wandira, Asavia. *Indigenous education in Uganda*. Kampala, Makerere University, Department of Education, 1971.

3639. Williams, Peter. *Aid in Uganda: education*. London, Overseas Development Institute, 1966.

Uganda—Elections

3640. Commonwealth Secretariat. *Uganda elections December 1980: the report of the Commonwealth Observer Group*. London, Commonwealth Secretariat, 1980.

Uganda—Employment

3641. Elliott, Charles M. *Employment and income distribution in Uganda*. Second edition. Norwich, University of East Anglia, Overseas Development Group, 1977.

Uganda—Energy

3642. Childs, P. E., and B. W. Langlands (eds.) *Energy in Uganda*. Kampala, Makerere University, Department of Geography, 1976.

3643. Wilson, Gail. *Owen Falls: electricity in a developing country*. Nairobi, East African Publishing House, 1967.

Uganda—Environment

3644. Kahimbaara, J. A., and B. W. Langlands. *The human factor in the changing ecology of Mwenge*. Kampala, Makerere University, 1970.

3645. Langdale-Brown, I., et al. *The vegetation of Uganda*. Entebbe, Government of Uganda, 1964.

Uganda—Ethnography

3646. Mafeje, Archie. *The theory and ethnography of African social formations: the case of the interlacustrine kingdoms*. Dakar, Codesria, 1991.

3647. Ray, B. *Myth, ritual and kingship in Uganda*. Oxford, Oxford University Press, 1991.

3648. Richards, Audrey I. (ed.) *East African chiefs: a study of political development in some Uganda and Tanganyika tribes*. London, Faber and Faber, 1960.

Uganda—Finance

3649. Bosa, G. R. *The financing of small-scale enterprises in Uganda*. Nairobi, Oxford University Press, 1969.

3650. Schneider-Barthold, W. *Uganda: Voraussetzungen und Möglichkeiten der privaten Investition*. Hamburg, Afrika-Verein, 1976.

Uganda—Food and Nutrition

3651. Amann, V. F., et al. (eds.) *Nutrition and food in an African economy*. Kampala, Makerere University, 1972.

3652. Hoorweg, Jan, and Ian McDowell. *The evaluation of nutrition education in Africa: community research in Uganda, 1971–1972*. The Hague, Mouton, 1979.

3653. Hyde, R. J., and B. W. Langlands. *Patterns of food crop production and nutrition in Uganda*. Kampala, Makerere University, Department of Geography, 1974.

Uganda—Foreign Aid

3654. Clark, Ralph, et al. *Aid in Uganda: programmes and policies*. London, Overseas Development Institute, 1966.

3655. Gitelson, Susan Aurelia. *Multilateral aid for national development and self reliance: a case study of the UNDP in Uganda and Tanzania*. Nairobi, East African Literature Bureau, 1975.

Uganda—Geography

3656. Dak, O. *A geographical analysis of the distribution of migrants in Uganda*. Kampala, Makerere University, Department of Geography, 1968.

3657. Langlands, B. W. *Inventory of geographical research at Makerere, 1947–1972*. Kampala, Makerere University, Department of Geography, 1972.

3658. Langlands, B. W. *Notes on the geography of ethnicity in Uganda*. Kampala, Makerere University, Department of Geography, 1975.

3659. Langlands, B. W., and G. Namirembe. *Studies on the geography of religion*. Kampala, Makerere University College, Department of Geography, 1967.

3660. Ojo, O. *Water balance in Uganda*. Kampala, Makerere University, Department of Geography, 1974.

Uganda—Handbook

3661. Byrnes, Rita M. (ed.) *Uganda: a country study*. Second edition. Washington, Library of Congress, Federal Research Division, 1992.

Uganda—Health and Medicine

3662. Dodge, Cole P., and P. D. Wiebe (eds.) *Crisis in Uganda: the breakdown of health services.* Oxford, Pergamon Press, 1985.

3663. Foster, William Derek. *The Church Missionary Society and modern medicine in Uganda: the life of Sir Albert Cook, 1870–1951.* Prestbury, the Author, 1978.

3664. Foster, William Derek. *The early history of scientific medicine in Uganda.* Nairobi, East African Literature Bureau, 1970.

3665. Hall, S. A., and B. W. Langlands (eds.) *Uganda atlas of disease distribution.* Nairobi, East African Publishing House, 1975.

3666. Holden, P. *Doctors and other medical personnel in the public health services in Africa, 1930–1965: Uganda, Tanganyika/Tanzania, Nigeria.* Oxford, Rhodes House Library, 1984.

3667. Holden, P. *Nursing sisters in Nigeria, Uganda, Tanganyika/Tanzania, 1929–1978: a report on the memoirs collected by Alison Smith for the Oxford Development Records Project on public health in Africa.* Oxford, Rhodes House Library, 1984.

3668. Hooper, Ed. *Slim: a reporter's own story of AIDS in East Africa.* London, Bodley Head, 1990.

3669. Musere, J. *African sleeping sickness: political ecology, colonialism and control in Uganda.* Lewiston, Edwin Mellen Press, 1990.

3670. Templeton, A. C. *Tumours in a tropical country: a survey of Uganda, 1964–1968.* Berlin, Springer-Verlag, 1973.

Uganda—History

3671. Adoko, Akena. *From Obote to Obote.* New Delhi, Vikas, 1983.

3672. Adoko, Akena. *Uganda crisis.* Kampala, African Publishers, 1970.

3673. Agami, John B. *The roots of political crisis in Uganda.* Copenhagen, the Author, 1978.

3674. Cohen, David William. *Womunafu's Bunafu: a study of authority in a nineteenth-century African community.* Princeton, Princeton University Press, 1977.

3675. Elizabeth, Princess of Toro. *Elizabeth of Toro: the odyssey of an African princess. An autobiography.* New York, Simon and Schuster, 1987.

3676. Jørgensen, Jan Jelmert. *Uganda: a modern history.* London, Croom Helm, 1981.

3677. Karugire, Samwiri Rubaraza. *A political history of Uganda.* Nairobi, Heinemann, 1980.

3678. Kato, Wycliffe. *Escape from Idi Amin's slaughterhouse.* London, Quartet Books, 1989.

3679. Lhoest, Bernard. *L'Ouganda sous Idi Amin Dada, 1971–1979*. Bruxelles, Université Libre de Bruxelles, Faculté des Sciences Sociales, Section des Sciences Politiques, 1985.

3680. Medeghini, Alessandro. *Storia d'Uganda*. Bologna, Editrice Missionaria Italiana, 1973.

3681. Mukherjee, Ramkrishna. *Uganda: an historical accident? Class, nation, state formation*. Trenton, Africa World Press, 1986.

3682. Mutibwa, Phares. *Uganda since independence: a story of unfulfilled hopes*. London, Hurst, 1992.

3683. Roden, D. (ed.) *Readings in the historical geography of the East African interior. Vol. 1*. Kampala, Makerere University, Department of Geography, 1975.

3684. Stacey, Tom. *Summons to Ruwenzori*. London, Secker and Warburg, 1965.

3685. Thomas, H. B. and Samwiri Rubaraza Karugire. *The story of Uganda*. Nairobi, Oxford University Press, 1973.

3686. Tumusiime, James (ed.) *Uganda 30 years: 1962–1992*. Kampala, Fountain, 1992.

3687. Twaddle, Michael. *Kakungulu and the creation of Uganda, 1868–1928*. London, James Currey, 1993.

3688. Webster, James Bertin (ed.) *A history of Uganda before 1900*. Nairobi, East African Publishing House, 1979.

3689. Weyel, V. *Interaktionen von Politik und Religion in Uganda nach 1875, dargestellt an ausgewählten Beispielen auf der nationalen Ebene und der lokalen des Landes Kigezi, inbesondere seines Regierungsbezirkes Ruzhumbura*. München, Karl Renner, 1976.

3690. Zwanenberg, Roger M. van. *An economic history of Kenya and Uganda, 1800–1970*. London, Macmillan, 1975.

Uganda — Housing

3691. Ouma, Sylvester J. *The politics of housing policy in Uganda*. Glasgow, Strathclyde University, Department of Government, 1992.

Uganda — Human Rights

3692. Amnesty International. *Uganda: six years after Amin, torture, killings, disappearances*. London, Amnesty International, 1985.

3693. Amnesty International. *Uganda: the failure to safeguard human rights*. London, Amnesty International, 1992.

3694. Amnesty International. *Uganda: the human rights record*. London, Amnesty International, 1989.

254   Bibliography

Uganda—Industry

3695. Halbach, Axel J. *Industriestruktur und Industrialisierungspolitik in Uganda, 1963–1972.* München, Weltforum-Verlag, 1974.

3696. Stoutjesdijk, E. J. *Uganda's manufacturing sector: a contribution to the analysis of industrialization in East Africa.* Nairobi, East African Publishing House, 1967.

3697. UNIDO. *Uganda: industrial revitalization and reorientation.* Vienna, UNIDO, 1992.

Uganda—Islam

3698. Kasozi, Abdu B. K. *The spread of Islam in Uganda.* Nairobi, Oxford University Press, 1986.

3699. King, N., et al. *Islam and the confluence of religions in Uganda, 1840–1966.* Tallahassee, American Academy of Religion, 1973.

3700. Oded, Arye. *Islam in Uganda: Islamization through a centralized state in pre-colonial Africa.* New York, Wiley, 1974.

3701. Soghayroun, Ibrahim el-Zein. *The Sudanese Muslim factor in Uganda.* Khartoum, Khartoum University Press, 1981.

Uganda—Journalism

3702. Gariyo, Zie. *The press and democratic struggles in Uganda, 1900–1962.* Kampala, Centre for Basic Research, 1992.

Uganda—Labor

3703. Elkan, Walter. *Migrants and proletarians: urban labour in the economic development of Uganda.* Kampala, East African Institute of Social Research, 1960.

3704. Grillo, Ralph D. *African railwaymen: solidarity and opposition in an East African labour force.* Cambridge, Cambridge University Press, 1973.

3705. Josephine, A. *Workers' struggle, the labour process and the question of control: the case of United Garment Industry Limited.* Kampala, Centre for Basic Research, 1991.

Uganda—Land Use

3706. Langlands, B. W. *A preliminary review of land use in Uganda.* Revised and corrected edition. Kampala, Makerere University, Department of Geography, 1973.

Uganda—Language

3707. Ladefoged, Peter, et al. *Language in Uganda.* London, Oxford University Press, 1972.

Uganda—Law

3708. Allen, P. *Days of judgement: a judge in Idi Amin's Uganda*. London, Kimber, 1987.

3709. Barya, J. J. B. *Workers and the law in Uganda*. Kampala, Centre for Basic Research, 1991.

3710. Kanyeihamba, George W. *Urban planning law in East Africa, with special reference to Uganda*. Oxford, Pergamon Press, 1973.

3711. Morris, Henry Francis, and James S. Read. *Uganda: the development of its laws and constitution*. London, Stevens, 1966.

3712. Odoki, Ben J. *A guide to criminal procedure in Uganda*. Second edition. Kampala, Law Development Centre, 1990.

Uganda—Local Government

3713. Barkan, Joel D., et al. *Uganda: district government and politics, 1947–1967*. Madison, University of Wisconsin, African Studies Program, 1977.

3714. Burke, Fred George. *Local government and politics in Uganda*. Syracuse, Syracuse University Press, 1964.

3715. Sathyamurthy, T. V. *Central-local relations: the case of Uganda*. Bergen, Chr. Michelsen Institute, Development Research and Action Programme, 1981.

Uganda—Military History

3716. Mmbando, S. I. *The Tanzania-Uganda war in pictures*. Dar es Salaam, Longman Tanzania, 1980.

Uganda—Missionaries

3717. Butler, Bill. *Hill ablaze*. London, Hodder and Stoughton, 1976.

3718. Hansen, Holger Bernt. *Mission, church and state in a colonial setting: Uganda, 1890–1925*. London, Heinemann, 1984.

3719. Tiberondwa, Ado K. *Missionary teachers as agents of colonialism: a study of their activities in Uganda, 1877–1925*. Lusaka, Neczam, 1978.

Uganda—Music

3720. Brandel, Rose. *The music of central Africa, an ethnomusicological study: former French Equatorial Africa, the former Belgian Congo, Ruanda-Urundi, Uganda, Tanganyika*. The Hague, Nijhoff, 1961.

Uganda—Planning

3721. GATT. *The Uganda development plan, 1961–1966*. Geneva, GATT, 1966.

3722. Safier, Michael, and B. W. Langlands (eds.) *Perspectives on urban planning for Uganda*. Kampala, Makerere University, Department of Geography, 1969.

Uganda—Politics

3723. Aasland, T. *On the Move-to-the-Left in Uganda, 1969–1971: the Common Man's Charter, dissemination and attitudes.* Uppsala, Scandinavian Institute of African Studies, 1974.

3724. Apter, David. *The political kingdom in Uganda: a study in bureaucratic nationalism.* Princeton, Princeton University Press, 1961.

3725. Avirgan, Tony, and Martha Honey. *War in Uganda: the legacy of Idi Amin.* London, Zed Press, 1982.

3726. Barkan, Joel D. *An African dilemma: university students, development and politics in Ghana, Tanzania and Uganda.* Nairobi, Oxford University Press, 1975.

3727. Bwengye, Francis W. *The agony of Uganda from Idi Amin to Obote. Repressive rule and bloodshed: causes, effects and the cure.* New York, Regency Press, 1986.

3728. Bwengye, Francis W. *The price of freedom: the assassination of Dr. Lutakome Andrew Kayiira, Uganda's great fighter for freedom and democracy.* Baden Baden, Uganda Human Rights Union, 1988.

3729. Expedit, Ddungu. *Popular forms and the question of democracy: the case of resistance councils in Uganda.* Kampala, Centre for Basic Research, 1989.

3730. Gertzel, Cherry J. *Party and locality in northern Uganda, 1945–1962.* London, Athlone Press, 1974.

3731. Gukiina, Peter M. *Uganda: a case study in African political development.* Notre Dame, University of Notre Dame Press, 1972.

3732. Hansen, Holger Bernt. *Ethnicity and military rule in Uganda: a study of ethnicity as a political factor in Uganda, based on a discussion of political anthropology and the application of its results.* Uppsala, Scandinavian Institute of African Studies, 1977.

3733. Ingrams, Harold. *Uganda: a crisis of nationhood.* London, H.M.S.O., 1960.

3734. Karugire, Samwiri Rubaraza. *The roots of instability in Uganda.* Kampala, New Vision, 1988.

3735. Kasfir, Nelson. *The shrinking political arena: participation and ethnicity in African politics, with a case study of Uganda.* Berkeley, University of California Press, 1976.

3736. Low, Donald Anthony. *Political parties in Uganda, 1949–62.* London, Athlone Press, 1962.

3737. Mamdani, Mahmood. *Imperialism and fascism in Uganda.* London, Heinemann, 1983.

3738. Mamdani, Mahmood. *Politics and class formation in Uganda.* London, Heinemann, 1976.

3739. Mazrui, Ali A. *Soldiers and kinsmen in Uganda: the making of a military ethnocracy.* London, Sage, 1975.

3740. McKenzie Smith, Justin. *Breaking with the past? A consideration of Yoweri Museveni's National Resistance Movement, and of social and political action in Uganda during its government.* Edinburgh, University of Edinburgh, Centre of African Studies, 1993.

3741. Mittelman, James H. *Ideology and politics in Uganda from Obote to Amin.* Ithaca, Cornell University Press, 1975.

3742. Museveni, Yoweri Kaguta. *Consolidating the revolution.* Kampala, Government Printer, 1990.

3743. Museveni, Yoweri Kaguta. *Selected articles on the Uganda resistance war.* Second edition. Kampala, NRM Publications, 1986.

3744. Museveni, Yoweri Kaguta. *What is Africa's problem? Speeches and writings on Africa.* Kampala, NRM Publications, 1992.

3745. Nabudere, D. Wadada. *Imperialism and revolution in Uganda.* London, Onyx Press, 1980.

3746. Obote, Milton. *Myths and realities.* Kampala, African Publishers, 1970.

3747. Obote, Milton. *The common man's charter, with appendices.* Entebbe, Government Printer, 1970.

3748. Omara-Otunnu, A. *Politics and the military in Uganda, 1890–1985.* Basingstoke, Macmillan, 1987.

3749. Richardson, Michael Lewis. *After Amin: the bloody pearl.* Atlanta, Majestic Books, 1980.

3750. Robertson, A. F. *Uganda's first republic: chiefs, administrators and politicians, 1961–1971.* Cambridge, African Studies Centre, Cambridge University, 1982.

3751. Rupesinghe, K. (ed.) *Conflict resolution in Uganda.* Oslo, International Peace Research Institute in association with James Currey, London, 1989.

3752. Rutiba, Eustace Gashegu. *Towards peace in Uganda.* Kampala, Nile Valley Pyramids Publishing House, 1986.

3753. Sathyamurthy, T. V. *The political development of Uganda, 1900–1986.* Aldershot, Gower, 1986.

3754. Seera-Muwanga, Lance. *Violence in Uganda: what is inside Museveni's Uganda?* Vaxjo, Vaxjo University Program for Human Rights and Refugee Studies, 1989.

3755. Segall, Marshall H., et al. *Political identity: a case study from Uganda.* Syracuse, Syracuse University, Maxwell School of Citizenship and Public Affairs, 1976.

3756. Uzoigwe, G. N. (ed.) *Uganda: the dilemma of nationhood.* New York, NOK Publishers, 1982.

Uganda—Population

3757. Hirst, M. A., et al. *Studies in the population geography of Uganda and Tanzania.* Kampala, Makerere University, 1970.

3758. Langlands, B. W. *Atlas of population census for 1969 for Uganda.* Kampala, Makerere University, Department of Geography, 1974.

3759. Langlands, B. W. *The population geography of Kigezi District.* Kampala, Makerere University, Department of Geography, 1971.

Uganda—Railways

3760. Hardy, Ronald. *The iron snake.* London, Collins, 1965.

3761. O'Connor, Anthony M. *Railways and development in Uganda: a study in economic geography.* Nairobi, Oxford University Press, 1965.

Uganda—Refugees

3762. Trappe, Paul. *Social change and development institutions in a refugee population.* Geneva, United Nations Research Institute for Social Development, 1971.

Uganda—Religion

3763. Abidi, Syed A. H. (ed.) *The role of religious organisations in development of Uganda.* Kampala, Foundation for African Development, 1991.

3764. Castelli, E. *La difficile speranza: testomonianze dall'Uganda.* Milano, Jaca Book, 1986.

Uganda—Roads

3765. Hawkins, Edward Kenneth. *Roads and road transport in an underdeveloped country: a case study of Uganda.* London, H.M.S.O., 1962.

Uganda—Rural Conditions

3766. Brett, Edwin Allan. *Providing for the rural poor: institutional decay and transformation in Uganda.* Brighton, University of Sussex, Institute of Development Studies, 1992.

3767. Coninck, John de, and Roger C. Riddell. *Evaluating the impact of NGOs in rural poverty alleviation: Uganda country study.* London, Overseas Development Institute, 1992.

3768. Jackson, R. T., et al. *Essays on rural marketing in West Nile.* Kampala, Makerere University, Department of Geography, 1972.

3769. Langlands, B. W. (ed.) *Geographical studies on rural markets in East Africa from Makerere.* Kampala, Makerere University, Department of Geography, 1975.

Uganda — Rural Development

3770. Hutton, C. *Reluctant farmers: a study of unemployment and planned rural development in Uganda.* Nairobi, East African Publishing House, 1973.

3771. Trappe, Paul. *Development from below as an alternative: a case study in Karamoja, Uganda.* Basel, Social Strategies Publishers Cooperative Society, 1978.

Uganda — Social Conditions

3772. Brandt, Hartmut, et al. *The industrial town as factor of economic and social development: the example of Jinja/Uganda.* Munich, Weltforum-Verlag, 1972.

3773. Hansen, Holger Bernt, and Michael Twaddle (eds.) *Uganda now: between decay and development.* London, James Currey, 1988.

3774. Hills, Denis. *The white pumpkin.* London, Allen & Unwin, 1975.

3775. Jacobson, David. *Itinerant townsmen: friendship and social order in urban Uganda.* Menlo Park, Cummings, 1973.

Uganda — Sport

3776. Andresen, Rolf, et al. *Sportstrukturen in Afrika: Sambia und Uganda.* Ahrensburg, Czwalina, 1988.

Uganda — Trade Unions

3777. Grillo, Ralph D. *Race, class and militancy: an African trade union, 1939–1965.* New York, Chandler, 1974.

3778. Scott, Roger. *The development of trade unions in Uganda.* Nairobi, East African Publishing House, 1966.

Uganda — Tsetse Control

3779. Jahnke, H. E. *The economics of controlling tsetse flies and cattle trypanosomiasis in Africa examined in the case of Uganda.* Munich, Weltforum-Verlag, 1974.

Uganda — Wildlife

3780. Baumgartel, Walter. *Up among the mountain gorillas.* New York, Hawthorn Books, 1977.

3781. Jahnke, H. E. *Conservation and utilization of wildlife in Uganda: a study in environmental economics.* Munich, Weltforum-Verlag, 1975.

3782. Neal, Ernest. *Uganda quest.* New York, Taplinger, 1971.

Uganda — Women

3783. Abidi, Syed A. H. (ed.) *Uganda women in development.* Kampala, Foundation for African Development, 1990.

3784. Obbo, Christine. *African women: their struggle for economic independence*. London, Zed Press, 1980.

3785. UNICEF. *Children and women in Uganda: a situation analysis*. Kampala, UNICEF, 1989.

Vegetation—East Africa

3786. Lind, E. M., and M. S. Morrison. *East African vegetation*. London, Longmans, 1974.

Wadai—Description and Travel

3787. Nachtigal, Gustav. *Sahara and Sudan. Vol. IV: Wadai and Darfur*. London, Hurst, 1972.

Water Supply—East Africa

3788. Warner, D. (ed.) *Rural water supply in East Africa*. Dar es Salaam, University College, 1970.

3789. White, Gilbert F. *Drawers of water: domestic water use in East Africa*. Chicago, University of Chicago Press, 1972.

Werizoid Languages

3790. Amborn, Hermann, et al. *Das Dullay: Materialen zu einer ostkuschitischen Sprachgruppe*. Berlin, Dietrich Reimer, 1980.

Wildlife—East Africa

3791. Huxley, Julian. *The conservation of wild life and natural habitats in central and east Africa*. Paris, UNESCO, 1961.

3792. Vaucher, C.-A. *East African wildlife*. Lausanne, Marguerat, 1967.

Woga—Ethnography

3793. Klausberger, Friedrich. *Woga: Recht und Gesellschaft in Süd-Äthiopien*. Frankfurt am Main, Peter Lang, 1981.

Women—East Africa

3794. Wright, Marcia. *Strategies of slaves and women: life stories from East/Central Africa*. London, James Currey, 1993.

Woodfuel—East Africa

3795. Bradley, P. N. *Woodfuel, women and woodlots. Vol. 1: a basis for effective research and development in East Africa*. London, Macmillan, 1991.

Yao—Language

3796. Whiteley, W. H. *A study of Yao sentences*. Oxford, Clarendon Press, 1966.

Yimbo—History

3797. Ochieng', William Robert. *A history of the Kadimo chiefdom of Yimbo in western Kenya.* Kampala, East African Literature Bureau, 1975.

Zaghawa—Ethnoarchaeology

3798. Tobert, Natalie. *The ethnoarchaeology of the Zaghawa of Darfur, Sudan: settlement and transience.* Oxford, British Archaeological Reports, 1988.

Zaghawa—Ethnography

3799. Tubiana, Marie-José, and Joseph Tubiana. *The Zaghawa from an ecological perspective: food gathering, the pastoral system, tradition and development of the Zaghawa of the Sudan and the Chad.* Rotterdam, A. A. Balkema, 1977.

Zanaki—Ethnography

3800. Bischofberger, Otto. *The generation classes of the Zanaki, Tanzania.* Fribourg, Fribourg University Press, 1972.

Zande Scheme

3801. Reining, C. C. *The Zande scheme: an anthropological case study of economic development in Africa.* Evanston, Northwestern University Press, 1966.

Zande—Description

3802. Piaggia, Carlo. *Nella terra dei Niam-Niam, 1863–1865.* Edited by E. Bassani. Lucca, Maria Pacini Fazzi, 1978.

Zande—Ethnography

3803. Evans-Pritchard, E. E. (ed.) *Man and woman among the Azande.* London, Faber and Faber, 1974.

3804. Giorgetti, Filiberto. *Death among the Azande of the Sudan: beliefs, rites and cult.* Bologna, Editrice Missionaria Italiana, 1968.

3805. Singer, André, and Brian V. Street. *Zande themes: essays presented to Sir Edward Evans-Pritchard.* Oxford, Blackwell, 1972.

Zande—History

3806. Evans-Pritchard, E. E. *The Azande: history and political institutions.* Oxford, Clarendon Press, 1971.

3807. Thuriaux-Hennebert, Arlette. *Les Zande dans l'histoire du Bahr el Ghazal et de l'Equatoria.* Bruxelles, Institut de Sociologie de l'Université Libre, 1964.

Zande—Language

3808. Claudi, U. *Zur Entstehung von Genussystemen: Überlegungen zu einigen theoretischen Aspekten, verbunden mit einer Fallstudie des Zande.* Hamburg, Helmut Buske, 1985.

Zanzibar—Agriculture

3809. Nelson-Richards, M. *Beyond the sociology of agrarian transformation: economy and society in Zambia, Nepal and Zanzibar.* Leiden, E. J. Brill, 1988.

3810. Wirth, Frigga (ed.) *A baseline survey for the identification of farming systems in Zanzibar.* Weikersheim, Josef Margraf, 1988.

Zanzibar—Colonial History

3811. Sheriff, A., and E. Ferguson (eds.) *Zanzibar under colonial rule.* London, James Currey, 1991.

Zanzibar—Documentation

3812. Walker, Audrey. *Official Publications of British East Africa. Part 3: Kenya and Zanzibar.* Washington, Library of Congress, 1962.

Zanzibar—History

3813. Ayany, Samuel G. *A history of Zanzibar: a study in constitutional development, 1934–1964.* Nairobi, East African Literature Bureau, 1970.

3814. Bennett, Norman R. *A history of the Arab state of Zanzibar.* London, Methuen, 1968.

3815. Bennett, Norman R. (ed.) *The Zanzibar letters of Edward D. Ropes, Jr., 1882–1892.* Boston, Boston University, African Studies Center, 1973.

3816. Bhacker, M. Reda. *Trade and empire in Muscat and Zanzibar: the roots of the British dimension.* London, Routledge, 1992.

3817. Birken, A. *Das Sultanat Zanzibar im 19. Jahrhundert.* Tübingen, Eberhard-Karls-Universität, 1971.

3818. Gray, John. *History of Zanzibar from the Middle Ages to 1856.* London, Oxford University Press, 1962.

3819. Harkema, R. C. *De stad Zanzibar in de tweede helft van de negentiende eeuw: en enkele oudere Oostafriukaanse kuststeden.* Loenen aan de Vecht, Van Kralingen, 1967.

3820. Lodhi, Abdulaziz, et al. *A small book on Zanzibar.* Stockholm, Fortfakkares Bokmaskin, 1979.

3821. Sheriff, A. *Slaves, spices and ivory in Zanzibar: integration of an East African commercial empire into the world economy, 1770–1873.* London, James Currey, 1987.

Zanzibar — Labor

3822. Cooper, F. J. *From slaves to squatters: plantation labor and agriculture in Zanzibar and coastal Kenya, 1890–1925.* New Haven, Yale University Press, 1980.

Zanzibar — Land

3823. Middleton, John. *Land tenure in Zanzibar.* London, H.M.S.O., 1961.

Zanzibar — Land Reform

3824. Shao, Ibrahim Fokas. *The political economy of land reform in Zanzibar.* Dar es Salaam, Dar es Salaam University Press, 1992.

Zanzibar — Politics

3825. Aumüller, Ingeborg. *Dekolonisation und Nationwerdung in Sansibar: Prozesse zur Unabhängikeit und territorialen Integration.* München, Weltforum-Verlag, 1980.

3826. Clayton, Anthony. *The Zanzibar revolution and its aftermath.* Hamden, Archon Books, 1981.

3827. Lofchie, Michael F. *Zanzibar: background to revolution.* Princeton, Princeton University Press, 1965.

3828. Martin, Esmond Bradley. *Zanzibar: tradition and revolution.* London, Hamish Hamilton, 1978.

3829. Okello, John. *Revolution in Zanzibar.* Nairobi, East African Publishing House, 1967.

Zanzibar — Slavery

3830. Lodhi, Abdulaziz. *The institution of slavery in Zanzibar and Pemba.* Uppsala, Scandinavian Institute of African Studies, 1973.

Zanzibar — Social Conditions

3831. Middleton, John, and Jane Campbell. *Zanzibar: its society and its politics.* London, Oxford University Press, 1965.

Zaramo — Art and Artists

3832. Felix, Marc Leo. *Mawana hiti: life and art of the matrilineal Bantu of Tanzania.* Munich, Fred Jahn, 1990.

Zaramo — Ethnography

3833. Swantz, Lloyd W. *The Zaramo of Tanzania.* Dar es Salaam, Nordic Tanganyika Project, 1965.

3834. Swantz, Lloyd W. *The medicine man among the Zaramo of Dar-es-Salaam.* Uppsala, Scandinavian Institute of African Studies, 1990.

3835. Swantz, Marja-Liisa. *Ritual and symbol in transitional Zaramo society, with special reference to women.* Second edition. Uppsala, Scandinavian Institute of African Studies, 1986.

Zaramo—Psychology

3836. Forssén, Anja. *Roots of traditional personality development among the Zaramo in coastal Tanzania.* Helsinki, Lastensuojelun Keskusliitto, 1979.

Zigua—Ethnography

3837. Grohs, Elisabeth. *Kisazi: Reiferriten der Mädchen bei den Zigua und Ngulu Ost-Tanzanias.* Berlin, Dietrich Reimer, 1980.

Zinza—Spirit Possession

3838. Bjerke, Svein. *Religion and misfortune: the Bacwezi complex and the other spirit cults of the Zinza of northwestern Tanzania.* Oslo, Universitetsforlaget, 1981.

Author Index

About the Author

HECTOR BLACKHURST (M.A. in economics; Ph.D.) studied social anthropology at the University of Manchester, completing both his undergraduate and postgraduate degrees there. His anthropological research took him to Ethiopia between 1969 and 1971, where he worked with a group of the Oromo people in the south of the country. On his return to Manchester he held various teaching posts in the Department of Social Anthropology and is now an honorary lecturer there. In 1978, he joined the John Rylands University Library of Manchester where he is currently social sciences librarian. Since joining the library he has maintained his anthropological interests, publishing journal articles and contributing to edited volumes in the fields of Ethiopian and Oromo studies. He has also developed an interest in African bibliography and was involved in the setting up of the *Africa Bibliography,* the bibliographical publication of the International African Institute in London, which he also edited for seven years.